Corpora and Lexis

Language and Computers

STUDIES IN DIGITAL LINGUISTICS

VOLUME 81

The titles published in this series are listed at *brill.com/lc*

Corpora and Lexis

Edited by

Sebastian Hoffmann
Andrea Sand
Sabine Arndt-Lappe
Lisa Marie Dillmann

BRILL
RODOPI

LEIDEN | BOSTON

The Library of Congress Cataloging-in-Publication Data is available online at http://catalog.loc.gov
LC record available at http://lccn.loc.gov/2018001128

Typeface for the Latin, Greek, and Cyrillic scripts: "Brill". See and download: brill.com/brill-typeface.

ISSN 0921-5034
ISBN 978-90-04-36112-6 (hardback)
ISBN 978-90-04-36113-3 (e-book)

This book is printed on acid-free paper and produced in a sustainable manner.

Contents

List of Figures and Tables

Figures

Tables

Notes on Contributors

Karin Aijmer

is Professor Emerita in English Linguistics at the University of Gothenburg, Sweden. Her research interests focus on pragmatics, discourse analysis, modality, corpus linguistics and contrastive analysis. Her books include *Conversational routines in English: Convention and Creativity* (1996), *English Discourse Particles: Evidence from a Corpus* (2002), *The Semantic Field of Modal Certainty: A Study of Adverbs in English* (with co-author, 2007) and *Understanding Pragmatic Markers: A Variational Pragmatic Analysis* (2013). She is co-editor of *Pragmatics of Society* (*Handbook of Pragmatics*, Mouton de Gruyter, 2011) and *Corpus Pragmatics: A Handbook* (Cambridge University Press, 2014), and co-author of *Pragmatics: An Advanced Resource Book for Students* (Routledge, 2012).

Moisés Almela

graduated in German Studies from the Complutense University of Madrid (UCM), and in English Studies from the Spanish National Distance Education University (UNED). He holds a PhD in English Studies from the University of Murcia (UMU), in Spain, where he works as a tenured professor teaching English Linguistics. He has authored and edited several publications on corpus linguistics and lexical studies. In 2008, he was co-founder of the Spanish Association for Corpus Linguistics (AELINCO), for which he served as a member of the executive board until 2014.

Sabine Arndt-Lappe

is a Professor of English Linguistics at Trier University. Before she came to Trier in 2015, just before the ICAME conference, she had worked as a doctoral and post-doctoral researcher at the universities of Marburg, Siegen, and Düsseldorf. Her research interests include aspects of variation in the English lexicon from a structural linguistic perspective, with a particular focus on morphological structure and its interfaces, which she is studying from both an empirical and a theoretical perspective. She is currently one of the editors of the *Zeitschrift für Sprachwissenschaft* and a member of the editorial board of *Morphology*.

Yves Bestgen

is a Research Associate of the National Fund for Scientific Research (F.R.S.-FNRS) and part-time Professor at the Catholic University of Louvain (Belgium) where he teaches courses in statistics and research methods. He is a member of the Centre for English Corpus Linguistics and of the Institute for Psychological

Sciences. His main research interests focus on the development of techniques for automatic text analysis, especially in the field of multilingualism and opinion mining. He also develops statistical methods for corpus linguistics.

Pascual Cantos
is Full Professor in the Department of English Language and Literature at the University of Murcia (Spain). His main research interests are in corpus linguistics, quantitative linguistics and computational lexicography. He has published extensively; his most recent book is *Statistical Methods in Language and Linguistic Research* (Equinox Publishing, 2013). Presently, he is co-editor of the *Journal of Research Design and Statistics in Linguistics and Communication Science*; Head of the LACELL (Applied Computational Linguistics, Second Language Learning and Lexicography) Research Group; President of the Spanish Association of Corpus Linguistics (AELINCO); and Dean of the Faculty of Humanities (University of Murcia).

Lisa Marie Dillmann
obtained her Master's in English Linguistics and Chinese Studies. She is a PhD student and Research Assistant in the Department of English Linguistics at Trier University. Her PhD thesis takes a mixed method approach to multilingual practices in Singaporean online discussion forums and the changing role of English in Singapore. Some of her current research interests are multilingualism, the field of sociolinguistics, World Englishes, specifically Asian Englishes and English in Singapore, and computer-mediated communication.

Maïté Dupont
is a PhD candidate in linguistics at the Centre for English Corpus Linguistics (Université catholique de Louvain). In her PhD thesis, she investigates cohesive markers of contrast in English and French, adopting a combined Systemic Functional and corpus approach. Her research interests include corpus linguistics, contrastive linguistics and translation studies, Systemic Functional Linguistics, syntax and discourse.

Costas Gabrielatos
is Senior Lecturer in English Language at Edge Hill University. His general research interests are in the development of corpus approaches to issues in theoretical and applied linguistics. More specifically, his research combines the following areas: corpus linguistic methodology (topic-specific corpora, annotation techniques, metrics), lexicogrammar (conditionals, modality, tense-aspect, construction grammar, lexical grammar), language education (peda-

gogical lexicogrammar, learner language), and (critical) discourse studies. He co-edits the *Journal of Corpora and Discourse Studies*, and organises the annual symposium *Corpus Approaches to Lexicogrammar*.

Sylviane Granger
is Professor Emerita of English Language and Linguistics at the University of Louvain. Since launching the International Corpus of Learner English project in 1990 she has played a key role in defining the various facets of the field of learner corpus research. Among her main research interests are the analysis of phraseology in learner language, with a particular focus on collocations and lexical bundles, and the design of electronic dictionaries and writing aids tailored to learners' attested difficulties. Her recent publications include *Phraseology: An Interdisciplinary Perspective* (Benjamins, 2008) and *The Cambridge Handbook of Learner Corpus Research* (Cambridge University Press, 2015).

Sebastian Hoffmann
is Professor of English Linguistics at Trier University. He received his doctoral degree from the University of Zurich, where he also worked for several years as a post-doctoral researcher. Before moving to Trier, he spent three years at Lancaster University (UK) as Lecturer in English Linguistics (2006–2009). His research predominantly focuses on the application of usage-based approaches to the study of language; main areas of interest include the pragmatics of tag questions, World Englishes (with a particular focus on lexico-grammatical phenomena and the diachrony of New Englishes) and corpus linguistic methodology. In May 2017, he was elected Chair of the ICAME board.

John M. Kirk
was a Lecturer, later Senior Lecturer, in English and Scottish Language at Queen's University Belfast from 1983–2013 and from 2015–2016 a Senior Research Fellow in English Linguistics at the Dresden University of Technology. He is a dialectologist (especially of Scottish and Irish English and increasingly World Englishes) and corpus linguist, combining both interests in much of his research. He is a founder participant in the International Corpus of English project, about which he recently completed a major review. In 2016, he guest-edited a special issue of the *International Journal of Corpus Linguistics* on spoken corpora.

Gabriele Knappe
is Professor of English Linguistics at the University of Bamberg. She teaches Old and Middle English language and literature, diachronic English linguis-

tics and also classes on Present-day English morphology, lexicology, lexicography and phraseology. Her publications cover rhetorical traditions in Anglo-Saxon England (PhD thesis, published 1996), several aspects of the history of English language scholarship, in particular phraseology (habilitation thesis, published 2004), (anti)lexicalisation, historical phonology and, recently, historical phraseology and construction grammar.

Antoinette Renouf
is Research Professor Emerita for English Language and Linguistics. Her research interests include lexis and lexical semantics, textual word patterning and meaning, and automated text analysis. She is a pioneer in the field of English corpus linguistics. At the Universities of Birmingham, Liverpool and Birmingham City, she has directed the Research and Development Unit for English Studies (RDUES) in the creation of the first automated systems to identify features including neology and change, lexical attraction and repulsion, in large diachronic news corpora, and to manage the extraction of very large corpora from the web. Since 2012, she has been using these systems and data to study aspects of lexical neology.

Andrea Sand
is Professor of English Linguistics at Trier University. She received her doctoral and post-doctoral degrees from the University of Freiburg, where she also worked as Assistant Professor and was involved in the compilation of several corpora, such as *The Freiburg Update of the Brown Corpus of Written American English* or *ICE-Jamaica*. In 2005, she became Associate Professor of English Linguistics at Leibniz University Hanover before moving on to Trier in 2007. She has worked repeatedly as a visiting professor or visiting research scholar at universities in the United States and in the Caribbean. Her research is mainly focused on World Englishes, and largely based on corpus linguistic methodology.

Julia Schlüter
is Professor of English Linguistics at the University of Bamberg. Her teaching covers major areas of Present-day English (especially phonology, grammar and cognitive aspects), international varieties as well as earlier forms of English, and includes a focus on empirical methodologies. Her research revolves around the effects of rhythm on grammatical variation and change (PhD thesis, published 2005), grammaticalisation, differences between British and American English, phonotactically conditioned allomorphy in Middle and Early Modern English, and quantitative methods in linguistics.

Edmund Weiner
has been a member of the staff of the Oxford English Dictionary since 1977. He was Co-Editor, with John Simpson, of the Second Edition of the OED (1989). He took a leading role in the digitisation of the OED, its publication in electronic form (1993), and the subsequent planning of its ongoing revision. He is currently part of the team overseeing the quarterly publication of the Third Edition, and specialises in the editing of entries for grammatical words. Since 1984 he has taken an interest in the implicit structures of the dictionary's data.

Introduction

Sebastian Hoffmann, Andrea Sand, Sabine Arndt-Lappe and Lisa Marie Dillmann

Over the past decades, the use of electronic corpora has revolutionised lexical studies. Today's linguistic resources are several orders of magnitude greater than those of only 50 years ago, but dramatically increased computing power has resulted in processing times that are nevertheless often measured in milliseconds. Beyond the obvious advantages of improved expediency in dealing with large amounts of data, however, the corpus revolution has also revealed fascinating facts about language that would have eluded researchers who approach the study of language by way of purely manual analyses.

Two well-known issues figure prominently in the linguistic study of lexis—one is paradigmatic, one is syntagmatic (however, with considerable overlap between the two—see below): The first is that, paradigmatically, words form a highly connective network, with relations between words pertaining to virtually all levels of structural linguistic description (both formal and semantic) and language usage (e.g. pragmatic, stylistic). Here corpus linguistics has opened up new pathways of studying relations and links between words, and with that, the structure of the lexicon. For example, the frequency profiles of words in representative corpora are standardly used as a proxy for measuring the word's psycholinguistic activation profile in the mental lexicon.

Syntagmatically, there is the question of how co-occurrence of words actually shapes meaning, to the extent that the status of the word as the primary meaning-bearing unit in language has become a matter of debate in much pertinent work. Bolinger's (1968, p. 127) insight that "a difference in syntactic form always spells a difference in meaning" and Goldberg's (1995, p. 67) "Principle of No Synonymy", stating that "if two constructions are syntactically distinct, they must be semantically or pragmatically distinct" have in the meantime been conclusively confirmed by corpus-linguistic studies (see e.g. the work by Gries and Stefanowitsch (2004) on collostructions). Also, Sinclair's (1996, 1998) model of the "extended lexical unit", which is a combination of lexical, syntactic, semantic and pragmatic components, provides further understanding of the syntagmatic interrelatedness of words.

Needless to say, no clear-cut distinction can be drawn between paradigmatic and syntagmatic foci in research on lexis. Instead, recent corpus-linguistic work has highlighted the important connections between these approaches, as more and more contextual knowledge is assumed to be part of the cognitive

 | DOI: 10.1163/9789004361133_002

representation of lexis. All this has important practical applications e.g. in the areas of lexicography and second language pedagogy.

One of the prominent researchers in this field of study is Michael Stubbs, who recently retired from his position at Trier University. His influential studies on collocations, phraseology and semantic prosody have further expanded our knowledge of the intricate interactions of lexis and meaning (see e.g. Stubbs, 1995, 2001, 2002 and 2007), a fact that was also celebrated in a special issue of the *International Journal of Corpus Linguistics* (Hoffmann, Fischer-Starcke & Sand, 2013) which was dedicated to Michael Stubbs. When it was decided that the annual ICAME conference—the longest-established conference for corpus-linguistic research—was to be held in Trier in 2015, it was a natural decision to honour his work by giving the conference a lexical focus. As a result, the theme of the 36th ICAME conference was set to "Words, Words, Words—Corpora and Lexis". It took place from 27 to 31 May 2015 and was attended by about 200 international participants. The papers in this volume were all first presented at this conference.

As is typical for ICAME, the theme did not heavily restrict the range of topics presented at the conference. However, the selection of papers presented here is a carefully chosen set of studies that explicitly relate to the central theme of the conference. They thus represent a showcase of the breadth of corpus approaches in current research on both dimensions of interest, paradigmatic and syntagmatic. At the same time, they confirm the very strong interwovenness of the two dimensions that was mentioned above.

The paradigmatic dimension is particularly relevant to lexicographers of course, as dictionary makers have long known that an alphabetical list of individual words—although essential for many reference purposes—is a serious misrepresentation of how a language is organised. It hides relations between words, which exist in networks of synonymy, antonymy and hyponymy, of narrower and wider semantic fields, of stylistic contrasts, and so on, and which are constitutive of how words are processed by speakers. The opening paper "Modelling Lexical Structures in the Oxford English Dictionary", by Edmund Weiner, the deputy chief editor of the most famous English-language dictionary, discusses what is involved in representing such networks of relations in electronic versions of the OED. Weiner was himself centrally involved in the first computer-readable versions of the OED in the 1990s, but points out that there are still central conceptual structures which are not represented in the current versions.

All other contributions to this volume use syntagmatic co-occurrence patterns as they occur in natural language samples to study lexical properties and aspects of their usage in context. Antoinette Renouf's paper "Investigating the

Circumstances of Coinage" shows how nowadays, very large longitudinal corpora and specialised access software can be used to gain new insights into the process of word creation in context. Contextual information in data extracted from Webcorp, a corpus of 1.3 billion words of British newspaper text, is used to establish a typology of signalling devices, which allows the author to study the speaker's perspective on neology in more detail. Both the findings and the paper's methodological contribution are particularly relevant to theoretical work on the nature of neologisms and their status in the lexicon, and to lexicographers interested in tracking emergent new words in running text of authentic English.

Absolute synonyms may not exist, but near synonyms are quite frequent in English. Providing evidence of the criteria in the selection of near synonyms is something which is notoriously difficult but for which corpus data can provide observable evidence. Very often, it can be shown that near synonym selection relies on semantic co-occurrence restrictions or stylistic differences. The paper by Julia Schlüter and Gabriele Knappe ("Synonym Selection as a Strategy of Stress Clash Avoidance") takes a less well-researched route and explores the influence of rhythm and stress on the selection of near-synonymous adjectives on the basis of 19th and 20th century data from the *Corpus of Historical American English* (COHA), the *Corpus of Contemporary American English* (COCA) and the *British National Corpus* (BNC). In a case study of a selected set of near-synonymous adjectives, they find robust evidence for a distributional split according to the rhythmic properties of the adjectives. Information about co-occurrence in context is thus argued to testify to syntactic specialisation among English adjectives.

As indicated above, there are aspects of word meaning which are evident only from a study of connected text, written and spoken. Furthermore, words have not only denotations and connotations, but also discourse functions and social functions: for example, they structure discourse and signal social solidarity. Three papers in the present volume are mainly concerned with the discourse functions of individual lexemes: Karin Aijmer looks at "Intensification with *Very, Really* and *So* in Selected Varieties of English", exploring the frequencies and functions of these adjective intensifiers on the basis of data from Inner and Outer Circle components of the *International Corpus of English* (ICE-GB, ICE-NZ, ICE-SIN) as well as American data. She shows differences in the relative frequencies of the intensifiers across the varieties, but also their individual functional profiles and collocational patterns, including the different semantic categories (e.g. positive or negative evaluation) of the adjectives modified by the forms under analysis. Differences between the varieties under analysis are linked to the status of the variety and their developmental paths.

John M. Kirk studies "The Pragmatics of *Well* as a Discourse Marker in Broadcast Discussions" in ICE-GB and SPICE-Ireland, the Irish corpus component marked for pragmatic functions, comparing his findings to Aijmer's (2013) study. While Kirk reports similar pragmatic functions with regard to coherence, involvement and politeness as Aijmer, the categorisation of the individual examples does not yield identical results. This serves to show the difficulty in assigning clear-cut pragmatic functions to potentially multi-functional discourse markers.

Maïté Dupont's contribution "Between Lexis and Discourse: A Cross-register Study of Connectors of Contrast" unites the areas of lexical, grammatical and discourse research by investigating the textual functions of contrastive connectives such as *however* or *on the other hand* in a corpus consisting of three registers (parliamentary debates, newspaper editorials and academic writing). Her contribution is particularly innovative as it develops the theme/rheme concept of Systemic Functional Linguistics further by adding more detail to the analysis of rheme position.

Even the earliest work with computer-readable corpora made it abundantly clear that individual words are not usually the main units of meaning. Words are co-selected in phrases and extended lexical units of various kinds, including collocations and n-grams. The paper "Towards a Model of Co-collocation Analysis: Theory, Methodology and Preliminary Results" by Moisés Almela and Pascual Cantos addresses those cases in collocational analysis in which the collocational cohesion is not contained in the relationship between node and collocate. They review current theoretical and methodological approaches and introduce a new category, the co-collocate, suggesting a 6-step methodology for extracting co-collocates from large mega-corpora such as the *English Web Corpus* (here: enTenTen2013) and illustrating it with a sample analysis of the lexeme CONSEQUENCE.

The two final papers in the present collection showcase recent research in the field of lexicogrammar, paired with potential application in the teaching of English as a foreign language. Costas Gabrielatos looks at "The Lexicogrammar of *BE Interested*: Description and Pedagogy" on the basis of British English data from the BNC and learner data from *The International Corpus of Learner English* (ICLE) and the *Louvain International Database of Spoken English Interlanguage* (LINDSEI), showing that the teaching materials used in EFL do not fully cover the complex differences between spoken and written usage native speakers of English exhibit. The paper by Yves Bestgen and Sylviane Granger is based on learner data from the *Longitudinal Database of Learner English* (LONGDALE) which allows researchers to study the development of English language learners over time. In "Tracking L2 Writers' Phraseological Development Using Collgrams: Evidence from a Longitudinal EFL Corpus" they assess the acquisition process by using collgrams, comparing the learner data bigrams to native speaker data from the BNC. In addition to yielding interesting results on the progress of the learners from year 1 to year 3, the study also contributes to the methodological inventory of corpus linguistics in a significant way.

In sum, the contributions in this book provide up-to-date examples of

- the uses of major corpus resources, both corpora and software tools
- findings—especially about frequency—which are simply not accessible without such corpus resources
- practical—especially pedagogical—applications of corpus findings
- new theoretical concepts relating to both lexical units and word meanings.

We would like to thank the reviewers—all ICAME board members and other long-time ICAMErs—who evaluated the submissions for the conference papers and posters and the anonymous reviewers who provided valuable feedback on the contributions to this volume for their time, effort and constructive input. Another big *thank you* is due to our senior advisor Mike Stubbs and the entire ICAME 36 conference team (Anne-Katrin Blass, Lisa Marie Dillmann, Denis Gusakov, Franziska Hackhausen, Daniela Kolbe-Hanna, Lilian Lee Hoffmann, Kerstin Lunkenheimer, Jennifer Ramberger and Isabelle Reinhardt), who helped to make the conference in Trier such a great success.

References

Aijmer, K. (2013). *Understanding pragmatic markers*. Edinburgh: Edinburgh University Press.

Bolinger, D.L. (1968). Entailment and the meaning of structures. *Glossa*, 2, 119–127.

Goldberg, A.E. (1995). *Constructions: A construction grammar approach to argument structure*. Chicago, IL: The University of Chicago Press.

Gries, S., & Stefanowitsch, A. (2004). Extending collostructional analysis: A corpus-based perspective on 'alternations'. *International Journal of Corpus Linguistics*, 9(1), 97–129.

Hoffmann, S., Fischer-Starcke, B., & Sand A. (2013). *Current issues in phraseology*. Special issue of the *International Journal of Corpus Linguistics*, *18*(1).

Sinclair, J. (1996). The search for units of meaning. *Textus*, 9(1), 75–106.

Sinclair, J. (1998). The lexical item. In E. Weigand (Ed.), *Contrastive lexical semantics* (pp. 1–24). Amsterdam: John Benjamins.

Stubbs, M. (1995). Collocations and semantic profiles. On the cause of the trouble with quantitative studies. *Functions of Language*, *2*(1), 23–55.

Stubbs, M. (2001). *Words and phrases: Corpus studies of lexical semantics*. Oxford: Blackwell.

Stubbs, M. (2002). Two quantitative methods of studying phraseology in English. *International Journal of Corpus Linguistics*, *7*(2), 215–244.

Stubbs, M. (2007). Quantitative data on multi-word sequences in English: The case of the word *world*. In M. Hoey, M. Mahlberg, M. Stubbs & W. Teubert (Eds.), *Text, discourse and corpora* (pp. 163–189). London: Continuum.

CHAPTER 1

Modelling Lexical Structures in the Oxford English Dictionary

Edmund Weiner

1 Introduction

The founding of ICAME and the start of my lexicographical career occurred in the same year, 1977. But as an OED lexicographer I have not had very much contact with ICAME. And this in a way is strange because there has been so much overlap between our interests, especially since 1984 when computerisation of the Oxford English Dictionary began. Like ICAME, the OED is *international* in its scope, it is *computer*-based, it is, surely, an *archive*, even if a selective one, and its field is *Modern and Medieval English*. Nonetheless, our main businesses are rather different. And although in the 1980s my colleagues and I were suddenly transported to the cutting edge of new technology, I do not write as an expert in digital matters. We now have specialists in our team who interact with many different text corpora in many ways and assist ordinary editors like me. The purpose of this paper is to show that there are numerous structural information networks implicit in the Dictionary, both within the individual entry and (especially) crossing the boundaries from one entry to another, and to examine the extent to which these are accessible.

2 The OED as a Public Database

I would like to go back some years. Not to 1977, but to the mid 1980s, when the original computerisation of the OED was planned. I'd like to look at our aspirations for the development of the database at that time. To refresh my memory I consulted a paper that I gave in March 1986 at a conference sponsored by IBM (then the world's leading computer company) (Weiner, 1987). Thirty years ago, we made some predictions about the way we planned to develop the OED as an electronic database in the near future. We said that:

1. A query language would be designed that would work on the OED's embedded tagging system to answer user queries which do not start from

 | DOI: 10.1163/9789004361133_003

a known headword and which are almost impossible to perform on the conventional dictionary.

2. The computerised dictionary would be housed in a database management system, and this would facilitate these non-headword queries.
3. Algorithms would combine information pigeonholed in different parts of the database in order to do any of three things:
    1. to pinpoint a unique answer,
    2. to build a list or table, or
    3. to calculate statistics of occurrence.
4. The database would actively help the user to understand his or her findings: there would be no need for the database to serve up the information in the form to which the conventional printed dictionary has inured us.
    1. Condensed or abbreviated information would be expanded.
    2. There would be a help facility which would translate every term in the dictionary's metalanguage at the touch of a key.
    3. For quotations in particular, another facility would take us straight to its entry in the dictionary's bibliographical database, which, in the fullness of time, would be linked to the computerised catalogues of the major libraries.
5. Intelligence would be introduced into the execution of the user's queries: advances in natural language processing would enable the database software to understand the user's queries with the minimum of translation into algorithmic language.
6. It should be possible for every keyword used in every definition to be linked to its own appropriate definition in the dictionary.

We began in 1984–1985 with the definite intention of building a relational database. This meant that we needed to think very carefully about the categories into which the data in the OED should be placed, and equally, about the relationships between those categories (Tompa, 1985). In order to facilitate this, we needed to envisage the ways the OED would be searched. Accordingly, in collaboration with the University of Waterloo, Ontario, we commissioned a user survey (Benbow et al., 1990). We designed questions, conducted the survey, and analysed the results statistically. The drawback, however, was that practically no one, apart from lexicographers, had any aspirations about the kinds of search they might make or, really, any inkling of the immense wealth of information locked away in the OED. Very few people at this time thought that they wanted to carry out this kind of research. There existed very few large textual databases, and those that existed were tucked away inside research institutions.

There was no World Wide Web. There were few online databases (between two and three thousand, I believe)—and "online" meant dialling up through a modem.

But already by the time the results of the survey were analysed, this line of approach was out of date. The march of progress swept us in a different direction, one that offered great prizes in a much more immediate way. Our partners at the University of Waterloo had developed one of the first rapid textual search engines, named Pat. It could search simply-structured text of any kind almost instantaneously and with well-tagged text it was miraculously powerful. As was said at the time, we didn't need to build the intelligence into the database as it could be built into the search engine.

As I understand it, this is pretty much how things have continued ever since. The search engines have become faster and more powerful, but the model is the same, and not only in online dictionaries, but in all online databases and websites. What we can now do with incredible rapidity and accuracy is locate relatively short strings of text within ultra-long strings of text, and, if there are meaningful tags embedded in the source document, we can locate particular categories of string; and we can do many ingenious and useful things with proximity, sequence, and nesting to identify subsets of the type of string we are interested in. But all this is, as it were, in two dimensions. We have an ultra-long sequence of characters in one dimension, we can look forward and backwards along the sequence, and we can apply various mechanisms that slice this sequence from a second dimension.

What I think is missing, at least within the database of the OED, is a third dimension, one that connects similar things to each other. In our original vision we were going to construct a relational database that would store similar items together for examination and analysis. The aim of this was to enable users to discover systematic structural facts about the English vocabulary that are implicit in the dictionary text but very hard or impossible to find by conventional means. In order to highlight this missing dimension, I will first consider and compare the two major steps in the development of the OED in electronic form before looking at the relational question in more detail.

These two steps are: the version issued on CD-ROM in 1993 (*The Oxford English Dictionary, Second Edition, on Compact Disc* (1993)), and the current OED Online, which was last redesigned in 2010.[1] I will compare the two versions

1 It's important to stress that I'm not primarily considering the *content* of the dictionary. It is beyond all dispute that the information contained in the OED has undergone an utter transformation since 1993, when revision began. This is, of course, especially true of the parts

under three headings. I will have to oversimplify enormously, and I hope that readers will make allowances for this. The headings are: Elements used in searching, access, and results.

2.1 *Elements Used in Searching*

In OED Online (2010), searching allows the correlation of strings in any of the main information categories. There are three variables:

1. Search in Entries, Senses, or Quotations
2. Drop-down menus to search in specific areas: for Entries: Full text, Lemma, Headword, Variant, Definition, Etymology (sub-areas: Language, Cited form), Label, Quotation (sub-areas: First quotation, Quotation date, Quotation author, Quotation title, Quotation text); for Senses and Quotations, the appropriate subset of these
3. Restrictions by Subject, Language, Region, Usage, Date of entry, Part of speech, entry letter or range for Entries and Senses, but only the last two for Quotations.

In the 1993 CD-ROM, searches were grouped into five kinds related to the general organisation of the dictionary, but it was possible to compile searches using all the items in the above categories, though they were distributed and named slightly differently: Full text; Headwords, Main and Subordinate, and Phrases (these three being equivalent to Lemmas); Variants; Definition text; Language names in etymologies; Cited forms; Etymology text; Quotation author names; Quotation work titles; Quotation text; and Pronunciations. Two other categories, Date and Part of speech, were available as filters that could be applied to the so-called word look-up (i.e. searching for anything that might be a lemma or lexical item).

Comparison shows that the set of elements used in searching has remained almost the same between 1993 and 2015. One has actually been dropped, namely Pronunciation. One important field has been added, that of Label, giving the extremely useful categories of *subject*, *region*, and *usage*.

---

that have been fully revised, but even the apparently unrevised parts have been transformed through restructuring and bibliographical research, all of which appears in the quarterly updates.

2.2 *Access*

The 1993 CD-ROM offered three kinds of search. You could type queries into a text search box, or you could make selections from the complete list of items, or you could highlight any word in the displayed results and click on a button *xref* and get a headword or a set of headwords matching that word.

You could also do advanced searches. This required you to use a specially devised query language, and to specify a file into which search results were saved, where they could be sorted by date and from which they could be output to your own file.

The OED Online of course offers text search and advanced search, but you cannot make selections from lists as in the 1993 CD-ROM. On the other hand, OED Online does provide access to some aspects of the relational nature of the data, both in its clickable cross-references, which are a properly constituted network, and in the new feature that allows selection from the Historical Thesaurus, Sources, Timelines, and Categories.

2.3 *Results*

The 1993 CD-ROM offered three kinds of result. The *display window* showed the dictionary entry where the selected result occurred (always opening on the context where the search item was located). The *results window* showed the results of a search as a KWIC display. The *list window* showed a complete list of items in a given category (such as headwords or authors' names: more about what these were below). So, output to the user was either as a conventional dictionary context, or as a set of keyword in context results, or as a complete list of all the items in a particular textual category.

In OED Online you can view results as either *list* (default) or *timeline*; you can sort the results by *entry* (default) or *date*. *List* is a quasi-KWIC format, but not a series of lines that can be readily scrolled or reordered. It is still assumed that the reader wants to end up with a conventional page-style display of individual entries. If, for example, one does an advanced search to find out what words the form *marry* is a variant of, the results one gets look like this:

1 marigold, *n.* and *adj.* View full entry. a1400
....ssion error mary goule mary gowle marry-gold Mary-Gold Mary G...

2 marrow, *n.*[1]. View full entry. eOE
...ghe maree marie mariȝ mary marye mery marry also Sc. marrie merurh transmission...

3 marrow, *n.*[2]. View full entry. 1440
...owe marrow marra marrah marrer marro marry marruh moro moroo morra Sc. mairow...

4 marry, *v.* View full entry. a1325
...ies mare mariȝe mari marye marie mary marry mareye marre marrye marrie mery Sc...

5 marry, *int.* View full entry. a1375
...mari ˈmɛri mare mari marie mary marye marry mayry marrie marrye marra also Brit....

6 marry-muff, *n.* View full entry. 1604
...ry-muff, n. marry-muffs marimuffe marry -muffemary-muffe Origin uncertain;...

7 † marry-muff, *int.* View full entry. 1602
...† marry muff, int. marry muffmarry muffe mary muffe mar...

8 Mary, *n.*[1] (and *int.*) View full entry. OE
...ȝe Ormulum Mariæ Mare Mari Marye Mary Marry Sc. Mair Mare Mari Marie Marries pl...

The assumption is that the user wants to click through to *each separate* entry where this is one of several variants, not to analyse this actual collection of hits *for its own interest*, e.g. to explore what range of lexical items might be represented by a particular string of characters.

2.4 *Advances since 1993*

None of this, of course, is to imply that there have been few significant advances since 1993. Of course, there have been many.

The biggest change between the 1993 electronic OED and that of 2010 was the addition of the *Oxford Historical Thesaurus* to the dictionary data. A large number of senses and nested items within the OED were linked into the semantic hierarchy of the Thesaurus. It then became possible to carry out reverse look-up, i.e. going from meaning to word, as well as to find synonyms, near synonyms, and words within related semantic fields. At the time, this was regarded within OED circles as an important breakthrough; it is surprising how little response there seems to have been in user circles. Exploiting or exploring the Historical Thesaurus is one of the five principal ways in which users are invited to browse OED Online. This is a step change in functionality: a much-needed semantic index. It fulfils one of the aspirations that we expressed in a different form in 1986, i.e. that every keyword used in every definition should be linked to its own appropriate definition in the dictionary.

There are four other ways of browsing OED Online. *Browsing sources* offers the user the chance to explore the top 1,000 authors and works quoted in the OED. The problem with this is that it implies that every OED quotation has been selected on some kind of underlying system. This is not, on the whole, the case. A given quotation is present largely for reasons unrelated to its actual identity. It may be there because it is the earliest or latest example of a use that we have found, or because it is one of very few examples apparently in existence, or because it fills a gap in the evidence for a particular period, or because it happens to illustrate the meaning in question particularly well, or for any of a large number of reasons that are quite arbitrary. *Browsing sources* is an example of a feature that is easy to provide but not part of the serious purpose of the OED.

Timelines enables one to discover when words entered the English language. The date of the earliest quotation for a headword is linked to that headword and the results are presented in graph form. The results can be filtered by the categories Subject, Region, and Origin. This is a neat function, but it is entirely headword-based. It doesn't get down to the level of individual meanings and it doesn't deal with multi-word lexical items. Hence, it's not really a tool for serious lexico-semantic research.

Categories enables one to browse words by subject, usage, region, or origin. In other words the dictionary's embedded labels and the first language name in the etymology field are used to categorise the OED's entries (and senses, which is very useful) into sets.

It is possible to browse the entire headword list. All 275,000 entries can be browsed with the first few words of the first definition visible for identification. There is also a complete list which gives headwords and dates of first use. But this is the only list which you can browse. In the 1993 CD-ROM you could browse the complete list of all items in all 12 information types. Not only was this incredibly useful to the user wanting to find out what kind of information could be found in the database; it was also a very courageous risk, considering that the data at that time was unrevised and inconsistent in the extreme.

A tremendous step forward has been taken in the OED Online in providing mouseovers and links to supporting data in the following contexts:

1. Pronunciation key
2. Cross-references (which both display and click through to the target)
3. Thesaurus
4. Categories
5. Middle English dating
6. Citation details (with bibliographical details and a link to the author's DNB entry)
7. Links to online dictionaries: *Dictionary of Old English* and *Middle English Dictionary*

Of these, the citation details (6.) and the external links (7.) both fulfil 1985 aspirations.

Another feature of OED Online is the option to find the word you have searched as a headword in any of the following further categories: Phrases, Definitions, Etymologies, Quotations, and Full text. For any headword search you make, say **portrait** (which offers you two main entries), you are offered these five categories and told how many hits there are in each.

Quick search results

Showing 1–2 of 2 results in 2 entries

Widen search? Find 'portrait' in: Phrases (37) Definitions (140) Etymologies (33) Quotations (1613) Full Text (1402)

View as: List | Timeline Sort by: Entry | Date

1. portrait, n., adv., and adj. View full entry 1560
   ... A drawing, painting, or other (broadly) two-dimensional representation of an object, scene, etc.; a picture, a design. Now *rare*....
2. portrait, v. View full entry 1548
   ... *trans*....

Whatever the usefulness of this feature may be in itself, it has two big drawbacks: (a) the results are presented as raw text strings, and (b) these results are classified under the entries where they may be found. Here, for example, are the results of choosing the Phrases option from the above Results:

1. composite adj. and n. View full entry 1943
   ... composite photograph or portrait composite photograph composite ...
2. draw, v. View full entry c1374
   ...ords, describe. Also to draw a portrait or picture of to draw a portrait ...
3. family portrait *in* family, n. and adj. View full entry 1732
   ... family portrait family portraits a portrait of ...
4. fancy, n. and adj. View full entry 1801
   ...cy picture, fancy piece, fancy portrait, fancy sketch. 1801 M. Edgewor ...
5. full length, n. View full entry 1760
   ...ull-length figure, full-length portrait, etc. Also ellipt. a full-len ...

This encapsulates the weakness of the string-searching model: it can only tell you what the result looks like in its raw form and where it happens to be placed within the main entry (an editorial artefact) and not how it relates (in linguistic terms) to similar items. The result is shown as part of a longer string of characters, mixed up with other stray data that happens to occur to the left and right of it; it is not picked out as an item in its own right and can't be taken out and manipulated along with other data.

2.5 *Aspirations Still to be Realised*

So, what is the gap between our original aspirations, based on the implicit structure of the OED, and the current resources available?

1. Users still have to translate what they want to know into arguments and algorithms that the search engine can use.
2. Owing to the limits on what categories can be browsed, the user cannot become familiar with the kind of data which is embedded within each category.
3. The output information mostly comprises strings extracted from the text with a small amount of context. These can't be readily manipulated by the user.
4. The output usually re-creates the printed entry, which means that a computer window cannot display the full picture.
5. The most serious objection is that the output is presented in the sequence in which it is held in the database (and as printed), rather than in a way that reflects its implicit structure.

3 The OED as an Explorable Electronic Archive

If the OED is to develop into an explorable computer archive it will be necessary to reconsider the principles of the OED's structure which need to be reflected in any complete model. In the remainder of this paper I will briefly discuss some of these.

3.1 *Individual Entry Structure*

In its printed form, at first sight, the OED is just a very long piece of rather complex text. On a second look, it is of course a series of discrete articles, each one dealing with an English word. On further examination, each article proves to be a word biography tracing the life story of a word. Each article is made up of a collection of units, most of which occur at least once in every article, some of them over and over again. On the printed page the units are laid out in a conventional order which has to be linear. But in actuality each kind of unit is related in its own special way to the subject of the article, the word being described. So, there is a non-linear hierarchical structure linking elements within each article to the headword and to each other, which in the printed form is mainly conveyed by sequence on the page.

3.2 *The Structure of the Whole Vocabulary*

The aim of the electronic OED is to present the historical structure of the English language from the lexical angle, not simply the story of each word individually. Such a comprehensive historical inventory of all the words in the language has a comparative purpose. No word is an island. The individual word, word meaning, or multiword item is always to be viewed within a matrix of all the others that may have a relationship with it. Such a relationship may be semantic, grammatical, morphological, etymological, or chronological, or it may be due to common membership of a lexical set constituted by register, region, or subject.

The individual word stories are not completely separate: there are bits of text in each one that link to other bits of text in other articles, some explicitly, others only by implication. These links (while we are still considering the printed book) are entirely in the reader's head, though suggested by the text. Hence the whole work is interconnected by these implied links. If the links within each article and those between articles could be made visible, we could see that the entire OED is a network of interconnected items.

Needless to say, it was especially for the sake of tracing these relationships that developing the OED as a computer resource was deemed to be a good idea. Equally, the success of the OED digital project should be judged by the degree to which it models and encapsulates this network of relationships for the benefit of the user.

3.3 *Entry Components*

Let's look at the highest-level components of an individual OED entry. Arranged on the page, or on the screen of OED Online, they are sequenced as follows:[2]

> headword lemma* (normally called just "headword")
> headword pronunciation
> headword inflections

2 The asterisked elements must be present. I use "headword lemma" as a reminder that headwords are simply lemmas provided with full entry treatment.

headword variant forms
etymology*
sense section*
lemma sections

This is the top-level structure and it is a simple one. The elements appear on page or screen in the above sequence, as if they formed a chain, each sequentially linked to its neighbour. But the real and primary relationship between them is not like this at all: each of the other six elements relates separately and in its own individual way to the headword lemma. A better diagram would be like a flower or a wheel, with the headword as the centre or hub, and the other sections as petals or spokes.

3.3.1 Headword Lemma

Conventional dictionary layout privileges the entry headword. Traditional entry look-up treats the entry headword as the highest level in the hierarchy of dictionary items, so that all entries are handled independently. This is quite reasonable as a way of organising the information associated with a particular word: to put it in corpus terms, the *type*. It's most important to realise that the hierarchical entry organisation is not merely a matter of convenience: it neatly embodies a network of inheritances which it would be very cumbersome indeed to have to spell out for each of the inheriting items.

However, the type-based approach doesn't adequately reflect the world of tokens, which is where the dictionary user is actually located, because they are trying to identify a token about which they are uncertain or with which they are unfamiliar.

From the uninformed user's point of view, there is no way of knowing whether a word being looked up is, in lexicographical terms, the headword of a single entry or of more than one entry, or a nested lemma, a variant form, or an inflected form. In a well set up digital environment, they shouldn't have to know.

As things stand, entering a homographic headword leads the user to a series of snippets of several entries and leaves them there to make a choice. This seems to me to treat homography as some kind of tiresome accident rather than a fact of inherent interest. But actually some members of homograph clusters are related to each other (obviously), while some pairs of homographs may or may not be the same lexical item in origin (there are some cases where the historical data which would enable us to decide does not exist). Many homographs have all but merged in the popular mind despite their utterly different origins (the anatomical *ear* and the *ear* of corn, for example).

But as I have just indicated, the complexities don't end there. Compound and derivative words are quite often treated as main headwords, but in the OED there are hundreds and hundreds that are treated as subordinate entries and nested within main entries. This is simply a matter of economy, but it does mean that headword lemmas and sub-lemmas do not share a level playing field in terms of their status as members of the vocabulary.

Finally, there are the variant forms and inflections of each headword lemma. As I have just suggested, faced with an unfamiliar token the user doesn't necessarily know whether this is actually a token of a type, (in OED terms the variant of a headword lemma), or if it is in fact a headword lemma in its own right. So, from the point of view of user access, a presentation of the vocabulary set in terms of a series of headword lemmas is an incomplete strategy. (We will return to this below.)

3.3.2 Variants

The variants section has potentially a highly complicated structure, conveying a great deal of explicit and implicit information about the way the headword has been spelt throughout its history, but at the lowest level the most important unit is the variant unit containing the form and its date range. The significance of these forms within the history of the language is twofold: (1) each of them is an instantiation, in a given text at a given time, for the form which has become, through standardisation, the headword lemma; (2) any of them may be a homograph of any variant of a different headword lemma (including the variant that is the headword lemma).

Here are the variants of the headword **ballad** *n.*

lME–15	balade	*U.S. regional*		
lME–15	balett	19–	ballet	*east.* and *south.*
15	balat	19–	ballit	*South.*
15	balate	19–	ballot	*Midland*
15	balette	*Sc.*		
15	ballatt	Pre-17	balat	
15	balled	Pre-17	ballatt	
15	ballete	Pre-17	balleit	
15	ballette	Pre-17	ballett	
15	ballytte	Pre-17 17 19–	ballat	
15–16	ballade	Pre-17 17–	ballad	
15–16	ballat	Pre-17 18	ballet	
15–16	ballet	18	ballan'	

15–	ballad		18–	ballant
Eng. regional				
17–	ballet			
18	ballat	*Cumberland*		
18–	ballant	*North.*		
18–	ballit	*Lancs.*		

In reality, it is not the lemma section as a unitary set that has a direct relationship to the headword lemma: this is an artificial result of page organisation. Each variant *individually* relates directly to the headword lemma; it has no necessary link to any other.

On the other hand, many of these variants given at **ballad** *n.* are also found as variants of other words. If we take just these variants and map them to their headwords we get a network of potentially many-to-many relationships, of which the figure presents only a small extract (see Figure 1.1). This is a more accurate picture of the reality of the language, where the variants (in the circles) are the actual tokens that we meet in the real world, while the headwords (in the rectangles) are the types that they instantiate. And this may well be the way in which many users want to visualise and explore the vocabulary of English.

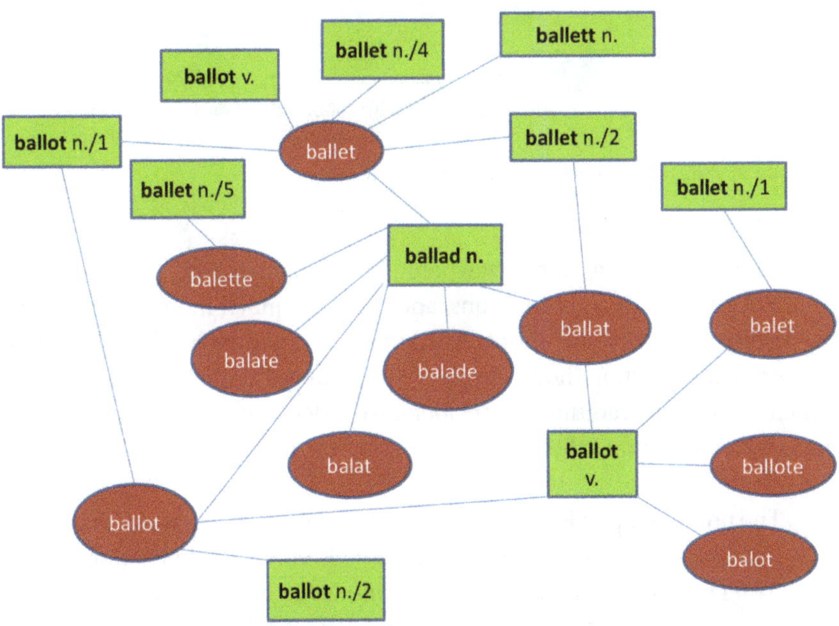

FIGURE 1.1 *Variants as a network*

Let's imagine that the user could enter a given string (say *balled*) and be given a map of all the roles this item plays in the history of English (see Figure 1.2, intended only to present the conceptual framework).

The actual visualisation could be, and would need to be, more sophisticated and flexible, enabling you to zoom in from the higher level presented at the outset to the further details which you wanted to discover. Although these further steps could be the OED entry where the information is held, there's no need for this to be the only result from your access.

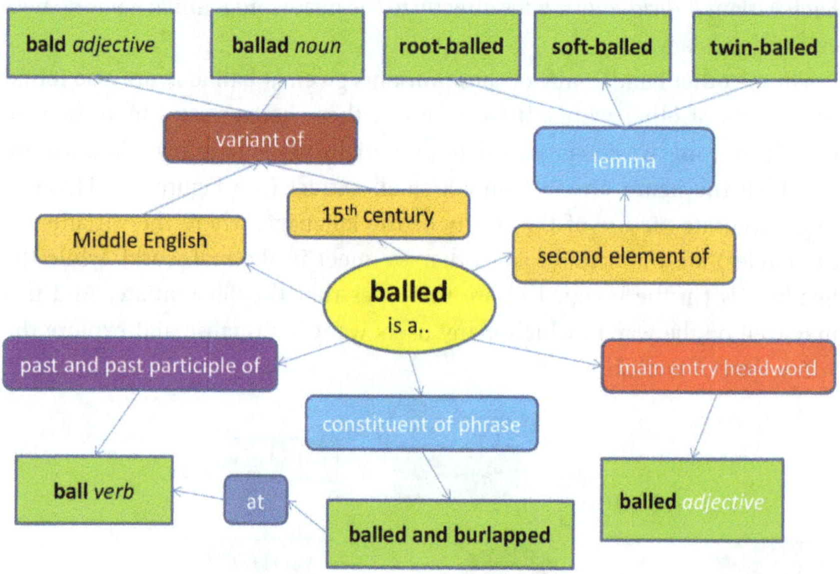

FIGURE 1.2 *Data roles played by a single orthographic string*

3.3.3 Pronunciation

From the conventional entry viewpoint, the pronunciations (which, in the OED, are phonemic representations, and therefore much more abstract than the spelling variants) are simply attributes of the entry headword lemma, answering the question "how is the word pronounced?". But this is a very one-dimensional view. Traditional entry look-up overlooks an important statement made by James Murray, the first editor of the OED, in 1884.

> The pronunciation is the actual living form or forms of a word, that is, *the word itself*, of which the current spelling is only a symbolization ... This living form is the *latest fact* in the form-history of the word, the starting-point of all investigations into its previous history, the only fact in its form-history to which the lexicographer can personally witness.
>
> MURRAY, 1884, p. xxiv

The logic of this—i.e. to enter words under their transcribed spoken form—has been followed by very few printed dictionaries. The main example known to me is *A Phonetic Dictionary of the English Language*, published by Hermann Michaelis and Daniel Jones in 1913. If the spoken form is "the word itself", at least two things follow.

Firstly, it ought to be possible to access entries via their pronunciation. I mentioned above that it was possible to search pronunciations in the 1993 CD-ROM by entering IPA symbols (using conventional keyboard equivalents). Ideally one ought to be able to employ voice recognition, but I shall pass by this particular avenue, interesting though it is. For users unfamiliar with phonemic notation, keying words phonemically is obviously problematic. However, OED Online already employs a very simple system of transcription based on English spelling as an alternative to IPA. And of course, many OED users are specialists who can handle IPA.

Secondly, in parallel with using the orthographic form as the node of all homographic forms, whether headword lemmas, sub lemmas, variants, etc., we can envisage using the phonemic form as the node of all the homophonous forms recorded in the dictionary, whatever their status. So, for example, entering /bɔːld/ would take one either to the headwords **bald** (of which there are three homographs) and **balled**, or to the past and past participles of the verbs *ball* and *bawl* (see Figure 1.3).

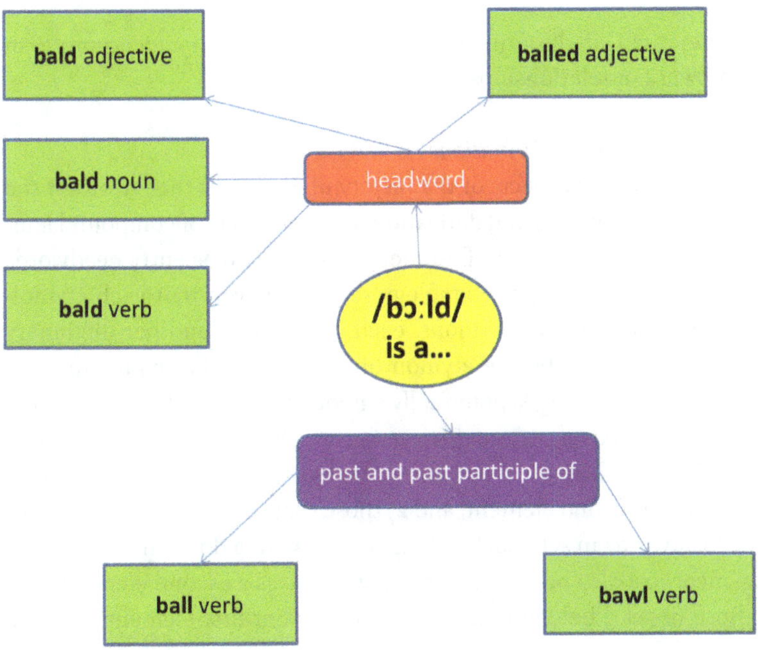

FIGURE 1.3 *Data roles played by a single phonetic string*

If dictionary content were accessible via pronunciation, it might well raise questions about the range and ordering of regional and other variants. But as this is a policy question, it will not be pursued here.

3.3.4 Etymology

The etymological section of an OED entry is, one might say, the most diverse habitat of all the sections in the dictionary. While it is very rich in content and very variable in arrangement, it is, arguably, insufficiently provided with internal structure within the current OED database. Much of the etymology text appears to be free-form discourse, but in fact it is highly formulaic.

To simplify a great deal, OED etymologies can be roughly divided into three types:

1. Internal English formations: the typical formula is X + Y, where X and Y are etymons consisting of cross-references to other entries.
2. Loanwords: the typical formula is {language-name} {cited form} {gloss}, a tripartite sequence representing an etymon which is usually followed by further information about the transmission involving numerous other etymons which may be direct ancestors in the line of transmission or related or relevant items in other languages.
3. Inherited words: the typical opening formula is "cognate with" followed by one or more sets of etymons in other (normally Germanic) languages.

If we consider each of these in turn, we can see that they incorporate an extended network of relationships.

3.3.4.1 *Internal English Formations*

One of the fundamental aspects of the history of English is the growth of the vocabulary by compounding and derivation. The parentage of compound lemmas that are fortunate enough to find themselves treated as entry headwords can be tracked by way of their etymology sections. Given that each etymology consists typically of two etymons, each of which is another dictionary headword and may itself be the etymon of numerous other compounds or derivatives, every such entry is potentially a node on an extended derivational network. Hence, for example, **meatball** *n.* is etymologised as from MEAT *n.* + BALL *n.*[1] As Table 1.1 shows, it thus belongs to two sets of words, 1) those that consist of *meat* + a second element, and 2) those that consist of a first element + *ball*. The headwords in set 1 each belong to a set with a different second element; e.g. **meat-axe** also belongs to a set 3 with *axe* as a second element; and each of those in set 3 belong to a set with a different first element, so if we

TABLE 1.1 *Extended derivational network of* ***meatball***

4 POLL *n.*[1] +	3 + AXE *n.*[1]	1 MEAT *n.* +	2 + BALL *n.*[1]	5 MOTH +	6 + -PROOF *adj.*
			baseball		
			basketball		
			cannon-ball		
	battle-axe		eyeball		
	boat-axe		football		
	hand-axe		handball		bombproof
	meat-axe	**meat-axe**	lowball		childproof
	pickaxe	**meatball**	**meatball**		fireproof
poleaxe	**poleaxe**	meat-board	**mothball**	**mothball**	fool-proof
poll bill	stone-axe	meatcorn	netball	moth-eaten	gas-proof
poll deed		meathead	oddball	moth-fretten	moisture-proof
poll evil		meathook	punchball	**mothproof**	**mothproof**
poll money		meat wagon	rollerball	moth-wing	

take as a random example **poleaxe** (despite the spelling of its first element), we find that it belongs to a set 4 with *poll* as the first element. Meanwhile the headwords in set 2 each belong to a set with a different first element: again, randomly selecting **mothball** from the list, it also belongs to a set 5 with *moth* as first element, and each member of this set belongs to a set with a different second element, e.g. **mothproof** belongs to a set 6 with *proof* as second element.

It's very clear from this chart that almost every word listed belongs to two such sets, initial and terminal, some of which are extremely large. Hence the implied network is vast and open-ended, but also an object of enormous interest. The numbers of members that each set has, and why some sets are bigger than others, and whether there is any synchronic or semantic factor involved—all are interesting questions that are not pursuable under the current model. With the current OED Online, you can of course click on the cross-references to jump to the parent elements, and you can use an advanced search (filtered by part of speech if necessary) to find the child elements. But it would be much more useful to have the network available as an inbuilt feature to be explored (a partial sketch of this is shown as Figure 1.4).

Another aspect of this question that must be borne in mind is the fact that many hidden members of these sets exist not as headword lemmas but as sub-

FIGURE 1.4 *Network of first and second elements of compounds*

ordinate entry lemmas, and, in the majority of cases, have no etymology and therefore no cross-references out to the parent headword: the first element, of course, is implicitly derivable by the mere fact of the lemma being nested, but the second element is not linked into the implied network at all. This brings problems of disambiguation: *archery ball, assize ball, charity ball, commemoration ball, county ball, court ball*, etc., of course contain another noun *ball* (BALL n.^{2}, meaning 'a dance'). And in fact, with both first and second elements, the hidden number that exist in subordinate entries is normally much larger than the acknowledged number that exist as headword lemmas. For example, the *meat* first element set contains about 23 compounds and derivatives as headwords, but the entry for MEAT *n.* contains about 50 undefined and 70 defined compounds, while the *ball* second element set contains about 65 headword members but somewhere between 200 and 300 subordinate entry members.

It's not difficult to think of further aspects of these networks which it would be really interesting to model. For example, the words compounded with *ball* seem to fall into several subsets: 1) things that are kinds of ball (e.g. *cannonball, eyeball, mudball, musket ball, puffball*), 2) kinds of ball game (*baseball, basketball, handball, softball*, etc.), 3) kinds of pitch or throw (*fastball, low ball, moonball*), 4) kinds of people (*nutball, oddball, screwball*). But to reflect this in any way would require bringing in the semantic dimension.

3.3.4.2 *Loanwords*

The typical formula, {language-name} {cited form} {gloss}, is by no means limited to loanword etymologies, of course; it is found wherever comparisons or connections are made to words in other languages. The point is that this sequence, or in some cases {language-name} {cited form} without following gloss, is an etymological unit that the user may well wish to use, for example, as a viewable item in result lists. At the moment it is possible to find all words whose immediate etymon is from a given language, which is extremely valuable. The actual result of the search, however, gives the identifying features of the headword, not the etymons.

2. aberglaube, n.View full entry 1873
   ...bəglaʊbə ˈɑbərˌglaʊbə aberglaubes German Aberglaube (13th or 14th cent....
3. abichite, n.View full entry 1850
   ..., n. ˈabɨkʌɪt ˈæbəˌkaɪt abichites German Abichit (attributed to J.J. Bernhardi...
4. † abietite, n.View full entry 1869
   ...† abietite, n. abietites German Abiëtit (F. Rochleder 1868, in...
5. Abitur, n.View full entry 1918
   ...ur, n. abiˈtʊə ˌæbiˈtʊ(ə)r Abiturs German Abitur (1897), shortened Abit...
6. Abiturient, n. and adj.View full entry 1842
   ...ts also with lower-case initial. German Abiturient candidate for the Abitur...
7. ablaut, n.View full entry 1849
   ...blaut, n. ˈablaʊt ˈæˌblaʊt ablauts German Ablaut (1819 in the specific sense...
8. abraum salt, n.View full entry 1872
   ...ˌsɔlt ˈæbraʊm ˌsɑlt abraum salts German Abraumsalz (1861 or earlier in...
9. abseil, n.View full entry 1923
   ...bˌseɪl abseils Either abseil, or German Abseilen action of abseiling,...
10. abseil, v.View full entry 1908
    ...abseils absail nonstandard abseil German abseilen to descend a rock face...

The output we need at least as much, if not more, however, would be more like this (though this realisation is not ideal, as the foreign word is not currently glossed in every case):

2. German *Aberglaube*
3. German *Abichit*
4. German *Abiëtit*
5. German *Abitur*
6. German *Abiturient* candidate for the Abitur
7. German *Ablaut*
8. German *Abraumsalz*
9. German *Abseilen* action of abseiling, descent made by abseiling
10. German *abseilen* to descend a rock face or other near-vertical surface using a rope

3.3.4.3 *Inherited Words*

The etymologies of inherited words have a rich internal structure which combines something of both the foregoing types of etymology. This is best shown by an example (the running text is tabulated, but not reordered, to show the inherent structure):

meal *n.*[1] **etymology**

Cognate with
  Old Frisian *mele*,
  Middle Dutch *mele* (Dutch *meel*),
  Old Saxon *melo* (Middle Low German *meel, mehel, mel, mele*),
  Old High German *mel, melo* (Middle High German *mel*, German *Mehl*),
  Old Icelandic *mjol* (Icelandic *mjöl*),
  Old Swedish *miöl, miol* (Swedish *mjöl*),
  Old Danish *miel* (Danish †*meel, mel*)

< an Indo-European base with numerous reflexes
  (as classical Latin *mola* mill),
and variants in other ablaut grades
  (compare from the o-grade
    Dutch *malen* grind, whirl;
  from the zero-grade
    MOULD n.[1],
    ancient Greek *mule, mulos* mill, millstone,
    and probably also Russian *blin* blin n.[2])

and with various root extensions
(compare
MALM *n.*,
MELT *v.*[1],
MILD *adj.*,
Old Icelandic *melr* sandbank, bentgrass).

Notice in the first section a series of foreign language etymons whose relation to the headword is that of cognate, not source, which a researcher might well wish to know about. ("What are the cognates of *meal*?", "Is there an English cognate of German *Mehl*?", for example).

Notice in the second section the mention of "Indo-European". OED Online no longer gives reconstructed Indo-European etymons, but is careful always to mention the parent language if there are cognates to the Germanic ancestral form.

Notice also a mixture of etymons here: some are cognates in Indo-European languages, and some are English words related via much earlier systems of word formation. Some of the cognates have themselves been borrowed as loanwords into English (for example *blin* at **meal** n.[1]). These loanwords and the cognate English words, expressed as cross-references, form another implicit network similar to the one we noted previously linking internal English formations, although of course much more limited in extent. In the above case, the headword **meal** n.[1] (at the bottom of Figure 1.5) would then be linked to an etymological tree showing cognate words (with the languages they belong to and their meanings) at the different levels of relationship (Germanic and Indo-European), together with links to other entries where some cognates are discussed further.

Additionally, the cross-references within etymologies in general constitute an interesting network. You can trace these by clicking on them, but of course you can only move in one direction, from source to target. How much more interesting to see the items that link in as well as out, graphically presented (see Figure 1.6). So, for example, after moving from **ballot** n.[1] to the suffix *-ot*, or from **balloon** n. to the suffix *-oon*, you could discover the many other entries that share these suffixes. This would not be difficult to arrange, since, for editing purposes, the inhouse OED database records both ends of every cross-reference.

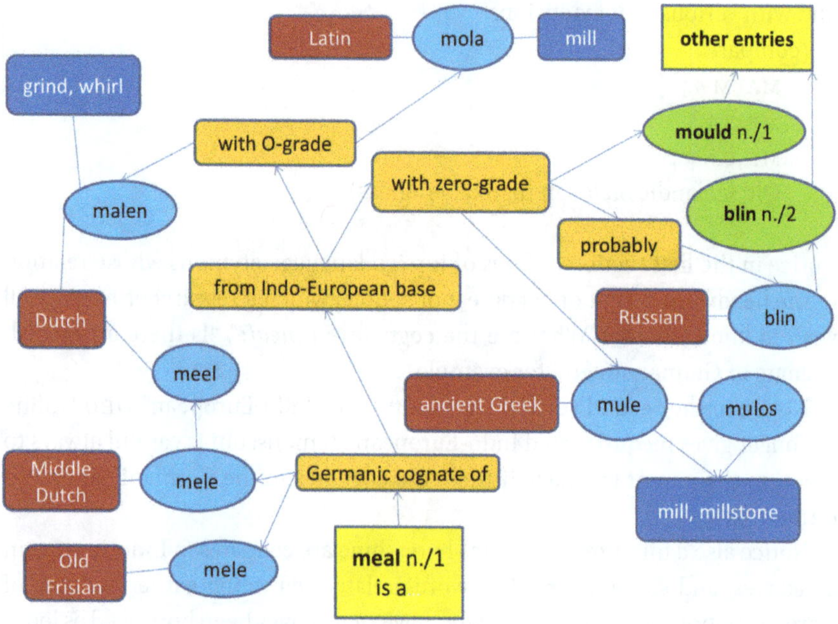

FIGURE 1.5 *Etymology tree structure*

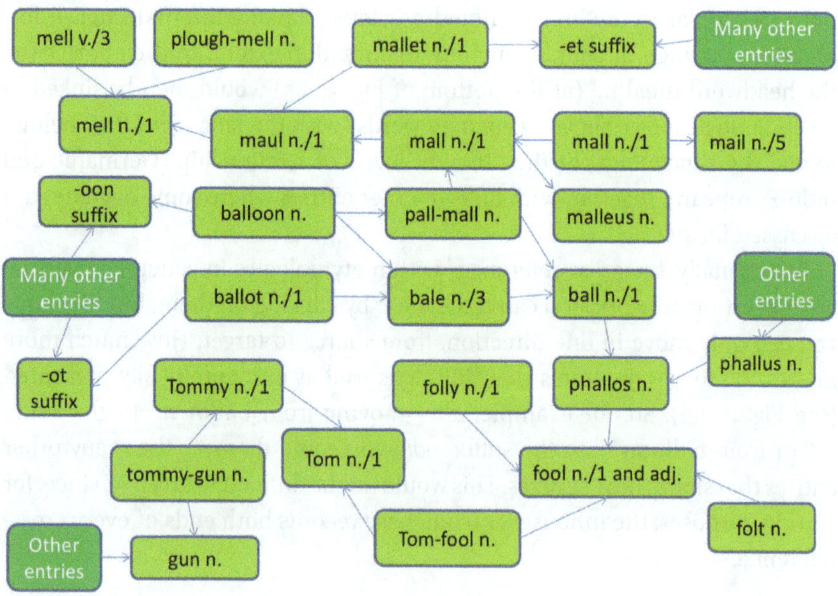

FIGURE 1.6 *Entries connected by etymology*

3.3.5 Quotations

The quotation element of the OED well exemplifies the tendency, which the sequential arrangement of information fosters, to assume that the system of structural tagging adequately reflects all the functions that the elements that it represents carry out in the notional structure of the dictionary. As I have tried to show already, some elements have multiple functions, and a good example of this is the date element in the quotation.

Within an OED quotation the function of the date is to be a key bibliographical identifier; its comparative chronological value has no significance. For example, the date, as well as the title, distinguishes **1936** J. Dos Passos *Big Money* from **1931** P.G. Wodehouse *Big Money*, while date alone distinguishes **1990** *New Age* Oct. from **1980** *New Age* Oct.

But within the quotation paragraph of the individual sense section, the date's function, together with the dates of all the other quotations, is to show the existence of that sense at a particular time and over a particular period, and if it is the oldest or youngest date, to show the rise, and potentially the demise, of that sense. From this point of view, the actual quotation to which the date is attached may well be irrelevant, and for this very reason the current OED editing software shows quotation paragraphs, when collapsed, as simply a date range. This is a simple example of multiple functionality.

Quotations are presented in the conventional OED layout as the lowest item in the hierarchy, the last thing you come to in the individual sense section. In OED Online the quotation paragraph can be suppressed so as to show only the date range.

By contrast, in terms of the construction of the OED, quotations are what drives everything. To put it in very simplified terms, while the interpretation of a set of quotations determines the definition of a sense, it is the date of the earliest of that set of quotations that determines the position of the sense in the chronological structure representing the word's history. For example, the entry for **ballot** *n.*[1] has three senses, determined and exemplified by the quotations. The date of the earliest quotation determines the place of the sense in the structure of three senses. The 1549 date (see below) makes this sense the earliest, numbered 1.

Part of **ballot** *n.*[1], sense 1:

1. Originally: a small coloured ball placed in a container to register a secret vote; (hence, by extension) a ticket, paper, etc., so used.

1549 W. THOMAS *Hist. Italie* f. 79, Boxes, into whiche he will, he maie let fall his ballot, that no man can perceiue hym.

1660 MILTON *Readie Way Free Commonw.* (ed. 2) 58 To convey each man his bean or ballot into the box.
1673 J. RAY *Observ. Journey Low-countries* 176 Each one of the *Pregadi* puts his ballot into what box he pleases.
1710 *London Gaz.* No. 4646/1 Elected by a great Majority of the Ballots.

3.3.6 Sense Section

In the printed dictionary, the sense section is made up of a series of senses; each sense is made up of a definition and a quotation paragraph. The structure of the sense section is controlled by three main factors: the number of distinct senses, the logical relationship of these senses to each other, and their chronological distribution. As has just been indicated, the number and relationship of the senses is determined by the content of the definition within each sense, while the chronological relationship is determined by the date of the first exemplifying quotation.

The history of a word is often pictured as a tree, with the various meanings as greater and lesser branches. It is a good image, but its main drawback is the limitations of the page, whether as a screen image on a website or in print. The image relies on two features of word development: the emergence of new meanings from existing ones, and the continuance of each meaning through a certain period of time, so that two or several or many meanings are all in being at the same time. The image is inherently three-dimensional, but the page, of course, is only two-dimensional. The senses can only be enumerated on the page in succession, but only parts of this successive list exactly mirror the chronological emergence of meanings: in reality, they may emerge in different parts of the tree at the same time as or at an earlier time than others that have already been enumerated. Moreover, a sense listed with its chronological sequence of quotations early on in the entry may be in continued existence while the subsequent senses are emerging and continuing, or it may become obsolete during that time. The screen or print representation simply cannot mimic the real picture. This is not a serious problem with the large number of entries (the great majority) which have only a few main meanings, but when these are discounted you are left with the most central words of the language, some of which have vast entries, whose shape is extremely difficult to grasp. Leafing through the pages of the print dictionary one can build up a mental picture with some effort, but if anything this is harder on the computer when the entry can only be viewed two or three sense sections per screen. It's impossible to demonstrate this in a written article: let the reader simply make the experiment of viewing any longish entry—say **measure** *n.*—in the printed OED Second Edition and in OED Online and he or she will quickly see that it's much easier to get an overall idea of the entry's structure leafing through the printed entry than scrolling down the online one.

The OED Online provides an *entry profile* for every entry you look up, giving as it were the vital statistics including a list of entries to which it links and which link to it. As part of this profile it offers users a two-dimensional graph of the chronology of senses, but as a visualisation this does not go far enough. No aspect of a historical dictionary is more central than this, and so it is of the utmost importance that a way be found of presenting this multidimensional tree of word meanings in an alternative and more intuitive form, one that would be more helpful than the serial format into which they were originally constrained by the print medium, and in which they are retained in electronic format.

One solution that would help but not fully solve the problem would be a way of drilling down or zooming in from higher to lower levels of sense structure. I offer the following illustrative sequence for the word **measure** *n.* (see Figures 1.7–1.11). Figure 1.7 shows the highest sense level: the four most general sense categories with a timeline above. Wherever there is a right-pointing arrow, users could then zoom in progressively on lower and lower levels of detail. For example, Figure 1.8 zooms in on Branch III showing the five main senses (14 to 18) that it comprises. Figure 1.9 zooms in on sense 17 and shows its three subsenses (only one is still current). Figure 1.10 zooms in on sense 17b and puts in schematic form the components that are at present given in connected prose. Figure 1.11 shows a more structured way of envisaging the quotations listed for sense 17b, shown below in their dictionary layout.

1625 N. CARPENTER *Geogr. Delineated* II. xiv. 247 The Northerne mans humour consortes best with the Phrygian measure, a loud and stirring harmonie.

1697 DRYDEN *Alexander's Feast* v. 5 Softly sweet, in Lydian Measures, Soon He sooth'd his Soul to Pleasures.

1776 C. BURNEY *Gen. Hist. Music* I. 60 The Lydian measure was appropriated to..songs of sorrow.

1854 *Littell's Living Age* 7 Oct. 1/2 Through the orchestra with slow advance The Dorian measure led the choral dance.

1890 *Atlantic Monthly* Sept. 401/2 Cassiodorus..indulges in a rather trite disquisition on the peculiarities of Dorian, Phrygian, Ionian, Ætolian, and Lydian measures.

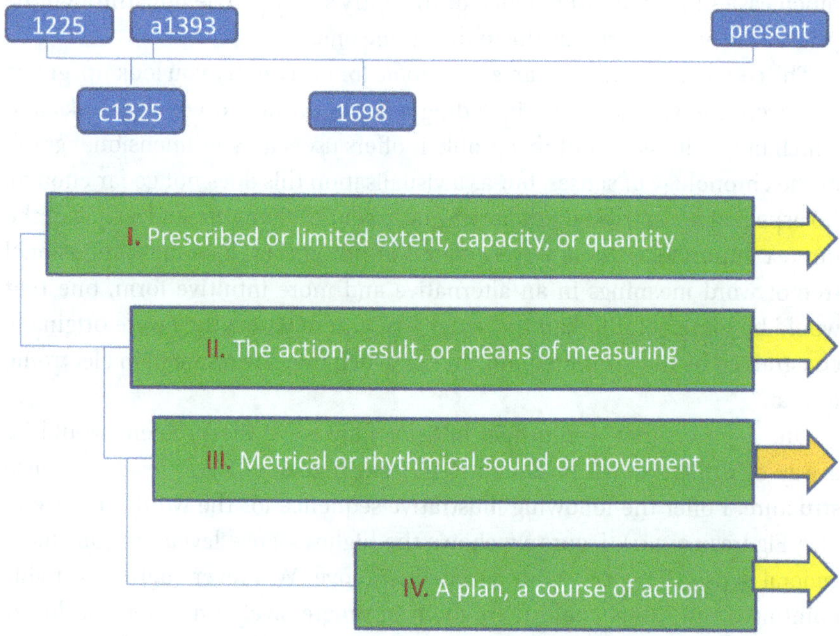

FIGURE 1.7 ***measure*** n.: *major sense branches*

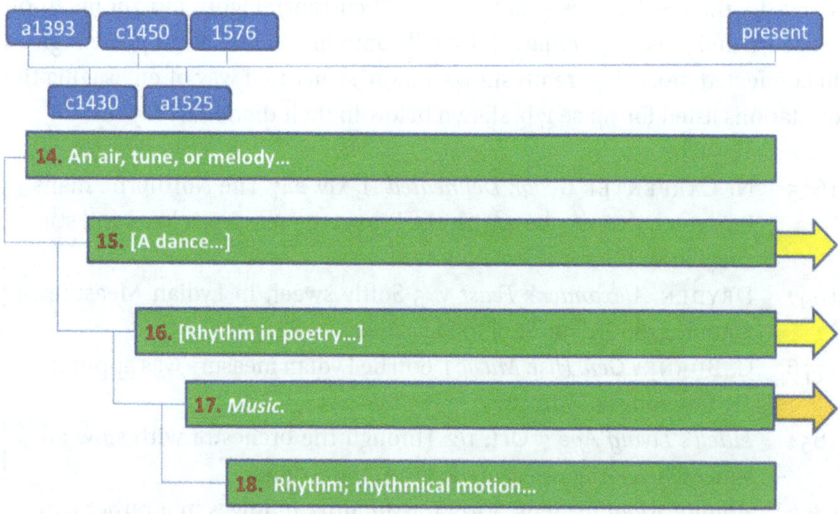

FIGURE 1.8 ***measure*** n.: *branch III outline*

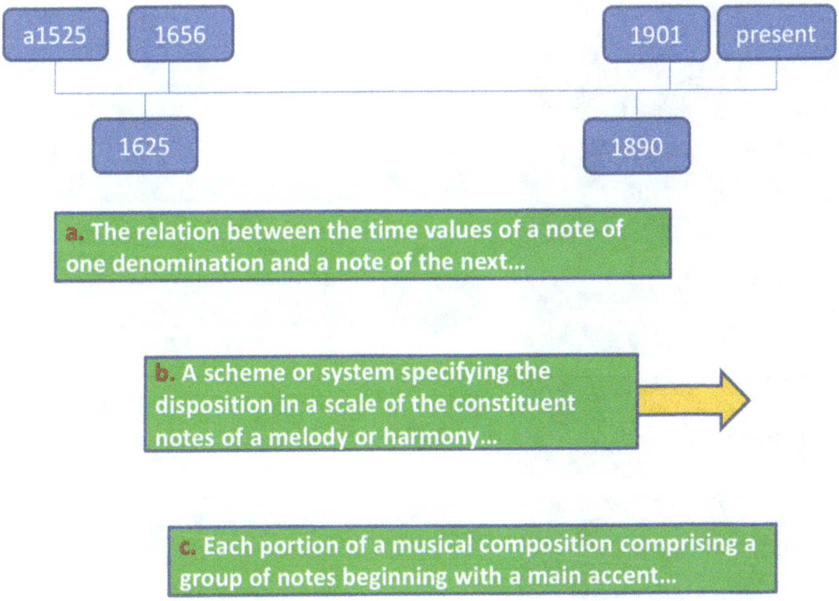

FIGURE 1.9 *measure* n.: *sense 17 outline*

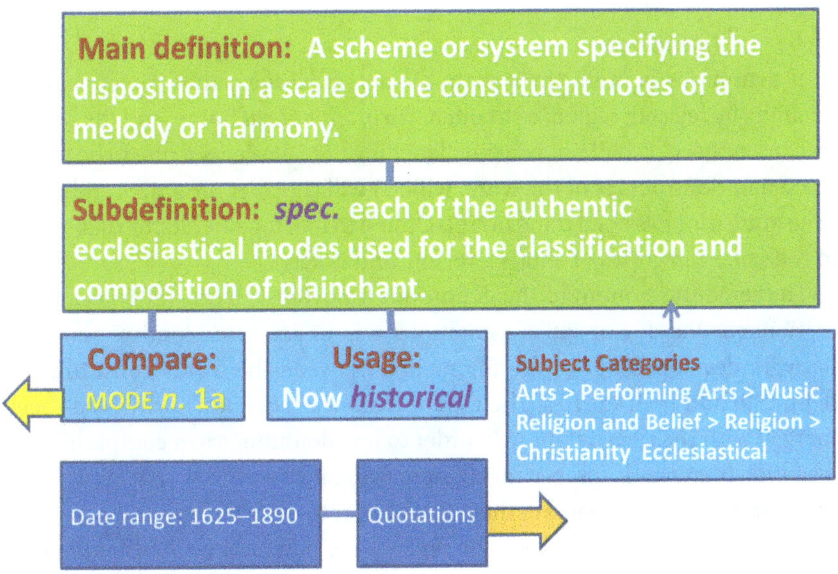

FIGURE 1.10 *measure* n. *17b: detail view*

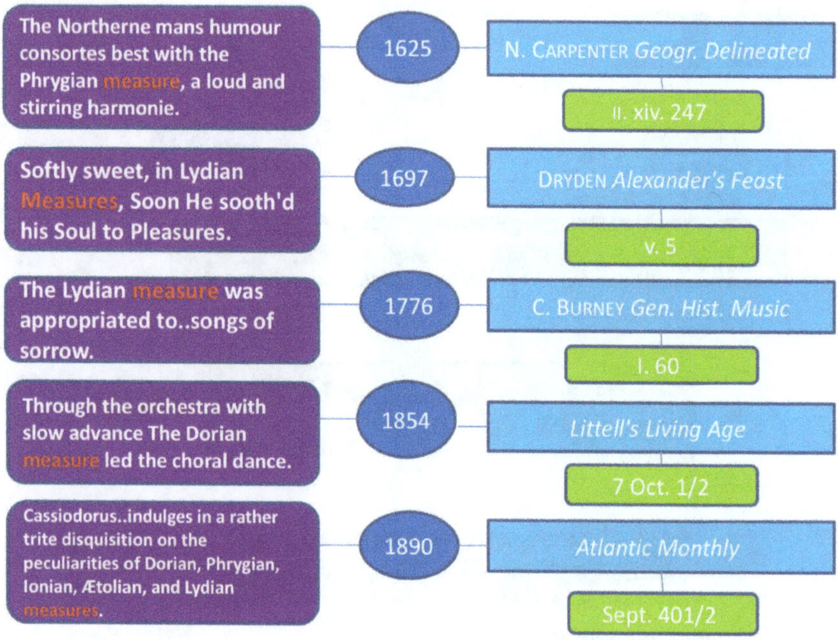

FIGURE 1.11 *measure* n. *17b: quotations*

3.3.6.1 *Definitions*

OED definitions contain three main elements: *labelling* that categorises the meaning by register, region, or frequency, a *grammatical* frame, and the *semantic* content itself. I shall not consider labelling here. It seems to me to be part of the semantic structure of the word, which I will consider presently, and moreover, quite a lot has been done in OED Online to link together items that belong in the same categories of subject, region, and usage.

The semantic content of the definitions is obviously a central aspect of the dictionary. One of our 1980s aspirations was to see some kind of semantic network developed out of the interaction between the words constituting a definition and their entries. The *Oxford Historical Thesaurus*, which has been merged with the OED database in order to link definitions to a comprehensive semantic framework, offers a much more workable route to such a network. At the moment the materials are there for the user to carry out their own network building. A great advance would be made if the potential were turned into an actual, visible, and explorable network. So, in Figure 1.12, for **portrait** n., the thesaurus tells us that sense 1a (in the ellipse) is a synonym of sense 1a (in the rectangle) of **picture** n., and also of sense 14a of **piece** n. (the lines show entry membership of senses; the arrows show synonymy).

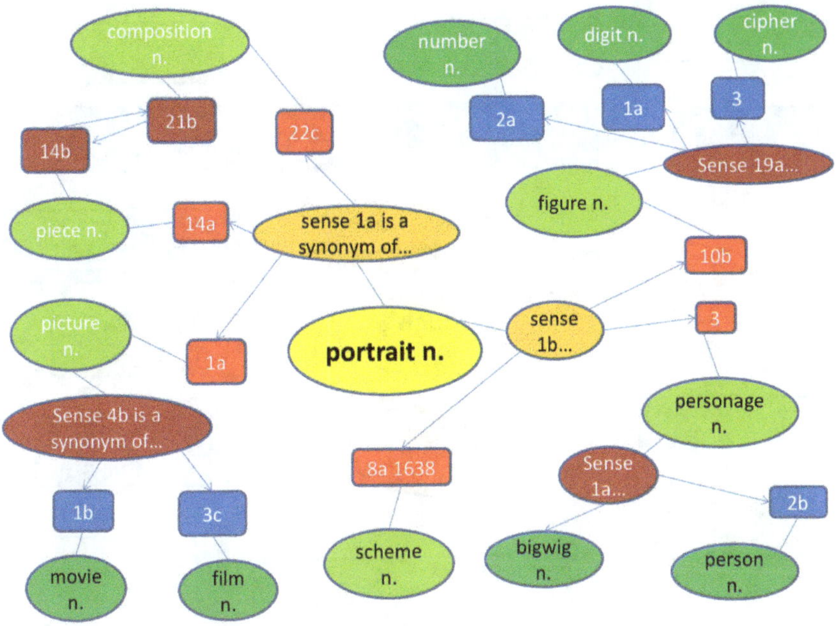

FIGURE 1.12 *Part of a semantic network*

3.3.6.2 *Grammatical Structures*

The OED's definitions include various kinds of grammatical information, all of which could be exploited so as to offer users valuable insights into the kinds of lexical or semantic item that enter into particular grammatical categories or relationships. To take collocation of headwords with particles (prepositions and adverbs) as an example: the OED deploys various different strategies to show how a headword is combined with prepositions and adverbs. The particle may be embedded in the definition or added to it; the combination of headword and particle may appear as a nested lemma, or as a phrase, or as a phrasal or prepositional verb. Essentially there are three structures:

Definitional constituent:

> **page** *v.*[2] 4. To leaf ⟨cf⟩*through*⟨/cf⟩ a book …
> **skin** *v.* 8.b. To pass ⟨cf⟩*through*⟨/cf⟩ … with little room to spare …

Definitional collocate:

> **rust** *v.*[1] 1.a. To become corroded, covered, or marked with rust. Also with … ⟨cf⟩*through*⟨/cf⟩ …
> **root** *v.*[2] 3.b. To rummage around … Freq. with ⟨cf⟩*through*⟨/cf⟩ …

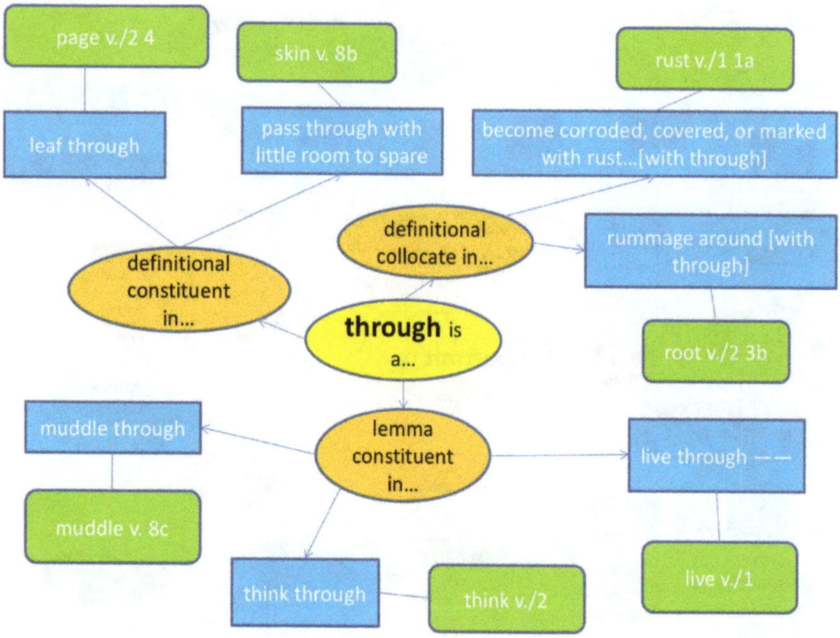

FIGURE 1.13 *Network of grammatical collocates*

Lemma constituent:

> **muddle** *v.* 8.c. ⟨lm⟩*to muddle through*⟨/lm⟩: to attain one's object by good fortune rather than good management
> **think** *v.*[2] PV ⟨sub⟩⟨lm⟩*to think through*⟨/lm⟩
> **live** *v.*[1] PV2 ⟨sub⟩⟨lm⟩*to live through*——⟨/lm⟩ ... To endure or survive ...

In other words the particle can be:

1. embedded in the definition (definitional constituent)
2. cited in its own clause (definitional collocate)
3. embedded in a lemma, either embedded in a definition or in its own subordinate entry (lemma constituent)

There are very good reasons why a single method of treatment is not used; if it were attempted, the dictionary would be very hard to compile and to understand. But nevertheless there are occasions when the user would like to be able to combine all the information about a particle held in disparate ways. When you consider that *through* occurs as a definition particle about 340 times and as part of a lemma about 430 times, and you extend this to all the other prepositions and adverbs in English, you realise that the OED contains an unparalleled archive of information about the use of particles in combination with other words. Freed from the straitjacket of sequential text, the relationships look something like Figure 1.13, illustrating the participation of *through* in different contexts.

The development of grammatical networks might well have implications for both the descriptive grammatical terminology used in the OED, and for the way grammatical notation and labelling is structured within the text. These questions are under active review within the OED project.

4 Summary

I have attempted to show that there are numerous structural information networks implicit in the dictionary text both within the individual entry and crossing the boundaries from one entry to another.

I have presented numerous diagrams with entities scattered around and connected by lines and arrows. It should not be thought that this is the way I think that the contents of the OED should *necessarily* be presented to the user, or (heaven forbid) that we should *substitute* such a representation for the current print-like presentation where they are arranged in linear fashion. What I have been trying to get across is the idea that *conceptually* the contents of the OED exist in a completely different mode, in which the constituents are not simply to be read from left to right and top to bottom. Cross-textual searching has become straightjacketed by the treatment of the dictionary as a sequential string of text, or at best, a small set of sequences frequently reiterated. We need to develop the dictionary along the lines of its inherent conceptual structure, which involves a great number of interconnections that, at present, are present to the minds of readers but are not modelled by the database itself.

How could we develop the OED along the lines of its inherent conceptual structure? In several of my diagrams I have presented the relationship between entities with a formula such as "X is-a-Y-of Z", or "X has Y". This resembles the entity-attribute-value model or semantic triple used in data modelling. I merely guess, as a non-expert, that some such approach might encapsulate the structural richness of the OED.

It hardly needs to be said that cross-textual searching, which has become available to us as a result of digitisation, is an indispensable tool of the comparative enterprise. In the past we had to collect data painstakingly, one entry at a time, but now there are tools that can do this instantaneously. But it does need to be said that individual entry look-up should not be contrasted with cross-textual searching, as if they were fundamentally different approaches to the dictionary. They are not: both involve the formulation of a query, which has to be accurate to obtain the correct information, both involve appropriate data structure and search tools, and both result in output which needs to answer the user's question intelligibly. I think it is all too easy to short-change entry look-up with the assumption that all we need to do is to model on the screen what the user of the print dictionary used to do and the results they used to find. To do this is a disservice to the user, who requires assistance in both encoding their query and decoding the results, and to the dictionary, whose rich contents need to be structured and presented analytically. At the moment, the output of straightforward lexical look-up provided by most electronic or online dictionaries is a representation of the print dictionary page, slightly adapted to the exigencies of the digital environment. It is true that we have also introduced alternative output formats (the print look-alike), which are ingenious and not to be decried, but they are a limited and rather random set. This may or may not be acceptable for the workaday desk dictionary equivalent, but for any historical or scholarly dictionary it is inadequate and undersells the potential of the product.

As regards the nature of the cross-textual searches offered and the interface for input and output, though much has been achieved, there hasn't been the kind of progress in the past twenty years that we have seen in most other areas of digital technology. We have stuck rather unadventurously to a set of possible searches dictated by the most obvious categories of data. Lexicographers themselves are well placed to advise on this subject, because they are aware of many ways in which, in the course of their work, they wish to interrogate their own dictionary database. Their potential queries are also the kind of query that any serious researcher would want to use, because lexicographers, OED ones at least, are engaged in essentially the same kind of work as their audience: they are students of the development of speech, grammar, literature, and culture. The tools need to be developed to stimulate the market. This is not the kind of situation where market forces lead. As someone once said: if Henry Ford had canvassed people on whether or not he should build a motor car, they'd probably have told him that what they really wanted was a faster horse.

References

Benbow, T., Carrington, P., Johannesen, G., Tompa, F., & Weiner, E. (1990). Report on the New Oxford English Dictionary user survey. *International Journal of Lexicography, 3*, 155–203.

Murray, J.A.H. (1884). General explanations. In J.A.H. Murray, H. Bradley, W.A. Craigie & C.T. Onions (Eds.), *A new English dictionary on historical principles, Part I: A-Ant* (pp. vii–xxiv). Oxford: Clarendon Press.

Oxford English Dictionary Online (2010–). Oxford University Press. Retrieved from http://dictionary.oed.com/. Last accessed 13 March 2017.

Oxford University Press. (1993). *The Oxford English Dictionary second edition on compact disc*. Oxford: Oxford University Press.

Tompa, F.W. (1985). A preliminary glance towards the design of the new OED database. Department of Computer Science. University of Waterloo.

Weiner, E.S.C. (1987). A conversation with a dictionary. In S. Nash (Ed.), *Science and intelligence* (pp. 117–132). Northwood: Science Reviews Ltd. (Paper given in March 1986).

CHAPTER 2

Investigating the Circumstances of Coinage*

Antoinette Renouf

1 Introduction

In studying lexis and lexico-grammar in a large, diachronic text corpus, it is possible to observe the "life-cycle" of new words (Renouf, 2013). But while a word in its full flush of use may be clearly observable, the circumstances of its birth, or coinage, are typically hazy. By coinage as a process, we mean the construction of a new word through the novel combination of existing words and affixes. We deem coinage to be a special case of neologism, distinct in that the act of creation itself is our focus. By circumstances of coinage, we mean the way that it is performed or reported in text, by the coiner or quoter. We also mean the degree of provenantial precision available.

The aim of this study is to develop a methodology to pinpoint new word coinages in a large corpus, and thereby to gain a clearer idea of the nature and typology of coinage. We base our study on a big data corpus of 1.5 billion words of UK *Guardian* and *Independent* newspaper texts from 1984 to 2014.

1.1 *Definitions*

In order to clarify what we mean in this study, we begin with brief definitions of key technical terms.

1.1.1 Coin

The *Oxford English Dictionary* online definition of *coin* is:

> ***coin*** *v* (*1*) *c. spec.* "To frame or invent (a new word or phrase), usually implying deliberate purpose; and occasionally used depreciatively, as if the process were analogous to that of the counterfeiter".

* We thank the Engineering and Physical Science Research Council (EPSRC) for research grants GR/L08243/01, GR/R16884/01 and EP/E001300/1, which funded the infrastructure for this study.

 | DOI: 10.1163/9789004361133_004

The allusion to falsehood is archaic, exemplified only in the earliest OED citation, though illustrative of the evolution in meaning. Bauer qualifies this definition, adding that the term "will not necessarily imply deliberate purpose, and it will not be intended to have any depreciative connotations" (Bauer, 2001, p. 38). We concur, and suggest as our own definition of COIN: 'to invent a new word, term or phrase, purposely or incidentally, which may go on to be used or re-coined by other people'.

1.1.2 Coinage

Bauer (2001) reflects on a suitable superordinate term for 'new words', saying that "it is probably not possible to tell at the point when a word is coined whether it will turn out to be a nonce word or a neologism" (Bauer, 2001, p. 39), where nonce words are defined by Zandvoort (1972) as "spontaneous creations by a speaker or writer coined for the occasion" (1972, pp. 43–44), and a neologism by Bauer as "a word which becomes part of the norm of the language" (2001, p. 39). Bauer (ibid.) settles on the alternative term coinage (proposed by Marchand 1969, p. 9; Strang, 1970, p. 27), as "rather more suitable as a technical term".

In this light, our own definition for this study is somewhat different. We define COINAGE (when used as a mass noun) as the act of coining or inventing a new word or phrase, and in addition, deem it to be a special case of neologising, distinct in that the act of creation itself is our focus. We define coinage (when used as a count noun) as being a product of that act: a new word, but one which may or may not recur or enter the language.

1.1.3 Signal

In Renouf and Bauer (2001, p. 235), we identified "various types of anchoring which are provided or available in the contexts of new words". CONTEXTUAL ANCHORING was Baayen and Neijt's (1997) term for different kinds of overt information to allow readers to interpret the functions of words. Our classification differentiated between overt and incidental help. Overt help consists of typographical and linguistic clues to meaning, including quotation marks, glosses and introductory and following phrases.[1] However, we were not focussed then, as we are now, on identifying actual acts of coinage, to which quotation marks, glosses and introductory and following phrases are not unambiguous clues.

1 Bullet-point listed in Renouf and Bauer, 2001, on page 236.

Thus, in this study, we adopt the term SIGNAL, by which we mean 'a metatextual device or indicator which marks a word or phrase as being a coinage, and communicates to the reader how the writer assesses it in terms of novelty and importance'. The following phrases are found to be likely signals of current coinage: [*I*|*we*] *dub, hereby, new* [*word*|*term*], [*I*|*we*] *call this*; and as signals of past coinage, we find: *was invented* [*in*|*by*|*at*|*on*], *came up with the* [*word*|*phrase*|*term*], *was originally used.*

1.1.4 Provenance

By PROVENANCE, we mean details of the circumstances of birth of a new word, in terms of its coiner, the time and date of its coinage, the place or event concerned, and any other information on its source. Such information is provided at two stages: firstly, when a word is coined within an article itself, so that it shares its date of creation with the article; secondly, when a past coinage is being reported on.

1.2 *Motivation*

The topic emerges from our recent diachronic corpus study of neologisms in news text, with particular reference to the nature of the life-cycle of a word in text (Renouf, 2013), or what Bauer et al. (2013, p. 29) call tracing "a new word through its own individual history". The study focuses on the earliest stage of neological formation, with reference both to the types of signalling involved, and to information on the provenance, or the circumstances of birth, of a coinage.

In this context, Bauer et al. (2013, p. 30) say that "the moment of coining (or the written or spoken record of it) is rarely observable …". This accords with our experience, but the hypothesis which we wish to put to the test is that coinage is nevertheless sometimes discoverable, especially in conjunction with certain words and phrases that signal the act of coining with varying degrees of purposefulness and precision.

Beyond our own curiosity as motivating force lies our awareness of the expressed needs of language professionals to gain access to the circumstances of word coinage, and thereby a yardstick by which to judge and represent the status of new vocabulary more accurately.

In the field of lexicology, for instance, Schmid et al. (2014) of the EnerG neology project investigate the factors influencing the success and failure of neologisms, asking, "What are the circumstances under which new words are coined? What are the coiners' motives and aims?". In lexicography, the OED team strives "to track down the first appearance of a given work in English", "to pinpoint the genuine birthday of a word in English", saying that "it can be difficult to trace exactly when a word first made its appearance on paper (and when it was used in speech is even harder to ascertain) and so it is rare to be able to give a definitive date for a word's first appearance" (Shea, 2012). Terminologists, meanwhile, need information on the provenance of a new word in order to predict its future validity for archival inclusion and use. NLP-based researchers, including Baayen and Sproat (1996), require information on the provenance of a recurring orthographic form, since it might represent fractionation (Baayen et al., 2002) in the form of semantic variation, which complicates statistical profiling.

We hope in this paper to give an insight into the processes of finding coinages by signal search, and into the types of signals involved in present and past coinage.

2 Data, Software and Method

2.1 *Data*

The principal data at our disposal consist of a diachronic corpus of 1.5 billion words of *Independent* and *Guardian* news text, dating from 1984 until the end of December 2014. This big data source combines the language benefits of variety with the analytical challenges of size. We base our study on three sets of data. The first consists of the first thousand candidate neologisms automatically identified in the corpus time-chunk December 2013, the total amounting to 10,077 first-occurrence items (including errors) for just that one month. The second is a list of potential words identified by Bauer (2001, pp. 40–41), from which signals of potential coinage are extracted and tested against our corpus. The third is a selection of candidate signals of past coinage, together with their contextualisation across the corpus.

In the presentation of data, a great many contextualised examples have been employed to exemplify features of coinage. Where this involves long contexts, these have regretfully often been cut to the minimum required to allow the relevant point to be made.

2.2 *Software*

The software consists of the APRIL morphological analyser (http://rdues.bcu.ac.uk/april.shtml) and WebCorp Linguist's Search Engine (WCLSE) corpus processing tools (http://www.webcorp.org.uk).

2.2.1 APRIL Software

APRIL identifies words which occur for the first time in the evolving corpus of news text. They are recorded in monthly batches relating to time-chunks of text. These words are not necessarily nonce formations, or neologisms, or first-occurrence words in the language as a whole (spoken or written), or hapaxes or coinages; they are simply words not previously encountered in the diachronic corpus.

A sample of 10 bona fide (i.e. not typographical errors) words arriving in the APRIL time-chunk December 13, 2013, is presented in Example set 1, displaying their morphological and grammatical analyses. The system only deals in single orthographic units, so multi-word neologisms are not recorded. The two items marked "N/A" are unparseable because the system only parses words with recognisable components, either existing words in a master wordlist, or affixes from an affix list. The items can be seen to represent a familiar range of word formation types in Example set 1. We shall examine these words in their contexts of use later.

EXAMPLE SET 1 Sample first-occurrence words in APRIL data on December 13, 2013

– top-of-the-milk-coloured	(top-of-the) '-' (milk) '-' (coloured)	|JJ|	201312
– singleless	(single) -less	|JJ|	201312
– custodying	(custody) -ing	|VVG|	201312
– nibblettes	(nibble) -ette -s	|NN2|	201312
– screen-blur	(screen) '-' (blur)	|NN1|	201312
– wirepulled	(wire) (pulled)	|VVD|	201312
– out-Kyle	out- '-' (Kyle)	|VVO|	201312
– pre-blocking	pre- '-' (blocking)	|VVG|	201312
– proto-McMansions	N/A	|NN2|	201312
– metalloproteins	N/A	|NN2|	201312

2.3 *Method*

The study is based on the observation that writers sometimes use a lexical signal to characterise a word in text as being a new or possibly new coinage. This practice is complicated by a series of factors, such as that the signal may not be literally intended, but serve a rhetorical or stylistic purpose. Equally, the new word may only be new in the immediate context of reference. Moreover, many words may not receive a signal because the writer does not view them as new or does not view the act of coinage as relevant in the context. Nevertheless, our aim is to focus on the nature of the signals accompanying selected sets of neologisms, in order to shed light on their role as markers of different types of coinage; as well as of source information.

The method involves a number of stages. The study begins with a search for candidate neologisms. The first search stage involves the selection of candidate coinages from those extracted automatically from the above corpus, followed by a contextualised investigation of coinage signalling devices accompanying them, if any. The second line of search finds the candidate signalling devices of potential coinage in the context of Bauer's (2001, pp. 40–41) list of potential words, followed by a test of the potential of these devices to signal further instances of imminent coinage in the corpus.

The third stage search process involves the discovery of past coinages. Since it is not obvious how to deal with this huge body of words and phrases in the abstract, or to identify past coinage without the aid of some signalling device, the search process involves the selection of some search terms intuitively associated with past coinage, such as *coined in*, and the iterative testing of these against retrieved corpus results to accumulate a working set of signals.

The study then proceeds to analyse the above retrieved coinages and signals, and develop a provisional typology of coinage, classifying coinages manually on the basis of their treatment by coiners and quoters, in terms of the lexical signalling used, if any, and the source detail provided. Coinages are classified within a framework of *no signalling, tentative signalling, performative signalling* and *past signalling*.

3 Findings

3.1 *No Signalling*

We defined the term signal earlier as 'a meta-textual device or indicator which marks a word or phrase as being a coinage, and communicates to the reader how the writer assesses it in terms of novelty and importance'. At first sight, it seemed to follow that the absence of signalling was an indicator of a coinage which was incidental or accidental. It was hoped that a clear correlation would emerge between the two, and that the language professions could be assured that unsignalled new words could probably be disregarded, not just for their lack of provenantial back-up, but because they probably were not important in terms of making a lasting impression on the language.

However, it is clear that, in the context of our newspaper journalism, whatever the coinages are, whether they are ad-hoc or planned, fleeting or intended for posterity, or in between, the signals which are potentially available to guide the reader to interpret their importance will not be consistently applied. Words will not be signalled if it does not occur to, or suit the purpose of, the writer.

Journalists probably coin relatively few lasting neologisms. Much of what they produce is ephemeral commentary and reportage. Creative gems are coined every day, but it is probably only once a journalist is responsible for more substantial reporting on some major, topical and ongoing issue that his/her coinages in the headline and following body of text will play a real role in "expanding the lexicon" (Hohenhaus, 2007, p. 17).

We shall try to glean an impression of the state of affairs regarding signalling, or rather the absence of it, with reference to the WCLSE news corpus. We return to the sample of ten candidate neologisms occurring on December 13, 2013, contextualised in Example set 2.

EXAMPLE SET 2 Contextualised candidate neologisms in the news corpus on Dec 13, 2013[2]

1. Kenwood House … the **top-of-the-milk-coloured** pile, available to wander through
2. Beyoncé's released a **singleless**, multi-layered, head-spinning album
3. Who is the **custodian** of my investments? If someone is **custodying** their own investments, it is a big red flag.
4. HENRY CONWAY … nothing brings out more social judgment than **nibbles** etiquette. The phone-hacking trial has thrown up many **nibblettes** of celebrity ephemera but the most extraordinary latest reveal is that Her Majesty is a stickler for her snacks.
5. the higher frame rate … ability to eliminate the **screen-blur** effect during fast-paced action sequences
6. It was none other than Jang who **wirepulled** behind scene
7. Merrick made sure to really **out-Kyle** Kyle by making two fat jokes in five minutes.
8. users worry as much about **post-blocking** retaliation as **pre-blocking** abuse
9. the kind of **proto-McMansions** you see on Hampstead Lane
10. Hemoglobins (Hbs) are large iron-containing **metalloproteins**

2 Throughout the paper, example sentences may have been abbreviated or otherwise slightly amended to improve readability.

The items in Example set 2 are deemed to be candidate neologisms at first point of entry, and it is possible that each new arrival represents a new coinage. In fact, we see that none of these carries a signal of such coinage, and we now look at each item in its context, to try to establish a reason why not.

In 1, *top-of-the-milk-coloured* is a multi-word adjectival compound. The writer, a literary critic, entertains readers here with a novel colour term, contextually very specific. In 2, *singleless* is a derived adjective, comprising *single* (N) + *less*,[3] created by a music journalist to fit grammatically into a set of premodifying epithets to *album*. In 3, *custodying* is a derived verbal form, comprising *custody* (N) + *-ing* based on *custodian*, and filling a lexical gap. It is unlikely to be intended as a new coinage, since it is incidental to the main topic focus, of guiding women in money dealing. In 4, *nibblettes* is a derivation of *nibbles*, which normally refers to small party snacks. Here, the society journalist applies it metaphorically to items of gossip. It occurs previously and since on the internet, once using the same pun.[4] In 5, *screen-blur* is a hyphenated noun modifier in this text, quoting a film director, but *screen blur* itself is an established technical term. In 6, *wirepulled* is a derivational variant of an established term, *wire-pulling*. In 7, *out-Kyle* is a compound verb consisting of the proper name *Kyle* + amusing productive prefix *out-* (at ca. 880 hapax types). It follows the word *Kyle-alikes* in the text. In 8, *pre-blocking* (as indeed *post-blocking*) is part of a quotation on text blocking policy by the Twitter chief. In 9, *proto-McMansions* is not new, appearing since 2006 on the internet, and is based on *McMansion*, coined in 1985 by Joni McWinn. In 10, *metalloproteins* is an established technical term, the concept having been discovered in the 1950s.

So, in Example set 2, we see a range of first-occurrence words, all coined by journalists except in 5, coined by a film director, and all of which are hapax formations as far as our corpus goes, except *metalloproteins*, in 10, which occurs twice. Of these, examples 1 *top-of-the-milk-coloured* and 7 *out-Kyle* are amusing nonce formations; but the remainder are either established in the language, or are new grammatical variants of existing words. Probably for these reasons, none of this diverse group of words attracts a coinage signal.

Continuing the search for signals of coinage, we examine each of the first 1,000 first-occurrence words for December 2013 in context. We identify among

---

3 Preceded by four instances of *singles* in the text, and by 192 instances of *single* and *singles* across the corpus, and thus primed for coinage.

4 "Two final *nibblettes*: [...] marsh mallows are called cheeses [...] [a]nd the mineral malachite is named after the mallow"; see http://www.eattheweeds.com/mallow-madness-the-false-roselle. Last accessed 18 June 2017.

them only six items which are arguably signalled as coinages. The signalled items are displayed in Example set 3.

EXAMPLE SET 3 Six signalled words found in the first 1,000 items in December 2013 data

1. 12/13 SAM WALLASTON TV critic a proper Italian sports car. **My little boy calls it** the **farty-farty** Maserati
2. 12/13 DANIEL HOWDEN journalist the smaller communities resent **what they see as** Dinka domination, or a "**Dinkocracy**"
3. 12/13 MATTHEW JENKIN editor careers **Lucy Burnford** set up a company **called Motoriety**, an online platform
4. 12/13 GRAEME WEARDEN technology journalist **Colm Tracey**, the **founder** of '**eishtech**', a call company centre
5. 12/13 With all the talk of 'selfies', 'lelfies' and 'belfies', **was that a 'selvie'**, ponders CHARLES EVISON of that Selvey-with-fan shot
6. 12/13 MOLLY GUNN "Mum Dressing" **means** the "**frumpification**" of one's style after having children

In Example set 3, we present the six examples with any claim to coinage signals. In 1, we see the reduplicative, onomatopoeic and scatalogical term *farty-farty*. This is introduced by the verb *call*, associated with coinage, but not signalling that *farty-farty* is an intended coinage; it is simply reporting it as a word that has already been coined. In 2 and 3, there are two proper nouns, *Dinkocracy* and *Motoriety*. *Dinkocracy* (blend of *Dinka* and *-cracy*) characterises South Sudan's domination by the Dinka tribe, and *Motoriety* (blend of *motor* and *notoriety*) names an online platform for vehicle owners. Though they are the topic words of the respective texts, they are extant words, and are not being coined. As with 1, the potential signal *call* introduces them, but is not in performative mode. In 4, there is a third noun, another brand name though printed in lower case, *eishtech* (later known as *Eishtec*, which itself receives several hits on Google), introduced by the term *founder*, which possibly signals that the founder named the company, but which is not coining the company name. In 5, the word *selvie* is the only candidate for coinage in Example set 3, since it seems to be proposed as a possible coinage in situ, signalled by the tentative question *was that a ...?*, and inverted commas. In 6, the candidate coinage *frumpification* appears as part of a definition of another neologism, *Mum Dressing*. *Frumpification* is thus not coined, although signalled as still new (or perhaps odd) by inverted commas (though *WebCorpLive* dates it back to 2007).

So, with the exception of example 5, Example set 3 examples are not signalled as acts of coinage. They contain possible coinage signals, but these are not performative, instead reporting existing and past coinages. Ironically, the only new signalled coinage, *selvie*, in 5, is coined by the only non-journalist in that data sample; all other writers are journalists.

Obiter dicta, Example set 3 does give us a sense of the fleeting coinage and the ad-hoc coinage signals in everyday journalistic text. This is clearer if we move our focus to the more linguistically-aware *Independent* and *Guardian* regular columnists, whose job it is to cast ordinary things in a new light, and who can decide whether or not to celebrate a coinage event with a signal.

The arbitrariness of the assignment of signals in respect to coinage is demonstrated by instances in Example sets 4 and 5. Example set 4 contains journalistic coinages apparently created on the fly by two journalists prone to neologising at speed. Lucy Mangan is a star *Guardian* columnist; Euan Ferguson a columnist for *The Observer*. These were found among the automatically retrieved neologisms for December 2013.

EXAMPLE SET 4 Examples of unsignalled coinage by journalists

1. 12/13 LUCY MANGAN a production in which some over-leveraged reality TV star is being desperately stretched to fill another **hour-shaped** hole in the schedules
2. 12/13 EUAN FERGUSON I **seesaw-grunted** out of bed at 8.30 am
3. 12/13 EUAN FERGUSON I had tried to speak, and hadn't been too **unstutteringly** successful
4. 12/13 EUAN FERGUSON "Get thee to a **Nambulance**". I got me to a **nambulance**

It can be seen in Example set 4 that none of the coinages shown is signalled as new. Perhaps to journalists, these relatively everyday formations do not seem to warrant special attention, or perhaps the coinages achieve a more amusing stylistic effect for being casually dropped into the running text.

In contrast, in Example set 5, the cited journalist Lucy Mangan has certainly signalled her awareness of deliberate, performative coinage. Her coinage of *enhappyfying* is explicitly signalled three times in one text:

EXAMPLE SET 5 Examples of journalistic coinage signalled as deliberate

1. 07/10 has there ever been a more delightful, a more and I shall coin a whole new word here, in honour of this most ... **people-enhappyfying** invention, than a cafe that supplies kittens to play with
2. 07/10 it was by some margin the most, ah yes, already I feel it slipping seamlessly into my personal lexicon, **enhappyfying** story of last year
3. 07/10 the set-up has about it something slightly, um, well, let's call it **unenhappyfying** for the moment.

3.2 *Tentative Signalling*

By tentative signalling of coinage, we mean signalling the fact that the writer or speaker perceives (or affects to perceive for rhetorical or stylistic purposes), a coinage as being questionable in one way or another. This can be a word which the speaker has struggled to find during a discussion, but has not found, so has invented one on the fly, without complete conviction. It could be a rarer derived word, which does not easily come to mind in the context of its base form; or a lacuna in the language (for instance, English lacks the equivalent of the French adverb *difficilement*, so a speaker on the topic might produce *with difficulty*, but if searching for a single-word alternative, might venture *difficultly*, together with a suitable disclaimer or hedge).

We extrapolate the concept of tentativeness from Bauer's (2001) discussion of potential words. In discussing the notion (referring to Halle, 1973, p. 6; Aronoff, 1983), Bauer lists a series of quotations which he says "illustrate the filling of what is perceived as a real or perceived gap in the speaker's lexicon" (Bauer, 2001, pp. 40–41).

Bauer is concerned with the status of these words as potential rather than actual formations, as "words which might exist, even though they do not" (Bauer, ibid.). What is interesting from our perspective is that Bauer's potential coinages are actually accompanied by signals which could be argued to express tentativeness on the part of the coiner—being, for instance, interrogative rather than assertive in form. Bauer's list of examples, containing both coinage and signal, is reproduced in abbreviation in Example set 6.

EXAMPLE SET 6 Bauer's list of potential words (Bauer, 2001, pp. 40–41)

1. ... it was all eminently postponeable, **if that's a word.**
2. ... increased ... electronification—**if there is such a word.**
3. '**Do we call her a** hit person,' I said.

4. The very unattainableness ... **is there such a word**? Anyway, you can see what I mean.
5. char-a-bancers, **as** Teesdale **called them** ...
6. **What do you call** a woman who does the same thing—a manizer?
7. He was kind of Zenny, **I guess you'd call it.**
8. Is there also an ethicisation of the poor **if I can coin the word?**
9. '**There's no such word** ... as attentionist. ... **Anyhow,** I've coined the word.'

We have expanded the signals found in Bauer's data in Example set 6 into more comprehensive search strings to garner more results, as shown in Example set 7, and applied them to the news corpus, to test the quality of tentativeness attributed to the signals. Tentative signals 8 and 9 from Example set 7 are not explored here, since they are used in searches in Section 3.3 of this paper.

EXAMPLE SET 7 Expanded signals of tentativeness

---

1. **if that's a word** (expanded to include "if that is a word")
2. **if there is such a word** (expanded to include "if there's such a word")
3. **do we call her a** ... (expanded to include "do [we|I] call [her|it|them|him] [a|an]"; also "do we call [it|him|her|them|us|ourselves]")
4. **is there such a word?**
5. **as X called them** (expanded to include "as X called [them|him|her|us]")
6. **what do you call** a X who (expanded to include "what do [you|we|they] call [a|an] *3 [who|which|that]")
7. **I guess you'd call it** (expanded to include "I [guess|imagine|suppose] you* call it"; also "I [guess|imagine|suppose] * call it", with filter "-you")
8. **if I can coin the word?** (expanded to include "if [I|we] can coin the [word|term|phrase]?")
9. **Anyhow, I've coined the word** (expanded to include "[I*|we*] coined the [word|term|phrase]")

Matching Bauer's tentative signals to our news data, we find many instances accompanying potential coinages (defined here as occurring once only in the corpus, although "potential" is a perception of the coiner, and, according to Bauer (1988, p. 65), also of the speech community). A selection is shown in Example set 8.

EXAMPLE SET 8 Sample signals of tentativeness in context

1. 10/05 The best programme of all, however, is Ultimate Fighting ... other major sports could be revitalised by being **ultimatised** (if that's a word).
2. 07/10 On the net, comedy can be done without the **blandinisation**, if that's a word, that comes about when you've got committees overseeing comedy and when it's all about ratings
3. 01/11 her tributes to Beuys, wooden boxes filled with bottles of sacred water ... "It's to do with the way he **sacramentalised**—if that's a word—materials. It's a celebration but also a critique of him, because collecting sacred water is a very common practice".
4. 01/12 Murray meets it at the back post, and the ball goes **zgltyuyfajkfg**, if that's a word. Or 'wide', if it's not ...
5. 09/87 The camera is not lying. It is first extrapolating and then **intrapolating**, if there is such a word.
6. 04/93 I was getting very **palpitative**, if there is such a word
7. 04/06 'English rugby has been extremely cyclical ... we need [to] get away from that ... is there such a word as **cyclicality**?'
8. 02/10 what do you call a play that uses vichyssoise as its central metaphor? A **soup opera**, perhaps.
9. 08/92 Mark Frost ... directed some episodes and—**reverse nepotism**, I guess you'd call it—cast his father, a professional actor, in the role of Doc Hayward.
10. 08/02 I want to build a boat, and float around rescuing people, especially aspiring French actresses with ... mucky flood-rescue fantasies ... **Flood envy**, I suppose we should call it.

Example 1 in Example set 8 ventures *ultimatised* as a new verb. It is preceded by six instances of *ultimate*. So, the tentativeness signalled here concerns whether *ultimatised* is the acceptable derived form from *ultimate*. In 2, *blandinisation* is a process noun derived from *bland*, which is odd in requiring the linking syllable, *-in-*, to facilitate pronunciation, and is thus signalled as a possible formation. In 3, as in 1, a verb must be derived from the adjective *sacramental*, and the closest candidate to come to mind is the lengthy *sacramentalised*, signalled as an uncertain choice. In 4, *zgltyuyfajkfg*, and the querying of its word status, is clearly a joke. In 5, *intrapolating* is invented to contrast with *extrapolating* by the elegant means of substituting *extra* with *intra*, but the writer feels the need to signal its probable novelty. In 6, the novelist Vikram Seth is quoted as saying that he was "getting very *palpitative*", which he seemingly preferred to the more prosaic *I was developing palpitations* or *my heart was palpitating increasingly* or similar. This formulation brought him to add a signal of tentativeness. In 7, *cyclicality* is derived from the nearby *cyclical*, a fairly standard move, which is nevertheless queried as to its existence (It exists: in our corpus 74 times). In 8, we meet a particular case of potential coinage, in the form of a pun: *soup opera*. This is a possible outcome of the question form *What do we call a* N *that* V *?*, which can function as a framing question to open a joke. The closing modal adverb *perhaps* then completes the punchline. In 9, *reverse nepotism* is apparently unknown to the writer,[5] and thus queried. In 10, *Flood envy* combines the words *flood* and *envy* (*envy* being a productive word which also generates *penis-envy* and 102 further compound types in the news corpus). The coinage is used by this journalist as a sort of punch-line, casualised by *I suppose we should call it*.

The signals found in Bauer's (2001) list are not exhaustive, since they are limited to the potential words he is focussing on. Inevitably there are further cases. These include, as shown in Example set 9:

EXAMPLE SET 9 Further tentative signals of coinage

1. **"if there is such a* [noun|adjective|verb]"**
   02/95 the perceived need to **cotton-wool** (if there is such a verb) the England players
2. **"or whatever you call it"**
   02/93 Outside it was broad daylight, or **foglight**, or whatever you call it when visibility is down to a few feet.
3. **"or whatever it's called"**
   03/09 Radio 3 continues to celebrate Henry Purcell's **three-and-a-half-centenary**, or whatever it's called

3.3 *Performative Signalling*

As we have seen above, word coinage can take different forms, according to the perceptions of the coiner within the particular context. In Section 3.1, we showed that it can be incidental; in Section 3.2, that it can be tentative. In this section, we examine coinage which we deem to be performative.

5 Though *reverse nepotism* is in use on the Internet, with several senses: see http://www.urbandictionary.com. Last accessed 19 June 2017.

We observe this performativity of coinage to obtain in cases which are signalled by certain characteristic phrases.[6] The most immediate and unambiguous case of coinage is probably signalled by a combination of three elements: deictics (or "referential indexicals": Peirce, 1932) including *I*, *here* and *now*, which indicate some state of affairs (i.e. *I* refers to whoever is writing; *now* refers to the time at which the word is coined; and *here* refers to the place of utterance); a performative verb such as *coin*, and the adverbial indexical *hereby*.

Yet, in the whole of the 1.5 billion-word corpus, we find only one instance of this formulation, shown in Example set 10 as:

EXAMPLE SET 10 Phrasal signal of the act of coinage: "[I|we] hereby coin"

07/11 LEO BENEDICTUS. Helm insists on staging her own "fictionalised memoir" (**I hereby coin the word "semoir"** to describe these kinds of capers.)

In Example set 10, the *semoir* is intended as a blend of *semi* + *memoir*. This sole example shows that the signal *I hereby coin* is a rare event in news text, and used humorously or ironically.

Mey argues that "performativity is a property that is not specifically bound up with SAVs [speech act verbs]", and that "indirect speech acts [...] in many cases are the most 'direct' realizations of what we have come to know as 'illocutionary force'" (Mey, 2001, p. 109). However, corpus observation suggests that the explicit performance of word coinage is a special case. While the verb COIN itself is in practice rarely used in direct speech acts (except in law), other institutionalised speech act verbs or verbs pressed into quasi-performative roles occur. These verbs are more obvious vehicles for retrieving performative coinage from the corpus than albeit more habitual indirect speech acts. They are retrieved via the search string "[I|we] hereby", and comprise *declare* (3 occs.), *name* (3 occs.), *dub* (2 occs.), *announce* (1 occ.), *propose* (1 occ.), *christen* (1 occ.) and *rename* (1 occ.). They are exemplified, one for each verb, in Example set 11.

---

6 Though there are cases where a new word or phrase alone can effect its own signalling, such as "Port Isaac is the new Padstow", rather than the more explicit "Port Isaac ... is utterly glorious. I hereby declare it The New Padstow". Austin (1956, pp. 26–27) recognises the existence and similar function of the reduced performative utterance, provisionally calling it a "primary" as opposed to "explicit" performance utterance.

EXAMPLE SET 11 Putative performative signal search string "[I|we] hereby + verb"

1. 11/08 Port Isaac ... is utterly glorious. I hereby **declare** it The New Padstow.
2. 10/05 Grant and Phil in EastEnders ... playing a pair of pigs ... I hereby **name** these pigs Grunt and Phil the Grease.
3. 08/05 owner of Waterstone's ... to buy Ottakar's—Wottakar's, as I hereby **dub** it
4. 08/08 BRIAN LOGAN. I hereby **announce** my own awards, the Logans
5. 11/95 Anderssen's win, which I hereby **propose be known** as 'the Deciduous'
6. 07/93 My particular prejudice, which I hereby **christen**—whoops sorry, **name** 'socwism'.
7. 05/10 mascots for the Olympic Games ... two giant phalluses ... I hereby **rename** them The Peniods

The verbs exemplified in Example set 11 are a mixed bag. With reference to example 1, Mey (2001, p. 108) questions the performative status of *declare*. In 2, *name* is a fairly standard performative verb, though not synonymous with *coin*. In 3, *dub* echoes *name*, with the added sense of 'nickname'. In 4 and 5, the verbs *announce*, and *propose + be known as*, are regarded by Austin (1956, p. 28) not as performative but as descriptive verb types, not delivering performative utterances but statements. In 6, *christen* also falls into the latter category; it is changed to *name*. Finally, in 7, *rename* echoes *name*.

In the context of *declare* as in *I hereby declare my innocence*, Mey (2001) goes on to question the status of *hereby* as "a practical criterion for a true, 'performative' SAV", saying that the utterance "seems to indicate that the use of 'hereby' at best is an indicator of SAVs in general, not exclusively of performativity[...]" (p. 108). However, our opinion is that *hereby* itself conveys a sense of occasion and immediacy which can transfer itself to verbs which are not performative, bringing a reflected aura, or even perlocutionary force, of performativity (even if ironically). Incidentally, *herewith* can function like *hereby*,[7] in the sense of 'by this means', as shown in the single example found:

> 10/29 How about the Coolidge recovery? ... I herewith **dub** it the **Coolidge recovery**. So let it be written. So let it be done.

7 Otherwise used to mean 'together with this (e.g. letter)': see Collins English Dictionary (2014).

Though the verbs in Example set 11 are mainly quasi-performative, and supported by *hereby*, some also feature in the corpus in a performative capacity without the support of *hereby*. See, for instance:

> 01/08 the house is warm enough (except the shower room, which I **rename** Siberia).

Reviewing the power of signals containing the first person singular and plural pronouns, together with a present tense performative verb, to identify the act of coinage, we move on to examine other verb forms of COIN, to discover whether they also retrieve further instances of coinage enactment. We begin with future reference, in the search terms "[I|we] shall coin"[8] and "going to coin". In the contexts shown in Example set 12, these verb forms can be seen to perform coinage within the text itself.

EXAMPLE SET 12 Examples of future reference performative signalling function

1. 07/10 and I **shall coin** a whole new word here, in honour of this most innovatory creation, **people-enhappyfying** invention
2. 01/12 There is a word for this: "anhedonia" ... but we're **going to coin** a neologism for their version of it: **Manhedonia**, to describe that genus of Manchester band who seem to relish their own discontent.

Next, we inspect present perfect forms, with the search string "[I#have|I've|we've] (*) just (*2) coined";[9] results are shown in Example set 13. Based on full-text search, we observe that, while the present perfect verb form dates the coinage as being of the immediate past, it can still perform the coinage of words. This requires the presence of *just, only just* or *just this minute*, as a marker of the time span from the immediate past up until the present, and that the coinage is actually taking place within the boundary of the host text itself.

8 "[I|we] will coin" does not occur.

9 In this notation, the hashtag finds separate, hyphenated and solid variants of the phrase, employed here to preserve the integrity of *I have* in the string, while the asterisk plus number is a wildcard of specified maximum span.

EXAMPLE SET 13 Signal search string: "[I#have|I've|we've] (*) just (*2) coined", case insensitive, 5 occs.

---

1. 07/97 RICHARD EHRLICH Picnicking **rhodophiles** (a word **I've just coined** for people who like red better than white) will want to drop in to Marks & Spencer
2. 01/99 As a vindication, too, of a proverb which **I've just this minute coined**: If at first you do succeed, don't try again.
3. 03/06 JOHN PATTERSON Unfortunately, **auto-plagiarism** is not my idea of a mitigating circumstance, so it is with ... regret that I sentence Loncraine under this ... arbitrary new law **I've just coined**
4. 03/11 IAN MCMILLAN The limericks are Lear's crowning glory. These **Learmericks** (a term **I've just coined**) have an odd shape
5. 12/11 TIM DOWLING Got secrets you want to keep? There is an obvious next step: the **meta-injunction. I have only just coined** the term

---

Detailed provenance is rarely provided in the process of word coinage, but it occurs de facto when coinage occurs (as far as we can judge) within the confines of the article. The author of the article is thereby identified as the coiner; the date of coinage equates to the date of the article itself.

Being aware that the presence of the first or third person pronoun, together with a performative verb in the simple present or present perfect, seem to be the hallmarks of coinage, we next modify the search string to see whether verb modality can mark the act of coinage, as shown by the three out of a total of six corpus occurrences in Example set 14.

EXAMPLE SET 14 Modalised performative signal: "[I|we] * coin", with filter "minus *if*", case insensitive

---

07/88 ENOCH POWELL **I might coin** a word for this tendency and call it **'awardism'**

09/10 HASSASSIAN/KAUFMAN Perhaps, then, **we could coin** a new phrase for our class: **"Israelis and Palestinians are blessed to be neighbours."**

03/10 I **would like to coin** a phrase: **'end-to-end stuff'**.

The verb modality, without *hereby*, in Example set 14 is still seen to mark coinage. This modality at first bears some resemblance to our category of tentative coinage in Section 3.2. The difference is that here, the tentativeness is not directed at the status of the coinage itself, but at the propriety of coining in the first place. Furthermore, most of the signals in Bauer's (2001) list of potential words occur in clause-final position, which brings a lesser force to them than to those here which are clause-initial, and thus seem more assertive. This string also supports the use of *dub* in a performative function, as shown in Example set 15, but not *name, declare, announce, propose*; they are only attested with different, phrasal meanings; e.g. *I could name names*.

EXAMPLE SET 15 Modalised performative signal: "[I|we] * dub", 4 occs.

1. 03/96 another theory for the fall in fertility levels, which **we might dub** the **Larkin proposition**
2. 07/04 a problem that I think **we should dub "When Bad Celebrities Happen to Good Fashion".**
3. 10/11 the Dow Jones (which **perhaps we should dub** the **Gow Jones**) index
4. 03/13 The desolate atomisation of **what we might dub "generation self"**

Our next search string, "if [I|we] * coin", exemplified in Example set 16, is closer still to one of Bauer's tentative signals, the sentence-final *if I can coin the word?* Nevertheless, we retain it here with our performative signals of coinage because the examples in 1–3 commence with the politeness formula *if I*, followed by a modal auxiliary verb with deontic function, and are thus expressing polite intention rather than existential uncertainty; while the signal *can* in 4–5 strikes us similarly as deontic, not conveying quite the epistemic tentativeness brought to the original Bauer signal with its final question mark.[10]

EXAMPLE SET 16 Signal: "if [I|we] * coin", case insensitive, 12 occs.

1. 11/01 **if I may coin a term, "Performance Criticism"** not Performance Art
2. 01/08 What is not **Reaganesque, if I might coin a term**, about proclaiming "the era of big government" as "over"?
3. 07/12 the summer's second **"escape memoir" if I may coin the term.**
4. 12/93 The ... symptoms of this **Santafysing, if I can coin a word**, is the donning of the white beard of wisdom
5. 04/12 there's a **Richienne (if I can coin that phrase)** poem about death

10 Bauer's original example was *Is there also an ethicisation of the poor if I can coin the word?* (2001, p. 40).

So, in Section 3.3, we have examined the concept and practicality of performative signalling of definitive coinage. We show that the moment of coinage is signalled by a performative verb, together with first person singular or plural pronominal reference, and often supported by the adverbials *hereby* and *now*. We have also argued that the act of coinage can be signalled by performative verbs like *coin* in an apparently non-performative mode—normally a descriptive or reporting mode—by using verbs in the future and present perfect forms, or modal verbs in present and past tenses.

3.4 *Past Signalling*

We now turn to past coinages, as quoted in the news corpus. By past signalling, we refer to the act of signalling words or phrases as having been coined in what is deemed by a particular writer at a particular point as being in the past. The purpose here is to trace a methodology for finding past coinages via relevant signals, then to move towards a working typology by observing these in context.

3.4.1 Methodology of Search for Past Coinage Signals

A sensible method of selecting and dealing with the vast percentage of past coinages which make up the corpus has to be found. In principle, every word in the corpus which was once coined or first used qualifies for inspection. The search for signalled past coinage thus has to be targeted, so we begin with a working list of past coinage signals.

We have found that the only verb which unambiguously signals past coinage is COIN, or rather *coined* and *had coined* (and exceptionally the historic present tense *is coined*). It seems reasonable in the first instance to assume that our working list comprises synonyms of *coined*, accumulated iteratively by thesaural search, collocational cross-referencing between signalling verbs, and attention to syntactic variability in context.

We have observed that the performative act of coinage passes into the reporting of past coinage rather quickly. The switch or progression can take place within a day, and seems to be governed by the verb form involved: in contrast with performative coinage, signalled primarily by the use of present or present perfect forms, reported coinage typically starts when the verb shifts into simple past and past perfect forms. The data search thus focuses on the synonyms in the past tense. In order to give some idea of quantitative facts in this case, a manual analysis of past tense synonyms retrieved by the two search strings shown in Example set 17, was carried out.

EXAMPLE SET 17 Search strings designed to retrieve synonyms of *coined* in past tense usage

- "was [authored|built|composed|conceived|concocted|conjured|created|minted]",
  with filter "[word|phrase|term]" (at position left 1)
- "[authored|built|composed|conceived|concocted|conjured|created|minted]
  the [word|phrase|term]" (within a single sentence)

These synonym search terms were expanded to include phrasal verb forms, as well as some periphrastic formulations such as the nominalised *first use*. The frequency counts are provisional because of the size and complexity of working manually with big data. One economising measure employed above was to increase precision by restricting the coinage labelling inventory to *word, phrase,* and *term,* thereby excluding rarer alternatives such as *name, slogan, expression* and *acronym*. Another was to control the nature and length of context. Both measures rendered the analytical task more feasible, though inevitably limiting the insights gained.

Verbs, active and passive voice, which have functioned as signals to retrieve past coinages are enumerated in Table 2.1.

TABLE 2.1 *Verbs which signal past coinage*

Transitive verbs							
invented	287	minted	9	built	1	generated	1
created	19	formed	6	conceived	1	initiated	1
made	17	produced	4	conjured	1		
originated	12	designed	4	formulated	1		
devised	10	concocted	2	framed	1		
Phrasal verbs				**Intransitive verbs**			
came up with	75	made up	5	first appeared	46	came into existence	2
gave birth to	11	thought up	6	emerged	4	first use	6
dreamed up	8			occurred	3		

3.4.3 Ambiguity of Some Past Coinage Signals

Bona fide examples of coinage reported by the verbs in Table 2.1 are seen in Example set 18.

EXAMPLE SET 18 Coinage signals of bona fide past coinage

1. 06/92 the term '**producer capture**' was **invented** in the Sixties by the United States's Public Choice analysts
2. 12/87 'I **constructed** the name **Thomas Bowen Chandler** from two past senators,' he replied.
3. 06/87 He **acquired** the name **'Henry Streep Porter'** after a hoax interview with a lady purporting to be Meryl Streep.
4. 01/04 It is almost exactly two years since George Bush **conjured** the phrase "**axis of evil**" to demonise Iraq, Iran and North Korea.
5. 09/09 Michael Harrington, the democratic socialist, first **came up with** the word "**neoconservatism**".
6. 08/11 Reynolds points out that the British rave label Ibiza had "**the first use of** the word '**jungle**' on their [12-inch] sleeves"
7. 04/13 **the word "feminist" came into existence in 1895**
8. 04/14 His 2011 book **The Precariat** set out its story: the term was **originally used** in 1980s France to denote temporary and seasonal workers

However, it emerges from the study that many synonyms of *coined* are of limited reliability in reporting past coinage signals, since, unlike COIN, they do not unambiguously signal authorship of past word coinage. In Example set 19, we see some verbs of this kind.

EXAMPLE SET 19 Some verbs which do not unambiguously signal past coinage

1. 03/97 that Bentley had called out **'Let him have it, Chris.'** Bentley insisted that the police **concocted** the phrase
2. 06/98 At least, until Martin Bell **added** the phrase **'ethnic cleansing'** to our vocabulary.
3. 06/99 **Carillion** was **chosen** because, Tarmac says, of its 'connotations with a peel of bells, suggesting the new clarity of the construction business'.
4. 03/01 Rowling, who ... told the New York judge in January that she **came up with** the word **muggles** after hearing people call each other "mugs".
5. 11/15 Californian farmers **came up with** the name **avocado** in the early 20th century. They adopted the name, but did not coin it.

6. 08/05 In 1925, the nation ... **adopted** the term "**universal time**" to avoid international confusion

---

In Example set 19, example 1, *concocted* means 'coined—but also manipulated the truth in doing so'. In 2, *added the phrase to our vocabulary* means this journalist 'took the existing phrase and popularised it'.[11] In 3, *chosen* means 'selected from other existing word candidates'.[12] In 5, *came up with* is subsequently explained as meaning 'adopted' (of an existing name).[13] In 6, *adopted* means 'officially accepted', of a long existing term evolving in meaning internationally.

Similarly, some adverbials are not always reliable signifiers of past coinage. The adverb *first* is a case in point, as seen in Example set 20.

EXAMPLE SET 20 The adverb *first* as unreliable signal of past coinage

---

1. 02/97 Incidentally, John Roberts was incorrect when he wrote that the term **'Grand Slam'** was **first applied to** tennis in 1938. It was first used in the 'New York Post' in 1933.
2. 04/07 The marines were called **skinheads** in the Second World War, but the term was **first applied to** British youth towards the end of the Sixties
3. 03/03 he has a "personal commitment" to a Palestinian state. But he has said much the same before. Nor does **this first use of** the word **"personal"** make it any more likely to happen.
4. 04/08 **the first use of the word "radical"**, in a political sense, is ascribed to the English Whig parliamentarian, Charles James Fox ... in 1797

The adverb *first* does refer to the first occurrence of the use of a word, but not necessarily to its birth. It can refer to the first use of a word in a particular context or to the earlier use in the same text, and so on. In examples 1 and 2 in Example set 20, the phrase *first applied* does not signify the first use or coinage of a word. In 3, the phrase *first use of* in combination with the

11 See https://en.wikipedia.org/wiki/Ethnic_cleansing (last accessed 19 June 2017) for the earliest antecedents to the present-day sense.

12 *Carillion* is the misspelling of carillon, 'a bell', which is however a common proper name for companies.

13 As a matter of interest, as seen in 4, *came up with* often means 'coined as a result of external prompting.'

epithet *personal* similarly does not signify coinage. In 4, the phrase *first use of* is qualified by *in a political sense*, thus identifying a case of semantic change rather than of neology.

What we have found with past signalling using the simple past and past perfect forms in terms of the prevalent verb choices, both unambiguous and ambiguous, seems to apply also in the case of the historic present tense. The range of verbs functioning in this way, however, is very limited. Examples are shown in Example set 21, and seem to favour *first* as a prompt.

EXAMPLE SET 21 Examples of the historic present tense used to signal past coinage

1. 02/90 'I was a Rich Man's Plaything' (1947) is a patchwork of pulp-mag bimbo and Coca-Cola ad. In it, incidentally, the word **'Pop' makes its first appearance** in art.
2. 02/14 The phrase **'consent of the governed' first appears** in the Declaration of Independence.

3.4.4 Reasons for Past Coinage Signalling

We next consider why past coinages are ever signalled as such. The answer, as shown in Example sets 22 and 23, is that irrespective of their vintage, earlier coinages can become relevant as background information in present-day text wherever the topic has a historical perspective. This occurs, for instance, in book reviews and in articles on past phenomena. Another use of early coinages is a stylistic one: to bring a sense of gravitas to a current issue. A peculiarly mediatic phenomenon is the appearance of past coinage information to answer readers' queries on various topics.

EXAMPLE SET 22 References to past coinages

1. 05/90 **Subsidiarity** ... **The term was minted** not in Brussels but **in Rome, by Pope Pius XI in** an encyclical of **1931.**
2. 09/13 'Outsider house' is the latest dance music subgenre ... **The term was created** to pull together US producers who embrace lo-fi techniques. Hessle Audio's BenUFO **first playfully coined the term "outsider house" during a Rinse FM show.**
3. 11/93 What is the origin of having 40 **winks?** *Wink* ... The word seems to have been used for brief eye-closing or sleep since the middle ages ... The curious thing is that the phrase '40 winks' seems to have **made its first appearance** in 1828

4. 02/90 the ICA Fun House **1956**. Its in house critic, Lawrence Alloway **invented the designation 'Pop Art'**

In Example set 22, in example 1, the term *subsidiarity* is dated back to 1931 in a 1990 report on a meeting of European Community leaders to discuss political union. In 2, the coinage *outsider house* is attributed to a record company head in the context of an album review. In 3, the coinage *40 winks* is dated in answer to a reader query. In 4, the coinage *pop art* is attributed, and approximately dated to the 1950s, in a 1990 art review. A similar rationale revives very early coinages, as exemplified in Example set 23.

EXAMPLE SET 23 References to early coinages

---

1. 12/08 Although the term **macaronic verse** was **coined in 1488**, as a literary practice it can be dated back at least to Ausonius (born in about 310).
2. 10/06 The term "**grand tour**" was **coined in 1670** to denote an institutionalised pilgrimage of juvenile lords.
3. 05/12 the word '**nostalgia**' originally had a rather different meaning: **coined in 1678**, it described expatriate injured soldiers overcome by longing for their native land ...
4. 07/90 More important was the appearance of the **restaurant, a word** inadvertently **coined in 1765** by an enterprising Paris soup-seller.

In Example set 23, example 1 mentions and dates the term *macaronic verse* to 1488 in the course of advertising a new English translation of a poem in 2007. Example 2 mentions and dates the coinage of *grand tour* to 1670, in a new text narrating the history of the "grand tour". Example 3 provides the etymology of the coinage *nostalgia* in a new text on the same topic. Example 4 dates the coinage of *restaurant* as 1765 in a new report on cooking with simple ingredients in London.

3.4.5 Favoured Anchorings for Past Coinage

A final aspect of past coinage which we shall investigate concerns the features or circumstances of birth which seem to be most salient and thus cited by writers over the intervening years, decades or centuries. It is useful to take a closer look at provenance, given the utility of such information to lexicographers, translators, and terminologists, specialists in documenting the life-cycle of neologisms.

The form *coined* is an unambiguous marker of authorship, more so than COIN in simple present and present perfect forms (when it is both very rare, and potentially ambiguous as to sense and function). When interrogated for details on time and date by the search string "coined + at", the corpus yields relevant information, as sampled in Example sets 24 and 25.

EXAMPLE SET 24 Sample of past coinages provenanced historically by date

---

1. time—at an approximate time (4 occs):
   05/14 The term "**pinkification**" seems to have been coined **at around this time**
2. time—at a contextually deducible time (3 occs):
   01/15 The army interludes ...ram home Lodge's New Man credentials by placing him sideways-on to "**the establishment**", a phrase coined **at almost exactly the time he set off** for basic training at Bovington Camp in Dorset.
3. time—at an exact time (1 occ):
   08/92 To pay due credit to my fellow panellists, the anthologists will ... wish to record the gorgeous waterfall of aphorisms coined **at 7.35 on the night of Friday 30 September 1978.**
4. time—specified to the nearest century (3 occs):
   08/95 The word [smog] was coined **at the turn of the century** to describe the acidic smoke-plus-fog that regularly blighted the London winter.

It might be thought that "coined + at" would retrieve the precise moment of coinage. In fact, such detail is retrieved by this search string only once in the entire corpus, as seen in example 3 in Example set 24. More typically, the time and date are less precisely identified, if at all.

In Example set 25, we are shown that a past coinage can also be recalled via an associated event or location.

EXAMPLE SET 25 Sample of past coinages associated historically with events and places

---

1. event plus year (6 occs):
   09/98 The term '**New Queer Cinema**' was coined **at the Sundance film festival in 1992 by Ruby Rich**, a Village Voice journalist.
2. institution plus [year|decade] (5 occs):
   06/10 the word "**soccer**" was coined **at a British university in the 19th century.**

3. event only (3 occs):
   08/11 "**Austerity chic**" was surely a gift catchphrase coined **at the first script meeting.**
4. place only (1 occ):
   03/87 **Fresh**, an **acronym** coined **at Sainsbury's** ... standing for 'friendly, responsive, enthusiastic, sincere, helpful and positive'.

Since "coined + at" restricts the source details to those retrievable by the preposition *at*, we show briefly in Example set 26 that a more articulated search string such as "coined by *9 at *9 in" can achieve greater precision of provenance.

EXAMPLE SET 26 "coined by *9 at *9 in" with greater precision of source details

---

1. 03/08 "**post-classic**" wines ... The term was coined **by** the world's leading viticulturist Dr Richard Smart, **at** the second World Conference on Global Warming and Wine **in** Barcelona last month
2. 07/09 "**platonic lover**" (a term coined **by** the Florentine philosopher Marsilio Ficino) **at** a chivalric tournament ... **in** 1475.
3. 12/10 The term **octothorpe** was coined **by** engineers **at** Bell Laboratories **in** the early 1960s
4. 05/15 **growth hacker** ... The term was coined **by** Sean Ellis, who was the head of growth **at** Dropbox, in 2010.

In the sample output in Example set 26, it is notable that strategic search filtering can indeed coax precision out of the corpus. The search string "coined by *9 at *9 in", where *9 means 'up to 9 tokens',[14] yields 15 instances of detailed provenance, including coiner, location and date. In addition, the coiner is usually a famous person in recent or remote history.

In this final part of the study, with a view to providing a typology of past signalling, we have tried to reveal some of its characteristics by examining which signals of past coinage are active and which reliable, the reasons for past coinage signalling, and the preferred points of reference for past coinage as they emerge in our corpus searches.

---

14 A wildcard span of 9 words is the largest currently allowed in our system.

4 Closing Remarks

In this study, we have attempted to provide an overview of the circumstances under which new words are coined, and by which means. We have studied a series of words presented as candidate neologisms by our automated corpus monitoring system, as well as potential words in Bauer's (2001) study. We have retrieved from these a range of lexical and phrasal signals of coinage, supplemented by words intuitively associated with word coinage, and synonyms of proven coinage signals. These data have been analysed to create a framework for a working classification of coinage types.

Within this framework, we have attempted to convey our observations about the stages of treatment of word coinage at the start of its life-cycle, as well as in the post-coinage, later-life citation phase. We have tried to illustrate how first occurrence words are not necessarily deliberate coinages, created to name a major new invention or concept, and adopted in the public arena; but are often incidental formations, accompanied inconsistently by coinage signals and source information. We have observed that potential word coinages (Bauer, 2001) can be marked by tentative signalling, indicating that they are not yet deemed to properly exist (i.e. to have entered into the lexicon). We have demonstrated that performative signalling occurs where the act of coinage takes place within the text itself. Finally, we have tried to show some of the character of past signalling, in terms of its purpose, the signals involved, and source information provided.

The study is inevitably impressionistic, for reasons of corpus size, extensive manual analysis, and the possible semantic and functional ambiguity of candidate signals. Nevertheless, we hope to have arrived at a reasonable working typology of coinage signalling. In terms of future work, there are many additional ways of expressing the same classes of signalling, as well as many unconventional signals and aspects of word coinage to account for. There is also much still to be discovered about the signalling of phrases, semantic neology, re-coinage and other features of lexis. These will be the focus of our continuing search for finer definitions of neology.

References

Aronoff, M. (1983). Potential words, actual words, productivity and frequency. *Proceedings of the Thirteenth International Congress of Linguists*. 163–171.

Austin, J.L. (1956). Performative utterances. In J.O. Urmson & G.J. Warnock (Eds.), *Philosophical papers of J.L. Austin*, 1961 (pp. 220–239). Oxford: Oxford University Press.

Baayen, H.R., & Sproat, R. (1996). Estimating lexical priors for low-frequency morphologically ambiguous forms. *Computational Linguistics, 22*(2), 155–166.

Baayen, H.R., & Neijt, A. (1997). Productivity in context: A case study of a Dutch suffix. *Linguistics, 35*, 565–587.

Baayen, H.R., van Halteren, H., Neijt, A., & Tweedie, F. (2002). An experiment in authorship attribution. Paper given at *JADT 2002*.

Bauer, L. (1988). *Introducing linguistic morphology*. Edinburgh: Edinburgh University Press.

Bauer, L. (2001). *Morphological productivity*. Cambridge: Cambridge University Press.

Bauer, L., Lieber, R., & Plag, I. (2013). *The Oxford reference guide to English morphology* (Oxford Linguistics). Oxford: Oxford University Press.

Collins English dictionary—Complete and unabridged (12th ed.). (2014). HarperCollins Publishers.

Halle, M. (1973). Prolegomena to a theory of word formation. *Linguistic Inquiry, 4*(1), 3–16.

Hohenhaus, P. (2007). How to do (even more) things with nonce words (other than naming). In J. Munat (Ed.), *Lexical creativity, texts and contexts* (pp. 17–36). Amsterdam & Philadelphia: John Benjamins.

Marchand, H. (1969). *The categories and types of Present-Day English word formation* (2nd ed.) Munich: Beck.

Mey, J.L. (2001). *Pragmatics: An introduction* (2nd ed.). Mass. US & Oxford: Wiley-Blackwell.

Shea, A. (2012, April 25). Tracing the birth of words: from 'open' to 'heffalump'. Retrieved from http://blog.oxforddictionaries.com/2012/04/tracing-the-birth-of-words/. Last accessed 19 June 2017.

Oxford English Dictionary Online. (2016) Oxford University Press. Retrieved from http://www.oed.com/. Last accessed 19 June 2017.

Peirce, C.S. (1932). Division of signs. In C. Hartshorne & P. Weiss (Eds.), *Collected papers of Charles Sanders Peirce, Vol.* II (pp. 134–155). Cambridge: Harvard University Press. [1897]. OCLC 783138

Renouf, A., & Bauer, L. (2001). Contextual clues to word-meaning. *International Journal of Corpus Linguistics, 5*(2), 231–258.

Renouf, A. (2013). A finer definition of neology in English: the life-cycle of a word. In H. Hasselgård, S.O. Ebeling & J. Ebeling (Eds.), *Corpus perspectives on patterns of lexis* (pp. 177–208). Amsterdam/Philadelphia: John Benjamins.

Schmid, H.-J. et al. (2014). EnerG—English Neologisms Research Group. Retrieved from http://www.neocrawler.anglistik.uni-muenchen.de/crawler/html/index.php?abfrage=about. Last accessed 17 June 2017.

Strang, B. (1970). *A history of English*. London: Methuen.

Zandvoort, R.W. (1972). *Handbook of English grammar* (6th ed.). Harlow: Longman.

CHAPTER 3

Synonym Selection as a Strategy of Stress Clash Avoidance

Julia Schlüter and Gabriele Knappe

1 Introduction and Hypothesis

The Principle of Rhythmic Alternation holds that

> [...] stressed and stressless syllables tend to alternate at *rhythmically ideal disyllabic distances*. Rhythmic alternation manifests itself by the avoidance of sequences of stressed syllables, as well as of long sequences of stressless syllables.[1]
>
> KAGER, 1989, p. 2, italics in the original

Schlüter (2005) and subsequent studies[2] have provided quantitative evidence of the influence of rhythm on grammatical variation and change. This paper is an attempt to determine to what degree stress clash avoidance can also determine lexical choices, which is an area that has so far been almost completely neglected. The basic idea for this study is inspired by Bolinger's (1965b, p. 149) observation that *a glád dáy* seems objectionable, while *a glád occásion* or *a háppy dáy* are acceptable.[3] He surmises that in cases where speakers or writers plan to use a sequence of lexemes that would result in the adjacency of two strongly stressed syllables, they may replace one of the words with a rhythmically more fitting one. Needless to say, such a bypass will be adopted only if it does not substantially alter the intended meaning.

1 For some further, largely congruent, formulations of the principle, see Jespersen (1909, p. 156; 1972, p. 97); Fijn van Draat (1910, p. 9); Behaghel (1924, pp. vi–vii); Bolinger (1965b, p. 139); Selkirk (1984, p. 37); Nespor & Vogel (1989, p. 69, 82); Couper-Kuhlen (1986, p. 60).

2 Cf. Lee & Gibbons (2007); Schlüter (2008, 2015); Anttila, Adams & Speriosu (2010); Speyer (2010); Mollin (2012, 2014); Lohmann (2014); Ehret, Wolk & Szmrecsanyi (2014); Shih, Grafmiller, Futrell & Bresnan (2015).

3 In the examples here and elsewhere, acute accents are added to indicate primary lexical stress.

 | DOI: 10.1163/9789004361133_005

Putting Bolinger's impressionistic (albeit very perceptive) observation to an empirical test is not an easy task since in the lexical domain semantic equivalence is harder to establish than in the domains of morphological and syntactic variants. To counterbalance these difficulties, we will focus on rhythmic and syntactic constellations that can be predicted to exhibit the strongest impact of the Principle of Rhythmic Alternation. Its effect strength has been shown to depend both on the degree of stress (primary, secondary, no stress) and the degree of syntactic bonding (i.e., the width of the prosodic juncture). We will adopt a binary division between primary and non-primary stress and focus on attributive adjectives immediately preceding the nouns they modify. Prenominal uses (also referred to as attributive uses in this paper) represent the critical contexts, where the two elements are syntactically and prosodically tightly bound to each other. Combinations of adjectives + nouns are relatively frequent, as c. 65% of adjectives occur prenominally (according to a POS-tag-based search of COCA, on which see below). What makes the situation even more liable to stress clashes is that initial stress is prevalent in English nouns: Approximately 85% of noun tokens in the Brown corpus have initial stress (cf. Schlüter, 2005, p. 330; cf. also Cutler & Carter, 1987). Two examples of such critical contexts are given in (1a) and (2a).

(1) a. ***glád*** *péople* ***háppy*** *péople*
b. *they were* ***glád*** *they were* ***háppy***

(2) a. ***rích*** *péople* ***wéalthy*** *péople*
b. *they were* ***rích*** *they were* ***wéalthy***

When adjectives appear in other, i.e. predicative and otherwise postnominal, positions, as in (1b) and (2b), they are typically followed by (unstressed) function words or pauses. Even in the few occurrences where this is not the case, they are rarely part of a phrase with the same degree of syntactic and prosodic bonding as an attributive structure. Thus, other contexts can be considered as rhythmically uncritical and will serve as control contexts. To test Bolinger's (1965b, p. 149) suggestion, we can therefore formulate two hypotheses, aiming to reject the null hypothesis and to support the alternative hypothesis:

> H_0: Two adjectives with equivalent meanings and different rhythmic shapes (monosyllabic and end-stressed or plurisyllabic and non-end-stressed) occur equally often in all syntactic functions.

> H_1: Two adjectives with equivalent meanings and different rhythmic shapes (monosyllabic and end-stressed or plurisyllabic and non-end-stressed) do not occur equally often in all syntactic functions.

If it was only the meaning of an adjective that determined its placement in sentences, details of its phonological (or rhythmic) shape should be irrelevant. But if H_1 holds true, we expect a monosyllabic or end-stressed adjective (like *glad* or *rich*) to occur less often in a rhythmically critical context than a non-end-stressed adjective with an equivalent meaning (like *happy* or *wealthy*). Their occurrence in control contexts should remain unaffected by their rhythmic shapes.

One complication of our proposal lies in the fact that words cannot be studied irrespective of their individual histories, including their baseline frequencies, deep-rooted co-occurrence patterns, established semantic ranges, etc. In order to assess the time-depth and relative stability of our findings for Present-Day English, we will therefore compare the syntactic uses of adjective pairs (and a triplet) over the past 200 years. In addition, we will, in a case study, fathom the role of specific fixed collocations (phraseological units) by looking at their developments from the 16th century onwards. If the Principle of Rhythmic Alternation turns out to have explanatory potential, we predict a contrast between critical and control contexts that should be stable diachronically, across different varieties (British and American English) and across spoken and written modes, as discussed in the concluding section.

Our prediction is reflected in the corpus selection and search procedures described in Section 3. Before turning to the considerable methodological challenges posed by our research question, in the following Section 2, we will briefly discuss our choice of adjectives and the notion of synonymy that we employ. Section 4 looks at the results for the synonym pairs and the triplet individually and for *happy—glad* in greater historical depth, and ends with a synopsis of spoken and written data from Present-Day English. In the concluding section, we will throw into relief the theoretical relevance of our findings and point out shortcomings and avenues for further research.

2 Choice of Items for Analysis and Notes on Synonymy

Besides the seminal remarks in Bolinger (1965b, p. 149), who—among some other examples—draws attention to the pair *glad—happy*, the small selection of adjectives to be scrutinised in this paper takes *Oxford Learner's Dictionaries Online* as its starting point. This resource contains a list of lemmas where special notes about synonyms, defined as "words with similar meanings",[4] can be found. From the considerable number of adjectives listed, we selected the pair *rich—wealthy* and the triplet *fast—quick—rapid* on the grounds that the adjectives a) involve a rhythmically relevant difference, b) constitute sufficiently close synonyms, and c) can be retrieved from a corpus with reasonable precision. (For some additional candidates, see Section 5.) The pair *shut—closed*, which will receive special consideration in Section 4.4, is adduced by Bolinger (1965a, p. 135) in a different but comparable context: Though both members of the pair are monosyllables, they will allow us to extend and supplement our notion of rhythmic alternation to include the impact of syllable length.

Following Cruse (2002, p. 486), we understand synonymy as "a relation of similarity/identity of meaning between senses associated with two (or more) lexical forms", or, in cognitive terms, two or more lexical forms that are mapped onto the same concept. For our analysis of pairs (and the triplet) of adjectives, Cruse's (1986, p. 88) notion of cognitive synonymy is particularly useful (cf. also Paradis, 1997, p. 67; for further discussion cf. Cruse, 2002, pp. 489–490 on propositional synonymy):

> X is a cognitive synonym of Y if (i) X and Y are syntactically identical, and (ii) any grammatical declarative sentence S containing X has equivalent truth-conditions to another sentence S[1], which is identical to S except that X is replaced by Y.

The adjectives we consider may be interchanged in declarative sentences without changing the equivalence of the truth conditions of the sentences involved, and this goes for both types of syntactic contexts (i.e., prenominal and postnominal). The following examples will show the relevance of Cruse's cognitive synonymy in terms of mutual entailment for our approach:[5]

(3) a. The Arabian sheik was **wealthy**.
 b. The Arabian sheik was **rich**.

(4) a. He was a **wealthy** man.
 b. He was a **rich** man.

4 Cf. the "usage notes" at: www.oxfordlearnersdictionaries.com/wordlist/english/usage_notes/UsageNoteList_Synonyms/.

5 Sentences (3a) and (3b) were used by Lyons (1968, p. 450) to illustrate his concept of synonymy, which is propositional synonymy.

If sentence (3a) is true, sentence (3b) is true, and if sentence (3b) is true, sentence (3a) is true; if sentence (3a) is false, sentence (3b) is false, and if sentence (3b) is false, sentence (3a) is false. The same mutual entailment can be shown for (4a) and (4b). Since all conditions apply, *wealthy* and *rich* are cognitive synonyms in the contexts relevant for our analysis. As opposed to absolute synonymy, not all senses of the lexemes have to match in this way; the denotational ranges of the lexemes may in fact differ in size (cf. also Section 4.1). In addition, the notion of cognitive synonymy tolerates collocational restrictions (e.g., *filthy rich*, but **filthy wealthy*; cf. Cruse, 1986, pp. 279–282) and will for the present purposes be extended to cover the merely partial equivalence of prenominal *happy* and *glad* (cf. 4.3).

Cognitive synonyms form the second of three levels of synonyms in Cruse, which are differentiated by frequency. The most frequent kind of synonymy is plesionymy (near synonymy; cf. Cruse, 2002, pp. 490–491), where the senses connected to word-forms show a relatively minor meaning difference. The relation of plesionymy can be found out by the *or rather* test, as in *He was murdered, or rather executed.* Plesionyms yield sentences with different truth-conditions and are therefore not relevant for our study. The third type, absolute synonyms—"two distinct lexical forms being associated with senses that are identical" (Cruse, 2002, p. 488)—belong into the smallest, "vanishingly rare" (Cruse, 2002, p. 490) group of synonyms.

"Absolute synonymy is rare—and when found mostly fleeting" (Dolezal, 2013, p. 255). This transience as well as instances of cognitive synonymy may give way to splits. Two types of splits have been discussed in the literature so far: First, they can be of a semantic nature (cf. Cruse, 2002, p. 489), and possibly result in stylistic divergence. For instance, the native word *hearty* and the foreign loan *cordial* both were in late Middle English used to express feelings that were supposed to spring from the heart. But then *hearty* came to imply a certain physical vigour and downrightness, as in *a hearty dinner*, and *cordial* a more quiet or conventional manifestation, as in *a cordial reception* (cf. Baugh & Cable, 2013, p. 176; *cordial* is labelled "formal" in *Oxford Learner's Dictionaries Online*). A second form the split can take is (idiosyncratic) collocational restriction, for example in the pair *flawless* and *impeccable*. *Flawless*, according to Cruse (2002, p. 489), shows collocational restrictions: While the noun *performance* can be modified by either adjective, *impeccable*, but not *flawless*, collocates with the noun *behaviour*.[6] The present contribution suggests a

6 Viewed from a historical perspective (cf. OED, s.v. *impeccable* adj. and *flawless* adj.), this split might go back to the original uses of these adjectives. *Impeccable* is first attested in 1531

third type of split, namely syntactic specialisation, and investigates the factors underlying such instances of syntactic split.

3 Corpora, Search Expressions and Sampling Methods

In order to test the assumed diachronic stability of the contrasting distributions of synonymous adjectives, the main parts of the following analyses (4.1–4.4) are based on a diachronic corpus spanning two centuries: The *Corpus of Historical American English* (COHA) comprises a total of 400 million words of written American English taken from fiction, popular magazines, newspapers and non-fiction books, and is subdivided into 20 decades (1810s–2000s). To manage the large amount of data and retain reasonable control of the hits that entered our counts, we picked five more or less evenly spaced decades from which we retrieved the adjectives under investigation.[7] In most cases, attaching the part-of-speech tag for adjectives [j*] proved useful to enhance the precision of the search. However, for the item *fast*, which was frequently mistagged, all ambiguous tags that incorporated the adjective tag [j*] among their options were included in the search. For *closed*, which is highly ambiguous between past participles, past tense forms and adjectives, and *shut*, which in addition serves as the present tense and infinitive, it was found that part-of-speech tagging was extremely unreliable. To obtain the full range of results, all instances marked with adjective [j*] and past participle [v?n*] tags (in the case of ambiguities, including all tags containing either [j*] or [v?n*]) were retrieved.

with the meaning 'of persons: not capable of or liable to sin; exempt from the possibility of sinning or doing wrong'. This meaning is last attested in 1849; from 1620 onwards *impeccable* developed the meaning 'of things: faultless, unerring'. *Flawless*, on the other hand, is first attested in 1659 with the meaning 'free from flaws; without a crack, defect, or imperfection'. It seems to have never referred to persons. While the meanings can be seen to partly converge from 1620 onwards in 'faultless, without imperfection', *flawless* (still) cannot collocate with a noun relating to persons, such as *behaviour*.

7 For details of corpus structure, see the link in the reference section. As indicated by the tabular overview available from that website, our earliest decade (1820–1829) contains no newspaper data and our second decade (1860–1869) contains a smaller share of newspaper data than the later decades. However, while normalised frequencies of the adjectives under investigation vary between genres (for extralinguistic reasons), sporadic checks on our data revealed no influence of genre on the rhythmic effects targeted in this study.

Further, the hypothesis proposed in Section 1 distinguishes not only between mono- and disyllabic adjectives, but also between hits preceding a stressed syllable within a noun phrase and such where this is not the case. In order to isolate rhythmically critical examples of the former type, every corpus search was followed up with another search where the adjective in question preceded a word tagged as a noun [nn*].[8] On this basis, the percentage of prenominal occurrences (defined above as "critical contexts") out of all occurrences of the adjective in question was calculated as the crucial parameter of comparison in this study.

For both types of contexts, irrelevant hits had to be excluded. For example, due to ambiguous tagging, the search for *fast* retrieved more instances that represented the adverbial use than the adjectival one, and among instances of the latter numerous examples that did not mean 'quick, rapid' but 'firm, constant, steadfast' (as in *fast friend, hard and fast rule*, etc.). Moreover, some of the hits preceding nouns were not adjectival premodifiers of the nouns in question. Thus, manual checks of all hits (in the case of low numbers) or of (one or occasionally two) random samples of 100 examples were carried out to assess the quota of irrelevant hits, which was then, by way of extrapolation, subtracted from the total numbers of hits in that corpus subsection. To exemplify this procedure, the search for the ambiguous item *closed* tagged as an adjective or past participle yielded 2436 hits for the decade 1990–1999. A sample of 100 of these was checked, producing a relatively high proportion of 33 hits (= 33 %) that were irrelevant, i.e. verbal rather than adjectival uses (e.g. *They must have closed their windows* ..., COHA 1997). Further, the search for the same item immediately followed by the tag for a noun produced 429 hits, 100 of

8 While this search retrieves virtually all instances of the item in question followed by a common noun, it misses other potentially relevant hits that also involve attributive uses preceding a stressed syllable, where this syllable belongs to an adjective, nominalised numeral or proper noun (e.g. *a wealthy Dutch family*, COHA 1999; *the wealthy few*, COHA 1995; *a wealthy Prague family*, COHA 1992). In a sample of 100 hits for the adjective *wealthy*, 46 hits preceded a common noun and thus were correctly retrieved by our search for critical contexts, but there were another potentially relevant 12 hits of the three abovementioned types that escaped the search. The recall for the search for critical contexts was thus 46/58 = 79 %. Conversely, of a random 100 hits retrieved by a search for *wealthy* immediately preceding a noun, 13 preceded a noun that was not initially stressed: The precision of the search for critical contexts was 87 % and thus not significantly different from the average of 85 % of noun tokens with initial stress. Precision and recall rates vary between adjectives as well as corpus sections. The analyses in Section 4 will show to what extent rhythmic effects remain stable in the face of these error margins.

which were manually checked, yielding an error rate of 3% (e.g. *He ... hung the* CLOSED *sign from the hook*, COHA 1997; *they had quietly closed ranks against him* COHA 1993). Thus, the crucial parameter *percentage of prenominal use* was calculated as (429*0.97) / (2436*0.67) = 416/1632 = 25.5% (see Figure 3.5 below).

In an extension of the results to Present-Day English retrieved from COHA, in Section 4.5 the same search procedures which were applied to COHA were repeated for the *Corpus of Contemporary American English* (COCA; 450 million words from the period 1990–2012 at the time of retrieval, May 2015). The results will allow us to compare written and spoken usage. While the spoken component (20%) is considerably smaller than the written one, the hits for the adjectives investigated are plenty in both the spoken and written sections.

These searches, sampling procedures and extrapolations produce highly reliable results where overall numbers of occurrence are not too high and part-of-speech tagging produces low error rates. For those adjectives that are highly frequent and often mistagged, samples of 100 hits per subcorpus and adjective can provide indications as to the direction of the contrast, but larger samples would be necessary to draw firmer conclusions. What can partly make up for high error rates is the large number of independent samples that have been drawn (at least 100 hits per adjective per decade in COHA and per corpus section in COCA). To check the statistical significance of differences observed between pairs of synonymous adjectives, we will thus report results of chi-square tests in footnotes for every single corpus subperiod. The tests calculate the error probability if we reject H_0, that is if we assume that the rhythmic shape of the adjectives analysed does have an influence on their use in different syntactic functions. Where our samples of prenominal occurrences yielded an error rate of 0%, chi-square results for the proportion of prenominal uses per adjective will be indicated straightforwardly. Where the samples produced error rates (i.e., occurrences of the search word preceding the POS tag [nn*] that did not represent actual attributive adjectives), these will be reported as percentages and the chi-square results for the extrapolated proportions of prenominal uses will be indicated in brackets. Since the chi-square results cannot be taken at face value after extrapolation, we will thus adopt a careful interpretation. In total, the cumulative evidence from all case studies we have performed so far points in the same direction so that the findings seem to mutually support each other.

In Section 4.3 we extend the diachronic study by a case study on the development of *glad tidings* vs. *happy tidings* and *glad news* vs. *happy news*, based on the corpus *Early English Books Online* (EEBO; version of July 2016). This collection includes "virtually every work printed in England, Ireland, Scotland, Wales and British North America and works in English printed elsewhere from 1473–1700" (http://eebo.chadwyck.com/about/about.htm) and covers 130,000 titles and more than 17 million scanned pages. In the EEBO corpus we searched for absolute numbers and relative percentages of competing word-form tokens, including spelling variants.

4 Analysis and Discussion

The four case studies to be presented in this section each focus on one particular synonym pair or triplet. Since lexical items—even such belonging to the same grammatical class—differ vastly from each other in their formal, semantic and collocational characteristics, each of the following subsections will have a different focus. Thus, the contrastive study of *rich* and *wealthy* will deal with differences in the denotational range of the adjectives. The comparison of *fast, quick* and *rapid* will include some notes on the lexicalisation of collocations and on stylistic levels. The analysis of *glad* and *happy* will address the historical dimension of collocations and the question of how to weigh collocational fixations against free choice of synonyms. Finally, the investigation of the two monosyllables *shut* and *closed* will allow us to extend the hypothesis to effects of syllable duration. Far from being exhaustive, these alternating perspectives will serve as mere pointers to the various influences involved in the choice of synonyms.

4.1 *Rich—Wealthy*

The usage note on synonyms in *Oxford Learner's Dictionaries Online* (s.v. *rich, wealthy*) defines *rich* in the sense relevant here as follows: "(of a person) having a lot of money, property or valuable possessions; (of a country or city) producing a lot of wealth so that many of its people can live at a high standard". The definition of *wealthy* is simply phrased in terms of its synonym: "rich". In addition, the dictionary site answers the question "rich or wealthy?" by stating that "[t]here is no real difference in meaning between these two words." It furthermore notes that *wealthy* is less frequent than *rich* and is not interchangeable with the latter in "fixed phrases" such as *stinking/filthy rich* or *the rich and famous*. The assumption of synonymy is corroborated by a large number of comparable examples from our corpus searches where the choice of adjective appears more or less random (bold emphasis in all examples is ours):

(5) a. Are the **rích péople** just going to keep those loaves to grow mold? (COHA nonfiction, 1998)
b. There are very, very **wéalthy péople** in the neighborhood and some who are just regular old middle class folks ... (COHA news, 1992)

(6) a. Westerners have heard many times that Shanghai has grown **rích** and adopted Western culture ... (COHA news, 1997)
b. Market studies suggest that 10 percent of Hungarians have grown **wéalthy** under capitalism ... (COHA news, 1994)

Interchangeability can generally be posited in collocations with humans (e.g. *people, kids, girl, widow*) and collectives (e.g. *countries, city, family*). However, *rich* (but not *wealthy*) in the corpus data also combines with a wider range of collocates (e.g. *soil, literature, fabric, flavour, history, resource, experience*), which exemplify its wider denotational range.

Predictably, our corpus searches confirm the lower frequency of *wealthy*, which—despite substantial gains in frequency—is still outnumbered by *rich* three- to fourfold in the early 21st century. In view of our research hypothesis, however, the more interesting comparison is between the relative percentages of prenominal uses of both adjectives: If the null hypothesis is to be rejected, examples like (5a), where *rich* premodifies and immediately precedes a noun, should make up a smaller percentage of the total occurrences than examples like (5b), where *wealthy* occurs prenominally and thus resolves the rhythmically critical situation.

Figure 3.1 presents the results of this analysis. For each decade investigated, the share of instances occurring in rhythmically critical positions (5a/b) out of the total number of instances is indicated. For instance, *wealthy* occurred 105 times in total in the COHA section for the 1820s and all occurrences were examined. 44 of these (41.9%) were in prenominal, i.e. rhythmically critical positions. In the same subperiod, the adjective *rich* occurred 1157 times in total. Of these, 397 hits (34.3%) preceded a word that was tagged as a noun, of which 100 were manually checked. As the random sample contained no spurious example, the error rate was determined to be 0 and, by extrapolation, the number of 397 hits was not adjusted. The graph for *rich* demonstrates that this adjective has of course always been used attributively; actually, attributive uses have constantly accounted for 30 to 42% of the occurrences. Needless to say, attributive use is one of the canonical positions for adjectives, irrespective of their length and despite the fact that with monosyllables this position regularly provokes stress clashes with the following nouns, as in example (5a). However, as Figure 3.1 shows, the synonym *wealthy* dis-

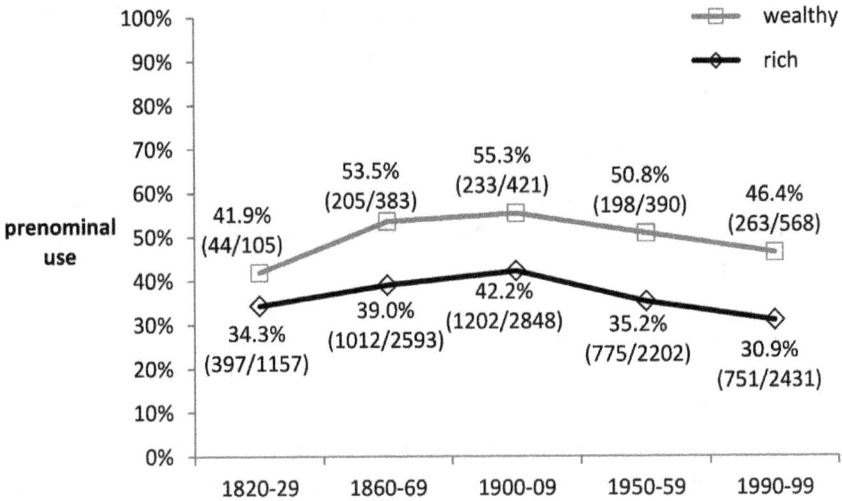

FIGURE 3.1 *The distribution of* rich *and* wealthy *in* COHA*, selected decades*

plays a consistently stronger affinity with prenominal uses, occurring in such positions in 42 to 55% of its occurrences. The difference between the adjectives is statistically highly significant for each of the subperiods investigated, except the first, where *wealthy* is still too infrequent.[9] In line with what was found for adjectives in general (cf. Schlüter, 2005, p. 330; cf. also Cutler & Carter, 1987), both *rich* and *wealthy* are followed by initially stressed nouns in between 84 and 95% of their attributive occurrences across all subperiods. Considering the substantial synonymy of the adjectives, the distributional difference displayed in Figure 3.1 can thus be attributed to the difference in their rhythmic shapes: *Wealthy* is more apt to serve in prenominal position because its disyllabic form effectively prevents the adjacency of stressed syllables.

A further hypothesis that will not be pursued here is that in its other senses, *rich* in prenominal position might be partially replaced by alternative adjectives that fit the rhythmical conditions better. For instance, in its sense 'full of variety', *rich* might yield to *varied*; when referring to food, *nutritious* or *luxurious* may express the same meaning; when referring to soil, *fertile* is an option;

9 For the last subperiod, we have to factor in a certain sampling error, which is why the χ^2 result is only given in brackets. The significance levels for the differences in proportions of prenominal use between *rich* and *wealthy* are: 1820–1829: $\chi^2 = 2.44$ (n.s.), 1860–1869: $\chi^2 = 29.01^{***}$, 1900–1909: $\chi^2 = 25.71^{***}$, 1950–1959: $\chi^2 = 34.27^{***}$, (1990–1999: $\chi^2 = 48.86^{***}$, error rates: *rich* 8%, *wealthy* 1%).

when describing colours or sounds, *vivid, vibrant* or *resonant* could be substituted; in yet other contexts, *gorgeous, splendid, elegant, expensive, precious* or *priceless* may step into the breach prenominally.[10]

4.2 *Fast—Quick—Rapid*

As in the case of *rich* and *wealthy*, for *fast, quick* and *rapid* corpus examples can easily be found that suggest a potential synonymy of the three adjectives in question.

(7) a. ... an inferior force can, through **fást móvement**, surprise attack, and intelligent use of the terrain, mount a successful campaign ... (COHA magazines, 1993)
b. ... she saw, or thought she saw, the same **quíck móvement**, that hesitation, that almost involuntary act of pulling back from something. (COHA fiction, 1996)
c. In addition to an anthropomorphic head-eye system capable of **rápid móvement**, the Waseda teams are combining voice recognition software and speech synthesizers ... (COHA magazines, 1993)

(8) a. She never felt the blow, it was too **fást**. (COHA fiction, 1999)
b. One's rapprochement is never as **quíck** and as charming as it is when one is en route. (COHA magazines, 1997)
c. When the buildup began, the Pentagon tried to make it appear more **rápid** than it actually was, ... (COHA magazines, 1990).

However, a quantitative analysis of the triplet incurs a number of difficulties. The adjective *fast* is particularly problematic since its use in the sense of 'rapid' developed in late Middle and Early Modern English from the homonymous adverb illustrated in *stand fast, run fast* etc. (cf. OED, s.v. *fast*, adj.). Its earlier sense, still well represented in all decades of our corpus though with declining frequency, is that of 'firm, constant, steadfast'. While the automatic tagging supplied by COHA is often ambiguous between adverb and adjective, this disambiguation as well as that between the two senses of the adjective was easy to perform when inspecting the random samples.[11]

---

10 The examples are partly taken from Thesaurus.com (2016).

11 Due to the large number of irrelevant hits that are actually adverbs or adjectives representing the older meaning not synonymous with *quick/rapid*, the high error rates for *fast* lead to considerable insecurity when extrapolation to hundreds or thousands of hits is based

In contrast, *quick*, which can likewise function as an adverb, is rarely mistagged in the data, and *rapid* is wholly unproblematic.

To complicate matters further, co-occurrence preferences limit the interchangeability of *fast, quick* and *rapid. Oxford Learner's Dictionaries Online* (s.v. *fast, quick, rapid*) discuss the three in a note labelled "Which Word?" and explain differences of usage primarily in terms of the nouns with which they collocate. In fact, our data demonstrate that towards the end of the 20th century, *fast* becomes increasingly involved in a number of fixed collocations (phraseological units, cf. Section 4.3). In the 1950s, frequent reference is made to the *fast breeder* (a type of nuclear reactor), while in the 1990s, three collocations alone (*fast food, fast lane, fast track*) make up around two fifths of the prenominal occurrences (and well over half in spoken American English, which will be sketched in Section 4.5). The first of these recent phraseological units may represent a deliberate formation involving an attention-grabbing alliteration plus stress clash (*fást fóod*).[12] The latter two even show evidence of being compounds, with their main stress on the initial element (*fást làne, fást tràck*).[13]

Thus, we have to allow for various distorting factors impinging on the distribution of the three adjectives studied. However, there is no *a priori* reason to expect that they should differ in the syntactic positions they take—if not the rhythmic shape that sets the disyllable *rapid* off against the monosyllables *fast* and *quick*. Figure 3.2 provides further evidence for this research hypothesis.

In the earliest subperiod, *fast* is generally very rare as an adjective in the sense of 'rapid', and in the later subperiods, it produces massive error rates. Yet, visual inspection of the results for *fast* and *quick* on the one hand and *rapid* on the other, and statistical testing of the distributional contrast between *quick* and *rapid* reveal a diachronically stable and statistically convincing contrast: *Fast* and *quick* appear in rhythmically critical positions between 34 and 54% of

on samples of only 100 hits. This insecurity also prohibits an application of the chi-square test to the figures for *fast*.

12 See Section 4.3 for a consideration of the possible poetic function of such phraseological units.

13 As before, primary lexical stress is indicated by acute accents on the syllable nuclei. The more reduced secondary stress usually found in the non-initial component of compounds is symbolised by grave accents (Compound Stress Rule; cf. Hayes, 1995, p. 368). The stress assignment in the given phraseological units and compounds follows the EPD (s.v. *fast*). This raises the question of whether *fast lane* and *fast track* should be excluded from the counts on account of being compounds, which would reduce the number of prenominal uses of *fast* substantially for the 1990s and reinforce our conclusions.

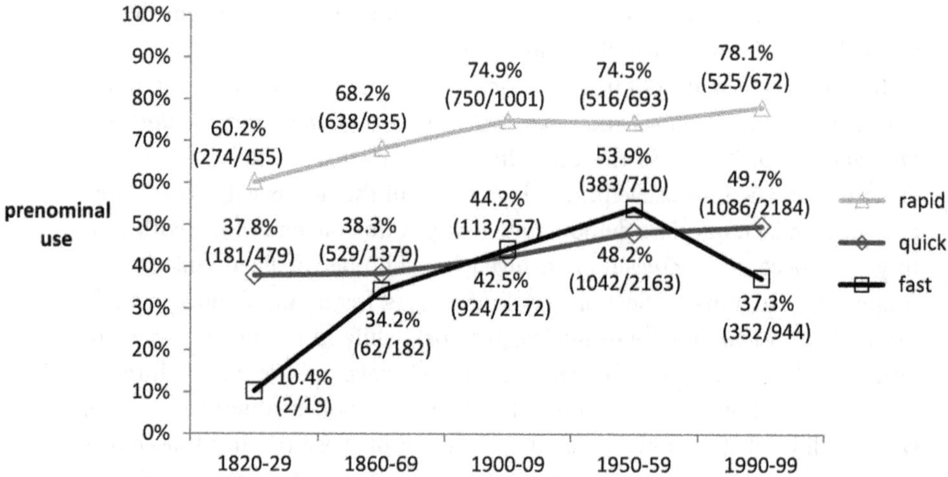

FIGURE 3.2 *The distribution of* fast, quick *and* rapid *in* COHA, *selected decades*

their total occurrences, while *rapid* figures extremely often prenominally.[14] This finding supports the hypothesis that the syntactic distribution of synonymous adjectives is at least partly governed by the avoidance of stress clashes.

An inspection of the random samples for *rapid* however leads to a supplementary explanation: This adjective, borrowed from Latin or French as late as in the 17th century (cf. OED, s.v. *rapid*, adj., adv. and n.) is not only the preferred choice to characterise the speed of processes of change (rather than of movements or actions; cf. *Oxford Learner's Dictionaries Online*, s.v. *rapid*), but it often premodifies nouns of Latinate origin, too (e.g. *ráte, páce, chánge, devélopment, evolútion, succéssion, expánsion, impróvement, reáction, demíse, transítion*). These nouns often have abstract meanings, belong to rather formal registers and, crucially, many of the nouns found in the samples lack the initial stress typical of Germanic words. Compared to the average of nouns in English, 85% of which are initially stressed, noninitially stressed nouns are thus massively overrepresented after *rapid* (21–37% in COHA; 38–45% in COCA). While this might lead us to expect a greater compatibility with *fast* or *quick* (which is not borne out by the data), stylistic and genre-specific affinities obviously have to be allowed for in accounting for the co-occurrence preferences of *rapid*.

14 Comparing the shares of prenominal uses between *quick* and *rapid*, we find low error rates and thus significant distributional differences throughout: (1820–1829: $\chi^2 = 47.00^{***}$, error rates: *quick* 2%, *rapid* 0%), (1860–1869: $\chi^2 = 198.93^{***}$, error rates: *quick* 1%, *rapid* 0%), 1900–1909: $\chi^2 = 288.31^{***}$, 1950–1959: $\chi^2 = 146.26^{***}$, 1990–1999: $\chi^2 = 168.560^{***}$.

In sum, while this case study has unearthed further factors impacting on the choice of adjectives in prenominal positions (the establishment of preferred collocations, their fixedness as compounds and stylistic attraction), the extraordinarily high incidence of *rapid* before nouns can still be ascribed to the Principle of Rhythmic Alternation: The majority of nouns following *rapid* in our data are, after all, initially stressed, so that the use of *rapid* helps to avoid stress clashes. For the minority of nouns that are not initially stressed, we might consider a carry-over effect from the larger number of rhythmically critical cases: *Rapid* is the one adjective among those investigated in this paper that is most strongly attracted to prenominal contexts, for which it shows a noticeable predisposition.

4.3 *Glad—Happy*

In contrast to the adjectives discussed so far (and *rapid* in particular), the pair *glad* and *happy* (as well as *shut* and *closed*, investigated in the next section) are substantially less frequent in attributive uses. Gladness and happiness in human beings (as well as the condition of being shut or closed in objects that can also be open; see below) tend to be transitory states. Thus, a closer look at the semantics of the adjectives under investigation and concomitant syntactic effects is in place.

Adopting a semantic approach, Leisi (1985, p. 54) argues that the meaning of *glad* is restricted to actual uses, i.e. to cases where the referent is currently in a state of gladness. This semantic feature is mirrored in the syntax of *glad* (with the exception of a few fixed collocations, on which see below): It can, according to Leisi, only be used in predicative positions, but not in attributive positions, which typically characterise the referent of the noun permanently. In contrast, *happy* is subject to no such restrictions; like the majority of other adjectives, it has actual and potential uses alike, meaning that it can also refer to a person in whom happiness is a trait of character, even though at the moment of speaking he or she may be in a less-than-happy mood. As a consequence, *happy* should occur unrestrictedly in predicative or attributive position (on semantic nuances of attributive and predicative adjectives, cf. also Bolinger, 1952, pp. 1133–1137; 1967, pp. 3–4; Jacobsson, 1996, p. 218). An inherent semantic difference between *glad* and *happy* is thus predicted to lead to the same distributional tendency as rhythmic considerations. Both motivations conspire to disfavour *glad* in prenominal position, and on both accounts *happy* can be expected to occur in prenominal as well as other (predicative and postnominal) positions.

A full semantic analysis of data samples is beyond the scope of the present study. However, the following examples have been selected so as to show that *glad* and *happy* do not necessarily occur in contexts forcing a different semantic interpretation, and examples like these are numerous.

(9) a. Sir John Maynard moved to make bonfires all over the town, and the House rose so that members could spread the **glád néws**. (COHA non-fiction, 1996)
b. We were housed in the Palace as the chief envoy went to carry the **háppy néws** to the Prince. (COHA fiction, 1997)

(10) a. Her mother was still talking with Marla's, who seemed **glád** to see Janice. (COHA fiction, 1999)
b. People seemed **háppy** to be out with their children, gazing at animals, drinking soda, … (COHA fiction, 1998)

Especially in the earlier decades, both adjectives frequently premodify nouns denoting time or temporally limited events, such as *time, hour, day, morning, moment, laughter, smile, songs, cries, voice, tidings, news, memories* or *heart* 'feeling', in which Leisi's (1985, p. 54) distinction between actuality and potentiality is inapplicable: The temporal extension of gladness/happiness coincides with the temporal extension of the referent: A particular piece of *news* is characterised as *glad*, an instance of *laughter*, while it sounds, is *happy* throughout, and so on. In contexts like these, *glad* and *happy* seem to be interchangeable, at least to a certain degree. However, it is true that *happy* also occurs as an attribute before nouns designating persons, where *glad* appears extremely rarely, for instance before *child, couple, face, family, man, people* and *person*.

Espousing Bolinger's (1965b, p. 149) presupposition that *glad* and *happy* are interchangeable in at least some of their uses, the analysis presented in Figure 3.3 follows up his hunch that *happy* may replace *glad* in rhythmically critical positions. As in the previous case studies, we will test whether *happy* occurs more frequently prenominally than *glad*.

The research hypothesis seems to be borne out by the data: For every decade, *happy* occurs clearly more often in prenominal position than *glad*.[15] At the same time, a further decline in the already low numbers of prenominal use of *glad* is noticeable. In the 19th century, *glad* seems to have been less problematic in prenominal use than later. This leads us to a subsidiary hypothesis,

15 The chi-square results are only slightly kerbed by small error rates: (1820–1829: χ^2 = 118.23***, error rates: *glad* 0%, *happy* 1%), 1860–1869: χ^2 = 745.72***, (1900–1909: χ^2 = 818.84***, error rates: *glad* 0%, *happy* 9%), 1950–1959: χ^2 = 666.67***, (1990–1999: χ^2 = 353.58***, error rates: *glad* 0%, *happy* 2%).

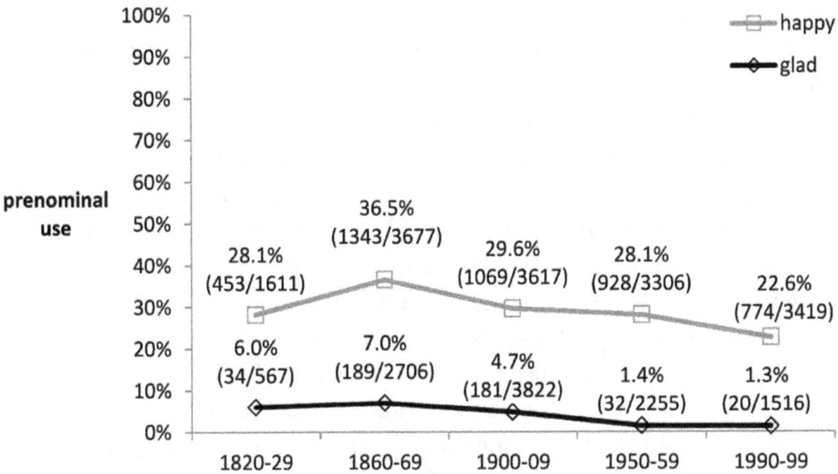

FIGURE 3.3 *The distribution of* glad *and* happy *in* COHA, *selected decades*

the testing of which is beyond the scope of this study since it would require a qualitative (semantic) analysis of a large number of examples reaching back further than the earliest COHA decade: We propose that the rhythmic inappropriateness of *glad* in prenominal position and its increasing restriction to predicative and postnominal uses may in its turn have led to a gradual loss of potential (characterising) meanings in the adjective. In other words, rhythmic constraints may have given rise to an ensuing semantic restriction of *glad*, which never affected *happy* thanks to its different rhythmic shape and continued prenominal occurrence. While the emergence of such a secondary semantic specialisation has—to our knowledge—never been supported with empirical data, there is the comparable case of so-called "predicative-only" adjectives (*alive, asleep, adrift, afraid, aware* etc.), which have been argued to be generally barred from attributive uses on account of both their semantics and rhythm (cf. Bolinger, 1965b; Jacobsson, 1996; Schlüter, 2008).

The most frequent collocation in our COHA and COCA returns for prenominal uses of *glad* is *glad tidings*. A closer look at this collocation leads us to a consideration of the role of (fixed) collocations in our study. In particular, we will study the combination *glad* + noun from two points of view. First, we will show in a deeper diachronic perspective how *glad tidings* developed from the rhythmically uncritical collocation *glad(d)e tiding(e)s* to the modern collocation with clashing stresses. Second, a look at more modern phraseological formations in our results, which appeared with a stress clash right from the start, such as *glad eye*, will lead us to a consideration of the potential impact of the poetic use of language on our findings. In the following, the cover term 'phraseological unit' will specifically refer to adjective + noun collocations that are habitually employed to express a given idea, and as such form a semantic unit.

Glad tidings is a well-known example of a phraseological unit. In Cowie, Mackin and McCaig's (1983) idiom dictionary, (*the*) *glad tidings* is labelled "formal" and defined as 'very good news' (cf. also OED, s.v. *glad* adj. 4). Among our few corpus returns for *glad* in prenominal use, *glad tidings* occurred most frequently. High string frequency may seem to be an obvious criterion of phraseological status, but we would argue that it is not a necessary criterion. Thus, the phraseological unit *glad eye* 'a look or movement of the eyes designed to attract a person of the opposite sex' (cf. OED, s.v. *glad* adj. 4) is much less frequent (only 2 occurrences in COCA) than *glad tidings* (33 occurrences), and also less frequent than the free combination *glad cry* (9 occurrences). Identifying phraseological units with the help of corpus linguistic means is a problematic issue: Taken on their own, neither String Frequency, nor the measures of Transitional Probability, T-scores or (Pointwise) Mutual Information help to reliably find these units.[16] Due to the lack of a workable exclusion measure for phraseological units with prenominal *glad*, we decided to adopt an inclusion strategy for practical purposes and for the general survey in Figure 3.3. As has been previewed above, it is worthwhile to study two probable phraseological units separately to exemplify possible reflexes of phraseological fixations. Our assumption is that the phraseological units *glad tidings* and *glad eye* constitute two different types of violation of the Principle of Rhythmic Alternation, which both result from their phraseological status. One is the retention of a phraseological unit despite a newly developing violation of rhythmic alternation (*glad tidings*); the other concerns phraseological units which have embraced the rhythmical prominence of two clashing monosyllables since their creation (*glad eye, glad hand, glad rags*).

The EEBO database lists different spellings of *glad tidings* in the 16th and 17th centuries. In Middle English, all adjectives were suffixed with *-e* (schwa) except those which were monosyllabic, ended in a consonant, had singular reference and were not preceded by a demonstrative pronoun, a possessive or the definite article (i.e. formerly strong adjectives, mostly in predicative position). Minkova (1991, ch. 7) suggests that the prolonged retention of *-e* in monosyllabic singular weak adjectives—and likewise in the plural (cf. 1991,

16 Cf., e.g., Roth (2014, pp. 28–29, 66, 71), who employs a combination of these measures together with Salience for his analysis. Cf. also the overview in Xiao (2015, pp. 108–112), and cf. Gray and Biber (2015) on possibilities of corpus-driven analyses of phraseology for Present-Day English.

p. 186)—goes back to the rhythmic preference of stress-clash avoidance in adjective + noun combinations. Thus, in the earliest attestation of *glad tidings* in the OED, *-e* indicates a rhythmically harmonious phrase:

(11) Let him in..he bringeð us **gleade tidinges.** (*Sawles Warde* in *Cott. Hom.* 257, *a*1240; OED, s.v. *glad* adj. 4b)

But by c. 1450 the last schwas in final position had disappeared, and there are no indications that final *-e* was still pronounced in the educated speech of London after the early 15th century (cf. Dobson, 1968, p. 879).

> A fifteenth century reversal of the strength of the eurhythmy rules relative to other rules would not [sic] surprising. Extremely powerful morphological analogy within the adjectives, demorphologization of *-e* in the other word classes, as well as sweeping changes in the syntactic structure of the language led to what may appear to be a tendency to "dysrhythmy" in the prosodic organization of monosyllabic adjective + initially stressed noun phrases in Modern English.
>
> MINKOVA, 1991, p. 180

One strategy to avoid this new stress clash was to substitute the disyllabic synonym *happy* for the now monosyllabic *glad.* This strategy is mirrored by the situation in Present-Day English described above (cf. Figure 3.3). However, as Figure 3.4 shows, with c. 8% of all occurrences in the 16th and c. 6% in the 17th century, *happy tidings* remained the rarer option, and the phraseological unit *glad tidings* was retained. The noun *news*, which developed as a synonym of *tidings* from the 15th century onwards (cf. OED, s.v. *news* n. 2a), also entered into a collocation with *glad* (here, final *-e* with only 2 out of 158 instances in EEBO was not extended to the new expression), but it can be seen that the rhythmically more satisfying collocation *happy news* was preferred over *glad news* in the first centuries of use (80% *happy* in the 16th century, 66% in the 17th century) and is again preferred in Present-Day English (c. 94% in COCA). As Figure 3.4 shows, however, *glad news* acquired some popularity in the 19th century (maybe inspired by the model of *glad tidings*), but the COCA data reveal that there was a steep decline again at the end of the 20th century in favour of the combination *happy news*, without stress clash.[17] In Present-Day

17 1500–1600: $\chi^2 = 201.81^{***}$, 1601–1700: $\chi^2 = 943.67^{***}$, 1810–1899: $\chi^2 = 5.04^{*}$, 1900–1989: $\chi^2 = 27.99^{***}$, 1990–2015: $\chi^2 = 76.96^{***}$.

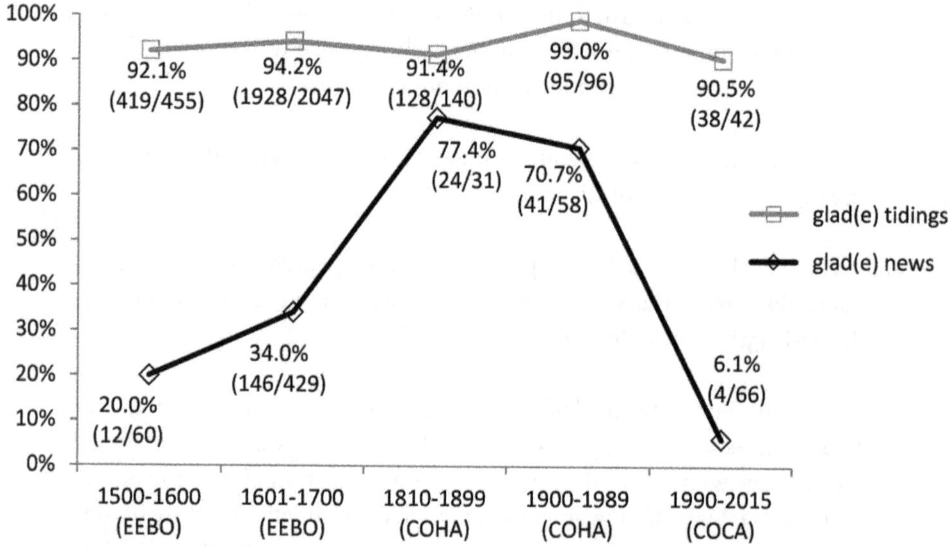

FIGURE 3.4 *The use of* glad(e) *as opposed to* happy *premodifying* tidings *and* news *in* EEBO, COHA *and* COCA

English, thus, the rhythmically marked phraseological unit *glad tidings* ultimately prevailed over its non-phraseological competitor *happy tidings*, while at the same time its non-phraseological synonym *happy news* with regular rhythm ousted the rhythmically marked but not phraseologically fixed collocation *glad news*.[18]

Interestingly, a manual check of all 1,951 occurrences of *glad(d)e* in EEBO revealed that in comparison with free collocations the adjective was comparatively slow to lose its *-e* in phraseological units: c. 12% of all instances of *glad(d)(e) tidings* (+ variants) in the 16th century (49 of a total of 419 tokens) and still c. 1% in the 17th century (16 of a total of 1,928 tokens) retained *-e*. The following quotations show the difference with regard to *-e* between the phraseological unit *glade tyding(e)s* and the free collocation *good things*, and how the phraseological unit, too, gradually lost orthographic *-e* in the course of the 17th century:

(12) And indeed if we had the sight of the fearcenesse of that eternall wrath of God for sinne, it could not be possible but we would say, *o hovv bevvtifull are the feete of them vvhich bring* **glade tydinges** *of peace, and bring* **glade**

18 For an overview of English historical phraseology and avenues for research, see Knappe (2012).

***tydinges** of **good things**!* (EEBO: Robert Rollock, *Lectures vpon the first and second Epistles of Paul to the Thessalonians* ..., 1606)

(13) *That faith is by hearing*, for which effect *preaching* is needfull, and therefore he with the Prophet sayeth there, *how beautifull upon the mountaines, are the feet of them that bring* ***glad tydings****, that bring* ***glade tydings*** *of* ***good things****?* (EEBO: James Sibbald, *Diverse select sermons upon severall texts of holy scripture* ..., 1658)

Most of the other instances of *glad(d)e* + noun also belong to recurring expressions (i.e. potential phraseological units); these are in particular: 1) glad facial expression: *(with [a] / of / maken) gladde chere / cheres, (with a) gladde vysage, (with a) gladde countenaunce*, 2) glad heart and mind: *(with [a]) gladde harte / hartis and mynde, with glade curage*.

Thus it seems that before the final fixation of spelling, phraseological units tended towards a more conservative spelling. Whether this is a sign of a somewhat prolonged time of stress-clash avoidance in these expressions cannot be judged from the sources at hand. In any case, the spelling is indicative of a special status of the unit.

Secondly, while time-honoured fixedness made the collocation *glad tidings* survive its acquired stress clash, newly coined phraseological units can actually be created with a stress clash right from the start, and then—we will argue—rhythmic marking complements pragmatic marking. The focus here is on three phraseological units which were coined around the turn of the 20th century (all OED, s.v. *glad* adj. 4): *glad hand* 'the hand of welcome, frequently used somewhat ironically' (first attestation: 1895), *glad rags* 'one's best clothes; very smart or fancy clothes; *spec.* formal evening dress. *colloq.* (orig. *U.S.*)' (first attestation: 1902), and *the glad eye* (first attestation: 1911).

(14) The lover, the elderly philanderer, the girl with the glad eye. (*Punch* 22 Nov. 382/2, 1911; OED, s.v. *glad* adj. 4)

Roman Jakobson (1960, pp. 356–357), in his famous discussion of the poetic function of language, draws attention to the political slogan *I like Ike*, which achieves its function through the combination of sound structure and sentence semantics (e.g. *Ike* being fully enveloped by *like*). On top of this, one may add, the double stress clash makes the slogan phonologically more salient. While a combination of adjective + noun is certainly a different kind of phraseological unit from a slogan, and although English phraseological units are often metrically well-formed (cf. Naciscione, 2010, pp. 37–38), in the case of *glad eye* and *glad hand* (as well as that of *fast food*, mentioned in 4.2) it can be hypothesised that in the process of coining the units, stress clashes were embraced as pragmatic markers.[19] In all three cases, according to the OED (*glad* adj. 4), *glad* denotes 'filled with, marked by, or expressive of joy or delight', and thus *joyful* or *delightful* could have been chosen instead of *glad* to produce rhythmically uncritical combinations. However, stress clashes persist, though with different leanings:[20] Phrasal stress seems to be retained in *glád éye* and *glád hánd* (as well as *fást fóod*, mentioned in 4.2), while *glád ràgs* (as well as *fást làne* and *fást tràck*, also in 4.2) has compound stress.[21] Though these examples, viewed superficially, appear to contradict the hypothesis proposed in the present contribution, the tendency to provoke stress clashes in phraseological units like these does not call the efficacy of the Principle of Rhythmic Alternation into question. Rather, the fact that rhythmic alternation can be interrupted for pragmatic marking underlines the importance of the phenomenon. An intentional infraction of rhythmic alternation is an appropriate means of giving the utterance more prominence, exactly because it is an effect that is normally avoided.

4.4 *Shut—Closed*

Oxford Learner's Dictionaries Online (s.v. *closed, shut*) flatly note that "[c]**losed** is used in front of a noun, but **shut** is not". Similarly, Jacobsson (1996, p. 209) remarks that *closed eyes* is fully acceptable as an attributive construction, while **shut eyes* is objectionable, although *shut* is largely synonymous with *closed.* Being concerned with explanations that are syntactic or semantic in nature, Jacobsson is unable to account for this phenomenon. An explanation in terms of the preference for alternating strong and weak syllables is not available either, since both *closed* and *shut* are monosyllabic. A clue to this phenomenon is provided by Bolinger (1965a, p. 135).[22] The two adjectives differ

19 Bolinger (1981, p. 29; 1986, p. 70) surmises that the purpose of such clashes is a vigorous and emphatic reinforcement of what is said.

20 The stress assignment in the given phraseological units and compounds follows the EPD (s.v. *glad*). Where the EPD lists no special stress pattern, ordinary phrasal stress is assumed, i.e. the adjectival premodifier and the nominal head retain their full lexical stresses (with the stress on the head exceeding that on the premodifier, in line with the Nuclear Stress Rule; cf. Hayes 1995, p. 368).

21 It is not uncontroversial in the literature on word formation whether adjective + noun combinations such as these started out as units with phrasal stress prior to their compound status (cf. Štekauer, 2000, p. 213, note 6).

22 Bolinger (1965a, p. 135) reports an elicitation experiment employing the pair of nonsensical sentences in (i) and (ii) to elicit preference judgements from consultants. As expected,

greatly in their phonetic duration: While *closed* contains a diphthong as its syllable nucleus and ends in a voiced consonant cluster, *shut* only has a short vowel, whose shortness is moreover reinforced by the voiceless stop in its coda. In consequence, the considerable duration of the monosyllable *closed* offers sufficient phonetic substance to be drawn out so as to accommodate a drop in articulatory energy from a stressed beginning to a much less stressed termination (cf. Bolinger, 1965a, p. 135; Hayes, 1984, p. 72). This effect is similar in nature to that of a second unstressed syllable: If followed by another stressed syllable, a long monosyllable incorporates the part of a buffer spacing out two stressed syllables.[23]

This section will thus put forward a supplementary hypothesis along the following lines: While ideally, two stressed syllables are separated by an intervening unstressed syllable, in the absence of an unstressed syllable, a long syllable in the first position will be preferable to a short one. The predicted outcome of this preference is that in our corpus, *shut* should be noticeably avoided in attributive uses, while *closed* should be more free to occur in such positions.

As pointed out in Section 3, the search procedure was far from unproblematic since the automatic tagging often failed to disambiguate instances of *shut* and *closed*. Instances not preceding a noun were frequently tagged as participles (prenominal position obviously being used as a clue to adjectivehood), so that our search for critical contexts as well as for general frequencies of *shut* and *closed* targeted all instances tagged as adjectives or past participles and all random samples were manually sorted into adjectival and adjective-like uses on the one hand and verbal uses on the other. In the process, other irrelevant hits such as the compound *shut eye* 'sleep' and the phraseological unit *open and shut case* 'legal case or other matter that is easy to decide or solve',[24] where *shut* is not a prototypical attribute, were eliminated. Figure 3.5 provides the results in the familiar format.

---

his consultants tended to prefer example (ii) with the phonetically long monosyllable *plam* in the clashing position to (i) with the considerably shorter *plap* in the same position.

(i) He lives in a *plám* and *pláp hóuse*.

(ii) He lives in a *pláp* and *plám hóuse*.

23 Compare also the phenomenon known as *raddoppiamiento sintattico* frequently described in Italian phonology: A consonant in the onset of the second of two clashing syllables can be lengthened so as to put more distance between the two stressed syllable nuclei (cf. Bayer, 1989, p. 16).

24 Definitions taken from *Oxford Learner's Dictionaries Online*.

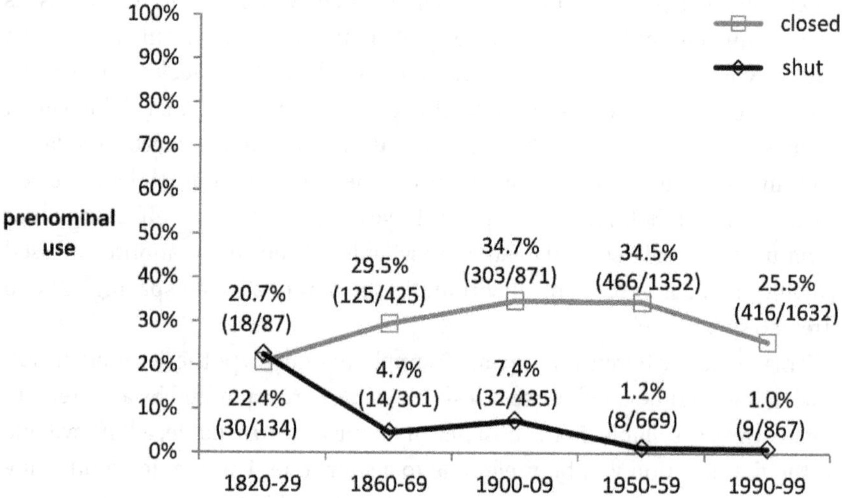

FIGURE 3.5 *The distribution of* shut *and* closed *in* COHA*, selected decades*

The results of the corpus analysis clearly show a consistent difference in the distribution of the two adjectives, except for the data from the early 19th century. *Closed* is used prenominally in between 25 and 35% of its occurrences and thereby contrasts sharply with *shut*, which hardly occurs in this position after the 1820s.[25] Detailed inspection of the sampled hits reveals that in all contexts where *shut* is used, *closed* could be used as well, since reference is typically made to *mouths, lips, eyes, lids, doors* and *windows*. The examples in (15) are representative in this respect.

(15) a. As I floated, the sun a red mist beyond my **shút éyelids**, I felt the slow, languid pace of life here ... (COHA fiction, 1995)

b. I covered my eyes while my wife read the article sitting on the **clósed líd** of our toilet. (COHA fiction, 1997)

c. But at eight o'clock, Daphne came to the **shút dóor**, waited a minute, creaked it open and said ... (COHA fiction, 1991)

d. Alice glanced at the **clósed dóor**, as if fearing Verna could see her. (COHA fiction, 1997)

25 Due to high error rates in the samples for *shut*, the insecurity introduced by extrapolation invalidates the application of chi-square tests. The results are given in brackets here for the sake of completeness: 1820–1829: χ^2 = 0.09 n.s., (1860–1869: χ^2 = 69.78***, error rates: *shut* 42%, *closed* 5%), (1900–1909: χ^2 = 114.47***, error rates: *shut* 29%, *closed* 3%), (1950–1959: χ^2 = 275.96***, error rates: *shut* 58%, *closed* 2%), (1990–1999: χ^2 = 239.85***, error rates: *shut* 71%, *closed* 3%).

The same collocates are found with the relatively numerous examples of prenominal *shut* from the 1820s. This raises the question of why the imbalance found in later decades is not yet in place in the earliest subperiod. Part of the answer may lie in the fact that the frequency of *closed* has more than tripled and thereby overtaken that of *shut* in the course of the past two centuries, as is revealed by a quick check in COHA: *Closed* was not as obvious a bypass then as it is now.

Beyond concrete uses such as those in (15), *closed*—but not *shut*—is also found in more abstract senses (describing *ranks, meetings, hearings, societies, parties, committees* etc.). The denotational range of *closed* is thus larger, but it properly includes that of *shut*, so that *closed* constitutes a viable alternative to *shut* in rhythmically critical contexts. The number of cases in which this (or some other) solution is not resorted to in the data—in other words, the residue of prenominal uses of *shut*—approaches the zero line in the course of the 20th century. The observations by Jacobsson (1996, p. 209) and *Oxford Learner's Dictionaries Online* quoted at the outset are thus confirmed and lend plausibility to the rhythmic account suggested by Bolinger (1965a, p. 135): A speaker or writer heading for a construction like (15a) or (15c) might run into rhythmic difficulties and in many cases substitute the short monosyllable *shut* with the longer form *closed* to avoid the imminent stress clash.

Incidentally, it should be noted that the corpus analysis yields some—statistically insignificant—support for the assumption that premodification of *shut* by an adverb might redeem the rhythmic situation to some extent. Thus, in examples like (16), *half* and *tightly* not only modify the meaning of *shut*, but also deflect the main stress from it, leaving it with no more than secondary stress (backshifted stress; cf. Bolinger, 1965b, pp. 141–145; Schlüter, 2005, pp. 29–30). This, in turn, separates the major stresses in line with the Principle of Rhythmic Alternation, with *shut* itself functioning as a buffer syllable.

(16) a. He did not see the gleam in Asbury's **hálf shùt éyes.** (COHA fiction, 1904)
b. On Oct. 21, the first trainload of oil from China's Kazakh holdings headed toward Chinese refineries across what until recently had been one of the most **tíghtly shùt bórders** in the world. (COHA news, 1997)

By way of a preliminary conclusion, the results from the four diachronic studies presented so far can be summarised as follows: Even though all the lexemes can in principle occur in single or complex attributive positions as well as in non-attributive positions, the rhythmically less appropriate members of the pairs (or triplet) are strikingly underrepresented before nouns. What is more, these differences have been in place throughout the two centuries investigated. The only statistically relevant exception is the earliest decade in the fourth case study, which may simply be explained by the fact that *closed* had not yet developed into an equally viable alternative to *shut*.

4.5 *Spoken and Written Present-Day English*

So far, we have exclusively used the written data contained in COHA, but they have provided consistent evidence in favour of the avoidance of stress clashes. When it comes to spoken data, we might predict a rhythmic effect that should be at least as strong, since infractions of the Principle of Rhythmic Alternation concern the spoken form of language rather than its written form. Thus, the previous four case studies will be repeated based on COCA, which allows us to distinguish between written and spoken data. For these analyses, all the procedures, caveats and restrictions adduced in Sections 4.1 to 4.4 apply identically, but will not be repeated here. The focus will be laid on the contrasting distributions of mono- vs. disyllabic and short vs. long monosyllabic adjectives in prenominal position, respectively.

The most striking result of the synopsis presented in Figure 3.6 is that the proportion of cases in which potentially synonymous adjectives are placed in prenominal position differs widely between the triplet *quick/fast/rapid*, all three of which are extremely frequent as noun premodifiers, and the pairs *glad/happy* and *shut/closed*, which have rather low prenominal shares across the board, with *rich/wealthy* taking an intermediate position. As mentioned above, this may be due to their different predispositions to encode actual or potential meanings. Not surprisingly, the distributions in COCA are also very similar to those found in the later subsections of COHA.

Crucially, however, all four panels show that the same contrasts as have been attributed to rhythmic constraints in the previous discussion are observable in the spoken as well as in the written mode: In each case, the disyllabic adjectives and *closed* are used comparatively often in prenominal position, while the proportions of prenominal *rich, quick, fast, glad* and *shut* are substantially smaller. The percentages by which longer adjectives differ from shorter ones are relatively constant across the pairs and the triplet considered: They oscillate between 15 and 30 percentage points, even for the pair of monosyllables that are merely distinguished by phonetic duration.[26] If anything, the contrast is strongest in the spoken data for *shut* and *closed*, which diverge by

26 COCA spoken: (*rich/wealthy*: $\chi^2 = 154.36^{***}$, error rates: *rich* 8 %, *wealthy* 0 %), *quick/rapid*:

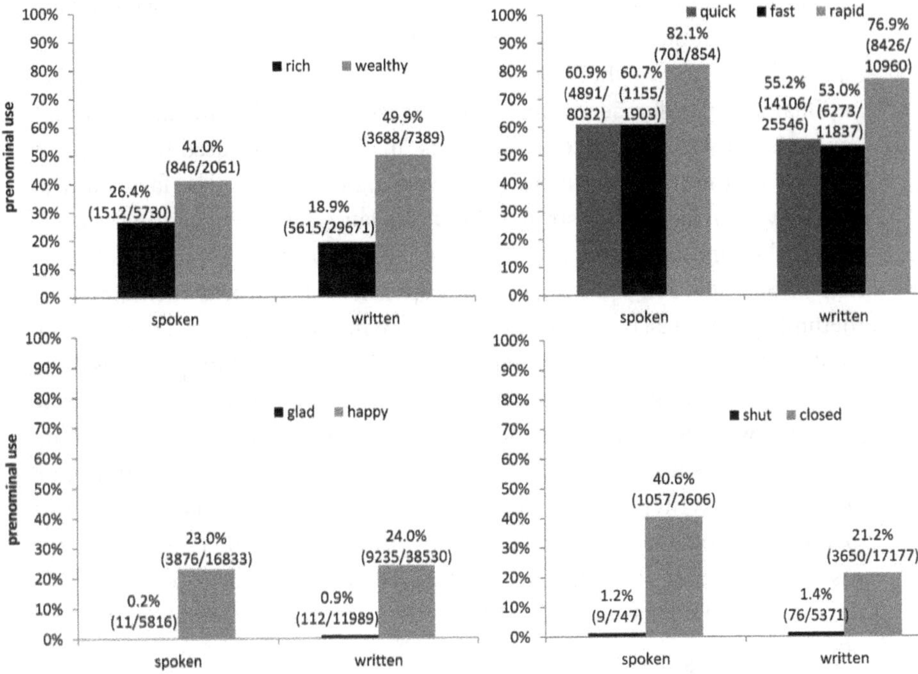

FIGURE 3.6 *The distribution of (near-)synonymous adjectives in* COCA, *spoken vs. written sections*

almost 40 %.[27] Without going into further detail here, it may be added that we have obtained parallel results from analyses of the same adjectives in the 100-million-word *British National Corpus* (BNC).

$\chi^2 = 148.58^{***}$, (*glad/happy*: $\chi^2 = 1585.70^{***}$, error rates: *glad* 0 %, *happy* 3 %), (*shut/closed*: $\chi^2 = 414.68^{***}$, error rates: *shut* 87 %, *closed* 0 %).

COCA written: (*rich/wealthy*: $\chi^2 = 3021.41^{***}$, error rates: *rich* 2 %, *wealthy* 0 %), *quick/rapid*: $\chi^2 = 1523.19^{***}$, (*glad/happy*: $\chi^2 = 3217.41^{***}$, error rates: *glad* 0 %, *happy* 2 %), (*shut/closed*: $\chi^2 = 1166.91^{***}$, error rates: *shut* 65 %, *closed* 5 %).

27 To account for this astonishing fact, we can offer a hypothesis that is suggested by the normalised frequencies of *shut* and *closed* in our control contexts: While the frequency of *closed* per million words is a multiple of that of *shut* in contemporary American English generally, *shut* is still better entrenched in speech than in writing (cf. *Oxford Learner's Dictionaries Online*, s.v. *shut*, *closed*, where it is noted that "[e]specially in *North American English*, **shut** can sound less polite [than **closed**]."). Thus, we propose that the use of *closed* in speech seems to be specifically triggered in rhythmically critical prenominal positions, where as many as 40 % of its occurrences can be found.

The fact that the same contrasts hold across diachronically spaced subsections of COHA and written and spoken parts of COCA and BNC (all of which have a differently weighted genre composition) and thus, across both major national varieties, further corroborates the assumption that the distributional contrasts between adjectives may at least in part be attributed to the preference for rhythmic alternation and the spacing of stresses. The fact that this tendency is not necessarily stronger in spoken language than in writing is in line with earlier findings about rhythmic alternation effects in grammatical variation (cf. Schlüter, 2005, p. 291): While the spoken form of words, including their rhythmic properties, is of course the only one relevant in speech, there is substantial evidence that subvocalisations also play an important part in writing and (silent) reading. What is more, speech often takes place under real-time pressures, while writing as a rule involves more intense pre-planning and monitoring, and thus may attain higher levels of well-formedness and optimisation of the output: Writers typically invest considerable effort in making their text *sound* good, which no doubt includes its rhythmic dimension (see also the discussion in Schlüter, 2005, pp. 50–55). Thus, it comes as no surprise that rhythm turns out to be no less influential in written data than in the spoken parts of COCA.

5 Conclusion and Perspectives

The analyses described in the present study have produced highly consistent results across speech and writing and across diachronic snapshots of written American English spanning almost two centuries. The results provide substantial cumulative support for our initial hypothesis H_1, to the effect that adjectives with equivalent meanings and different rhythmic shapes do not occur equally often in all syntactic functions: It has been found that monosyllabic or end-stressed adjectives occur less often before stressed syllables than their non-end-stressed (near) synonyms. The critical contexts for this hypothesis have been pinned down to attributive uses immediately preceding nouns, since nouns in English typically have initial stress. For the minority of nouns that have their primary stress on a later syllable (ca. 15% of tokens), a carry-over effect has been postulated, such that the avoidance of prenominal use in the large number of rhythmically problematic contexts spills over to unproblematic contexts through a generalised aversion to placement in grammatically equivalent (i.e. prenominal) positions. As a supplementary hypothesis, it has been argued that phonetic duration of a stressed syllable can, under certain circumstances, fulfil the same buffering function as an extra syllable. Some initial evidence has been presented, which suggests that the size of the effect is comparable to that of an extra buffer syllable. In sum, our data indicate that the Principle of Rhythmic Alternation has the potential to influence lexical choices.

While these results are supported by robust quantitative evidence, this is not to deny that there are important limitations to the impact of rhythm: Since our case studies have targeted individual lexemes and each one has idiosyncratic properties, the synonymy presupposed here has proved to be only partial in many respects. Some members of our synonym pairs have larger denotational ranges than others (*rich* vs. *wealthy*, *closed* vs. *shut*), some belong to different stylistic levels and involve slight referential nuances (*fast* vs. *quick* vs. *rapid*) and some lend themselves better than others to potential (characterising) or actual (temporary) interpretations, respectively (*happy* vs. *glad*). Fixed collocations (phraseological units), on the one hand, can be seen to survive in spite of stress clashes acquired through loss of final schwa (in the case of *glad tidings*), and on the other hand, newly coined units (such as *fast food*, *glad hand* and *glad eye*) may embrace this rhythmically critical condition to indicate pragmatic markedness.

Despite these restrictions, all four case studies have involved lexemes that are morphologically unrelated, but can at least part of the time replace each other, depending on the rhythmic context. These findings contribute important new insights regarding the scope of influence of the Principle of Rhythmic Alternation: The current state of research on the principle has accumulated evidence that it can trigger the avoidance of rhythmically inconvenient morphological or syntactic structures and their replacement by alternative grammatical forms whenever alternatives are available. It is of course easier to assume (near) semantic identity between morphologically marked or unmarked instances of the same lexeme in the same grammatical function, e.g. (17)–(23), or between syntactic constructions containing the same words, e.g. (24)–(29), to name just some of the grammatical phenomena studied in recent literature. (Note, however, that even here specific semantic distinctions have been shown to exist between some of the pairs.)

(17) *worse* vs. *worser*,

(18) *drunk* vs. *drunken*, *broke* vs. *broken*, *struck* vs. *stricken*,

(19) *knit* vs. *knitted*, *lit* vs. *lighted*,

(20) *quick* vs. *quickly*, *scarce* vs. *scarcely*,

(21) *go fishing* vs. *go a-fishing*,

(22) *make someone (to) do something, bid someone (to) do something*,

(23) *dare (to) do something* (all in Schlüter, 2005, 2015),

(24) *give Jim the book* vs. *give the book to Jim* (Anttila, Adams & Speriosu, 2010),

(25) *the teacher's method* vs. *the method of the teacher* (Ehret, Wolk & Szmrecsanyi, 2014; Shih, Grafmiller, Futrell & Bresnan, 2015),

(26) *he knew (that) Lucy washed the dishes* (Lee & Gibbons, 2007),

(27) *green and yellow* vs. *yellow and green* (Mollin 2012, 2014; Lohmann, 2014),

(28) *colleges and universities* vs. *universities and colleges* (Mollin, 2012, 2014; Lohmann, 2014),

(29) *John likes beans* vs. *beans, John likes* (Speyer, 2010).

Going beyond these fairly well-established facts, we have provided the first pieces of quantitative evidence for Bolinger's impressionistic observation that the choice of lexical alternatives may equally be determined by their rhythmic properties (1965b, p. 149).

On a theoretical level, the present study supplies a phonologically induced limiting factor for synonym choice within theories of synonymy. More importantly in our context, our study contributes to a more comprehensive assessment of the influence of the Principle of Rhythmic Alternation, arguing that the scope is larger than has so far been shown. Without going into detail here, an assumption shared by many linguistic models and supported by massive and largely undisputed evidence is that language structure as well as language processing are characterised by a hierarchical organisation.[28] Thus, language involves a semantic, lexical, syntactic, morphological and phonological level of representation, with semantics at the top (second only to pragmatics) and phonology at the bottom.

28 See, for instance, Bock (1987), Levelt (1989), Lamb (1999), Berg (1988, 1998, 2009). For a review of some models, see Schlüter (2005, pp. 237–306) and Lohmann (2014, pp. 144–182).

- As has been argued by Schlüter (2015; cf. also 2005, pp. 285–291), inside the phonological component, various powerful stress rules are at work that remedy violations of rhythmic alternation (stress deletion, addition and shift).
- Morphological variants such as (17) to (21), being situated close to the phonological level, are numerous and examples of this kind could easily be multiplied, e.g. from among the many variants of weak and strong past participles and suffixed and suffixless adverbs. What is more, these are heavily influenced by rhythmic constellations, the avoidance of stress clashes not infrequently being the prime determinant of their distribution.
- Syntactic structures such as (22) to (29), despite being quite remote from the phonological level, have still been shown to reflect attempts to optimise the rhythm of the outcome. The effect strength is however more limited (cf. Schlüter, 2015; see also Lee & Gibbons, 2007; Shih, Grafmiller, Futrell & Bresnan, 2015; Ehret, Wolk & Szmrecsanyi, 2014) and there are a few studies that failed to produce evidence of stress clash avoidance in multifactorial settings (e.g. Lohmann, 2011, p. 510, 2014, p. 112).
- As for lexical choices, an empirical demonstration of rhythmic influences has been pending up until now—a gap that we hope to have filled with the present study.

We thus embrace a non-modular, though layered model of language and language processing where constraints and influences of one level of representation interpenetrate other levels.[29] Significantly, this influence is not all-pervasive, but decreases as the distance between levels increases.[30] With regard to rhythmic well-formedness constraints, this means that their influence is strongest on the adjacent level of grammatical morphology, moderately strong at the syntactic level and—as has been shown in the present contribution—still demonstrable at the level of lexical selection. While the four case studies selected here yield relatively homogeneous results as to the constancy and size of the rhythmic effects, it has to be admitted that with several other adjective pairs that were tried, POS-tag-based pilot studies did not produce any obvious

29 A fully accountable estimation of rhythmic effects on other levels than that of lexical choices is beyond the scope of the present article. For more detailed and comprehensive assessments of the range and strength of rhythm in grammatical morphology and syntax, the reader is referred to the book-length discussion in Schlüter (2005) as well as the overview in Schlüter (2015).

30 For a congruent model based on a quantitative study of coordinate constructions, see Lohmann (2014, pp. 168–173).

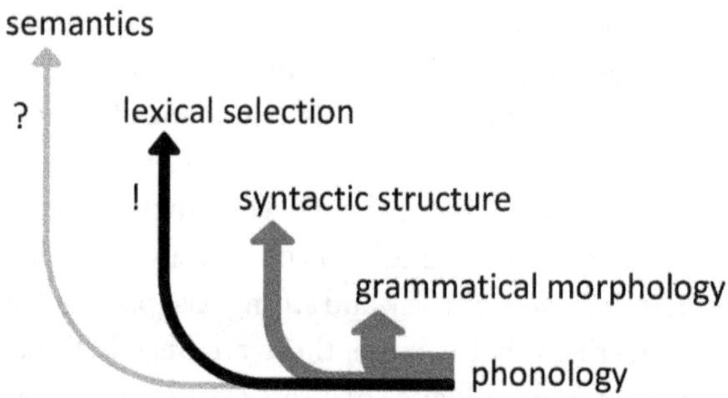

FIGURE 3.7 *The scope of the Principle of Rhythmic Alternation across levels of linguistic representation*

results. In these cases, no further attempts were made to tease apart potentially conflicting factors which may obscure the expected rhythmic effects. This indicates that the latter may become visible only in the absence of more cogent constraints of other kinds and can be used as a last resort in lexical choices, everything else being equal.

Figure 3.7 presents a rough sketch of the components of a model of language processing.[31] In language production, the major flow of information is from top to bottom.[32] The phonological component is the one that ultimately converts the string of lexemes, syntactic units and morphemes into pronounceable phonological structures. Violations of the Principle of Rhythmic Alternation will cause processing difficulties at this late stage. The width of the arrows symbolises the size of rhythmic effects, which diminish with increasing distance from the phonological level (where the rhythm factor is located). This can be conceptualised as a feedback mechanism that anticipates violations of rhythmic (and other phonological) principles following from constellations at higher linguistic levels, and works to pre-empt them by promoting competing (grammatical, syntactic or lexical) options. A potential influence of the Principle of Rhythmic Alternation on semantics will have to be explored in future research.[33]

---

31 For a more detailed elaboration of this model, see Schlüter (2005, pp. 257–306).

32 In language perception, the direction is reversed, but the focus of this contribution is on the choice of lexical items in the building of utterances.

33 It has been suggested, for instance, that the insertion of certain buffer elements between clashing stresses may serve primarily rhythmic purposes, but the semantic contribution of these elements—negligible though it may appear—leads to a slight modification of the originally intended communicative contents (cf. Bolinger, 1980, p. 57; Schlüter, 2005, p. 135).

On the diachronic plane, two kinds of hypotheses suggest themselves. First, as the detour into longstanding collocations (i.e. potential phraseological units) with *glad* has shown, the Middle English loss of unstressed final syllables in adjectives is likely to have increased dysrhythmy in sequences of attributive adjectives and nouns (cf. Minkova, 1991, p. 180, quoted above). For many pairs consisting of (now) monosyllabic or end-stressed adjectives and initially stressed nouns, the loss of endings has created loci for stress clashes that can no longer be averted. While in free collocations and newly developing phraseological units such as *happy news*, rhythmically critical adjectives have sometimes come to be replaced by uncritical ones with an unstressed final syllable (as has been argued throughout this paper), individual phraseological units (*fast food, glad eye, glad hand*) appear to have been coined with deliberate pragmatic marking supported by rhythmic deviancy. Second, we may hypothesise that a syntactic restriction caused by rhythmic difficulties may contribute to a secondary semantic specialisation: While *glad(e)* may once have been as common in attributive uses as *happy*, rhythmic inappropriateness may have progressively confined it to predicative uses. This, in turn, may have been a factor in obliterating potential (characterising) senses of *glad* and promoting actual (temporary) senses, since attributive position is typically associated with potential semantics. In other words, the subtle meaning distinction found in Present-Day English between *glad* and *happy* may in part have arisen from their rhythmic disparity.

The case studies presented in Section 4 have different degrees of statistical significance: In some cases, massive ambiguity led to imprecision of the searches (and concomitant statistical insecurity). What is more, some cross-cutting factors (in particular, phraseological fixations) could not be eliminated and may distort the picture. Be that as it may, taken together, all results appear to point in the same direction, in support of our leading hypothesis. In future research, it would thus be useful to study distributions of further adjective pairs with overlapping meanings and rhythmically relevant contrasts. Our search of the "Synonyms" section of *Oxford Learner's Dictionaries Online* yielded, among others, the following candidates: *afraid—frightened, mad—crazy, grave—solemn, fond—devoted, frank—outspoken, sour—acid, smart—clever, superb—excellent*. In view of the sheer size of the English lexicon, the number of (near) synonyms, the problems involved in their comparison, and the space allotted to this contribution, we have to leave this work undone for the time being.

References

Primary Sources

BNC: Davies, M. (2004–). *BYU-BNC*. (Based on the British National Corpus from Oxford University Press). Available online at http://corpus.byu.edu/bnc/. Last accessed 19 June 2017.

COCA: Davies, M. (2008–). *The Corpus of Contemporary American English: 450 million words, 1990-present*. Available online at http://corpus.byu.edu/coca/. Last accessed 19 June 2017.

COHA: Davies, M. (2010–). *The Corpus of Historical American English: 400 million words, 1810–2009*. Available online at http://corpus.byu.edu/coha/. Last accessed 19 June 2017.

Cowie, A.P., Mackin, R. & McCaig, I.R. (1983). *Oxford dictionary of current idiomatic English*. Vol. II: *Phrase, clause & sentence idioms*. Oxford: Oxford University Press. [Repr. 1993 under the title: *Oxford dictionary of English idioms*.]

EEBO: *Early English Books Online* (2003–2015). ProQuest LLC. Available online at http://eebo.chadwyck.com/home. Last accessed 19 June 2017.

EPD: Jones, D. (2011). *English pronouncing dictionary* (18th ed.). P. Roach, J. Setter & J. Esling (Eds.). Cambridge: Cambridge University Press.

OED: *Oxford English Dictionary Online* (2000–). Oxford University Press. Available online at http://dictionary.oed.com/. Last accessed 19 June 2017.

Oxford Learner's Dictionaries Online (2015). Oxford University Press. Available online at http://www.oxfordlearnersdictionaries.com/. Last accessed 19 June 2017.

Thesaurus.com (2016). Dictionary.com, LLC. Available online at http://www.thesaurus.com/. Last accessed 19 June 2017.

Secondary Sources

Anttila, A., Adams, M., & Speriosu, M. (2010). The role of prosody in the English dative alternation. *Language and Cognitive Processes*, 7/8/9, 946–981.

Baugh, A.C., & Cable, T. (2013). *A history of the English language* (6th ed.). London: Routledge.

Bayer, J. (1989). A note on alleged PRO-government. In D. Jaspers, W. Klooster, Y. Putseys & P. Seuren (Eds.), *Sentential complementation and the lexicon: Studies in honour of Wim de Geest* (pp. 1–20). Dordrecht/Providence: Foris.

Behaghel, O. (1924). *Deutsche Syntax: Eine geschichtliche Darstellung*. Volume II: *Die Wortklassen und Wortformen*. Heidelberg: Winter.

Berg, T. (1988). *Die Abbildung des Sprachproduktionsprozesses in einem Aktivationsflußmodell. Untersuchungen an deutschen und englischen Versprechern*. Tübingen: Niemeyer.

Berg, T. (1998). *Linguistic structure and change: An explanation from language processing*. Oxford: Clarendon Press.

Berg, T. (2009). *Structure in language: A dynamic perspective*. London: Routledge.

Bock, J.K. (1987). An effect of the accessibility of word forms in sentence structures. *Journal of Memory and Language*, 26, 119–137.

Bolinger, D.L. (1952). Linear modification. *Papers of the Modern Language Association, 67*, 1117–1144.

Bolinger, D.L. (1965a). Binomials and pitch accent. In D.L. Bolinger (Ed.), *Forms of English: Accent, morpheme, order* (pp. 129–138). Cambridge, Mass.: Harvard University Press.

Bolinger, D.L. (1965b). Pitch accent and sentence rhythm. In: D.L. Bolinger (Ed.), *Forms of English: Accent, morpheme, order* (pp. 139–180). Cambridge, Mass.: Harvard University Press.

Bolinger, D.L. (1967). Adjectives in English: Attribution and predication. *Lingua, 18*, 1–34.

Bolinger, D.L. (1980). A not impartial review of a not unimpeachable theory: Some new adventures of ungrammaticality. In R.W. Shuy & A. Shnukal (Eds.), *Language use and the uses of language* (pp. 53–67). Washington: Georgetown University Press.

Bolinger, D.L. (1981). *Two kinds of vowels, two kinds of rhythm*. Bloomington, IN: Indiana University Linguistics Club.

Bolinger, D.L. (1986). The English beat: Some notes on rhythm. In G. Nickel & J. Stalker (Eds.), *Problems of standardization and linguistic variation in Present-Day English* (pp. 36–49). Heidelberg: Groos.

Couper-Kuhlen, E. (1986). *An introduction to English prosody*. Tübingen: Niemeyer.

Cruse, D.A. (1986). *Lexical semantics*. Cambridge: Cambridge University Press.

Cruse, D.A. (2002). Paradigmatic relations of inclusion and identity III: Synonymy. In D.A. Cruse, F. Hundsnurscher, M. Job & P.R. Lutzeier (Eds.), *Lexikologie / Lexicology: Ein internationales Handbuch zur Natur und Struktur von Wörtern und Wortschätzen / An international handbook on the nature and structure of words and vocabularies*. Vol. I (pp. 485–497). Berlin: Mouton de Gruyter.

Cutler, A., & Carter, D.M. (1987). The predominance of strong initial syllables in the English vocabulary. *Computer Speech and Language*, 2, 133–142.

Dobson, E.J. (1968). *English pronunciation 1500–1700*. Volume II: *Phonology* (2nd ed.). Oxford: Clarendon Press.

Dolezal, F. (2013). Synonymy and sameness of meaning: An introductory note. *International Journal of Lexicography, 26*(3), 255–259.

Ehret, K., Wolk, C., & Szmrecsanyi, B. (2014). Quirky quadratures: On rhythm and weight as constraints on genitive variation in an unconventional data set. *English Language and Linguistics, 18*(2), 263–303.

Fijn van Draat, P. (1910). *Rhythm in English prose*. Amsterdam: Swets & Zeitlinger N.V. [Repr. 1967.]

Gray, B., & Biber, D. (2015). Phraseology. In D. Biber (Ed.), *The Cambridge handbook of English corpus linguistics* (pp. 125–145). Cambridge: Cambridge University Press.

Hayes, B. (1984). The phonology of rhythm in English. *Linguistic Inquiry, 15*, 33–74.

Jacobsson, B. (1996). A new look at 'predicative-only' adjectives in English. *Journal of English Linguistics, 24*, 206–219.

Jakobson, R. (1960). Closing statement: Linguistics and poetics. In T.A. Sebeok (Ed.), *Style in language* (pp. 350–377). Cambridge, Mass.: MIT Press; New York/London: J. Wiley & Sons.

Jespersen, O. (1909). *A Modern English grammar on historical principles*. Part I: *Sounds and spellings*. London: George Allen & Unwin/Copenhagen: Munksgaard.

Kager, R. (1989). *A metrical theory of stress and destressing in English and Dutch* (Doctoral dissertation). Rijksuniversiteit Utrecht.

Knappe, G. (2012). Idioms and fixed expressions. In L. Brinton & A. Bergs (Eds.), *English historical linguistics: An international handbook*. Vol. I (pp. 177–196). Berlin: Mouton de Gruyter.

Lamb, S.M. (1999). *Pathways of the brain: The neurocognitive basis of language*. Amsterdam/Philadelphia: John Benjamins.

Lee, M.-W., & Gibbons, J. (2007). Rhythmic alternation and the optional complementiser in English: New evidence of phonological influence on grammatical encoding. *Cognition, 105*, 446–456.

Leisi, E. (1985). *Praxis der englischen Semantik* (2nd ed.). Heidelberg: Winter.

Levelt, W.J.M. (1989). *Speaking: From intention to articulation*. Cambridge, Mass./London, UK: MIT Press.

Lohmann, A. (2011). *Help* vs *help to*: A multifactorial, mixed-effects account of infinitive marker omission. *English Language and Linguistics, 15*(3), 499–521.

Lohmann, A. (2014). *English coordinate constructions: A processing perspective on constituent order*. Cambridge: Cambridge University Press.

Lyons, J. (1968). *Introduction to theoretical linguistics*. Cambridge: Cambridge University Press. [Reprinted 1989.]

Minkova, D. (1991). *The history of final vowels in English: The sound of muting*. Berlin/New York: Mouton de Gruyter.

Mollin, S. (2012). Revisiting binomial order in English: Ordering constraints and reversibility. *English Language and Linguistics, 16*(1), 81–103.

Mollin, S. (2014). *The (ir)reversibility of English binomials*. Amsterdam: Benjamins.

Naciscione, A. (2010). *Stylistic use of phraseological units in discourse*. Amsterdam/Philadelphia: John Benjamins.

Nespor, M., & Vogel, I. (1989). On clashes and lapses. *Phonology, 6*, 69–116.

Paradis, C, (1997). *Degree modifiers of adjectives in spoken British English*. Lund: Lund University Press.

Roth, T. (2014). *Wortverbindungen und Verbindungen von Wörtern: Lexikografische und distributionelle Aspekte kombinatorischer Begriffsbildung zwischen Syntax und Morphologie*. Tübingen: Francke.

Schlüter, J. (2005). *Rhythmic grammar: The influence of rhythm on grammatical variation and change in English* (*TiEL* 46). Berlin/New York: Mouton de Gruyter.

Schlüter, J. (2008). Constraints on the attributive use of 'predicative-only' adjectives: A reassessment. In N. Gisborne & G. Trousdale (Eds.), *Constructional explanations in English grammar* (*TiEL*) (pp. 164–179). Berlin/New York: Mouton de Gruyter.

Schlüter, J. (2015). Rhythmic influence on grammar: Scope and limitations. In R. Vogel & R. van de Vijver (Eds.), *Rhythm in cognition and grammar: A Germanic perspective* (pp. 179–205). Berlin/Munich/Boston: Mouton de Gruyter.

Selkirk, E.O. (1984). *Phonology and syntax: The relation between sound and structure*. Cambridge, Mass./London, UK: MIT Press.

Shih, S., Grafmiller, J., Futrell, R., & Bresnan, J. (2015). Rhythm's role in genitive construction choice in spoken English. In R. Vogel & R. van de Vijver (Eds.), *Rhythm in cognition and grammar: A Germanic perspective* (pp. 207–233). Berlin/Munich/Boston: Mouton de Gruyter.

Speyer, A. (2010). *Topicalization and stress clash avoidance in the history of English*. Berlin/New York: Mouton de Gruyter.

Štekauer, P. (2000). *English word-formation: A history of research (1960–1995)*. Tübingen: Narr.

Xiao, R. (2015). Phraseology. In D. Biber (Ed.), *The Cambridge handbook of English corpus linguistics* (pp. 106–124). Cambridge: Cambridge University Press.

CHAPTER 4

Intensification with *Very, Really* and *So* in Selected Varieties of English*

Karin Aijmer

1 Introduction

There exists an overwhelming amount of research on intensifiers within different theoretical frameworks. It therefore requires some courage to look again at intensifiers and their combinations.[1] For this study I have been inspired by the reporting of ongoing variation and change in the intensifier system in English to compare the synonymous intensifiers *very, really* and *so* across some varieties of English. The starting-point is that region just like other pragmatic or social factors can account for differences in the choice of intensifier. Regional variation can be regarded as a special kind of social variation and where an individual comes from (along with other social factors) can be used in the social construction of an individual's identity.

Studies of cross-varietal differences have generally focused on new forms and innovative structures as the effect of the mutual cultural and linguistic accommodation resulting from the contact between founders and the indigenous population. Lately more attention has been given to the less noticeable variation involving quantitative differences. As Mukherjee and Gries (2009, p. 28) point out, "only recently has it been noted that structural nativisation not only refers to entirely new and innovative forms and structures in individual varieties, but also covers quantitative differences between varieties of English in the use of forms and structures that belong to the common core (cf. Quirk et al., 1985: 16) that is shared by all Englishes."

Intensifiers can be studied on many levels. Traditionally the focus has been on their uses as degree words modifying adjectives. They can also be regarded

* My heart-felt thanks to Sebastian Hoffmann for going through the manuscript so carefully and suggesting a number of constructive remarks.

1 See e.g. Bolinger (1972), Altenberg (1991), Partington (1993), Paradis (1997), Lorenz (1999), Xiao and Tao (2007), Méndez-Naya (2008). Earlier research taking a cross-varietal or sociolinguistic approach is discussed in Section 3.

 | DOI: 10.1163/9789004361133_006

as a more pervasive phenomenon concerned with the intensification of the speaker's attitudes and emotions. In a discourse-pragmatic perspective the focus has been on how intensified adjectives are used in the local interaction to take up a subjective positioning or stance and how they link indexically to contextual features. Speakers use linguistic devices such as evaluating (judgement-indexing) adjectives and adverbials with a second-order indexical (metapragmatic) function that "describes, explains and rationalises [their] appropriateness" in context (Silverstein 2003, p. 195). It follows that the choice of a particular linguistic variant can be motivated textually, interpersonally and socially.

The idea that one can study variation of pragmatic or discourse phenomena across languages or language varieties also comes from the new discipline of variational pragmatics (Barron & Schneider, 2009). Up till now we have seen a large number of cross-varietal studies especially on speech act variation strengthening the trend towards studying the effect of regional and social factors on language at different levels of analysis. However there have so far been only a few studies of intensifiers in a cross-varietal perspective.

The present study is concerned with comparing the frequencies and uses of combinations of (some selected) intensifiers with adjectives in data representing the English spoken in Britain, the US, New Zealand and Singapore. The reason for choosing *very, really* and *so* for the comparison is that they are frequent and have been shown to occur with different frequencies in several varieties of English. The focus is on the variation between the individual intensifiers or collocations of the intensifiers plus adjectives. In a cross-cultural perspective the intensifiers may have different constraints on usage.

The research questions focused on in this study are both quantitative and qualitative: Are the intensifiers used with the same frequency and distribution in the varieties compared? What is the meaning of the adjectives modified by one of the intensifiers? What types of evaluation (good or bad, strong or weak) do they express? How can we explain the differences between the patterns in terms of the variety of English and the social and linguistic norms the speakers adhere to?

The article has the following structure. Section 2 introduces the corpora and methodology. Section 3 is a short overview of previous work. Section 4 compares the frequencies of the intensifiers in some selected varieties of English. Section 5 deals with adjective intensification in general and how the notions evaluation and subjectivity are relevant for the description of adjectives and intensifiers in the different varieties. Sections 6–8 are devoted to the qualitative analysis of *very, really* and *so* in the varieties. Section 9 sums up the results and discusses some reasons for the quantitative and qualitative differences.

2 Methodology

Methodologically, the approach is based on corpora. We are lucky to have corpora of varieties of English which have been compiled within the *International Corpus of English* project (ICE).[2] By comparing patterns with intensifiers collocating with adjectives in the corpora we can get a better idea of the domain of intensification and the type and extent of variation in the varieties.

The corpora are of roughly the same size and were designed in a similar way to enable comparisons across varieties of English. The components of the ICE-corpus selected for this study are British English (ICE-GB), New Zealand English (ICE-NZ), Singapore English (ICE-SIN). New Zealand English is an Inner Circle variety of English (Kachru, 1992) which is spoken by the majority of the population and is used for both private and public communication. In Singapore English the speakers have a different first language than English (the Outer Circle: Kachru, 1992), which may influence their use of English. Singapore English is described as "without any doubt … the most advanced variety" among the so-called New Englishes (Mukherjee & Gries, 2009, p. 304). English is used in the education system and has become the default language of communication in formal and informal contexts for a large part of the population. Some elements of local linguistic usage (including characteristic grammatical constructions) are recognised as a way of representing a Singaporean identity.[3]

The compilation of an ICE-US is not yet complete. A subset of the *Santa Barbara Corpus of American English* (SBCAE, see http://www.linguistics.ucsb.edu/research/santa-barbara-corpus) will provide the main source of data for the face-to-face component of ICE-US. Since this selection has not yet been carried out, the complete SBCAE will be used for the present paper.

The ICE-corpora contain a number of spoken and written registers. However, the focus in this study is on colloquial language (the component of private conversation in the spoken part of the ICE-corpora) where intensifiers can be assumed to be most frequent.

Table 4.1 gives an overview of the corpora used to study patterns with intensifiers and adjectives and their frequencies. The data from the ICE-corpora are taken from Private Dialogue (face-to-face conversation and telephone calls), which represents the largest register of the ICE-corpora investigated (200,000 words). The American corpus has a total of 249,000 words and is therefore

2 For more information on the ICE-project see Greenbaum (1996).

3 In Schneider's (2003, 2007) evolutionary model, Singapore English would be described as having reached phase 4 "endonormative stabilization" (see e.g. Schneider 2007, p. 48 and Section 9 below).

TABLE 4.1 *Corpora used to study patterns with the intensifiers* very, really *and* so

ICE-GB	200,000 words	Inner Circle
SBCAE	249,000 words	Inner Circle
ICE-NZ	200,000 words	Inner Circle
ICE-SIN	200,000 words	Outer Circle

larger than the components of the ICE corpora and does not contain any telephone calls.

The intensifiers *very, really* and *so* plus adjective were extracted from the four corpora and investigated quantitatively and qualitatively.

3 Previous Work

Very, really and *so* have attracted a great deal of attention because of their variation across varieties and time. Tagliamonte and Roberts (2005) compared British English (data from the city of York in north-east England) and data from the North American television series *Friends*. In the British data, *very* was more frequent than *really* and *so* (in the order *very, really, so, absolutely, pretty*) whereas *so* was the new favourite in the American television data with the ranking *so, really, very*. In a follow-up study Tagliamonte (2008) showed that the intensification system was (also) changing in Toronto (Canadian) English. *Very* in the Toronto Corpus was moving out of favour and *really* had risen dramatically. Moreover, there was evidence to suggest that *so* (and *pretty*) were on the rise.

Bauer and Bauer (2002) carried out a large-scale investigation of schoolchildren's uses of the constructions *so cool, really cool, cool as, very cool* in New Zealand English. Their study suggested that there were changes in their frequency when they compared the frequencies of these forms with data from the Wellington Corpus of Spoken New Zealand English (Bauer, 1993). They found, for example, that the young speakers tended to avoid the use of *very* in favour of *really* and especially *so*. The authors also found some examples of regionalisation of intensifiers. The intensifier *sweet as* (not found in the other varieties) was more likely to be used in schools in the northern than in the southern part of New Zealand (Bauer & Bauer, 2002, p. 248).

As shown by several of these researchers, there may be contrasts in intensifier use from one major variety of English to another. The frequency of use and patterns of usage may in fact vary enormously between varieties (Tagliamonte

& Roberts, 2005). This is particularly the case for New Englishes. However there have so far been only few studies going beyond the Inner Circle varieties.

De Klerk (2005) was concerned with comparing a subset of intensifier combinations by speakers of Xhosa English (speakers of English as a second language in South Africa) with speakers of New Zealand English. It was found that the Xhosa speakers used fewer lexical variants of the intensifiers and a more restricted range of collocating adjectives. In particular, they used boosters (*very, hugely*) only half as often as NZ speakers. As a result of the differences in how intensification is expressed Xhosa speakers may come across "as less enthusiastic, less involved and generally more muted in expressing themselves" (De Klerk, 2005, p. 94).

Coronel (2011) used a similar research design as De Klerk to study intensifiers in a sub-corpus of Philippine English (ICE-PHI), which made it possible to compare second language learners with the speakers of New Zealand English. It was shown that there were differences between the varieties both with regard to the frequency of different intensifiers and their combinations with adjectives (and verbs). Coronel noted that the Philippine English (PhilE) speakers had developed their own strategies for reinforcing intensity such as reduplication of the intensifiers and the piling up of many intensifiers for more effect.[4] It was suggested that the reason why PhilE speakers used fewer intensifiers was that they were second language speakers who had learnt English through other Filipinos.

More recently Fuchs and Gut (2016) have contributed to corpus-based cross-varietal research by studying the effects of formality on intensifier frequency and variety-specific preferences for certain intensifier variants in Indian, Singapore, Philippine and British English. Their starting-point was an earlier study showing that intensifiers occurred around three times more frequently in Singapore English than in Indian English and Philippine English. On the basis of a study using cluster and phenogramme analysis they went on to show that in private and public conversations the distribution of intensifiers differed across the three varieties they studied. The study was based on the sub-corpora of the ICE-project, which makes the results comparable to other studies using the same data.

4 The Frequencies of *Very, Really, So*

I searched for occurrences of *very, really, so* with adjectives in the selected corpora. *Pretty* has not been included here since it is often difficult to decide

4 Reduplication is a productive feature in native Philippine languages (e.g. Tagalog) which suggests L1 interference in Philippine English (Blake, 1917).

whether it is being used as an intensifier (amplifier) or a compromiser expressing moderate degree (Tagliamonte, 2008, p. 370).

Collecting the data involved a certain amount of manual work since, for example, *really* and *so* have other uses than intensifiers. *Really* has only been included when it is followed immediately by an adjective (*it's a really good film*). On the other hand, I have not regarded *really* as an intensifier when it does not precede the adjective (*it's really a good film*). I have also set aside uses of *so* where *so* + adjective was followed by a *that*-clause. The analysis includes negative tokens as there may be differences between the varieties in how they use intensifiers in negative contexts (cf. however Ito and Tagliamonte (2003, p. 264) who exclude negative contexts since intensifiers do not express a high degree of a property when negated). Both predicative and attributive uses of the intensified adjective have been included.

The varieties differ both with regard to the overall number of intensifiers and the distribution of *very, really* and *so* (cf. Figure 4.1).

The low frequency of adjective intensification in American English is noteworthy and suggests that American English prefers adjectives without intensifiers or that it uses other intensifiers or strategies to express a high degree of a property or involvement. The ICE-SIN, on the other hand, has a high overall frequency of the three intensifiers compared with the other varieties. The high frequency of the intensifier variants in Singapore English is confirmed by Fuchs and Gut's (2016, p. 205) study of "boosters in general" (*so, too, very, really*) where they found that the intensifiers were more frequent in ICE-SIN than in the Indian and Philippine ICE-corpora (cf. Section 3).

Very has been regarded as "the intensifier *par excellence*" and it is also the oldest intensifier (Cacchiani, 2009b, p. 234). In the ICE-GB, *very* was the most frequent intensifier followed by *really*, which agrees with the distribution of the intensifiers in the British data discussed by Ito and Tagliamonte (2003) and Tagliamonte and Roberts (2005).

In Singapore English, *very* was by far the most frequent variant and it was found more often overall than in the other varieties. ICE-SIN also differs from British English in the preference for *so* rather than *really* (*very, so, really*).

The importance of *very* can however be overshadowed by one of the other intensifiers. The ICE-NZ was characterised by the popularity of *really* both in comparison with *very* and *so* and its frequency in the other varieties.[5] *So* was furthermore less frequent than in the other varieties. This result seems to agree

5 According to Coronel (2011), the high frequency of *really* was also characteristic of Philippine English.

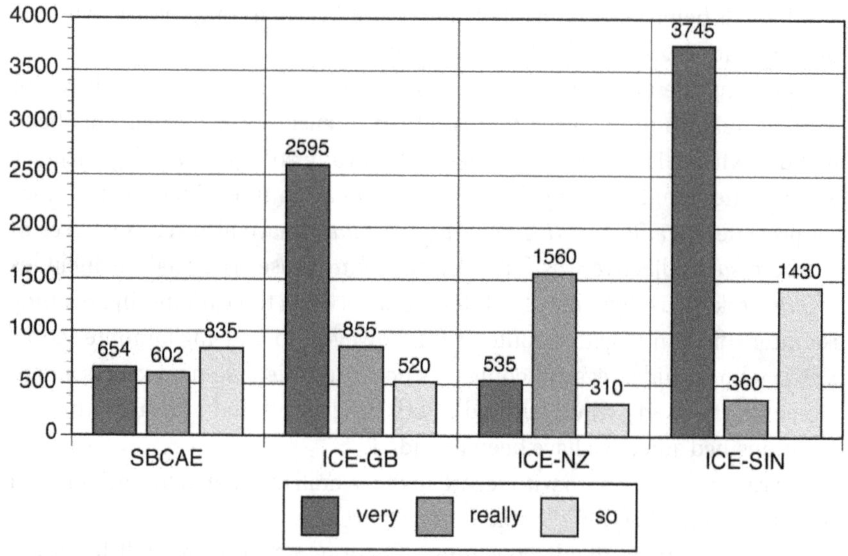

FIGURE 4.1 *The frequencies of* very, really *and* so *per one million words in four varieties of English*

with the patterns of frequency of the three intensifiers in Bauer and Bauer's (2002) study referred to in Section 3. The low frequency of *so* is also confirmed by D'Arcy's study of intensification on the basis of the ONZE Corpus (*Origins of New Zealand English*): "In ONZE, while *so* has clear longitudinal presence and its overall trajectory is one of increase, it remains less frequent overall than *very*, even among the youngest speakers" (D'Arcy, 2015, p. 469).

The Santa Barbara Corpus contained a high number of *so*. *Really*, on the other hand, was less frequent than both *very* and *so* which seems to go against the tendencies mentioned in earlier studies. According to Biber et al. (1999, p. 565), *really* was more frequent than *very* in American English conversation and Tagliamonte and Roberts (2005, p. 292) refer to *really* "as the most pervasive intensifier in North American English today".

5 Adjective Intensification

5.1 *Intensification, Subjectivity and Evaluation*

Intensifiers such as *very, really* and *so* have traditionally been treated as amplifiers with the function of moving adjectives or verbs upward on a scale from a norm (Quirk et al., 1985, p. 443). Quirk et al. (1985) further introduced a distinction between maximisers and boosters (*very, really* and *so*) where maximisers such as *totally* involve grading in terms of totality and the boosters involve scaling. The different types are said to have different structural and semantic properties. There are, for example, well-known restrictions on the possible combinations of boosters and adjectives. *Very awake* would be awkward because the adjective is a limit (either-or) adjective while *very beautiful* is acceptable since the adjective is scalar (can be positioned on an imaginary scale) (Paradis, 1997).[6] Intensifiers do not only express degrees of a property but they can be used to indicate different degrees of what Labov calls "intensity" (1984, pp. 43–44): "intensity operates on a scale centred about the zero, or unmarked expression with both positive (aggravated or intensified) and negative (mitigated or minimised) poles".

The semantic and pragmatic analysis of intensifiers is however complex and also involves notions such as subjectivity, evaluation or stance (cf. Thompson & Hunston, 2000, p. 2). Here the analysis recognises that intensifiers can have both subjective and intersubjective functions. In this perspective, intensifiers are viewed as resources which "negotiate relationships of alignment/disalignment vis-à-vis the various value positions referenced by the text and hence vis-à-vis the socially-constituted communities of shared attitudes and beliefs associated with those positions." (Martin & White, 2005, p. 136; quoted from Cacchiani, 2009a, p. 9)

We are also dealing here with ways of using intensifiers for exaggeration and being more expressive or subjective. Intensified adjectives can be characterised by more or less expressiveness. Speakers can, for example, show that they are more involved by using an extreme adjective such as *furious* which is placed at one pole of the scale rather than a central adjective like *angry*. Another way speakers can be more subjective and involved is by choosing expressive or colourful adjectives (*he is really groovy*), by repeating the intensifier, using2 the intensifier in unexpected contexts, exaggerating prosody, etc. The need to be expressive also accounts for semantic changes within the category of intensifiers. Since intensification "thrives on novelty and expressivity" (Lorenz, 1999, p. 87), old intensifiers become weakened and fall out of fashion and are replaced by new ones as a result. The more delexicalised or grammaticalised an intensifier becomes the more it loses in expressivity and needs to be replaced. "How long an intensifier lasts" (Tagliamonte, 2008, p. 301) may have to do with a variety of sociolinguistic factors and also be related to different developments

6 However, there are 9 examples of *very awake* in COCA (*Corpus of Contemporary American English*) which suggests that non-scalar adjectives show a great deal of flexibility with regard to gradability (Paradis, 1997, p. 64).

in the varieties of English. *Really* and *so* have, for example, become more frequent in some varieties while *very* has lost in importance.

5.2 *Classifying the Adjectives*

We may also expect that varieties of English use evaluative resources in different ways. The hypothesis is that the semantic quality of the adjective is a prominent feature of adjective intensification and that it is "a shibboleth of" (Lorenz, 1999, p. 60) different varieties of English. The classification here is based on the observation that the general function of adjective intensification in informal conversation is to negotiate the speaker's attitudes along different parameters.

Adjectives with emotional or evaluative qualities are, for example, "*beautiful, nice, great, interesting, terrible, despicable* and *important* and many others" (Hunston & Sinclair, 2000, p. 83). In order to classify the emotional adjectives semantically I have used the taxonomy (of adjectives and verbs) proposed in Martin's theory of Appraisal (Martin, 2001; Martin & White, 2005). In Appraisal theory adjectives (and other emotional words) are grouped into classes concerned with affect, judgement and assessment of good and bad.[7] The model has the advantage that it provides criteria and a large number of examples of adjectives in the different classes. Affect is expressed by adjectives covering emotions such as happiness or unhappiness (*happy, sad, miserable*), satisfaction or dissatisfaction (*interested, bored*), security or insecurity (*confident, anxious*). Adjectives in the domain of Judgement refer to basic human traits such as capacity (*clever, intelligent*), normality (*lucky, fortunate*), propriety (*good, nice*) or veracity (*honest*). Adjectives of Appreciation evaluate things or phenomena as good or bad, desirable or non-desirable, appealing, exciting, interesting (*funny, vile, nice*).

Intensifiers also collocate with non-evaluative adjectives. The classes of adjectives outside the evaluation domain indicate the relevance of what is said (e.g. *important, necessary, new, strange, familiar, different, special, strange*) as well as feasibility (e.g. *difficult, easy, hard, apparent, dangerous, impossible*) (Lorenz 1999). Dimensional adjectives (e.g. *large, small, tall, short, high, low, near, far, wide, narrow, cheap, expensive*) are also generally non-evaluative.[8] They "depict rather basic qualities" (Lorenz, 1999, p. 54) and have little meaning

---

7 For semantic subcategorisation of the adjectives see also Tagliamonte (2007, p. 377) based on Dixon (1977), Lorenz (1999) and Swales and Burke (2003).

8 Lorenz (1999) classifies *good* and *bad* as dimensional adjectives (appreciation adjectives in the classification suggested here).

in themselves. Physical properties are exemplified by *hairy, muddy, dog-eared, tatty*. Non-evaluative adjectives also refer to nation (*American*), political system (*democratic*), colour and various other qualities.

Another basis for grouping the adjectives which takes into account their evaluative properties has to do with whether the adjective collocating with the intensifier was positive (associated with evaluating something as good) or negative (and therefore evaluating something as bad). In this perspective the intensified adjectives are characterised by what Partington (2014) refers to as evaluative prosody. The adjectives *good* or *cool* help to express positive evaluation and *bad* or *annoying* express negative evaluation. It has been suggested that intensifiers may vary with regard to their ability to occur with adjectives which are associated with positive or negative evaluation. Bublitz (1998), for example, discussed intensifiers such as *perfectly* which have positive semantic prosody while for example *utterly* takes scope over negative adjectives and has negative semantic prosody (see also Partington, 1993).

However, many intensifiers occur with adjectives which have both positive and negative associations (or with adjectives which are neutral with regard to whether the adjectives are good or bad, e.g. *busy, sure*). In this case semantic prosody is associated with the high frequency of a certain pattern.[9] *Very, really* and *so* present, for example, a complex picture since they are found with both positive and negative adjectives but with different frequencies. It follows that correlations between intensifiers and the positive or negative prosody of the adjective can be tested by mapping how frequently the intensifiers appear with positive or negative words. Semantic prosody also has a diachronic aspect. This observation is based on the fact that intensifiers deriving from negative adjectives such as *awfully* may collocate both with negative and positive adjectives. For example, if an intensifier such as *awfully* co-occurs with positive adjectives this can be interpreted as indicating that it has lost the negative semantic content associated with *awe* and is more delexicalised (Partington, 1993; Tagliamonte, 2008, p. 375).

9 Partington (2014, p. 284) suggests that we need a statistical description of semantic (evaluative) prosody: "In other words, [an item] so co-occurs much more often than is to be expected by random probability."

6 *Very*

Very can be regarded as an old marker which has undergone complete delexicalisation. Cacchiani (2005, p. 407) describes it as "still subjective" but used for "relatively more rational evaluations". It conveys no traces of its original conceptual meaning 'true' or 'real' and can be characterised as "the unmarked adjective booster *par excellence*" (Lorenz, 1999, p. 214; italics in original). *Very* is however interesting from a comparative point of view because of the differences in frequency between the varieties. As indicated in Section 4, its frequency was especially high in Singapore English.

One explanation for this may be that Singaporeans in general intensify adjectives in order to convey more emphasis even when a single adjective would be enough. However, this points to a different language situation in Singapore from the Philippines. Coronel (2011) found that speakers of Philippine English generally used fewer intensifiers than speakers of New Zealand English (cf. Section 3). She suggested that one factor explaining this situation may be that most Filipinos learn English as a second language from other Filipinos and that Filipinos prefer a code-switching variety for informal conversation with other Filipinos.[10] In Singapore the situation for English is different. In a fairly short time English has become the language especially of the younger generation (Schneider, 2007, p. 157) and it is increasingly used in informal conversations within the family. However, despite the spread of English as a first language it is still correlated with social class and formality. As a result, a spoken variant (Singlish) is often used in informal contexts although this is generally discouraged by the government. The Singaporeans' frequent use of intensifiers (especially *very*) can therefore be viewed as a feature which has been appropriated by the informal local variety and indicates a Singaporean identity.

Nativisation may also refer to combinations of *very* and adjectives which are confined to certain regional varieties and can therefore be taken as signs of an accepted local structure. In (1) *very* followed by the extreme adjective *awful* was only found in Singapore English in the ICE-corpora.[11]

---

10 According to the *Concise Oxford Companion to the English Language* (1998) the code-switching register is confined to Manila and certain urban centres. It is used extensively on television and radio while English is used for business and education.

11 Cf. also *very terrible* (5 examples in ICE-SIN). *Very awful* was found in 21 examples in COCA (Corpus of Contemporary American English) and *very terrible* in 58 examples which suggests that the patterns are found in many varieties.

TABLE 4.2 *The most frequent adjectives with* very *in four varieties (tokens)*

SBCSAE	ICE-GB	ICE-NZ	ICE-SIN
good (24)	*good* (59)	*good* (29)	*good* (85)
nice (6)	*nice* (33)	*nice* (17)	*nice* (51)
important (5)	*difficult* (19)	*difficult* (5)	*cheap* (16)
true (4)	*funny* (7)	*different* (3)	*interesting* (16)

(1) That was *very awful* was when when he when he uhm when the guys grabbed the girls. (ICE-SIN:S1A-030#16:1:A)

Not very sure[12] occurred in 12 examples in ICE-SIN (but no example of *I'm very sure*)—also in the ICE-corpora representing Hong Kong English, Indian English and Philippine English—and may function as a sign of regional identity. From a semantic perspective, *sure* is a limit or either-or adjective which cannot normally "be laid out on a scale" (Paradis, 1997, p. 57).

(2) Probably because the support for it has uh uh is not there anymore I'm *I'm not very sure* (ICE-SIN:S1A-045#153:1:B)

(3) I think so but I'm *not very sure* (ICE-SIN:S1A-092#252:1:B)

Speakers both use *very* a lot and they use it with many different adjective types in the four corpora. Moreover the (two) most frequent adjectives were the same in the corpora. Table 4.2 shows the (four) most frequent adjectives occurring with *very* in the varieties.

Both *good* (and *nice*)[13] are highly frequent after *very* in all the varieties. However, in order to establish the strength of the relationship between *very* and one of the common adjectives in the list we need to take into account all the examples of the adjective where it can potentially be intensified. Table 4.3

12 Notice, however, that *not very sure* does not mean that the property of being very sure is absent but that the speaker is less than sure about what is said.

13 Cf. also Paradis (1997, p. 83) who found that of all the 1,464 occurrences of *very* in the London-Lund Corpus of Spoken English *very good* accounted for 9% of the occurrences and *very nice* for 6%.

TABLE 4.3 *The collocation between* very *and* good *in relation to all attestations of* good *which can potentially have intensifiers*

	SBCSAE	ICE-GB	ICE-NZ	ICE-SIN
very	24 (5.5%)	59 (28.6%)	29 (7.0%)	85 (33.7%)
really	22 (5.1%)	39 (18.9%)	109 (26.3%)	8 (3.2%)
so	16 (3.7%)	7 (3.4%)	10 (2.4%)	5 (2.0%)
All other intensifiers	39 (9.0%)[14]	31 (15.0%)	92 (22.2%)	34 (13.5%)
Unmodified *good*	334 (76.8%)	70 (34.0%)	175 (42.2%)	120 (47.6%)
Number of examples of *good* which can potentially have intensifiers[15]	435 (100%)	206 (100%)	415 (100%)	252 (100%)

compares the frequency of *very* with *good* in relation to all the examples of *good* which could potentially have modifiers.[16]

Considering all the tokens of *good* and their collocations with *very, really* and *so* we find that the predisposition for *very* to co-occur with *good* is not equally strong. In New Zealand English, *really good* was more frequent than both *very good* and *so good* (or all other intensifiers). In American English, *really good* would have been more frequent than *very good* if I had included *real good* (11 examples). We can also observe that *good* was less often modified in SBCSAE (76.8% unmodified) reflecting the general tendency that intensifiers seem to be used less often in American English (cf. Section 4). In ICE-GB and in ICE-SIN, the combination *very good* was represented more frequently than any of the other possibilities (ICE-GB 28.6%; ICE-SIN 33.7%).

Going beyond the quantitative analysis brings up problems of the meaning of the adjectives qualified. The semantic categories describing the adjectives

14 *Pretty good* was more frequent than *so good* (20 examples) in SBCSAE.

15 Examples which were not included are e.g. *for good, quite as good, good on you, no good, good morning, not good enough*.

16 The tendencies are the same when we consider the combinations between intensifier and *nice* in the varieties. *Very nice* (rather than *really nice* or *so nice*) was typical of Singapore English (49% vs. 3.8% for both *really nice* and *so nice*). In ICE-NZ *really nice* predominated (27.1%). *Very nice* was found in 14.4% and *so nice* in 4.4% of the examples. In American English *very nice* and *really nice* were represented by the same percentage (8.8%). In ICE-GB the differences were small (*very nice* 15.3%, *really nice* 13%).

here were chosen because they can be motivated by a theory of evaluation (Appraisal theory, see Section 5.2). Both synchronically and diachronically it is a matter of interest whether speakers use evaluative or non-evaluative adjectives with *very*.

The adjectives which occur most frequently with *very* are evaluative adjectives. These are found in fairly fixed phrases (constructions) expressing the speaker's evaluative or subjective attitudes to people or to things. The combinations of intensifier plus adjective are subject to categorisation depending on the type of evaluation. The phrases are exemplified by the following structures with BE with different subjects:

A. I am [INT] AFFECT ADJ
I'm very upset

B. You (he,she,they) BE [INT] JUDGEMENT ADJ
He is very honest

C. It (that) is [INT] APPRECIATION ADJ
NP is [INT] ADJ
That's wonderful

We are dealing with evaluative phrases (stored in the speaker's memory) much as if they are lexical items. However, the patterns are not completely routinised as shown by the fact that intensifiers collocate with many different evaluative adjectives. Moreover, intensifiers can be assumed to be at various stages of extending their uses to new, non-evaluative adjectives. In what follows, I will therefore focus on type rather than token frequencies, thus describing aspects of productivity and extension of range rather than mere frequency of use. Table 4.4 shows the proportions of *very* with evaluative and non-evaluative adjectives (types) in the four varieties.

In all the varieties *very* was found with both evaluative and non-evaluative adjectives. Intensifiers can also be seen to favour certain types of evaluative or non-evaluative adjectives. See Table 4.5.

By classifying the adjectives into semantic classes we can get a picture of how *very* combines with different adjectives expressing evaluation and non-evaluation in different varieties.[17] In New Zealand English *very* was, for example, particularly productive with adjectives expressing affect (*very lonely, very upset*) in comparison with the other varieties. The proportion of different non-

---

17 Naturally, a high percentage of *very* in Table 4.5 is not necessarily indicative of overall (token) frequencies: individual adjective types may be intensified frequently or only once.

TABLE 4.4 *Very with evaluative and non-evaluative adjectives (types) in four varieties of English*

	SBCSAE	ICE-GB	ICE-NZ	ICE-SIN
Evaluative	72 (61%)	102 (59.6%)	43 (66.2%)	174 (73.7%)
Non-evaluative	46 (39%)	69 (34.5%)	22 (33.8%)	62 (26.3%)
Total	118 (100%)	171 (100%)	65 (100%)	236 (100%)

TABLE 4.5 *Very with different categories of evaluation and non-evaluation adjectives (types) in four varieties of English*

	SBCAE	ICE-GB	ICE-NZ	ICE-SIN
EVALUATIVE				
Affect	12 (10.1%)	18 (10.5%)	15 (23.1%)	35 (14.8%)
Judgement	31 (26.2%)	33 (19.3%)	13 (20%)	67 (28.4%)
Appreciation	29 (24.5%)	51 (29.8%)	15 (23.1%)	72 (30.5%)
NON-EVALUATIVE				
Relevance	7 (5.9%)	10 (5.8%)	1 (1.5%)	12 (5.0%)
Feasibility	6 (5.1%)	3 (1.7%)	3 (4.6%)	6 (2.5%)
Dimension	20 (16.9%)	32 (18.6%)	13 (20%)	14 (5.9%)
Physical	3 (2.5%)	6 (3.5%)	2 (3.1%)	10 (4.2%)
Nation, political system, colour, other	10 (8.5%)	18 (10.5%)	3 (4.6%)	20 (8.5%)
Total number of adjective types	118 (100%)	171 (100%)	65 (100%)	236 (100%)

evaluative adjectives was generally low in all the varieties except for dimensional adjectives in SBCSAE, ICE-GB and ICE-NZ.

According to Cacchiani (2005, p. 403), *very* (and *really*) are neutral with regard to positive and negative connotations. However, like all other intensifiers, *very* can collocate with different frequencies with either positive or negative adjectives. I have therefore analysed the adjectives coming from the different evaluative domains (affect, judgement, appreciation) according to whether they are positively or negatively evaluated (cf. Table 4.6).

TABLE 4.6 Very *collocating with positive, negative or neutral evaluative adjectives (types)*

	SBCSAE	ICE-GB	ICE-NZ	ICE-SIN
positive	56 (77.8%)	66 (64.7%)	26 (60.5%)	98 (56.3%)
negative	16 (22.2%)	34 (33.3%)	17 (39.5%)	73 (42%)
neutral	–	2 (2%)	–	3 (1.7%)
Total	72 (100%)	102 (100%)	43 (100%)	174 (100%)

TABLE 4.7 Very *and repetition in four regional varieties, normalised to one million words within parentheses*

SBCAE	ICE-GB	ICE-NZ	ICE-SIN
8 (32)	–	15 (75)	27 (135)

In all the varieties positive semantic prosody was most frequent. Things were generally evaluated as *exciting*, *interesting* or *nice*, and people are said to be *clever*, *funny* and *reliable*. In the ICE-NZ data *very*'s mainly positive semantic prosody goes against the results of earlier research. For example, in Bauer and Bauer's (2002) study of New Zealand school children the majority of the adjectives had negative connotations (including examples such as *not very good*). However *very* was an infrequent intensifier in their data (Bauer & Bauer, 2002, p. 250).

Very has been delexicalised and does not itself contribute to intensity or to expressiveness. However it is still subjective and it can come to signal a higher degree of intensity depending on its prosody or if it is repeated. As shown in Table 4.7 repetition or reduplication of *very* was particularly frequent in ICE-NZ. There were no examples of repetition in the ICE-GB.

Coronel (2011) explains repetition of *very* (and *really*) in ICE-PHI as a strategy to express intensity compensating for the underuse of the two intensifiers in Philippine English. The same explanation could be given for the frequency of repetition in New Zealand English (and in Singapore English).

(4) i find that the fifth form maori paper is very easy eh ⟨,⟩ *very very easy* (ICE-NZ:S1A-080#371:1:N)

(5) And the set dinner is uh consists of it's a total of thirty—seven dollars plus plus and you can order anything from the main menu right and some of the *very very* uh expensive things you can order are salmon uh appetisers or uh or oysters and they're *very very* large fresh oysters. (ICE-SIN:S1A-074#141:1:B)

The frequency and use of *very* in the four varieties can be summarised as follows:

- *very* was the most frequent adjectival intensifier in ICE-GB (*very* > *really* > *so*) and in ICE-SIN (*very* > *so* > *really*). In American English *so* was more frequent than *very* (*so* > *very* > *really*) and in ICE-NZ it cannot compete with *really* (*really* > *very* > *so*)
- *very* had a higher overall frequency in ICE-SIN than in the other varieties resulting in over-intensification
- the number of examples of *very* was lower in ICE-NZ than in the other varieties indicating that other intensifiers are preferred
- *very* was found with a wide range of adjective types in all the varieties
- *very* co-occurred most frequently with common adjectives like *good* and *nice* in all the varieties
- there was also a strong predisposition for the collocation *very good* in ICE-SIN and in ICE-GB in comparison with other intensifiers (although occurrences without an intensifier were more common)
- *very* was most frequent in evaluative patterns with predicative adjectives indicating affect, judgement or appreciation
- *very* combined most often with evaluative adjectives having positive connotations but with different frequencies in the varieties. The tendency was, for example, less strong in ICE-SIN and in ICE-NZ
- *very* was associated with a low degree of expressivity and was used for rational evaluation rather than for emotional involvement or expressiveness
- especially in New Zealand English *very* could be reduplicated for more expressiveness. There were no examples of reduplication in ICE-GB
- *very* was found in unusual combinations such as *very awful* and *very terrible* in ICE-SIN possibly indicating regional specialisation

TABLE 4.8 *The most frequent adjectives collocating with* really *in four varieties of English*

SBCSAE	ICE-GB	ICE-NZ	ICE-SIN
good (13)	*good* (32)	*good* (70)	*good* (4)
nice (7)	*nice* (20)	*cool* (17)	*nice* (4)
bad (5)	*funny* (5)	*nice* (16)	*delicious* (2)
hard (4)	*interesting* (4)	*bad* (12)	*important* (2)

7 *Really*

7.1 *The Frequency of* Really *in Different Adjectival Patterns*

Really has attracted a great deal of interest as it has been claimed that it is on the rise in some varieties of English. Like *very* it is used about undistinguished emotions and adds to the degree of intensification of the adjective rather than to the expressive and subjective quality of the utterance (cf. Cacchiani, 2005, p. 407).[18] *Really* was the most frequent intensifier in New Zealand English and was also frequent in American and British English. On the other hand, it was infrequent in Singapore English (see Section 3). In addition to *really*, the zero form *real* is found in some varieties of English (see Section 7.3). It is dealt with separately since the conditions for its use are not the same as for *really*.

Really co-occurs with a wide range of adjectives in all the varieties. The most frequent adjectives are the ones we would expect from the similarity between *really* and *very* (cf. Table 4.8).

Good and *nice* were found in all the varieties among the most frequent adjectives.

The high frequency of *really cool* in ICE-NZ (slightly more frequent than *really nice*) agrees with Bauer and Bauer's observation that "the most frequent form with *really* + adj was *really cool*, which represented 8 per cent of the predicative 'tokens' of *really* + adj" (Bauer & Bauer, 2002, p. 250). Other intensifiers occurring with *cool* were: *quite cool* (6 examples), *so cool* (5 examples), *very cool* (1 example), *totally cool* (1 example), *pretty cool* (1 example).

18 Cacchiani (2005) analyses *really* as a high degree intensifier (an intensifier with high degree of expressive charge). Swales and Burke (2003, p. 1), on the other hand, find that *really* has been largely reduced by delexicalisation to an alternative for *very*.

TABLE 4.9 Really *collocating with evaluative and non-evaluative adjectives (types)*[19]

	SBCSAE	ICE-GB	ICE-NZ	ICE-SIN
Evaluative	69 (70.4%)	65 (84.4%)	72 (74.2%)	28 (62.2%)
Non-evaluative	29 (29.6%)	12 (15.6%)	25 (25.8%)	17 (37.8%)
Total	98 (100%)	77 (100%)	97 (100%)	45 (100%)

Among the collocates of *really* are both adjectives expressing subjective evaluation and non-evaluative adjectives specifying physical properties, dimensions, relevance and feasibility (cf. Table 4.9).

Table 4.9 shows that *really* was more frequent with evaluative adjectives in all the varieties. The proportion of evaluative adjectives was highest in ICE-GB and lowest in examples in ICE-SIN.

The intensifier can be further categorised with regard to adjective type (the meaning of the adjective)—cf. Table 4.10.

Among the collocates of *really* are both adjectives expressing subjective evaluation (affect or feelings, judgements of human traits, appreciation) and non-evaluative adjectives specifying physical properties, basic dimension and less frequent qualities such as relevance and feasibility.

The most productive category is Appreciation in SBCSAE, ICE-NZ, ICE-SIN (e.g. *it was really cool*). This can be assumed to be the category which best illustrates what intensifiers are doing in conversation (since it is used both about things and events). However, both judgement and affect also play an important role in conversation because of their orientation to the speaker or hearer.

Judgement was the most common evaluative meaning in ICE-GB. In other words, speakers used *really* plus adjective primarily to refer to a person's behaviour or human qualities (*he is really stupid, I was really lucky*). Affective meaning was the least frequent in all varieties (*I was really upset*) except Singapore English where Judgement had a lower proportion of examples.

Some intensifiers like *utterly* can be regarded as strong negative intensifiers since they nearly always occur with negative adjectives. *Really* (like *very*) has

19 *Really* could be negated (e.g. *not really bad*). However in these examples it has a downtoning or downscaling rather than upscaling effect; these instances have not been included here.

TABLE 4.10 Really *with different categories of evaluation and non-evaluation adjectives (types) in four varieties of English*

	SBCSAE	ICE-GB	ICE-NZ	ICE-SIN
EVALUATIVE				
Affect	20 (20.4%)	15 (19.5%)	11 (11.3%)	10 (22.2%)
Judgement	23 (23.5%)	27 (35.1%)	18 (18.6%)	5 (11.1%)
Appreciation	26 (26.5%)	23 (29.9%)	43 (44.3%)	13 (28.9%)
NON-EVALUATIVE				
Relevance	5 (5.1%)	1 (1.3%)	1 (1.0%)	4 (8.9%)
Feasibility	1 (1.0%)	1 (1.3%)	1 (1.0%)	1 (2.2%)
Dimension	9 (9.2%)	5 (6.5%)	13 (13.4%)	6 (13.3%)
Physical	10 (10.2%)	5 (6.5%)	7 (7.2%)	2 (4.4%)
Nation, political system, colour, other	4 (4.1%)	–	3 (3.1%)	4 (8.8%)
Total number of adjective types	98 (100%)	77 (100%)	97 (100%)	45 (100%)

TABLE 4.11 Really *collocating with positive, negative or neutral evaluative adjectives (types)*

	SBCSAE	ICE-GB	ICE-NZ	ICE-SIN
positive	30 (43.5%)	25 (38.5%)	31 (43.1%)	21 (75%)
negative	39 (56.5%)	40 (61.5%)	41 (57.0%)	5 (17.9%)
neutral	–	–	–	2 (7.1%)
Total	69 (100%)	65 (100%)	72 (100%)	28 (100%)

a more complex collocational profile since it co-occurs with both positive and negative adjectives.

The distribution of *really* with positive or negative collocating adjectives is shown in Table 4.11.

The negative tendency dominated in all the varieties except Singapore English. In the Santa Barbara Corpus the following adjective types were negative: something is (*really*) *annoying, awful, bad, bizarre, depressing, dumb, goofy, horrible, icky, lousy, mad, scary, terrible, weird* and speakers express a negative reaction to events or feelings: *I am* (*really*) *upset, frustrated, snubbed, bored, bummed*. Adjectives with positive connotations were also found (*beautiful, cool, cute, glad, hyper, lovely, neat, nice*). The present results can be compared with Biber et al. (1999, p. 564) who state that "[t]he most common [adjectives] have to do with positive value judgments (*good, cool, nice*) though negative judgments (*awful, bad, stupid*) are also relatively common".

In Singapore English *really* can be regarded as a (strongly) positive intensifier collocating with adjectives associated with positive evaluation: *advisable, amazing, cool, delicious, extraordinary, fun, good, heavenly, interesting, lucky, nice, nutritious, refreshing, resourceful, wonderful*. The only negative elements used with *really* were *bad* and *lousy at something*.

7.2 Really *with the Function of Turning Up the Emotional Volume*

As noticed above, *really* does not on its own signal a high degree of emotion. *Really* can however turn into a strong expressive intensifier by means of "pragmatic intensification" (Cacchiani, 2005, p. 410) for example by repetition:

(6) G: who cares if the quote that you're quoting has sexist language or whatever in it
M: because
M: because it's sexist language and you're not supposed
F: because sometimes *it's really really vile*
G: yeah but it's in a quote
(ICE-NZ:S1A-006# 164–168:1)

Really was repeated above all in the New Zealand data (20 examples). See Table 4.12.

Moreover *really* can occur in new contexts where the adjective is no longer scalar or when it is unusual in some other way. *Really* is emphasising when it combines with adjectives such as *wonderful* which are polarised (cf. *it is absolutely wonderful* with the same meaning).[20] Here *really* expresses the speaker's

20 Similar examples have also been discussed by Biber et al. (1999, p. 858) who treat them as ambiguous: "In the following example[s], *really* could have the stance meaning of 'in reality' or it could be interpreted as intensifying a verb or adjective with approximate meaning 'very (much)': *It's really wonderful* (CONV)." Cf. also Swales and Burke (2003) for a discussion.

TABLE 4.12 *Really and repetition in four regional varieties, normalised to one million words within parentheses*

SBCSAE	ICE-GB	ICE-NZ	ICE-SIN
3 (12)	–	20 (100)	4 (20)

strong commitment to the utterance by emphasising or reinforcing the evaluative meaning expressed by *wonderful* (cf. Paradis, 2003, "the emphasising *really*").

In both American English and in New Zealand English we find *really* used in ways associated with expressive language and hyperbole. As Lorenz (2002, p. 14) points out, "[c]rudely speaking, the more 'novel' or 'unusual' a linguistic item in a given function, the more expressive it will be perceived to be." I will illustrate this with data from ICE-NZ.

In New Zealand English *really* is used together with informal and unusual or slangy adjectives which can be understood as generational. *Really* was found in combination with adjectives such as *bizarre, crappy, mad, vile, cunning*. In examples (7) to (9) intensification of the following noun suggests that it has been mapped onto a scale of degree:

(7) but this book *is really top notch* (ICE-NZ:S1A-100#164:1:M)

(8) F: every day um i just i just really had a good time especially ⟨?⟩ hanging out our billets⟨/?⟩ you know
F: i mean you know cos you're ⟨unclear⟩word⟨/unclear⟩ choice too
T: and cos oh yeah i thought *it was really choice* oh guess what our billet um mele's coming up next week (ICE-NZ:S1A-058#97–99:1)

The speaker increases the force of *it's stink* by repeating it with *really*:

(9) G: last year was pretty good this year's got a real switch to it
M: oh it's stink man *it's really stink* (ICE-NZ:S1A-004#32–34:1)

The adjectives often ended in *-y*: *scary, icky, goofy, gorgey, dodgy, groupy, grotty, groovy, seedy, tacky, trendy, yummy*. Another group consisted of participle forms such as *cramped in* or *pissed off* which retain a verbal connotation and therefore are not scalar. Some *-y* adjectives are illustrated below:

(10) M: yeah all of their messages and ⟨,⟩ don't actually like them i got one of their albums but i don't like them
F: yeah *really messagey*⟨/?⟩ (ICE-NZ:S1A-001#263–264:1)

(11) and i think that a lot of people that really did that and *got really groupy and happy* (ICE-NZ:S1A-040:1:212:1:A)

The intensifier is needed not only to emphasise *groupy* (and *happy*) but to mark subjectivity and indirectly to strengthen the speaker's relations to other members of the social group to which the speaker belongs.

To sum up, we can make the following observations about the semantic patterns in which *really* expresses increased subjectivity and evaluation:

- *really* intensifying an adjective is typically associated with evaluative language
- the evaluative adjectives express emotional statements, judgements of the hearer's qualities and assessment of good and bad and are found in fairly fixed patterns
- many of the adjectives are colloquial, i.e. they would not be found in writing and many of them are associated with trendy young people
- the pattern *really* + adjective also contains polarised or extreme adjectives and can be interpreted in an emphatic or exaggerated way

The comparison between the varieties shows that they use *really* + adjective in different ways:

- *really* was most frequent in ICE-NZ and least frequent in ICE-SIN
- *really* co-occurred mostly with evaluative adjectives in all varieties
- *really* occurred most frequently with adjectives like *good* and *nice*. In ICE-NZ a frequent collocation was *really cool*
- in all the varieties *really* with adjectives was most frequently used to express the speaker's appreciation
- In SBCSAE, ICE-GB and ICE-NZ *really* was used (mostly) with negative semantic connotations but positive semantic judgements also occur.
- In ICE-SIN *really* overwhelmingly combined with positive adjectives

7.3 *Some Observations about* Real *plus Adjective*

Real can be used as an adverbial intensifier before adjectives as an alternative to *really*. It can be considered typically American although it was not as frequent as *really*. The differences between the two forms have been discussed in the

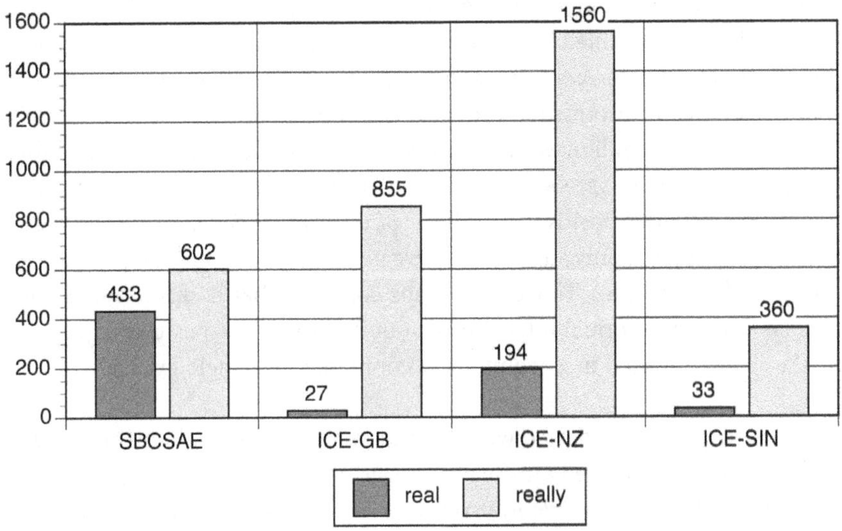

FIGURE 4.2 *Frequency of* real *and* really *in the varieties per one million words*

literature but mostly with regard to the whole class of dual form adverbs. Poutsma (1926, p. 63; referred to by Opdahl, 1997, p. 20) observed that there seems to be distinction of emotional language versus matter-of-fact style and style recurs as a factor mentioned by many scholars (see Opdahl, 1997, p. 20).[21] In a more recent study based on a corpus of American professional speech, Yaguchi et al. (2010, p. 594) established a correlation between "features of the interactive speech style in terms of negotiation of meaning as well as listener orientedness" and the ratio of usage of *real*. They also found that *real* was established as an acceptable intensifier in public speech.

In the SBCSAE *real* occurred 108 times to be compared with *really* (150 instances). In New Zealand English it was found 35 times which shows that it cannot compete with the frequency of *really*.[22] Figure 4.2 shows the distribution of *real* on the basis of figures normalised to one million words. The frequencies of *really* (including negated instances) have been added for comparison.

In SBCSAE *real* occurred more than twice as often with non-evaluative adjectives as with evaluative adjectives referring to properties such as size (*big*),

21 *Real* may have a different stylistic value depending on the variety. According to Bauer and Bauer (2002, p. 249), *real* + adjective was more likely to be reported by schools (in New Zealand) from predominantly high socioeconomic areas.

22 Coronel (2011) found five instances of *real* as an adjective modifier in Philippine English which in this respect is oriented to the American English pattern.

temperature (*hot*), price (*expensive*), relevance (*important*), etc. The most frequent adjectives modified by *real* were *good* (9 examples), *cute* (8 examples)[23] and *nice* (7 examples). A comparison can be made with Biber et al. who found that in American conversation the most common collocates of *real* occurring over five times per million words were *good, nice, hard, bad, big* and *crazy* (Biber et al., 1999, p. 543). In SBCSAE *real* was also more typical than *really* with adjectives associated with positive attitudes: *cool, cute, funny, good, interesting, lucky, nice, neat, sweet*. The only adjectives with a negative value were *bad* (1 example) and *stupid* (1 example). This can perhaps confirm Biber et al.'s (1999, p. 246) observation that informal intensifiers co-occur with more positive adjectives. *Real* was reduplicated in 3 examples as compared to a single example in ICE-NZ.

In the ICE-NZ *real* occurred with 30 different adjectives including *good, bad* and *nice*. *Real* co-occurred mostly with negative adjectives: *bad, bizarre, dumb, geeky, mental, nerdy, obnoxious, psycho, wicked*. Positively coloured adjectives were *awesome, fonzie* ('cool'), *choice* ('awesome beyond choice'). The adjectives generally have an expressive quality and are linked to informality, fashion, a trend to change and the expression of solidarity or youth.

8 *So*

So contributes to the emotional nature of the dialogue by signalling how strong the speaker's feelings are and by evaluating what is said as good or bad. In my data *so* was frequent above all in American English and Singapore English. It was less frequent in ICE-GB and ICE-NZ (cf. Section 4). However, according to Bauer and Bauer (2002, p. 249), *so* "appears to be the most usual form of booster in the spoken English of young Zealanders".

So has been described as "significantly tied to emotional adjectives" (Tagliamonte, 2008, p. 380). This is confirmed in my data where *so* co-occurs with evaluative adjectives more often than with non-evaluative adjectives. See Table 4.13.

So correlates strongly with emotional adjectives although non-emotional adjectives such as *cold, warm, young, close* were also found.

So was reduplicated for greater effect in Singapore English (5 examples) and in New Zealand English (2 examples):

---

23 This can be compared with only one example with *really* (*really cute*).

TABLE 4.13 *So collocating with evaluative and non-evaluative adjective types*

	SBCSAE	ICE-GB	ICE-NZ	ICE-SIN
Evaluative	75 (70.8%)	42 (64.6%)	45 (69.2%)	105 (68.6)
Non-evaluative	31 (29.2%)	23 (35.4%)	20 (30.8%)	48 (31.4%)
Total	106 (100%)	65 (100%)	65 (100%)	153 (100%)

(12) cos he looks married and like oh *so so cheeky*. (ICE-SIN:S1A-031#55:1:A)

Another way in which *so* can be strengthened is by the combination with other intensifiers (*just so* and *so really* mainly in ICE-GB and ICE-NZ,[24] *so bloody* and *so damn* in ICE-SIN).

So was most frequent in combinations such as *so funny*[25] and *so good*. In ICE-SIN a frequent combination was *so terrible* (12 examples), which is not found in the other varieties.[26] *So cool* was a frequent combination in New Zealand English although *cool* was intensified most often with *really* (cf. Section 7). The combination was also one of the most frequent collocations in Bauer and Bauer's (2002) study of New Zealand school-children's use of intensifiers, representing about 15% of the tokens. Table 4.14 provides the four most frequent adjectival collocates for the present data.

The type of evaluative adjective seems to be a factor distinguishing between the varieties although the differences between Affect and Appreciation are not very big (cf. Table 4.15).

So was used most productively with adjectives expressing affect in American English (and also in ICE-SIN). It was typically used in combinations such as *so happy, so tired, so miserable* describing the speaker's state or feelings. In New Zealand English *so* was most productive with appreciation adjectives and much less so with the function to make judgments about persons.

So also co-occurred with adjectives which are either positive, negative or neutral. See Table 4.16.

24 In ICE-NZ *just so* was found in 19 examples (cf. also *just so bloody hard* and *just so so naïve*). There were seven examples in ICE-GB.

25 *So funny* was the preferred alternative in SBCSAE (*really funny* 2 examples, *very funny* 1 example). In ICE-SIN, on the other hand, *very funny* was even more frequent than *so funny* (10 examples).

26 There were also 2 examples in ICE-HK.

TABLE 4.14 *The most frequent adjectives collocating with* so *in four varieties of English*

SBCSAE	ICE-GB	ICE-NZ	ICE-SIN
good (20)	*funny* (8)	*funny* (12)	*terrible* (12)
funny (10)	*good* (5)	*good* (10)	*funny* (9)[27]
tired (7)	*difficult* (3)	*cool* (5)	*nice* (6)
upset (5)	*sweet* (3)	*boring* (4)	*sad* (7)

TABLE 4.15 So *with different categories of evaluation and non-evaluation adjectives (types) in four varieties of English*

	SBCSAE	ICE-GB	ICE-NZ	ICE-SIN
EVALUATIVE				
Affect	29 (27.4%)	10 (15.4%)	17 (26.2%)	38 (24.8%)
Judgement	22 (20.8%)	14 (21.5%)	8 (12.30%)	30 (19.6%)
Appreciation	24 (22.6%)	18 (27.7%)	20 (30.8%)	37 (24.2%)
NON-EVALUATIVE				
Relevance	4 (3.8%)	5 (7.7%)	2 (3.1%)	6 (3.9%)
Feasibility	2 (1.9%)	4 (6.2%)	2 (3.1%)	5 (3.3%)
Dimension	16 (15.1%)	7 (10.8%)	11 (16.3%)	15 (9.8%)
Physical	8 (7.5%)	7 (10.8%)	5 (7.7%)	13 (8.5%)
Nation, political system, colour, other	1 (1%)	–	–	9 (5.9%)
Total number of adjective types	106 (100%)	65 (100%)	65 (100%)	153 (100%)

27 The following example was excluded: "thought you knew him uh then why *why why so funny* strangers could say hello to strangers". According to one of the reviewers, Singaporeans use the expression *why so funny* to express surprise or disbelief which is different from 'this is so funny'.

TABLE 4.16 So *collocating with positive, negative or neutral evaluative adjectives*

	SBCSAE	ICE-GB	ICE-NZ	ICE-SIN
positive	36 (48%)	18 (41%)	15 (33.3%)	36 (34.2%)
negative	38 (50.7%)	23 (52.3%)	28 (62.2%)	66 (62.9)
neutral	1 (1.3%)	3 (6.8%)	2 (4.4%)	3 (2.9)
Total	75 (100%)	44 (100%)	45 (100%)	105 (100%)

So is used with a higher percentage of negative adjectives in the four varieties. However in SBCSAE the number of positive and negative collocates is roughly the same which may suggest that *so* has been further delexicalised in that variety.

The observation in recent studies that *so* is increasing in frequency in American English also draws attention to its collocation with fashionable and novel adjectives. The SBCSAE contained the following combinations of *so* with an innovative or non-scalar adjective: *awesome, chubby, cool, crippled up, cute, geeky, goofy, gross, icky, mad, psyched, scary, sweet, weird.* People can for example be described as being or looking *goofy* (rather than *ridiculous*) or *geeky.*[28] In combination with *so* the adjective represents a particular style characteristic of speakers belonging to a group singled out by their shared norms and practices. The evaluative adjectives show a tendency to occur in certain predicative patterns (*she is so mad, it is so weird*) reflecting the fact that speakers use the collocations for expressing affect, judgements or appreciation. Since these patterns occurred most frequently in American English in my data the combinations may be understood as 'typically American' and associated with stances like informal, urban, trendy, etc. The preponderance of *so* in American English also stands out in Tagliamonte and Roberts' (2005) study of *so* in the American television series *Friends*. The authors argued that the current trends in the frequency and usage of *so* correlated with the fall and rise of the popularity of the television series. Another reason why *so* was so popular was because the speakers were young adults.

28 According to Wikipedia, the word *geek* comes from an English dialect *geek* or *geck* (meaning a 'fool' or 'freak'). Its meaning is said to have evolved to refer to "someone who is interested in a subject (usually intellectual or complex) for its own sake."

It is also of interest to observe that the same tendency to variation and growth is found in the other varieties (except New Zealand, the only example being *so hacked off*). *So* is understood as a new intensifier appearing together with slangy and trendy adjectives which are intended to attract attention.

Summing up, we can make the following observations:

- *so* collocates more strongly with evaluative adjectives than *very* and *really*
- *so* was often used with adjectives expressing affect (especially in American English)
- *so* was used primarily with negative semantic prosody. This tendency was particularly strong in Singapore English and New Zealand English
- *so* favours particular adjectives (*so funny*)
- *so* is used with adjectives in predicative patterns such as *I am/feel so* ADJ, *she is/looks so* ADJ or *it* (NP) *is so* ADJ with subjective and interpersonal functions (it is not normally found with attributive adjectives)
- *so* was found with trendy or slangy adjectives in all varieties except ICE-NZ indicating a current trend to change associated with young people

9 Conclusion

Intensifiers are subject to a great deal of variation synchronically and diachronically. They are therefore also interesting to study across varieties of English. The present study compared *very, really* and *so* in parallel corpora representing British and American English, New Zealand English and Singapore English. The focus was on the texts of private conversation from the spoken part of the corpora (and the conversations in SBCSAE for American English) where intensifier use can be expected to be most frequent.

The general findings of the comparison concerned differences in the frequency of *very, really* and *so* modifying an adjective. It was shown that the three intensifiers had a higher overall frequency in ICE-SIN than in the other varieties. On the other hand, American speakers used the intensifiers less frequently than speakers of the other varieties suggesting that other strategies are used for adjective intensification or that American English prefers the unmodified adjective. When one compares the distribution of *very, really* and *so* across the varieties ICE-SIN stands out because of the high frequency of *very*. *So* was also frequent but *really* was less frequent than in any of the other varieties. In New Zealand English *really* had a higher frequency than both *very* and *so*. In American English *so* was the most frequent intensifier which is in line with previous research showing that *so* is becoming more frequent.

Very was used more than *really*. However *real* was more frequent in American English than in the other varieties.

Another aim was to compare the types of adjectives the intensifiers co-occurred with. Interestingly, similar adjectives were found among the most frequent ones after one of the intensifiers in all the varieties. While *very* and *really* co-occurred most often with *good* and *nice* the most frequent adjective after *so* was *funny*. It was also shown that the intensifiers co-occurred with evaluative or emotional adjectives more than with non-evaluative adjectives and that the evaluative adjectives tended to occur in certain fixed patterns. A further research question concerned the kinds of adjectival meanings intensified by *very*, *really* and *so* and whether the adjectives had positive or negative connotations. The findings showed that *very* combined most often with evaluative adjectives having positive meanings in all the varieties. *Really*, on the other hand, was used most frequently with negative adjectives (with the exception of Singapore English). In Singapore English *really* tended to co-occur with positive adjectives and *so* with negative ones. In American English *really* collocated more often with negative than with positive adjectives while *real* preferred adjectives with positive connotations. *So* was above all used with adjectives expressing the speaker's emotional state (*so upset, so tired*).

The present analysis is synchronic only. However the results also have a diachronic aspect. In particular, the corpus data confirm findings that report on-going changes and restructuring in the intensification system mainly in American English. *So* is rising in frequency and is used with novel, fashionable adjectives by young speakers leading the current trend to change. A similar rise in frequency could be established in New Zealand English confirming previous research (Bauer & Bauer, 2002) that *really* is increasing in frequency with a start among young speakers.

The high frequency of intensifiers particularly in Singapore English needs to be explained. The explanation for the differences is socio-historical and associated with the development of new varieties through the spread of English. Thus, intensifiers in New Zealand English and in Singapore English have developed differently although the varieties share the history of colonisation by British settlers and having British English as the major influence. Similarities and differences between the varieties reflect both founding history, regional and culture parameters and the progression of English through time to a new dialect or indigenous variety. According to Schneider (2003, 2007), the post-colonial varieties pass through different phases in a dynamic, historical process which goes hand in hand with identity reconstruction in relation to others and indigenisation (adoption by the indigenous community of new grammatical structures and new vocabulary).

Singapore English has reached phase 4 in Schneider's model characterised by its greater degree of structural nativisation and identity construction. The high degree of intensifiers in Singapore English and the adoption of *very* as the Singaporeans' own intensifier may be explained by how speaker nativise the language for example by using a particular variant more frequently in relation to other varieties.

In New Zealand English *really* has established itself as a regional norm. *Really* was more frequent than both *very* and *so* and some patterns with adjectives (*really cool*) were more frequent than in the other varieties of English. In terms of Schneider's developmental stages (2007, p. 132) the linguistic orientation in New Zealand is endonormative, characterised by homogeneity and codification (phase 4).

New Zealand English has also shown signs of entering the most advanced stage in Schneider's developmental model (phase 5) characterised by differentiation, i.e. the establishment of sub-varieties and dialects. There are for example indications of regional differentiation in the use of intensifiers among New Zealand English school children as pointed out by Bauer and Bauer (2002) (cf. Section 3).

For American English the time depth is greater and extends over several centuries. As a result, American English has experienced both a tendency towards linguistic homogeneity and dialect diversification. It is also characteristic of American English that we need to go beyond regional differences and investigate how sociolinguistic conditions, mass media and youth culture create linguistic differentiation and can indicate a particular identity.

Appendix: Transcription Conventions[29]

⟨,⟩	short pause
⟨,,⟩	long pause
⟨.⟩ … ⟨/.⟩	incomplete words
⟨X … X⟩	uncertain hearing

29 Transcription of the individual examples has however been simplified. I have, for example, excluded non-transcribed material marked ⟨o⟩ ⟨/o⟩.

References

Altenberg, B. (1991). Amplifier collocations in spoken English. In S. Johansson & A.-B. Stenström (Eds.), *English computer corpora: Selected papers and research guide* (pp. 127–148). Berlin: Mouton de Gruyter.

Barron, A., & Schneider, K. (2009). Variational pragmatics: Studying the impact of social factors on language use in interaction. *Intercultural Pragmatics, 6*(4), 425–442.

Bauer, L. (1993) *Manual of information to accompany The Wellington Corpus of Written New Zealand English*. Wellington: Victoria University. Retrieved from http://clu.uni.no/icame/manuals/WELLMAN/INDEX.HTM. Last accessed 20 June 2017.

Bauer, L., & Bauer, W. (2002). Adjective boosters in the English of young New Zealanders. *Journal of English Linguistics, 30*(3), 244–257.

Biber, D., Johansson, S., Leech, G., Conrad, S., & Finegan, E. (1999). *The Longman grammar of spoken and written English*. London: Longman.

Blake, F.R. (1917). Reduplication in Tagalog. *American Journal of Philology*, 38, 425–431.

Bolinger, D. (1972). *Degree words*. The Hague: Mouton

Bublitz, W. (1998). 'I entirely dot dot dot'. Copying semantic features in collocations with up-scaling intensifiers. In R. Schulze (Ed.), *Making meaningful choices in English: On dimensions, perspectives, methodology and evidence* (pp. 11–32). Tübingen: Gunter Narr Verlag.

Cacchiani, S. (2005). Local vehicles for intensification and involvement: The case of English intensifiers. In P. Cap (Ed.), *Pragmatics today* (pp. 401–419). Frankfurt am Main: Peter Lang.

Cacchiani, S. (2009a). From narratives to intensification and hyperbole: Promotional uses of book blurbs. *Proceedings of the Corpus Linguistics Conference*. Retrieved from http://ucrel.lancs.ac.uk/publications/CL2007/paper/79_Paper.pdf. Last accessed 3 Feb. 2013.

Cacchiani, S. (2009b). Lexico-functional categories and complex collocations: The case of intensifiers. In U. Römer & R. Schulze (Eds.), *Exploring the lexis-grammar interface* (pp. 229–246). Amsterdam: John Benjamins.

Concise Oxford companion to the English language. (1998). Oxford: Oxford University Press.

Coronel, L. (2011). Patterns of intensifier usage in Philippine English. In M. Bautista & S. Lourdes (Eds.), *Studies of Philippine English: Exploring the Philippine component of the International Corpus of English*. (pp. 93–116). Manila: De La Salle University Centennial Book Series.

D'Arcy, A. (2015). Stability, stasis and change. The longue durée of intensification. *Diachronica, 32*(4), 449–493.

De Klerk, V. (2005). Expressing levels of intensity in Xhosa English. *English World-Wide, 26*, 77–95.

Dixon, R.M.W. (1977). Where have all the adjectives gone? *Studies in Language, 1*(1), 19–80.

Fuchs, R., & Gut. U. (2016). Register variation in intensifier usage across Asian Englishes. In H. Pichler (Ed.), *Discourse-pragmatic variation and change in English: New methods and insights* (pp. 185–201). Cambridge: Cambridge University Press.

Geek. (n.d.) In *Wikipedia: The Free Encyclopedia.* Retrieved from https://en.wikipedia.org/w/index.php?title=Geek. Last accessed 9 May 2017.

Greenbaum, S. (1996). Introducing ICE. In S. Greenbaum (Ed.) *Comparing English world-wide* (pp. 3–12). Oxford: Clarendon.

Hunston, S., & Sinclair, J. (2000). A local grammar of evaluation. In S. Hunston & G. Thompson (Eds.), *Evaluation in text: Authorial stance and the construction of discourse* (pp. 74–101). Oxford: Oxford University Press.

Ito, R., & Tagliamonte, S. (2003). '*Well* weird, *right* dodgy, *very* strange, *really* cool': Layering and recycling in English intensifiers. *Language in Society, 32*, 257–279.

Kachru, B. (Ed.) (1992). *The other tongue: English across cultures* (2nd ed.). Urbana: University of Illinois Press.

Labov, W. (1984). Intensity. In D. Schiffrin (Ed.), *Meaning, form and use in context. Linguistic applications* (pp. 43–70). Washington DC: Georgetown University Press.

Lorenz, G.R. (1999). *Adjective intensification—learners versus native speakers. A corpus study of argumentative writing.* Amsterdam: Rodopi.

Lorenz, G.R. (2002). *Really worthwhile* or *not really significant*? A corpus-based approach to the delexicalization and grammaticalization of intensifiers in Modern English. In I. Wischer & G. Diewald (Eds.), *New reflections on grammaticalization* (pp. 144–161). Amsterdam and Philadelphia: John Benjamins.

Martin, J.R. (2001). Beyond exchange: Appraisal systems in English. In S. Hunston & G. Thompson (Eds.), *Evaluation in text: Authorial stance and the construction of discourse.* (pp. 142–175). Oxford: Oxford University Press.

Martin, J.R., & White, P. (2005). *The language of evaluation: Appraisal in English.* London: Palgrave.

Méndez-Naya, B. (2008). Special issue on English intensifiers. *English Language and Linguistics, 12*(2), 213–219.

Mukherjee, J., & Gries, S. (2009). Collostructional nativisation in new Englishes: Verb-construction associations in the International Corpus of English. *English World-Wide, 24*, 147–173.

Opdahl, L. (1997). Ly *or zero suffix? A study in variation of dual-form adverbs in present-day English* (Doctoral dissertation). Department of English. University of Bergen.

Paradis, C. (1997). Degree modifiers of adjectives in spoken British English. *Lund Studies in English*, Vol. 92. Lund University Press.

Paradis, C. (2003). Between epistemic modality and degree: the case of *really*. In R. Facchinetti, F. Palmer & M. Krug (Eds.), *Modality in contemporary English* (pp. 197–220). Berlin: Mouton de Gruyter.

Partington, A. (1993). Corpus evidence of language change: The case of the intensifier. In M. Baker, G. Francis & E. Tognini-Bonelli (Eds.), *Text and technology. In honour of John Sinclair* (pp. 177–193). Amsterdam: John Benjamins.

Partington, A. (2014). Evaluative prosody. In K. Aijmer & C. Rühlemann (Eds.), *Corpus pragmatics* (pp. 279–303). Cambridge: Cambridge University Press.

Poutsma, H. (1926). *A grammar of late modern English II*. Groningen: Noordhoff.

Quirk, R., Greenbaum, S., Leech, G., & Svartvik, J. (1985). *A comprehensive grammar of the English language*. London: Longman.

Schneider, E.W. (2003). The dynamics of new Englishes. From identity construction to dialect birth. *Language, 79*, 233–281.

Schneider, E.W. (2007). *Postcolonial English. Varieties around the world*. Cambridge: Cambridge University Press.

Silverstein, M. (2003). Indexical order and the dialectics of sociolinguistic life. *Language and Communication, 23*, 193–129.

Swales, J., & Burke, A. (2003). 'It's really fascinating work': Differences in evaluative adjectives across academic registers. In P. Leistyna & C.F. Meyer (Eds.), *Corpus analysis. Language structure and language use* (pp. 1–18). Amsterdam and New York: Rodopi.

Tagliamonte, S. (2008). So different and pretty cool! Recycling intensifiers in Toronto, Canada. *English Language and Linguistics, 12*(2), 361–394.

Tagliamonte, S., & Roberts, C. (2005). So weird; so cool; so innovative: The use of intensifiers in the television series *Friends*. *American Speech, 80*(3), 280–300.

Thompson, G., & Hunston, S. (2000). Evaluation: An introduction. In S. Hunston & G. Thompson (Eds.), *Evaluation in text: Authorial stance and the construction of discourse*. (pp. 1–27). Oxford: Oxford University Press.

Xiao, R., & Tao, H. (2007). A corpus-based sociolinguistic study of amplifiers in British English. *Sociolinguistic Studies, 1*(2), 241–273.

Yaguchi, M., Iyeiri, Y., & Baba, Y. (2010). Speech style and gender distinctions in the use of *very* and *real/really*: An analysis of the Corpus of Spoken Professional American English. *Journal of Pragmatics, 42*, 585–597.

CHAPTER 5

The Pragmatics of *Well* as a Discourse Marker in Broadcast Discussions*

John M. Kirk

1 Introduction—Pragmaticalisation of *Well*

In recent years, the complexities of discourse structure and pragmatic interaction have attracted particular attention. The study of *well* as a pragmatic discourse marker has proceeded apace with the study of discourse markers in general, so that there has emerged some consensus about *well*'s formal features and pragmatic functions.[1]

As Schourup (2001, p. 1037) explains, in a sentence such as *Mary swims well*, what lexical *well* conveys is that Mary measures up favourably against a norm or standard of swimming. To describe something adverbially as *well*, a speaker considers or assesses something in relation to what is already known or believed about that phenomenon. Thus *well* expresses both an objective referential or ideational meaning of judgment as well as an inter-subjective meaning through the shared recognition of the validity of the judgment being made. In contrast, in the following exchange: *Is it raining? Well how do I know? I can't see out*, the use of *well* as a pragmatic marker functions against a set of

* This paper arises from a project on Pragmaversals at the Chair of English Linguistics at Dresden University of Technology (cf. https://tu-dresden.de/gsw/slk/anglistik_amerikanistik/as/forschung/forschungsprojekte/pragmaversals [last accessed 24 April 2017]). For discussion of the examples in this paper, I am particularly grateful to Ashleigh Dawn. I am also most grateful to two reviewers and the volume editors for their many helpful comments and useful suggestions on earlier versions of this paper. I'm also indebted to Kevin McCafferty and Carolina Amador-Moreno for inviting me to present a version of this paper at the *New Perspectives on Irish English 4* conference, Bergen, 5–7 July 2016.

1 Major studies of *well* include (alphabetically arranged) Aijmer (2011, 2013, 2014), Aijmer & Simon-Vanden-Bergen (2003), Blakemore (1987, 1992), Bolinger (1989), Carlson (1984), Cuenca (2008), De Klerk (2005), Finell (1989), Fraser (1987, 1999, 2010), Innes (2010), James (1983), Johansson (2006), Jucker (1993, 1997), Lakoff (1973), Owen (1981), Sakita (2006, 2013), Schiffrin (1985, 1987), Schourup (1985, 2001), Sperber & Wilson (1986, 1995), Svartvik (1980) and Watts (1986, 1989).

 | DOI: 10.1163/9789004361133_007

known or assumed communicative norms which function interpersonally and *a fortiori* inter-subjectively (Sakita, 2006, 2013). Speakers expect questions to be answered, and hearers feel obliged to answer questions. More specifically, speakers of sincerely-uttered direct questions usually expect a *yes* or *no* answer, and hearers also know that sincerely-uttered direct questions expect a *yes* or *no* answer. Whenever those general conditions cannot be fulfilled, *well* tends to be used. In the above example, the speaker cannot answer the question directly because they do not know the answer. In many cases what is being discussed are not truth-conditional propositions but matters of opinion or stance or attitude. By using *well*, the speaker fulfils the expectations of the exchange by providing a response but not the expected response. It is this link between shared assumptions and expectations that has transferred from lexical *well* to pragmatic *well*.

This paper looks at the pragmatic functions of *well* in the orthographic transcriptions of broadcast discussions (BRD) from two national varieties of the *International Corpus of English* (ICE): Ireland and Great Britain. The Irish data are taken from ICE-Ireland's pragmatically- and prosodically-annotated daughter corpus: SPICE-Ireland (Kirk et al., 2011; Kallen & Kirk, 2012). Broadcast discussions are an interesting genre for the investigation of *well* because, as we will see in this paper, many of the discourse-cohering functions of *well*, in particular its Janus-like function of relating preceding to following discourse, become particularly apparent in this register. The broadcast discussion data from the ICE-GB corpus has already been looked at by Aijmer (2013), whose study is based on the lexical theory of meaning potential put forward by Östman (1995), and Norén and Linell (2007). What the current paper offers is the application of a tried-and-tested model to both a new data set as well as to a re-analysis of the data upon which the model was developed. The Irish data set has its own intrinsic interest as phonological, lexical and syntactic items functioning pragmatically as discourse markers are already annotated as such, including *well*. Kallen and Kirk (2012, p. 108) record that in the SPICE-Ireland corpus as a whole there are 1,750 occurrences of *well* annotated as a discourse marker. To that primary-level analysis, this paper provides a fuller, more categorical, more descriptive, secondary-level analysis of one particular item: the discourse marker *well*, with copious exemplification and discussion. This paper will investigate how far, in Irish broadcast discussions, *well* has the coherence, involvement and politeness functions identified by Aijmer and how far the distribution of those functions compares with the British data. Once demonstrated, three hypotheses are then tested: homogeneity of function, compatibility of register (registerness), and regionality. Homogeneity is defined in terms of *well*'s pragmatic functions and frequencies of those functions being 'of a similar kind' and is tested by comparing the three major functions of *well* in each corpus; compatibility of register (registerness) is defined as having shared features of the discourse situation and is assessed by the distribution of functions carried out within that spoken register; regionality is defined as having shared or contrastive features which are attributable to regional or diatopic variation and is tested by comparing the distribution of those functions in each jurisdiction. In so doing, the paper provides a further contribution to the growing interest in the pragmatics of Irish English (cf. Amador-Moreno et al., 2015).

2 Objects of Investigation

2.1 *Pragmatic Features of* Well

As a pragmatic discourse marker, *well* has several features which researchers appear to be in agreement about. Firstly, *well* is mostly utterance-initial in typically two-party exchanges. In turn-initial position, *well* is responding to what went before and introducing what comes after—thereby relating what went before to what comes after. What comes before may largely be of three structural types: direct questions, *wh*-questions, or statements; in speech act terms they are most likely to be directives or representatives. A direct question sets up a proposition, with the expectation of a *yes/no* response. When *well* introduces the response, it signals that the answer is not going to be the expected one but a modified one, possibly even a divergent one. At the same time, *well* expresses the co-operation expected in the exchange and reduces any face-threat by doing so. By contrast, a *wh*-question sets up an expected frame of reference for a response. By beginning with *well*, a speaker expresses recognition of the many possible choices for a response and that what follows is to be regarded as just one of many possibilities. In so doing, by signalling the speaker's co-operation in providing an answer, *well* preserves the speaker's own face as well as that of the hearer. As for statements, in conversations and discussions, it is expected that participants will make statements and other participants will offer responses, sometimes agreeing, sometimes disagreeing, sometimes introducing other topics. For Levinson (1983) *well* is "a response to, or a continuation of, some portion of the prior discourse" (p. 88). For Schiffrin (1987), *well* is simply "a marker of response" as reflected in the title of her chapter dealing with it.

On a more general and abstract level, the bi-directional orientation of turn-initial *well* can be viewed as providing coherence to the unfolding discourse, like a "discourse connective" (Blakemore, 1987, chapter 4). Moreover, *well* indicates that the speaker is thinking about what to say. What is clear is that the speaker is both developing the discussion and maintaining the conversational engagement with the other participants. With regard to discussion development, a turn introduced by *well* may be indicating some kind of change—from simply a nuance or contrast of opinion to something more substantial, such as a change of topic or even direction. With engagement maintenance, *well* is both upholding positive face of the participants as well as mitigating or preventing any negative face threat. Thus *well* acts as a topicaliser or focusing device announcing a new topic or stage of development (what Svartvik (1980, p. 174) calls a "frame marker").

For some researchers, the connective function of *well* is to be explained through relevance theory where *well* signals to the hearer that what is about to be said (whatever it might be) is to be inferred as relevant to what has just been said because it is simply responding to it (cf. Sperber & Wilson, 1986; Jucker, 1993; Schourup, 2001). In other words, the relevance of that response is vouched for through the mere uttering of *well*, which simultaneously confers on that response what has been called "a guarantee of its own optimal relevance" (Jucker, 1993, p. 438). That guarantee of relevance removes any threat to negative face and accounts for the widespread popularity of *well* in spoken exchanges.

Well has been described in yet other ways: *well* has been considered as a staller or delaying device (Svartvik, 1980, p. 171) with the mere uttering of *well* providing a split-second of time for planning the utterance about to be made, rather like a filled pause. Finally, Svartvik (1980, pp. 174–175) discusses its function to mark the start of the citation of reported speech.

2.2 *Aijmer's Model*

As a basis for explaining the functions of *well*, while building on past consensus, Aijmer (2013) adopts the very general model of meanings or semantic parameters identified by Östman (1995). For Östman, to paraphrase Aijmer, pragmatic markers have three functions: 1) they construct both social and discourse coherence; the former because they relate to social conventions and norms and the latter because they provide "the 'grease' between parts of discourse"; 2) they express the speaker's active involvement in the interaction, especially emotions and attitudes; and 3) they enact politeness both with the establishment of interpersonal relations and the negotiation of face and occasionally by breaking them, i.e. with impoliteness (Aijmer, 2013, p. 31). Those three functions: coherence, involvement and politeness form the centre of Aijmer's analysis and the present one.

What underlies those general functions is not any fixed or core meaning which *well* has but its potential to mean different things in different situations or contexts, what has been called *well*'s "meaning potential" (Östman, 1995, p. 104; and also: Norén & Linell 2007, p. 390). Citing Norén and Linell (2007, p. 390), Aijmer writes: "A theory of meaning potentials assumes that parts of a word's meaning are evoked, activated or materialised, foregrounded or backgrounded, *in different ways in the different contexts,* in which it is exploited" (2013, p. 12, italics in the original source). The categories of coherence, involvement and politeness are thus "a fairly abstract representation of the speaker's knowledge about the meanings of a particular pragmatic marker" (ibid., p. 149).

Building on those foundations, Aijmer (2013) recognises that almost all research on *well* has been conducted on the basis of face-to-face, private, conversational data. Although she investigates *well* in conversational and telephone-conversational data, too, her primary aim is to study *well* in public speech and to draw comparisons between situations of use. To that end, she investigates broadcast discussions, courtroom cross-examinations and spontaneous commentaries. She finds that *well* is a crucial marker in those situations but that, in line with the theory of meaning potentials outlined briefly above, different situations confer on *well* their own special functions: what Gumperz (1982, p. 131) earlier calls "contextualization cues" or what Linell (2009) calls "opportunities for use" (p. 347, cited by Aijmer, 2013, p. 71). For instance, Aijmer cites doctor-patient exchanges where "[*w*]*ell* has to be interpreted against the background of the shared knowledge of societal and communal norms and conventions" (ibid., p. 35). The contention is that "[t]he functions of *well* in broadcast discussion can be explained by the social activity and the speaker roles" (ibid., p. 57)—moderator and participant roles alike.

To recap briefly, the basic premise is that pragmatic discourse markers such as *well* lend themselves to reinterpretation depending on the situational context. The pragmatic functions of *well* identified by Aijmer are based on *well*'s meaning potential, depending on the situation, to express coherence, involvement and politeness.

2.3 *Broadcast Discussions*

Broadcast discussions (BRD) are situations where the topic is invariably predetermined, and each speaker has been chosen to appear on the programme for their reputation as a desirable or crucial participant in an issue (e.g. a politician or trades unionist) or influential commentator on the subject (such as a journalist or clergyman) or as a subject specialist or expert, or simply an opinion-former or pundit. Most participants are well-known in the public sphere. Although the speakers usually know what they are likely to be saying on the programme in advance, and are thus prepared, the entire discussion is always spontaneous. With clear speaker roles, there is a distinct purpose to the discourse. There is considerable interaction, with speaker after speaker responding to the moderator and, to a lesser extent, each other. The moderator leads the discussion by introducing and allocating speaker turns and regularly introduces new topics or aspects of the present topic for discussion. Among the participants, there is shared knowledge of how the discourse situation works, with a shared metalinguistic knowledge, in which discourse markers play their part, when suddenly asked to speak. As we will see below, the many moderation and participant-response roles are reflected in the uses of *well*.

As a register of spoken language, BRDs have only relatively recently attracted investigatory attention and it is barely mentioned (certainly not as a genre) in the introductory, descriptive textbook *The Language of Television* (Marshall & Werndly, 2002). Within a critical discourse framework, spearheaded by Fairclough's study *Media Discourse* (1995), the focus has been more on news reporting than on news discussion, on institutional power and authority and on the creation and possibly manipulation of listening audiences. Earlier studies originated alongside a growing sociological and cultural-studies interest in television (cf. the papers in Scannell, 1991). Whereas radio had traditionally represented an institutional voice speaking to an unseen national listenership, television enabled viewers to listen to or eavesdrop on people talking to other people. Once the format of a discussion programme, with a presenter/moderator co-ordinating it and directing its progression, had been established, it was an easy step to adapt the format for radio.

2.4 *Discourse Markers in Broadcast Discussions*

Although 'broadcast discussions' is a text category in the original *Survey of English Usage Corpus*, later computerised as the *London-Lund Corpus of Spoken English* (cf. Svartvik, 1990), in the *Lancaster/IBM Spoken English Corpus* (cf. Knowles et al., 1996), and in the International Corpus of English, and has inevitably contributed to overall frequencies and distributional statistics of each corpus, there appear to be few specific investigations of the register itself. I am aware of only three such studies, two of which also deal with the register-specific use of discourse markers.

Perhaps the fullest corpus-based account of the range of broadcast discourse involving dialogue is O'Keeffe's monograph *Investigating Media Discourse* (2006), the primary material for which comes from the Irish radio phone-in talk show *Liveline* but which uses material from several British talk shows as well. Specifically using broadcast discussions from ICE corpora is the project investigating register variation being undertaken by Neumann (2012,

2014; cf. also Neumann & Fest, 2016).[2] Thirdly, the project by Aijmer (2013), already mentioned, who investigates broadcast discussions in the ICE-GB corpus as one of three spoken public registers which are contrasted with face-to-face conversation. Let us consider O'Keeffe in a little more depth.

O'Keeffe (2006) recognises that, for a theoretically-based descriptive account of broadcast discussions, there are "three facets" which need to be taken into consideration (p. 156). Firstly, the model needs to be more than that of traditional dyadic interactions. In its place, O'Keeffe

> propose[s] a participation framework model [cf. Goffman, 1981, p. 137 ff.] within which we can say that all media interactions take place between a presenter/host, one or more interviewee/guest and an audience. [...] There will be a non-present audience who listen to or view the interaction and this cohort is fully ratified within the participation framework.
>
> O'KEEFFE, 2006, p. 157

This triadic communicative constellation is very relevant for the usage of *well* in the data analysed in the present study. From the present data under investigation in this paper, for instance, (1a) shows that it is the listening audience that is being addressed by the moderator.

(1) a. ⟨I⟩[3] ⟨$A⟩ ⟨#⟩ **⟨rep⟩ Well** there are few subjects more emotive than fair employment and our panel tonight are passionate in their beliefs ⟨,⟩ both for and against **⟨/rep⟩** (ICE-NI-P1B-024)[4]

Moreover, *well* may introduce to the audience the broadcast's participants:

2 However, as Neumann (2012, 2014) and Neumann and Fest (2016) do not deal with discourse markers, their studies will not be treated further here.

3 In ICE markup, an ⟨I⟩ indicates the start of a new text, which in the context of BRDs is often the start of the broadcast.

4 In the SPICE-Ireland annotation scheme, speech act annotation comprises pairs of opening and closing cocoa brackets (e.g. ⟨rep⟩ for "Representatives", ⟨dir⟩ for "Directives", etc.). Discourse markers are annotated with an asterisk as in *well** (cf. Kallen & Kirk, 2012) (but here deleted at the request of the editors). ⟨#⟩ denotes a new sentence or utterance fragment. The examples in this paper will use bold to highlight the following: **well**, any relevant speech act annotations (e.g. **⟨rep⟩** ... **⟨/rep⟩**), and any other relevant text or markup which may help with a clearer understanding of the example.

b. ⟨I⟩ ⟨$A⟩ ⟨#⟩ **⟨rep⟩ Well** joining us in the Counterpoint studio here in Belfast is the Ulster Unionist MP for Strangford John Taylor ⟨,⟩ and from Belfast the Progressive Unionist David Ervine **⟨/rep⟩** (ICE-NI-P1B-030)

Each of those broadcast-initial occurrences would seem to connect with the expectations of the programme listeners, appealing for their assent in the choice of topic for discussion or speakers chosen, each being heard with a recognition of relevance, each an instance of a positive politeness strategy.

Secondly, O'Keeffe (2006) shows that through the use of discourse markers a "pseudo-intimacy" (ch. 5) is created between speakers and addressees in the programme,—"'pseudo'-intimate because the participants do not normally know each [other] and if they do, it is only at the level of public persona" (p. 90). Thirdly, O'Keeffe shows "how identities are encoded in the language of media interactions" (p. 156), e.g. via linguistic indices of shared knowledge such as vague markers or via pronouns as indices of audience identity (ch. 6).

We will see below how *well* is integral to the organisation of turns in broadcast discussions, and how *well* encodes people's feelings. After discussing various examples, O'Keeffe remarks that "[d]iscourse markers can indicate power-relations [...] in that the power-role holder in a media interaction usually manages the discourse and so will use markers such as *right let's turn to ...*, *okay*, and so on. They can be used as a means of both structuring and controlling the discourse" (2006, p. 122). We will again see below how that function is executed by *well*. O'Keeffe also discusses *right* as "a very common discourse marker in media discourse, which is normally used by the presenter to confirm information, create topic boundaries" (p. 122) and to make closures. O'Keeffe continues: "discourse markers can be found in situations of conflict" (p. 123), and yet again we will see *well* being used in such situations too. O'Keeffe's claim about pseudo-intimacy among strangers is based on the premise that the intimacy comes from the use of discourse markers which reflects their use in everyday conversation just as friends would do in a cosy chat and their help in "creat[ing] and sustain[ing] this illusion of an interpersonal relationship" (p. 125). O'Keeffe finds that discourse markers "are an indicator of interactivity" (p. 125).

From existing corpus-linguistic studies of broadcast discussions, several points emerge. Firstly, in the present paper, with its narrow focus on *well*, when *well* initiates a response to a previous utterance, in almost every case *well* could be analysed in terms of a dyadic model of conversational structure. However, *well* is also used by the moderator to address the listening audience, for instance, in beginning and ending programmes. It is to account for those differing audiences, which transcend the traditional model, that O'Keefe (2006) adopts Goffman's (1981) participation framework model. Note, however, that a full appreciation of that model to the present data is beyond the scope of the present paper.

A second important feature of discourse markers in BRDs is, as pointed out by O'Keeffe (2006), their interactivity. From the many examples cited in section 4, the interactivity between moderator and contributor, indeed the liveliness between speakers, will be affirmed over and over again. O'Keeffe contends that there is an "illusion" (2006, p. 125) of intimacy among participants in broadcast discussions, although the interactions in my data do strike me as very real and genuine, possibly because there is almost certainly in most cases some familiarity among participants not only because of public reputations but because the same people may have discussed the topic or similar topics on previous occasions.

A third important feature, again pointed out by O'Keeffe (2006), is their use in situations of conflict, including disagreements, to be illustrated below in § 4.2.5.

This section has set the scene for the analysis to follow. Firstly, it has provided an account of the research literature on *well*; in particular it has contextualised the scholarly background to Aijmer's (2013) model to be used here. Secondly, it has given an account of the triangulated discourse situation to be found in broadcast discussion texts.

3 Data and Methodology

The data for this analysis come from the *SPICE-Ireland Corpus* ('Systems of Pragmatic Annotation for the Spoken Component of ICE-Ireland') (Kirk et al., 2011; Kallen & Kirk, 2012), a daughter corpus of the Irish component of the International Corpus of English, and from ICE-GB (cf. ICE-GB, 1998; Nelson et al., 2002). Crucially, in the former, the material is divided equally between Northern Ireland and the Republic of Ireland. The spoken component of an ICE-corpus comprises 15 discourse situations, one of them Broadcast Discussions. Participation in such a situation presupposes a certain level of completed education beyond high school level, and in fact a great many speakers in ICE-Ireland and ICE-GB are university or college graduates. As for all text categories, speakers were not chosen for the way they spoke, but it may be inferred that the nature of the discourse exchange in each situation meant that speakers were approximating to some form of standardised English. In each corpus, the recordings come from the early 1990s: 1990–1991 (Nelson et al., 2002, pp. 312–313) in ICE-GB, and 1990–1994 in SPICE-IRL (Kallen & Kirk, 2012, pp. 84–85).

Most of the Northern Ireland texts deal with the 'Troubles', or civil war, which was raging at that time between the British Army and the terrorist organisation, the Irish Republican Army (IRA), and with attempts by politicians to reach solutions for ending the conflict and the future of the province. In this paper, all examples cited are from BRD texts and will be annotated as ICE-NI (for the Northern Irish component) or ICE-ROI (for the component of SPICE representing the Republic of Ireland), or ICE-GB.

In order to facilitate the study of pragmatic functions, an annotation scheme was developed. Four categories relevant for pragmatic analysis are distinguished: speech acts (after the defining notions by Searle, 1969; 1976), utterance tags (which include declarative as well as interrogative polarity-marking sentence tags, but also vocatives and discourse markers used sentence or utterance-finally), quotatives (citations of speech attributed to another speaker and supposedly rendered verbatim or directly) and, of course, discourse markers (as being discussed here with regard to *well*). As a fifth category, tone movements are also annotated. Pragmatic and prosodic annotation go a long way towards resolving the inadequacies of orthographic lexico-syntactic transcriptions. With prosodic and pragmatic annotation, it is possible objectively to capture in the transcription the illocutionary intentions of an utterance for an altogether deeper understanding of how communicative exchanges work. Key features are the many discourse markers associated with illocutionary force and a speaker's stance towards their utterance and their audience. Such information is expressed by pitch movement, discourse markers, and utterance tags, as well as by lexical and syntactic choices. By encapsulating such information, the annotation scheme complements and upgrades the transcription as a richer representation of the original spoken utterance (cf. Kirk, 2016).

The SPICE-Ireland annotation scheme was inserted manually by the present author and his team, primarily identifying those phonological, lexical and syntactic items which also had discourse marker functions. For the present, secondary analysis, the annotated instances of *well* were analysed by the author, again manually, while heeding the formal characteristics, primarily with regard to *well*'s three functional categories of coherence, involvement and politeness set out by Aijmer (2013).

Factors in the formal analysis were position (mostly utterance-initial), and prosody (tone movement—whether falling, rising, rise-falling, fall-rising, level, etc.—and accompaniment by filled or unfilled pauses). Other factors included collocations (especially with other discourse markers such as *oh, right, you know* and such like) and the syntax which accompanies *well*. In her analysis, Aijmer (2013) adds pronunciation, whether clipped or reduced as if uttered without a vowel, or full, possibly even elongated, articulation. In the analysis of the present data, pronunciation was noted in an impressionistic way, by the present author, based on collocational evidence, so that pauses—or pauses and discourse markers—surrounding *well* were interpreted as suggesting a full, even elongated, pronunciation, whereas *well* without the accompaniment of such markers was interpreted as suggesting a rapid pronunciation, as if it were merely a consonantal articulation.

4 Functional Analysis of *Well* in BRDs

This section will present the analysis of coherence, involvement and politeness functions in the BRDs of the SPICE-Ireland Corpus.

4.1 Well *and Coherence*

As indicated above, following Aijmer (2013) and behind her Östmann (1995) and Norén and Linell (2007), coherence is one of the main functions of *well*'s meaning potential. Coherence in spoken exchanges is created when a following utterance connects with a preceding one in a way which has been thought about and interpreted by the hearer as being considered by the speaker as relevant.

4.1.1 *Well* as a Turn-Initial Discourse Connective

As we have already seen, *well* may be the very first word of a broadcast, uttered by the moderator, introducing the general topic, as in (1a) and (1b) above. Moreover, *well* is used by the moderator to name a first or new speaker, to introduce the subject of the programme, or to state a new or change of topic, to invite a speaker to contribute or to state the name of a speaker who has just finished speaking, to end the discussion of a topic, and so on. A further use of discourse-connective *well* by the moderator is when he[5] wishes to move the discussion on, as in the following regulatory-declarative speech act:

(2) a. ⟨$A⟩ ⟨#⟩ ⟨**dec**⟩ **Okay well** ⟨,⟩ we'll have to leave it there ⟨.⟩ ⟨/**dec**⟩ ⟨#⟩ (ICE-NI-P1B-021)

Just as common is the use of *well* by a new speaker to start their turn, in response to a call to speak by the moderator, of which (2b) is typical. In this

5 In the SPICE-Ireland broadcasts, all moderators are male.

example, the speaker announces the type of speech act that he is about to perform before proceeding to do so.

b. ⟨$A⟩ ⟨#⟩ **⟨dir⟩ Gentleman beside you just two along ⟨/dir⟩** ⟨#⟩ **⟨dir⟩** Yes sir **⟨/dir⟩**
⟨$C⟩ ⟨#⟩ ⟨rep⟩ **Well** ⟨,⟩ I come from outside Lisburn ⟨/rep⟩ ⟨#⟩ ⟨dir⟩ **The question I would like to ask if given the opportunity** ⟨.⟩ wou ⟨/.⟩ is ⟨,⟩ can our politicians handle the peace ⟨,⟩ [...] ⟨/dir⟩ (ICE-NI-P1B-022)

A further discourse-connective use of *well* is after *wh*-questions, first noticed by Hale (1999, p. 59) and cited by Aijmer (2013, p. 60). *Well* enables speakers to gather their thoughts after a *wh*-question, the neutrality of which does not commit the speaker to a specific direction in their response. Thus a *why* question receives a *well because* response.

(3) a. ⟨$A⟩ ⟨#⟩ **⟨dir⟩** Uh **why** do you have a problem with health fascists **⟨/dir⟩**
⟨$C⟩ ⟨#⟩ ⟨rep⟩ **Well because** health fascists are engaged in a crusade of persecution against those who exercise their absolutely legal right to smoke ⟨/rep⟩ (ICE-NI-P1B-025)

In fact, after *wh*-questions a response-initiating *well* occurs frequently, no doubt because any answer to a *wh*-question has to be thought through on the spot and could well involve hesitation (*I think uh one one's one's view*) as in (3b), or could be potentially lengthy:

b. ⟨$B⟩ ⟨#⟩ **⟨dir⟩** Cashel **what're your own memories ⟨/dir⟩**
⟨$F⟩ ⟨#⟩ ⟨rep⟩ **Well I think uh one one's one's** view of Christmas ⟨&⟩ clears throat ⟨/&⟩ one has a changing perspective as you grow as you grow older ⟨/rep⟩ (ICE-ROI-P1B-035)

In a BRD, moderator and participants appear to know their roles and the rules of engagement. Turn-initial *well* aids the discussion by connecting the present utterance back to the previous, marking that the speaker is responding to what the previous speaker had just said. *A fortiori*, it could be claimed that, regardless of its other functions, *well* is always functioning as a connective.

4.1.2 *Well* as a Marker of Reported Speech

As noted above, a further coherence function of *well* is to mark the start of reported speech, even imagined reported speech. By marking the transition to a quotation, Aijmer (2013) claims that *well* "makes the description more vivid and emotional" (p. 36) and continues that *well* adds to "the vividness of the description by presenting what took place as happening before our eyes" (p. 36). In this function, *well* may collocate with other discourse markers or be accompanied by pauses, filled and unfilled. In (4) *well* introduces a direct quotation:

(4) ⟨$A⟩ ⟨rep⟩ And one listener **said**+ ⟨,⟩ to another lady who was on ⟨,⟩ **⟨quote⟩ well** do you agree with that **⟨/quote⟩** ⟨/rep⟩ ⟨#⟩ ⟨rep⟩ And she more or less said yes ⟨/rep⟩ (ICE-NI-P1B-028)[6]

4.1.3 *Well* as a Marker of Word Search and Self Repair

In this coherence function, when speakers search for the right word or interrupt their flow in order to start again, *well* is associated with hedging, as if filling a pause. In (5a) *well* is accompanied by several filled pauses until the speaker[7] finds the right words:

(5) a. ⟨$A⟩ **⟨dir⟩** Uhm what's your view to the to the **uh uh uh well uh** expression of of outrage that animals ought to be killed **⟨/dir⟩** (ICE-NI-P1B-025)

Other pragmatic uses of turn-medial *well* include self-interruptions, including self-repair, genuine stalling, particular speech acts (such as apologising), or for making certain references more explicit or precise (as for time references or numbers).

4.1.4 Coherence Functions of *Well* in SPICE-Ireland and ICE-GB

Table 5.1 compares the occurrences of *well* as a coherence marker for BRDs in SPICE-Ireland with those in ICE-GB and their percentage distribution.

Although there are considerably more occurrences in the British data, the percentage distributions among coherence functions displayed in Table 5.1 show that *well* is used in each corpus in a broadly similar way. For instance, 28 % of occurrences of *well* in Ireland and 27.9 % of occurrences in GB are used by speakers at the start their responses when called upon to speak. For the start of responses to *wh*-questions, no doubt for the reasons outlined above, the distributional figures for *well* are 24.0 % for Ireland and 18.6 % for GB.

---

6 (4) shows the SPICE-Ireland annotations for reported speech: a + symbol for the reporting word, and the pair of brackets **⟨quote⟩** ... **⟨/quote⟩** for the reported speech.

7 When specific speakers are discussed, the gender has been checked.

TABLE 5.1 *Occurrences of coherence uses of* well

Coherence functions	IRL		GB	
	N	%	N	%
Moderation	15	30.0	12	14.0
Named speaker starts	14	28.0	24	27.9
New speaker starts	1	2.0	8	9.3
Speaker changes topic	–	–	8	9.3
After a *wh*-question	12	24.0	16	18.6
Introduces direct speech	3	6.0	4	4.6
Word search (medial)	1	10.0	–	–
Self repair (medial)	4	8.0	9	10.5
Speaker changes topic (medial)	–	–	2	2.3
Unanalysable	–	–	3	3.5
Total	50	100.0	86	100.0

In each corpus, as outlined in § 4.1.1, moderators use *well* for a range of functions, which provide the central coherence of the programme. Those acts of moderation notwithstanding, participants use *well* far more than moderators. However, speakers in the British group are much more likely to respond to each other directly or to change the topic when they start to speak. And British speakers seem to interrupt themselves more than the Irish, either by changing the topic as they speak or to repair their speech in some way, as in:

b. ⟨$B⟩ ⟨#⟩ Thi This is a world-class piece isn't it ⟨#⟩ This is one of the things that that worries me of course and ⟨#⟩ and fortunately now that we **well** we both tour around abroad it's possible to gauge the impact of British music on foreign audiences and foreign orchestras (ICE-GB-S1B-032)

As Aijmer (2013) comments, picking up on Östman's (1995) image, *well* functions as if it were "'the grease' between the propositional parts of discourse making it work as discourse" and thus "creat[ing] coherence 'locally' within the speaker's turn." (p. 32)

4.2 Well *and Involvement*

Aijmer's (2013) second functional category for the study of the pragmatic uses of *well* in terms of its meaning potential is involvement. She bases her analysis on Östman who says that "[i]nvolvement is 'concerned with how to express or not to express feelings, attitudes and prejudices' (Östman 1995: 104)" (Aijmer, 2013, p. 37).

4.2.1 *Well* and Agreement

Involvement occurrences for BRDs include direct agreement, implied, partial (or qualified) agreement, disagreement, neither agreement or disagreement, and challenges. Following Haviland, Aijmer acknowledges that agreement is "a complex category" (2013, p. 38), and that "it is possible to express a reservation by agreeing with only part of, or something conditional on an utterance [...] an oppositional move in the garb of the agreement" (Haviland, 1989, p. 45, quoted in Aijmer, 2013, p. 38).

4.2.2 Direct Agreements

Well can preface responses which are in direct agreement with the proposition posed by the moderator or another participant. In (6a) the moderator (speaker A) seeks agreement through the tag question and receives it from Speaker G through a face-keeping *you know* and an explicit restatement of the proposition prefaced by *well*:

(6) a. ⟨$A⟩ ⟨#⟩ **⟨rep⟩** ⟨[⟩ **That was your experience ⟨/rep⟩ ⟨dir⟩ wasn't-it ⟨/dir⟩**
⟨$G⟩ ⟨#⟩ **⟨rep⟩ Well you know it was my experience** that if difficulties arose and I I was uh there I I Cabinet confidentiality I-suppose would would make ⟨unclear⟩ 4 sylls ⟨/unclear⟩ **⟨/rep⟩** (ICE-ROI-P1B-034)

In (6b) the speaker implicitly agrees with a *yes/no* question posed by the moderator through restatement of the proposition, prefaced not only by *well* but extended through a personal qualifier and a long speech act of mitigation the modality of which impels the speaker to agree:

b. ⟨$A⟩ ⟨#⟩ **⟨dir⟩** But does your religious uh identity impact on your politics **⟨/dir⟩**
⟨$E⟩ ⟨#⟩ **⟨rep⟩ Well** I would have to say that personally as a Christian ⟨.⟩ m ⟨/.⟩ my faith does influence my politics **⟨/rep⟩** (ICE-NI-P1B-028)

Direct agreements thus tend rarely to come with an explicit *yes* or *no* response; rather they come with a restatement of the proposition in terms of which the speaker expresses agreement either explicitly (*that's right*), or through restatement or paraphrase, or showing an understanding of the issue. By beginning with *well*, the speaker maintains coherence and face by signalling that the answer is going to be relevant.

4.2.3 Partial Agreements

Partial agreements (cf. Lakoff, 1973, p. 459 and Svartvik, 1980, p. 174) involve agreement with only part of a proposition, with some reservation about another part, often a quantification, or with some condition attached. Some partial agreements are structured around a *well … but …* collocation, with the *well* clause expressing agreement or at least acknowledgment, and the *but* clause expressing the reservation or condition. (7a) is a typical example of partial agreement involving quantities:

(7) a. ⟨$A⟩ ⟨#⟩ **⟨dir⟩** ⟨[⟩ Our panel ⟨,⟩ our panel ⟨.⟩ repre ⟨/.⟩ ⟨/[⟩ ⟨/{⟩ is not pro-war if that's your point **⟨/dir⟩**
⟨$G⟩ ⟨#⟩ **⟨rep⟩ Well** two of your speakers are pro-war **⟨/rep⟩** (ICE-ROI-P1B-038)

There are several other instances of partial agreement where *well* enables the respondent to revise one of the inherent factors and at the same time helps the speaker to maintain face. In (7b) a negative statement is partially agreed with by a contradictory fact, prefaced by *well*, and mitigated by final concessive *but*.

b. ⟨$C⟩ ⟨#⟩ ⟨rep⟩ But there are **no** Greeks **no** French **no** Germans in the IRA ⟨/rep⟩ ⟨#⟩ ⟨rep⟩ They're all Irish ⟨,⟩ and therefore they are a risk ⟨/rep⟩
⟨$A⟩ ⟨#⟩ ⟨rep⟩ **Well** there are Greeks and Germans in other terrorist organisations **but** ⟨/rep⟩ ⟨#⟩ (ICE-NI-P1B-030)

Some agreements are only partial because they depend on the fulfilment of a condition. In (7c), an exchange about the Northern Ireland Troubles hangs on the word *only*. Although each speaker agrees about the desirability of peace, they disagree about the ordering of priorities. For the moderator (speaker A), the only (and first) goal is peace, after which a political settlement can be discussed, whereas for speaker B the first goal is a political settlement only after which, if achieved, peace would follow. Aware of his contrastive view, speaker B tones down his contrastive view with the two occurrences of an epistemically-modalised pragmatic marker *I think*.

c. ⟨$A⟩ **⟨dir⟩** I mean you've got to separate **peace** from a united Ireland as **the only outcome of peace** and then take a look at who wants a united Ireland **⟨/dir⟩**
⟨$B⟩ ⟨#⟩ **⟨rep⟩ Well I think** that peace is **only likely to come** I I'm not saying that peace can only come with a united Ireland **but I think** that peace is **only likely to come when you have a settlement** which addresses the concerns of the the Nationalist uh minority in the North **⟨/rep⟩** (ICE-NI-P1B-021)

The collocation *well … but* is frequent and divides responses into two parts. Responses to questions often involve only partial agreement or both agreement and disagreement, where there is something else to be said which the speaker believes is relevant. *Well* enables the speaker to balance those mixed responses, letting the speaker uphold positive face by providing the desired response but it also protects the hearer's negative face by adding a new point.

4.2.4 Implied Agreements

Well can preface responses where agreement with the proposition posed by the moderator is implicit in what the respondent says. In (8a), the restatement of the question from the speaker's perspective shows the agreement inferred comes from the relevance of the response.

(8) a. ⟨$A⟩ **⟨dir⟩** Clifford Smyth ⟨,⟩ do you think as a committed Orangeman that it is possible to talk about this subject without being influenced by our bias **⟨/dir⟩**
⟨$B⟩ ⟨#⟩ ⟨rep⟩ **Well** each of us comes to a particular ⟨,⟩ situation or circumstance or indeed institution like the Orange Order ⟨,⟩ uh with certain preconceptions or presuppositions ⟨,⟩ and so uh I've yet to meet the person who can say I am not biased ⟨/rep⟩ (ICE-NI-P1B-023)

In (8b) there is implied agreement both about not knowing the actions of the incoming rainbow coalition government as well as about what might happen to the politician, Padraig Flynn:

b. ⟨$A⟩ ⟨#⟩ Avril Doyle the question we're on is Padraig Flynn ⟨/rep⟩ ⟨#⟩ **⟨dir⟩** Should he be retained or replaced **if that were possible by any incoming Rainbow** ⟨,⟩ **⟨/dir⟩**
⟨$J⟩ ⟨#⟩ ⟨rep⟩ **Well I'm not sure what the incoming Rainbow actually will do** with Padraig Flynn ⟨,⟩ ⟨/rep⟩ ⟨rep⟩ **but** uh if he was removed it's no reflection on Padraig's ability nor indeed his record ⟨/rep⟩ ⟨#⟩ (ICE-ROI-P1B-033)

In (8c) speaker B remarks that the Orange Order is a sexist organisation although he has reservations about calling it that (*not entirely*). By sharing those reservations, speaker D feels he cannot but agree with speaker B's claim (*well it may as well be*).

c. ⟨$B⟩ ⟨#⟩ ⟨rep⟩ It's it's not entirely a male sexist organisation though I understand ⟨{⟩ ⟨[⟩ there are women in it ⟨/[⟩ ⟨/rep⟩
⟨$D⟩ ⟨#⟩ ⟨rep⟩ ⟨[⟩ **Well** it may as ⟨/[⟩ ⟨/{⟩ well be because I mean ⟨&⟩ laughs ⟨/&⟩ the women are more like bunny girls ⟨/rep⟩ (ICE-NI-P1B-023)[8]

4.2.5 *Well* and Disagreement

For Aijmer (2013), *well* occurs both "when 'everything is as it should be' and when something has not taken place according to expectations" (p. 40). *Well* introduces disagreements as readily as agreement of any kind. *Well* seems able both to acknowledge what was said as if maintaining face, and to enable a disagreement despite the potential face threat. By accompanying disagreements, many of them overt, *well* enables the speaker to invoke whatever occurs to them as relevant to the situation and to maintain solidarity and politeness with their addresses, and to avoid threatening their negative face if they are uttering an answer that was contrary to what might have been expected. Disagreement *well* occurs as feedback to questions and marks answers as inappropriate, insufficient, or not giving the information sought.

In (9a), the moderator presents a case about the Irish political party, the SDLP, which speaker C does not accept. Although *well* helps to mitigate his disagreement, it is still asserted strongly, with authority, as modalised through *certainly*, itself stressed with a falling tone.

(9) a. ⟨$A⟩ ⟨#⟩ **⟨dir⟩** And whether you like it or not I think you've got to admit that the what the SDLP have done through John Hume in their talks with Sinn Fein is to try and get the gun out of that side of the equation which would lead to the gun being taken out of politics ⟨,⟩ full stop **⟨/dir⟩**
⟨C⟩ ⟨#⟩ ⟨rep⟩ **Well** the SDLP have been at it for twenty-five years ⟨/rep⟩ ⟨#⟩ ⟨rep⟩ They **certainly** haven't stopped the IRA killing ⟨/rep⟩ (ICE-NI-P1B-030)

8 Overlapping speech is marked up in an ICE-corpus using two sets of pairs of opening and closing brackets: ⟨[⟩ … ⟨/[⟩ for each speaker's words which overlap; and ⟨{⟩ … ⟨/{⟩ for the entire overlapping exchange.

In (9b) Speaker G believes that the days were numbered for Irish politician, Padraig Flynn. When the moderator (speaker A) suggests that the matter was still wide open, speaker G disagrees, prefacing his disagreement with *well*, and restates his earlier position.

b. ⟨$G⟩ ⟨rep⟩ So I think there's there's already strains there ⟨/rep⟩ ⟨#⟩ ⟨rep⟩ I mean if you look at at uh Michael Noonan on on on Saturday uh View ⟨,⟩ Rodney Rice's programme ⟨,⟩ he seemed to indicate to the to the populace that **Padraig Flynn was on the way out** and yet ⟨{⟩ ⟨[⟩ John Bruton ⟨/[⟩ ⟨/rep⟩
⟨$A⟩ ⟨#⟩ **⟨rep⟩** ⟨[⟩ No he was ⟨/[⟩ ⟨/{⟩ leaving a blank cheque actually ⟨{⟩ ⟨[⟩ for for his leader I thought ⟨/[⟩ **⟨/rep⟩**
⟨$G⟩ ⟨#⟩ **⟨rep⟩** ⟨[⟩ **Well** I think he was going ⟨/[⟩ ⟨/{⟩ very near to saying in effect that uh **Padraig was on the way out** or on the way back ⟨,⟩ and uh that uh ⟨,⟩ that uhm we were going to get a situation perhaps where one of the Fine Gael people were put in **⟨/rep⟩** (ICE-ROI-P1B-034)

4.2.6 Neither Agreement nor Disagreement

Sometimes agreement is not the issue but the need for clarification. In (10) the speaker shows implicit agreement to an embedded proposition by tentatively (his use of modalised *I think*) confirming the survey referred to by the moderator on the basis of reports he has known. However, the speaker doesn't actually address the moderator's question, so that no explicature can be drawn, leaving it open whether people would or would not be surprised about the size of the figure.

(10) ⟨$A⟩ **⟨dir⟩** Now Michael Farrell ⟨,⟩ do you think people would be surprised in the Republic uh by that opinion poll survey that says like only fifty-two percent of Catholics really want a united Ireland **⟨/dir⟩**
⟨$B⟩ ⟨#⟩ **⟨rep⟩ Well I think** there have been a few reports like that recently **⟨/rep⟩** (ICE-NI-P1B-021)

4.2.7 Challenges

Propositions can be challenged, and moderators sometimes do, prefacing but thereby downtoning their challenge with an initial *well.* To a general point about the welfare of animals made by the discussant, the moderator seeks clarification about particular types of behaviour towards animals. The *well* acknowledges the general point in question and enables the posing of questions about or querying the implications of it without seeming to be a face threat.

(11) a. ⟨$O⟩ ⟨#⟩ ⟨#⟩ **⟨rep⟩** However ⟨,⟩ we as farmers and human beings have responsibilities to raise animals in the most humane way possible **⟨/rep⟩**
⟨$A⟩ ⟨#⟩ **⟨dir⟩ Well** why is there a distinction drawn for instance between battering a seal or a a cuddly animal and standing on a beetle **⟨/dir⟩** (ICE-NI-P1B-025)

In (11b) the discussion focuses on the significance of bombing Baghdad. Speaker A poses the challenge that levelling Baghdad is hardly a victory. But for Speaker F that is the reality of war. Each contribution is prefaced by *well*.

b. ⟨$F⟩ ⟨#⟩ ⟨rep⟩ So they can actually go in and level the city ⟨,⟩ but ⟨/rep⟩
⟨$A⟩ ⟨#⟩ ⟨dir⟩ **Well** that's hardly victory ⟨,⟩ that's hardly liberating ⟨,⟩ Baghdad ⟨/dir⟩
⟨$F⟩ ⟨#⟩ ⟨rep⟩ **Well** that's war and it's happened before and there are precedents for this ⟨/rep⟩ (ICE-ROI-P1B-038)

4.2.8 Involvement Functions of *Well* in SPICE-Ireland and ICE-GB

Table 5.2 compares the occurrences of *well* as an involvement marker for BRDs in SPICE-Ireland with those in ICE-GB and adds their percentage distributions.

Table 5.2 shows that, although there are different numbers of occurrences, it is the percentage distributions which better highlight their different functions. While disagreements are in the minority (although there are more of them in ICE-GB), it is among the various subcategories of agreement where the biggest differences lie. In ICE-GB, 18 out of 22 agreements take the form of direct agreements, for which numerous collocations occur, as in (12a–c):

(12) a. ⟨$A⟩ ⟨#⟩ **Well** Stefan **is quite right** (ICE-GB-S1B-025)
b. ⟨$E⟩ ⟨#⟩ **Well I I agree** precisely with what Paddy Ashdown said just now (ICE-GB-S1B-027)
c. ⟨$A⟩ ⟨#⟩ Is it the pressure group like the Open Spaces Society **or** is it the farmer
⟨$B⟩ ⟨#⟩ **Well** I think it's **unquestionably** the farmer (ICE-GB-S1B-037)

By contrast, among Irish speakers, 10 out of 34 agreements are direct, the rest being implied or partial. In Table 5.2, in the British data, the responses from one participant to another, which are all the more common, are expressive of direct agreement, whereas in the Irish data participants seem rarely to comment on each other and only contribute when invited to do so by the moderator; when this happens, it is to the moderator's formulation of an issue that partic-

TABLE 5.2 *Occurrences of involvement uses of* well

Involvement	IRL		GB	
	N	%	N	%
Direct agreement	10	23.2	18	58.1
Implied agreement	9	20.9	3	9.7
Partial agreement	15	34.9	1	3.2
Disagreement	2	4.7	9	29.0
Challenges	6	14.0	–	
Confirmation	1	2.3	–	
Total	43	100.0	31	100.0

ipants are responding. Moderators, after all, are knowledgeable journalists and skilled presenters, capable of addressing issues from a range of perspectives or positions, so it strikes me that, in the Irish data, moderators present far more contentious statements about issues than their British counterparts, who seem merely to name the next speaker and let that person get on with it. In the Irish data, there are no fewer than six challenges to what the moderator has said, plus one confirmation, none of which categories occur in the British data. It would appear that British participants appear to comment more on each other than in the Irish data, so that the broadcasts come across more genuinely as discussions, whereas the Irish broadcasts more resemble question-and-answer sessions.[9]

4.3 Well *and Politeness*

For Aijmer (2013), the third pragmatic function of *well* in terms of its meaning potential is politeness. According to Östman upon whom Aijmer (2013) builds, politeness is "concerned with the interactional constraints we follow when establishing, maintaining or breaking interpersonal relationships (Östman 1995: 104)" (Aijmer, 2013, p. 42). Whereas politeness maintenance has been considered an implicit factor in the explanation of involved uses of *well* above, specifically polite uses of *well* are distinguished by accompanying harmonic

9 In her analysis of the same British data, Aijmer (2013, p. 57, Table 2.17) does not find any cases of agreement, which, given even the collocationally-reinforced examples cited above, is quite puzzling. For her, all 31 examples are categorised as disagreements.

collocations. Aijmer explains: "[t]he motive for *well* may be to soften a potentially face-threatening act or to reinforce it (e.g. in an argument). However," she continues, "something must be added to *well* to show how it is intended. Combinations such as *well I don't know, well I think, well perhaps, well maybe* and *well you know* [...] have the function of mitigating illocutionary force in contexts which can be experienced as face-threatening." (2013, p. 42). Thus the use of *well* "is reinforcing and as a result assertive and authoritative in contexts where it co-occurs with *certainly, surely, actually, really, as I say, unquestionably*, etc." (ibid.)

The present data indicate that *well*, besides being a marker of coherence and involvement, is also a politeness marker, when there is an interpersonal or face element involved. Through co-operation by answering a question or responding to a statement, *well* upholds positive face of both speaker and the hearer (which an abrupt answer without *well* would have threatened); and by providing what Sperber and Wilson call (1986, p. 158) "an optimally relevant answer or response", *well* simultaneously removes any threat to negative face, thus making the answer or response, as already mentioned, less "abrasive" (Bolinger 1989, p. 321). As a politeness marker, *well* is described by Jucker (1993, p. 444) as a "face-threat mitigator". When a speaker utters *well*, the hearer's co-operation is ensured. Moreover, when *well* has a face-saving, face-mitigating function, it holds the discourse together cohesively as well as coherently. Expectations or entailments raised by specific premises of the proposition in question may not be fulfilled, but *well* keeps the engagement with the hearer by upholding relevance and fulfilling general communicative strategies at a metadiscoursal level. These points are born out by the examples to be discussed.

In SPICE-Ireland, 10 instances of *well* as politeness marker are identified. For reason of space, only a few typical examples can be discussed here. In (13a), *well* occurs as an utterance-medial self-interrupt, to enable the speaker to change tack and offer an apology (*I'm sorry*) for what he is about to say, thereby mitigating a face-threatening act and protecting the hearer's negative face.

(13) a. ⟨$A⟩ **⟨dir⟩** [...] and if you think we can walk away and leave that **well I'm** ⟨{4⟩ ⟨[4⟩ **sorry** ⟨/[4⟩ you've got the wrong guy **⟨/dir⟩**
⟨$F⟩ ⟨#⟩ **⟨icu⟩** ⟨[4⟩ No ⟨/[4⟩ ⟨/{4⟩ **⟨/icu⟩** (ICE-NI-P1B-022)

In (13b) *well* (reinforced by *really*) serves to mitigate speaker F's disagreement with the moderator's (speaker A) view about the level of confidence in the community, thereby avoiding a face-threatening act.

b. ⟨$A⟩ ⟨#⟩ **⟨dir⟩** And that of course has decimated then the the uh the the streets uh ⟨.⟩ m ⟨/.⟩ made the kind of community life of those streets much less uh confident **⟨/dir⟩**
⟨$F⟩ ⟨#⟩ **⟨rep⟩ Well** there is really no confidence about employment **⟨/rep⟩** (ICE-NI-P1B-029)

In (13c), in an outburst of an expressive speech act, *well* is used pragmatically by the speaker, in the middle of his turn, with a harmonically modalised *I don't know*, to mitigate a possible face threat about the hearer's attitude to what is being discussed.

c. ⟨$D⟩ Lent I think uhm you know like Lorraine was saying it's about concentrating the mind and you know reaching a greater understanding ⟨/rep⟩ ⟨#⟩ ⟨xpa⟩ Uhm ⟨,⟩ I would ⟨{⟩ ⟨[⟩ hope that at the end of it I would have I will uh ⟨/[⟩ ⟨/xpa⟩ **⟨exp⟩ well I don't know** if it's if you would consider it good **⟨/exp⟩** ⟨com⟩ but I'm going to do something in my life ⟨,⟩ to make these forty days different to the rest of the year ⟨/com⟩ (ICE-ROI-P1B-036)

These few examples show politeness uses of *well* encompass a range of face-mitigating functions and are often qualified by epistemically-modalised expressions for hedging or tentativeness effects, as claimed by Aijmer (2013), as discussed above.

4.3.1 Politeness Functions of *Well* in SPICE-Ireland and ICE-GB

In both SPICE-Ireland and ICE-GB BRDs there are 10 occurrences of *well*. In the British data, the use of *well* to mitigate face threats is sometimes reinforced collocationally by pragmatic markers such as *actually* or *of course*. In several examples, *well* maintains positive face by accompanying agreements with the propositions being negotiated in tag questions. On other occasions, *well* mitigates against face threat by avoiding disagreement, as in (14a):

(14) a. ⟨$C⟩ ⟨#⟩ Surely that is wrong
⟨$E⟩All right ⟨#⟩ I Well uh that's a matter of opinion ⟨#⟩ Uhm I personally don't think that is wrong (ICE-GB-S1B-031)

or (14b) where *well* tones down any face threat or disagreement:

b. ⟨$A⟩Do you think a lot of other things are going to come out as time goes on
⟨$C⟩ Well I don't see it that way (ICE-GB-S1B-034)

5 Discussion

In any analysis of ICE-/SPICE-Ireland, an implicit agenda (indeed a further motivation) is invariably to detect any Irishisms. The distribution of occurrences lends itself to the inference that there is nothing peculiarly Irish about discourse uses of *well*.

At the centre of this study lies Aijmer's (2013) model of meaning potential where *well* has three main pragmatic functions: a discourse-connecting, textual or coherence function; an interpersonal, inference-generating function of involvement; and a face-addressing function as a marker of politeness. The present study, which is based on corpus material from a specific situation of public discourse, shows that claims about *well* (1) as a connective or frame or coherence marker, (2) as an interpersonal marker depending on conversational implicatures and relevance, and (3) as a politeness marker are by and large confirmed by the Irish data. By the above comparison of three major functions of *well* in each corpus, the functional homogeneity (defined as being 'of a similar kind') between SPICE-Ireland and ICE-GB data is demonstrated. Confirmation of an existing model through application to another data set is always a satisfying outcome.

There have been difficulties along the way, however, not least distinguishing uses of *well* which are only involved from those which are involved but show politeness, too. Politeness uses were identified in the Irish data by the presence of a face-addressing element, which was lacking in strictly involved cases, where the focus of the exchange was usually on the proposition; and in the British data by pragmatically-harmonious collocations or co-occurring epistemically-modalised expressions. The difficulty can be avoided if involvement and politeness are combined into one single interpersonal function, as in Brinton's (1996) study, as noted by Aijmer (2013, p. 17); after all many involved examples are explained in general politeness terms above.

What is more, Aijmer's synthesis does acknowledge that the categories are "not watertight", and that *well* "can have several functions simultaneously ('mixed' functions)[:] [...] [d]epending on the topic, social situation and sequentiality several [...] functions of *well* can be activated" (2013, p. 31). In characterising *well* in BRDs, the present analysis has had to determine its primary classification on the basis of which function clearly predominates in each instance, in avoidance of any possible overlapping or mixed categories.

Table 5.3 summarises the above findings. It shows that the distribution of those three main functions across corpora is consistent, with coherence predominating at 48.5% in SPICE-IRL and 67.7% in ICE-GB. That the highest scores are for coherence uses in each corpus is almost certainly attributable

TABLE 5.3 *Pragmatic functions of* well *in* BRDs

Pragmatic functions	IRL		GB	
	N	%	N	%
Coherence	50	48.5	86	67.7
Involvement	43	41.8	31	24.4
Politeness	10	9.7	10	7.9
Total	103	100.0	127	100.0

to the nature of the discourse situation, not simply the various roles of moderation but the way participants respond almost uniformly to the invitation to speak or, in the case of ICE-GB, how participants mark the start of their spontaneous, unelicited responses to other participants. Although the analysis presents a discrete distribution, it is possible to think of *well* as always having a discourse-connective function (as suggested in § 4.1.1) but not always having an involved or politeness function. In other words, connectivity is *well*'s basic function, whereas involvement and politeness are the marked forms, functioning interpersonally as well as textually.

Although Table 5.3 shows that the higher proportion of coherence uses is found in ICE-GB and those of involvement and politeness in SPICE-Ireland, it seems futile to speculate about possible explanations: whether Irish speakers are more engaged or respectful of each other; whether the discussions are simply livelier; whether Irish participants are more willing to express their feelings, attitudes and prejudices; whether British discussions are less concerned with feelings, attitudes and prejudices and more concerned about the discussion and the contribution of each participant; and so on. The Irish discussions are all broadcast live, and hence unedited, and the same would be the case for the British texts if broadcast live.

Table 5.3 raises a deeper question about corpus-linguistic methodology. Three of the principles of corpus linguistics established by Leech (1992) are verification, replication and objectivity. Although studies are often replicated on other data (like SPICE-Ireland here), it is quite rare for a study to be verified. For that, Aijmer's (2013) analysis in which all involved uses of *well* in ICE-GB expressed disagreement (cf. footnote 9) provided just such a motivation. That I find only 127 instances of pragmaticalised *well* and Aijmer 130 concerns me less than the considerable difference in functional distribution between the two analyses. In terms of corpus-linguistic objectivity, of which computer-based frequency searches are a prime example, searches for *well* as an orthographic word as in ICE-GB or annotated *well* as a discourse marker in SPICE-Ireland will always yield identical scores. But the interpretation of function would seem to be rather less objective. Whether based on face-negotiating criteria or reinforced by collocations, the discrimination between involved and politeness uses or between functions of agreement and disagreement of *well* are always going to be based ultimately on the analyst's own judgment, no matter how experienced the analyst may be. The functional interpretations reported here are all documented and, if necessary, open to further verification. By committing myself to written analyses using definable criteria, which have been refined in the course of doing so, I have tried to be as objective as possible. But the paradox remains that no matter how objective a corpus-linguistic methodology may be, parts of it may still depend on the analyst's subjectivity.

5.1 *Compatibility of Register (Registerness)*

The data being compared in this paper come from the same communicative situation: the broadcast discussion. Because of their "recurring characteristics of the situational context" (Neumann & Fest, 2016, p. 197), broadcast discussions do indeed constitute a register: "the specific constellation of features in a given situational context" (ibid., p. 198). The broadcast discussion is a familiar format for radio and television programmes in Great Britain and in Ireland, North and South. Between jurisdictions, broadcasters move freely and any producer or moderator could readily be responsible for such a programme in any jurisdiction. Participants, too, could well occur in the programmes of any jurisdiction. Thus from the outset the broadcast discussion is a linguistic event with which all the external parameters of the situation would appear to be shared and familiar.

Little surprise, then, that the role of the moderator can be characterised in identical terms: to introduce topics and speakers, to bring in new speakers and ensure participants get their turn, to challenge what participants say, to wind up and end discussions, and so on.

One of Aijmer's (2013) motivations was to discover uses of *well* which related to the public discourse context, which would not have been uncovered in analyses of face-to-face conversation. As shown, *well* plays a crucial role in moderation and management of the broadcast discussions, and the roles uncovered by Aijmer are confirmed afresh by the Irish data.

In some programmes, because it is radio, only members of the invited panel are present. However, in other programmes, where there is an actual audience present, some members may be called upon to speak, as happens several times in text P1B-022:

(15) a. ⟨$A⟩ ⟨#⟩ **⟨dir⟩** But you see **the gentleman over here** wants to know how come the Unionists can do business ⟨,⟩ with the Loyalists **⟨/dir⟩** (P1B-022)

b. ⟨$A⟩ ⟨#⟩ **⟨dir⟩ Gentleman beside you just two along ⟨/dir⟩** ⟨#⟩ **⟨dir⟩** Yes sir **⟨/dir⟩** (P1B-022)

c. ⟨$A⟩ ⟨#⟩ ⟨rep⟩ Yeah I I I don't know ⟨/rep⟩ ⟨rep⟩ uhm **I'm going to come to this gentleman over here** because I I'm not sure now ⟨/rep⟩ (P1B-022)

As previously mentioned, and as O'Keeffe (2006) points out, the ultimate audience is the listening or viewing audience, and occasionally, to that audience, remarks are specifically directed, as when a programme first starts. No doubt there are protocols in place for such programmes. Whereas the Republic of Ireland has its own state broadcasters, the broadcasters in Northern Ireland are part of UK-wide organisations: the British Broadcasting Corporation (BBC), and Independent Television Network (ITV), with common arrangements and protocols.

In those terms, the findings of the present paper would appear to deny much variation between the format or procedures of Irish and British broadcast discussions and rather to highlight their consistency and similarity, indicating membership of the same register type and thereby upholding the hypothesis about register compatibility. That "registers share some general similarities across varieties" (Neumann, 2012, p. 85) is also demonstrated by Neumann's (2012) research.

5.2 *Regionality*

The data under investigation here comes from the ICE corpora for Ireland and Great Britain, with the former covering two geo-political regions: Northern Ireland and the Republic of Ireland. However, in this paper, no significant distinction has been made between those regions. This is hardly surprising: there is nothing substratally or otherwise characteristically Irish about *well* as a form or its functions.[10] Just as this paper shows a similarity of distribution among functions of *well* between Ireland as a whole and GB, it may be inferred that this similarity extends to both parts of Ireland. Of the four hypotheses devised for explaining ICE-Ireland data, set out in Kallen and Kirk (2007, p. 122), the

10 Consider a different situation: for instance, substrate language influence is cited by Neumann (2012, p. 91) as an explanation by Xiao (2009, p. 443) for the high frequency of nouns in Indian English.

present findings conform to their "default hypothesis, whereby the standardised English of Northern Ireland and the Republic of Ireland are no different from standardised English elsewhere".[11] Thus region, although seemingly a potential variable, would appear not be a conditioning factor here; rather, as two near-neighbour L1 countries, region rather explains similarities and common functionalities thereby upholding the third research question. This hypothesis would appear supported by Neumann's (2012) research as well—the striking differences or "divergences" (p. 91) which she finds are between L1 and L2 varieties, not between L1 varieties. Neumann and Fest (2016, p. 195) find that the markers of register medium which they investigate (pronouns, conjunctions and lexical density) "show differences along both regional and functional lines which allow comparative conclusions about the speech societies in question" (p. 195).

6 Concluding Remarks

A major component of this paper is the close, contextualised reading of 230 examples of discourse marker *well*. Those examples are discussed in terms of Aijmer's theory of meaning potential by which *well* has three main pragmatic functions: a discourse-connecting, textual or coherence function; an interpersonal, inference-generating function of involvement; and a face-addressing function as a marker of politeness. The three main notions of homogeneity, register compatibility and regionality have been tested. Through close readings and frequency analysis, those functions are all shown to be shared between the British and Irish data sets.

This paper has triangulated the register of broadcast discussions, the discourse marker *well*, and the 'regions' of Ireland and Great Britain. By showing that, as far as Ireland and Great Britain are concerned, there is scant divergence in the pragmatic marker usage of *well*, the paper confirms similar conclusions

11 The alternative hypotheses are "the single-island hypothesis", whereby the standardised English of Northern Ireland and the Republic of Ireland are no different from each other but differ from standardised Englishes elsewhere; "the political hypothesis", whereby the standardised English from the Republic of Ireland differs from that of Northern Ireland, the difference being explained on political and identity grounds; and "the dialect-historical hypothesis", whereby the standardised English of Northern Ireland and the Republic of Ireland differ from each other in ways which can be explained by historical dialect evolution and different degrees of contact (pp. 135–136).

on other pragmatic uses of three other discourse markers: *just* in Kirk and Kallen (2009) and *kind of* and *sort of* in Kirk (2015).

It is claimed that discourse markers are under cognitive control (e.g. Sperber & Wilson, 1986, 1995; Haselow, 2016, 2017). According to Aijmer (2013, p. 32), "*well* [...] is closely associated with consideration, deliberation, hesitation and is used to gain time for cognitive processes 'connected with prompting of memory, search of memory, hesitation and planning' (Allwood et al. 1990: 11)." This paper shows that a speaker's use of *well* is linked to their metadiscoursal awareness about the ongoing communicative exchanges and their responsive cooperation. At the same time, from the use of *well*, speakers and hearers draw micro-contextual inferences regarding the relevance of what is being said to what has just been said in immediately preceding propositions. *Well* thus maintains the flow of discourse as well as harmonious relationships among speakers, each of which is crucial for an interactive broadcast situation. Nevertheless, it is hard to infer cognitive control from corpus data, attractive though it be to speculate.

This paper shows how *well* is both face-protecting and face-enhancing. *Well* is shown to stand at the confluence of both textual and interpersonal communicative functions, certainly in so far as BRDs are concerned. Put at its simplest, *well* functions as a "marker of response" (Schiffrin, 1985, p. 641) and shows that "the speaker is thinking about things" (Carter & McCarthy, 2006, p. 152), each a basic premise for Aijmer's (2013) and this analysis. Little wonder that *well* is the most complex and most studied of all pragmatic discourse markers.

References

Aijmer, K. (2011). *Well I'm not sure I think* ... The use of *well* by non-native speakers. *International Journal of Corpus Linguistics*, *16*(2), 231–254.

Aijmer, K. (2013). *Understanding pragmatic markers*. Edinburgh: Edinburgh University Press.

Aijmer, K. (2014). Pragmatic markers. In K. Aijmer & C. Rühlemann (Eds.), *Corpus pragmatics* (pp. 195–218). Cambridge: Cambridge University Press.

Aijmer, K., & Simon-Vandenbergen, A.-M. (2003). The discourse particle *well* and its equivalents in Swedish and Dutch. *Linguistics*, *41*(6), 1123–1161.

Allwood, J., Nivre, J., & Ahlsén, E. (1990). Speech management: On the non-written life of speech. *Nordic Journal of Linguistics*, *13*, 3–48.

Amador-Moreno, C.P., McCafferty K., & Vaughan, E. (Eds.). (2015). *Pragmatic markers in Irish English*. Amsterdam: John Benjamins.

Blakemore, D. (1987). *Semantic constraints on relevance*. Oxford: Blackwell.

Blakemore, D. (1992). *Understanding utterances: An introduction to pragmatics*. Oxford: Blackwell.

Bolinger, D. (1989). *Intonation and its uses: Melody in grammar and discourse*. London: Edward Arnold.

Brinton, L.J. (1996). *Pragmatic markers in English: Grammaticalization and discourse functions*. Berlin: Mouton de Gruyter.

Carlson, L. (1984). *'Well' in dialogue games: A discourse analysis of the interjection 'Well' in idealized conversation*. Amsterdam: John Benjamins.

Carter, R., & McCarthy, M. (2006). *The Cambridge Grammar of English*. Cambridge: Cambridge University Press.

Cuenca, M.-J. (2008). Pragmatic markers in contrast: The case of *well*. *Journal of Pragmatics, 40*(8), 1373–1391.

De Klerk, V. (2005). Procedural meanings of *well* in a corpus of Xhosa English. *Journal of Pragmatics, 37*(8), 1183–1205.

Fairclough, N. (1995). *Media discourse*. London: Arnold.

Finell, A. (1989). *Well, now* and *then*. *Journal of Pragmatics, 13*(4), 653–656.

Fraser, B. (1987). An approach to discourse markers. *Journal of Pragmatics, 14*(3), 383–398.

Fraser, B. (1999). What are discourse markers? *Journal of Pragmatics, 31*(3), 931–952.

Fraser, B. (2010). Pragmatic competence: The case of hedging. In G. Kaltenböck, W. Mihatsch & S. Schneider (Eds.), *New approaches to hedging* (pp. 15–34). Bingley: Emerald.

Goffman, E. (1981). *Forms of talk*. Philadelphia: University of Pennsylvania Press.

Gumperz, J.J. (1982). *Discourse strategies*. Cambridge: Cambridge University Press.

Hale, S. (1999). Interpreters' treatment of discourse markers in courtroom questions. *Forensic Linguistics, 6*, 57–82.

Haselow, A. (2016). Intensifying adverbs outside the clause: A cognitive analysis. In G. Kaltenböck, E. Keizer & A. Lohmann (Eds.), *Outside the clause: Form and function of extra-clausal constituents* (pp. 379–415). Amsterdam: John Benjamins.

Haselow, A. (2017). *Spontaneous spoken English: An integrated approach to the emergent grammar of speech*. Cambridge: Cambridge University Press.

Haviland, J.B. (1989). 'Sure, sure': evidence and affect. *Text* 9(1), 27–68.

ICE-GB. (1998). *The International Corpus of English: The British component* (ICE-GB). CD-ROM. London: Survey of English Usage, University College London.

Innes, B. (2010). *"Well, that's why I asked the question, sir": Well* as a discourse marker in court. *Language in society, 39*(1), 95–117.

James, A.R. (1983). *Well* in reporting clauses: Meaning and form of a lexical filler. *Arbeiten aus Anglistik und Amerikanistik, 8*(1), 33–40.

Johansson, S. (2006). How well can *well* be translated? On the English discourse particle *well* and its correspondences in Norwegian and German. In K. Aijmer & A.-M. Simon-Vandenbergen (Eds.), *Pragmatic markers in contrast* (pp. 115–137). Oxford & Amsterdam: Elsevier.

Jucker, A.H. (1993). The discourse marker *well*: A relevance-theoretical account. *Journal of Pragmatics, 19*(5), 435–452.

Jucker, A.H. (1997). The discourse marker *well* in the history of English. *English Language and Linguistics, 1*(1), 91–110.

Kallen, J.L., & Kirk, J.M. (2007). ICE-Ireland: Local variations on global standards. In J.C. Beal, K.P. Corrigan & H.L. Moisl (Eds.), *Creating and digitizing language corpora*, Vol. 1: *Synchronic databases* (pp. 121–162). Houndmills: Palgrave Macmillan.

Kallen, J.L., & Kirk, J.M. (2012). *SPICE-Ireland: A user's guide*. Belfast: Cló Ollscoil na Banríona. Retrieved from http://www.johnmkirk.co.uk/cgibin/generic?instanceID=11. Last accessed February 2017.

Kirk, J.M. (2015). *Kind of* and *sort of*: Pragmatic discourse markers in the SPICE-Ireland corpus. In C.P. Amador-Moreno, K. McCafferty & E. Vaughan (Eds.), *Pragmatic markers in Irish English* (pp. 89–113). Amsterdam: John Benjamins.

Kirk, J.M. (2016). The pragmatic annotation scheme of the SPICE-Ireland corpus. *International Journal of Corpus Linguistics, 21*(3), 299–323.

Kirk J.M., & Kallen, J.L. (2009). *Just* in Irish Standard English. In R. Bowen, M. Mobärg & S. Ohlander (Eds.), *Corpora and discourse—and stuff. Papers in honour of Karin Aijmer* (pp. 149–158). Gothenburg Studies in English. Acta Universitatis Gothoburgensis.

Kirk, J.M., Kallen, J.L., Lowry, O., Rooney, A., & Mannion, M. (2011). *The SPICE Ireland corpus: Systems of pragmatic annotation for the spoken component of ICE-Ireland*. Version 1.2.2. Belfast: Queen's University Belfast & Dublin: Trinity College Dublin.

Knowles, G., Williams, B., & Taylor, L. (Eds.). (1996). *A corpus of formal British English speech*. Harlow: Longman.

Lakoff, R. (1973). Questionable answers and answerable questions. In B.B. Kachru, B. Lees, Y. Malkiel, A. Pietrangeli & S. Saporta (Eds.), *Issues in linguistics in honour of Henry and Renée Kahane* (pp. 453–467). Urbana IL: University of Illinois Press.

Leech, G. (1992). Corpora and theories of linguistic performance. In J. Svartvik (Ed.). *Directions in corpus linguistics: Proceedings of Nobel symposium 82* (pp. 123–144). Berlin: Mouton de Gruyter.

Levinson, S.C. (1983). *Pragmatics*. Cambridge: Cambridge University Press.

Linell, P. (2009). *Rethinking language. Mind and word dialogically: Interactional and contextual theories of human sense-making*. Charlotte, NC: Information Age Publishing.

Marshall, J., & Werndly, A. (2002). *The language of television*. London: Routledge.

Nelson, G., Wallis, S., & Aarts, B. (2002). *Exploring natural language: Working with the British component of the International Corpus of English*. Amsterdam: John Benjamins.

Neumann, S. (2012) Applying register analysis to varieties of English. In M. Fludernik & B. Kohlmann (Eds.), *Anglistentag 2011 Freiburg* (pp. 75–94). Trier: Wissenschaftlicher Verlag Trier.

Neumann, S. (2014). *Contrastive register variation: A quantitative approach to the comparison of English and German*. Berlin: Mouton de Gruyter.

Neumann, S., & Fest, J. (2016). Cohesive devices across registers and varieties: The role of medium in English. In C. Schubert & C. Sanchez-Stockhammer (Eds.), *Variational text linguistics: Revisiting register in English* (pp. 195–220). Berlin: Mouton de Gruyter.

Norén, K., & Linell, P. (2007). Meaning potentials and the interaction between lexis and contexts: An empirical substantiation. *Pragmatics, 17*(3), 387–416.

O'Keeffe, A. (2006). *Investigating Media Discourse*. Abingdon: Rouledge.

Östman, J.-O. (1995). Pragmatic particles twenty years after. In B. Wårvik, S.-K. Tanskanen & R. Hiltunen (Eds.), *Organization in discourse* (pp. 95–108). Turku: University of Turku.

Owen, M. (1981). Conversational units and the use of "well". In P. Werth (Ed.) *Conversation and discourse* (pp. 99–116). London: Croom Helm.

Sakita, T.I. (2006). Parallelism in conversation: Resonance, schematization and extension from the perspective of dialogic syntax and cognitive linguistics. *Pragmatics and Cognition, 14*(3), 467–500.

Sakita, T.I. (2013). Discourse markers as stance markers: *Well* in stance alignment in conversational interaction. *Pragmatics and Cognition, 21*(1), 81–116.

Scannell, P. (1991). *Broadcast talk*. London: SAGE.

Schiffrin, D. (1985). Conversational coherence: The role of *well*. *Language, 61*(3), 640–667.

Schiffrin, D. (1987). *Discourse markers*. Cambridge: Cambridge University Press.

Schourup, L. (1985). *Common discourse particles in English conversation*. New York: Garland.

Schourup, L. (2001). Rethinking *well*. *Journal of Pragmatics, 33*(7), 1026–1060.

Searle, J.R. (1969). *Speech acts*. Cambridge: Cambridge University Press.

Searle, J.R. (1976). A classification of illocutionary acts. *Language in Society, 5*(1), 1–23.

Sperber, D., & Wilson, D. (1986). *Relevance: Communication and cognition*. Oxford: Blackwell.

Sperber, D., & Wilson, D. (1995). *Relevance: Communication and cognition* (2nd ed.). Oxford: Blackwell.

Svartvik, J. (1980). *Well* in conversation. In S. Greenbaum, G.N. Leech & J. Svartvik (Eds.), *Studies in English linguistics for Randolph Quirk* (pp. 167–177). London: Longman.

Svartvik, J. (1990). *The London-Lund Corpus of Spoken English: Description and research*. Lund: Lund University Press.

Watts, R.J. (1986). Relevance in conversational moves: A reappraisal of *well*. *Studia Anglica Posnaniensia, 19*, 37–59.

Watts, R.J. (1989). Taking the pitcher to the 'well'. Native speakers' perception of their use of discourse markers in conversation. *Journal of Pragmatics, 13*(2), 203–237.

Xiao, R. (2009). Multidimensional analysis and the study of World Englishes. *World Englishes, 28*(4), 421–450.

CHAPTER 6

Between Lexis and Discourse: A Cross-register Study of Connectors of Contrast

Maïté Dupont

1 Introduction

Connectives are lexical items that signal explicitly a logical relationship (such as addition, causality or contrast) between two clauses, sentences or paragraphs, thereby contributing to text cohesion. They form a broad functional category grouping members from various grammatical classes, viz. coordinators (*and, but*), subordinators (*although, because*), adverbial connectors (*therefore, nevertheless*), along with a number of signals that do not belong to a well-defined grammatical category (*despite the fact that, it remains that*), sometimes referred to as alternative lexicalisations (Prasad, Joshi, & Webber, 2010). The present study focuses on one of these categories of connective devices in particular, i.e. adverbial connectors. Adverbial connectors (also referred to as conjuncts by Quirk, Greenbaum, Leech, & Svartvik, 1985, or linking adverbials by Biber, Johansson, Leech, Conrad, & Finegan, 1999) are especially interesting, as they are syntactically mobile elements—unlike the other types of connectives, which are fixed at clause-initial position (see e.g. Quirk et al., 1985). In fact, together with adjuncts and disjuncts, in present-day English adverbial connectors are the only truly flexible constituents with respect to their position within the sentence (Lenker, 2014, introduction). The placement patterns of English adverbial connectors have been studied quite extensively, from a variety of perspectives. Statements on adverbial connector placement are found in structural descriptive grammars (Biber et al., 1999; Leech & Svartvik, 1994; Quirk et al., 1972, 1985), systemic functional linguistics (Halliday & Matthiessen, 2004), contrastive linguistics (e.g. Altenberg's 1998 comparison with Swedish), diachronic linguistics (Lenker, 2010, 2011, 2014) and learner corpus research, which has frequently looked at native-speaker data as a yardstick to evaluate the learners' awareness of the preferred syntactic positions of English connectors (e.g. Altenberg & Tapper, 1998; Field & Yip, 1992; Granger & Tyson, 1996; Tankó, 2004). In a large majority of these studies, English adverbial connectors have been shown to display a strong tendency to occur sentence-initially. The initial position has been referred to successively as the "normal", "unmarked" or

 | DOI: 10.1163/9789004361133_008

"natural" position for connectors.[1] According to Quirk et al. (1972), for instance, "[t]he normal position for most conjuncts is I [initial] [...]. M [medial] positions are rare for most conjuncts, and E [end] rarer still" (p. 526). Similarly, for Halliday and Matthiessen (2004), connectors are "what we might call characteristically thematic [...]. They are natural Themes:[2] if the speaker or writer is making explicit the way the clause relates to the surrounding discourse [...] it is natural to set up such expressions as the point of departure [of the message]" (p. 83).

While many studies contain fairly general statements on connector placement for the English language as a whole, some linguists hold more nuanced views and underline the role played by lexis and register on placement. In his study of adverbial positions in English, Jacobson (1964) provides an empirically-based word-order dictionary of English adverbs, whose "main purpose is to show how individual adverbs are actually placed by present-day writers" (p. 365). Based on a corpus of English written prose, he provides the proportion of use of each adverb in three main positions (i.e. initial, medial and final). A look at the various entries provided for connectors reveals that the different items do not behave in the same way with respect to placement. Although illuminating and highly innovative for its time, Jacobson's account is fairly limited empirically (e.g. only c. 100 occurrences of *however*; c. 50 occurrences of *nevertheless* are investigated). In a learner corpus research framework, Paquot (2010) compares the use of initial and final connectors in native and learner data. Her results show that the prominence of each position differs according to the lexical item. For example, *moreover* occurs initially in 73.7 % of the cases, against only 5.3 % for *therefore*. Some contrastive linguistic studies also provide valuable insights into the role of lexis on connector placement. In his study of English and Swedish connectors in second initial position, Altenberg (2006) notes that in his written corpus of fiction and non-fiction texts there is "clear evidence of individual positional 'profiles'" (p. 15) among the English connectors investigated. He observes the following:

> Some [connectors] have a strong tendency to occur at E [end] (*though, anyway, then*), others prefer M [medial] (*accordingly, therefore, still*), while others are never placed there in the corpus (*furthermore, consequently, moreover*). Some connectors are extremely mobile without any clear pref-

1 Some rare studies have nevertheless demonstrated the importance of medial positions for connectors, see Altenberg, 2006; Lenker, 2011, 2014.

2 See Section 2 for a definition of the Theme.

> erence for any position (e.g. *however, for example, for instance*), while others are practically restricted to one position (e.g. *besides* at I [initial]).
>
> p. 15

Likewise, in a previous study (Dupont, 2015), I compared the positional patterns of English and French connectors of contrast in a comparable corpus of editorials. The results showed that general statements on the positional preferences of connectors for languages as wholes are overly simplistic, as significant heterogeneity was uncovered between the connectors within each language system.

With respect to the impact of register,[3] many studies have demonstrated the highly register-sensitive character of connectors. They have shown that both the number and types of connectors used tend to differ markedly depending on the mode (spoken vs. written) or communicative situation (see e.g. Altenberg, 1984, 1986; Biber, 1988; Liu, 2008), and that some connectors are typical of some communicative situations while they are inappropriate in others (e.g. *so* and *anyway* are typical of speech; *thus* and *however* are specific to writing, see Altenberg, 1984, 1986). By contrast, relatively few studies have investigated register in relation to syntactic positioning. In an early study, Greenbaum (1969, p. 80) notes that, in his corpus of c. 100,000 words comprised of texts from a variety of registers, most of the final connectors occur in discussion and conversation, while a majority of the medial connectors come from scientific texts. Biber et al. (1999, p. 891) investigate the placement of adverbial connectors in conversation and academic prose. They observe that while the initial position is the most frequent one in both conversation and academic writing, the two registers differ markedly in their use of final positions (c. 40 % in conversation, against c. 10 % in academic writing) and medial positions (c. 40 % in academic writing, against less than 5 % in conversation; see also Conrad, 1999, p. 13). However, these studies have mostly noted differences in placement according to the mode (speech vs. writing) instead of investigating a possible influence of the communicative situation or register within a given mode (e.g. placement in written news vs. academic prose). In addition, I am not aware of any study investigating a possible interaction between lexis and register with respect to connector placement.

3 Following Biber et al. (1999), in the present article 'register' refers to a language variety defined by its situation of use. Thus, for example, fiction, academic prose and newspaper articles are considered as distinct language registers.

By underlining the role of both lexical and stylistic factors on connector placement, however, these studies have provided a major impetus for the present article, which intends to dig deeper into the influence of lexis and register on connector positioning by investigating this phenomenon on a large, stylistically-varied empirical basis. The study intends to address the following three research questions: (i) what is the role played by lexis in adverbial connector placement—or, in other words, to what extent do connectors of contrast display individual patterns of placement?; (ii) to what extent does connector placement vary across language registers (as opposed to language modes)?; and (iii) if both lexis and register play a part, do they interrelate, and how? The focus of the study is on adverbial connectors expressing contrast, such as *however* and *nevertheless*. In this study, contrast is defined as a broad semantic category subsuming three main meaning relations (namely opposition, concession and correction) which share the property of signalling a negation of either similarity or implication (i.e. one thing leads to another) between two events or situations[4] (see e.g. Foolen, 1991; Izutsu, 2008; Taboada & Gómez-González, 2012 for similar classifications). In relations of opposition, the connector simply signals the existence of a difference between the two segments S1 and S2 that it links, as in (1). In concessive relations, the marker indicates that the second segment S2 (or its implication) rejects the pragmatic inference that the receiver could be taken to have drawn from the first segment S1, as in (2). Finally, in correction S1 is an explicitly negative sentence, and S2 provides a correction of S1 in its affirmative form, as in (3).

(1) Tom is tall. His brother, **by contrast**, is very short.

(2) She studied hard. **Nevertheless**, she failed her exam.

(3) Lucy is not mean. **On the contrary**, she is the nicest person I know.

---

4 An overview of (some of) the literature on contrast reveals the existence of highly varied, frequently conflicting ways of defining and categorising discourse relations of contrast. More specifically, descriptions of contrast differ in (i) the number and types of relations of contrast that are identified; (ii) the ways in which these relations are classified; and (iii) the labels assigned to both the general category of contrast, and its various subtypes. It is, however, beyond the scope of this study to go into detail about such semantic considerations: the study does not aim to carry out any fine-grained semantic analyses, and the definition of contrast provided here mostly serves to delimit the object of study.

The present paper is made up of seven main parts. Section 2 introduces the analytical framework as well as the classification of adverbial positions adopted in the study; Section 3 presents the data and methodology. The results are discussed in Sections 4 to 7. Section 4 discusses the variation in frequency of connectors across registers. Sections 5 to 7 look successively at the influence of lexis, register, and the interaction between the two factors on connector placement. Section 8 provides some concluding remarks.

2 A Systemic Functional Approach to Connector Placement

The present study differs from most previous work on adverbial placement in that, instead of resorting to purely syntactic criteria of analysis (see e.g. Altenberg, 2006; Greenbaum, 1969; Hasselgård, 2010), it is grounded in the framework of systemic functional linguistics (henceforth: SFL) and relies primarily on the SFL notions of Theme and Rheme to investigate adverbial connector placement, according to a classification established in Dupont (2015). The SFL framework is combined with the powerful methods and solid empirical basis afforded by corpus linguistics, as advocated in Thompson and Hunston (2006). The two approaches share numerous properties which make their combination extremely promising, such as their concern for authentic language and the importance that they attach to corpus frequencies for language theorisation (see Halliday, 1991, 2006). As early as 1991, Halliday (1991) highlighted the "inherently probabilistic" nature of the linguistic system, which creates a "natural affinity between systemic theory and corpus linguistics" (2006, p. 293). SFL and corpus linguistics may in fact be seen as complementary: SFL contributes a theoretical grounding that is not always present in corpus linguistics, which in turn provides a solid and stylistically-varied empirical foundation together with powerful methods of extraction and analysis. In spite of the many arguments in favour of a synergy, to this day few studies have combined the advantages of SFL with those of corpus linguistics. The present study situates itself in a set of recent studies attempting to bridge the gap between the two approaches (e.g. Kunz & Lapshinova-Koltunksi, 2014 and the GeCCo project in general; Thompson & Hunston, 2006). Section 2.1 below briefly introduces the notions of Theme and Rheme, while Section 2.2 presents the classification of adverbial positions adopted.

2.1 *Theme and Rheme in Systemic Functional Linguistics*

In systemic functional linguistics, the Theme and the Rheme are the two constituent parts of a clause functioning as a message, referred to as thematic structure. In Hallidayan linguistics, the Theme is defined functionally as "the element which serves as the point of departure of the message; it is that which locates and orients the clause within its context" (Halliday & Matthiessen, 2004, p. 66). In English, the Theme thus corresponds to the sentence-initial position, and can be formally identified as "the first clause element which has a function in transitivity [i.e. subjects, objects, verbs, complements, adjuncts], along with any preceding elements" (Hasselgård, 2004, p. 64). The Rheme, on the other hand, corresponds to everything that follows the Theme; it is the part of the clause in which the Theme is developed (Halliday & Matthiessen, 2004, p. 66).

The Theme has been studied quite extensively in the SFL literature, which has distinguished between several types of Theme. The first relevant distinction with respect to the Theme is that between topical, textual and interpersonal Themes. The Theme of a clause always contains one, and only one, topical Theme, which refers to entities of the outside world such as participants and circumstances (e.g. *the dog, yesterday, in England*). Some clauses, such as (4), contain a simple Theme, solely made up of a topical Theme. However, a Theme may also include one or several textual and interpersonal Themes preceding the topical Theme, thereby making up a multiple Theme (see Bloor & Bloor, 2004; Hasselgård, 2004). Textual Themes are elements that indicate explicitly how a given clause relates to what precedes in discourse. Textual Themes are typically expressed by discourse connectives such as *but, and, however* and *in addition*. Interpersonal Themes, on the other hand, provide information about the stance of the writer or speaker towards the message (e.g. *frankly, luckily, unfortunately*). An example of a multiple Theme is provided in (5).

(4)	Kuala Lumpur	is the capital of Malaysia (Bloor & Bloor, 2004, p. 73)
	Theme	Rheme

(5)	But	unfortunately	the United Kingdom	is controlled by what we might refer to as the political undead.
	Textual	Interpersonal	Topical	Rheme
	Theme			Rheme

A second important distinction pertaining to the Theme is that between marked and unmarked Themes. When the topical Theme of a clause corresponds to its grammatical subject, as in examples (4) and (5) above, the Theme is unmarked. By contrast, when the topical Theme does not coincide with the subject, it is said to be marked. The most typical examples of marked Themes occur when the topical Theme corresponds to a fronted adjunct, as in (6).

(6)	For a long time,	the Spartans proved themselves invincible on land (Bloor & Bloor, 2004, p. 76)
	Theme	Rheme

While SFL provides an extensive body of research on the Theme, to this day scant attention has been devoted to the Rheme.[5] Unlike the Theme, in current SFL research the Rheme is generally viewed as one single entity, and no distinctions are made within it. Notable exceptions[6] include Fries's (1994) N-RHEME (defined as the last constituent of the clause, corresponding to the newsworthy part of the clause, as in (7)) and Morel and Danon-Boileau's (1998) intonational notion of POST-RHEME (i.e. an optional intonational constituent produced with a flat intonation, a low pitch and a reduced intensity at the end of an oral paragraph, as in (8)). In addition, Taglicht (1984) has put forward a rhematic equivalent to the marked Theme: the *marked Rheme*, defined as a rhematic element that attracts more attention than is usually the case through being detached from the rest of the clause—for instance by means of the insertion of a connector—and placed sentence-finally, as in (9), where *to England* emerges as the marked Rheme. Interestingly, however, all three studies have tended to focus on the end of the Rheme, leaving medial positions aside.

(7) Every day decisions are being made by local officials in our communities *that could drastically affect the quality of our lives* (Fries, 1994, p. 243).

(8) He's really weird, *that guy*.

(9) They are returning, however, *to England* (Taglicht, 1984, p. 25).

5 Symptomatic of this is the fact that the Rheme is systematically defined by exclusion with respect to the Theme. According to Bloor & Bloor (2004, p. 288), for example, the "Rheme is that part of the clause which is *not* Theme" (my italics). Similarly, for Thompson (2014, p. 147), while the Theme is the first constituent of the clause, "*all the rest* of the clause is *simply* labelled the Rheme" (my italics).

6 See Dupont (2015) for a more complete account.

Note that some distinctions made with respect to the Theme are in fact relevant for the study of the Rheme. This is the case of Hannay and Gómez-González's (2013) thematic parentheticals, i.e. "parenthetical elements, irrespective of form, which are marked off typographically, and occur immediately after, and are triggered by, a thematic element" (p. 99), as in (10), where the thematic parenthetical is italicised. Those parenthetical elements may be connectors, as in (11).

(10) Industry, *aside from its economic importance*, was also of course a bourgeois virtue (ibid., p. 113).

(11) By the early 1970s, *however*, this attitude was changing [...] (ibid., p. 104).

Since such parentheticals are considered to be triggered by a thematic element, Hannay and Gómez-González regard them as thematic themselves. Strictly speaking, however, they are rhematic, as they occur after the topical Theme.

In summary, so far research on the Rheme has been both scarce and scattered: there is no consensus on the kinds of subdivisions to be made within the Rheme or their denominations, and within the small community of researchers interested in the Rheme there is little or no acknowledgment of the existing work on the Rheme. If we accept the claims made in most of the literature on connector placement, the paucity of research on the Rheme should not be problematic for a study dealing with connector placement, as connectors have been said to occur predominantly in initial positions (see Section 1). However, a few studies have highlighted the significance of medial positions for adverbial connectors—especially when they express contrast (see Altenberg, 2006; Dupont, 2015; Lenker, 2011, 2014). As a result, in order to provide a detailed account of the placement patterns of adverbial connectors occurring after the topical Theme this study adopts a classification of adverbial positions which makes distinctions within the Rheme whenever relevant for the analysis, thus identifying three rhematic positions in addition to the thematic positions described in the SFL framework. The classification is presented in Section 2.2.

2.2 *A Systemic Functional Classification of Adverbial Positions*

The classification of adverbial positions adopted in this study was elaborated in a previous study investigating the placement of adverbial connectors of contrast in English and French editorials (Dupont, 2015). It identifies five main positions within the clause (or clause complex), i.e. two within the Theme, and three within the Rheme. The two thematic positions were identified on the basis of the distinctions within the Theme put forward by SFL (i.e. between the topical, textual and interpersonal subparts of the Theme). For the rhematic positions, by contrast, it was not possible to apply ready-made SFL criteria to identify relevant positions, due to the paucity of research on the Rheme. When relevant, inspiration was sought in the rare studies dealing with the Rheme discussed in Section 2.1, but not all of them were helpful (e.g. Morel and Danon-Boileau's post-rheme is restricted to spoken language). Distinctions within the Rheme were, therefore, to a large extent corpus-driven: based on the patterns observed in the corpus data, I was able to identify three rhematic positions that have identifiable functional relevance (in terms of information and thematic structure; see Dupont (2015) and Section 7 for an illustration of the functional properties of those positions).

The first position, labelled **thematic 1**, includes connectors occurring either at the very beginning of the clause or clause complex, as in (12), or after another textual Theme, as in (13). The thematic 1 position thus corresponds to the sentence-initial position.

(12) Since the hearing is taking place during a presidential campaign, it's unlikely that a spirit of bipartisan decorum will prevail. **Nevertheless**, it's good to bring this debate out in the open (Dupont, 2015, p. 99).

(13) Yesterday's feeble performance by Donald Anderson, the supposedly independent chair of the foreign affairs committee, added to the gloom. *But* **nonetheless** the game of trying to make the prime minister admit what he may not feel is probably fruitless (ibid.).

The second position identified is the **thematic 2** slot, which includes connectors occurring after an interpersonal Theme, as in example (14). Although Halliday and Matthiessen (2004) restrict the category of interpersonal Themes to comment adjuncts (e.g. *honestly, sadly, clearly*), vocatives and finite verbal operators in yes/no questions, in our classification the structures that Thompson (2014) refers to as thematised comments are also analysed as interpersonal Themes. Thematised comments are defined as introductory verbal constructions which "allow speakers to start their message with their own comment on the value or validity of what they are about to say" (ibid., p. 156). Examples include *it is important to, it is clear that, it is regrettable that*.[7] This means that connectors such as the one in (15) are categorised as thematic 2.

7 Such structures are viewed as interpersonal Themes because they seem to function as

(14)

Crucially, **though**, the US	was able to maintain the support of other countries (Dupont, 2015, p. 100)
Theme	Rheme

(15)

It is a regrettable, **however**, *that* a genuine difference	should be reported in such melodramatic terms.
Theme	Rheme

The first rhematic position, labelled **rhematic 1**, includes connectors used between the topical Theme (whether marked or unmarked) and the verb phrase of the clause (complex). Example (16) illustrates a rhematic 1 connector occurring after an unmarked Theme, while (17) exemplifies a rhematic 1 connector placed after a marked Theme. Rhematic 1 connectors are akin to what Hannay and Gómez-González (2013) refer to as thematic parentheticals.

(16) Past premiers would give just the occasional speech and the even more occasional one-to-one interview, and would otherwise make themselves accountable to MPs only at question time. *Mr Blair*, **on the other hand**, has rewritten the handbook on prime ministerial accessibility and accountability (Dupont, 2015, p. 100).

(17) *When the surplus evaporated and turned into a huge deficit*, **however**, Bush did not reverse his arguments (ibid.).

Rhematic 2 connectors occur within the verb phrase of the clause (complex), which is made up of the predicate along with all its complements. This category is fairly broad, as it includes connectors occurring within the predicate, as in (18); connectors used between the predicate and its complements, as in (19); and, more rarely, connectors placed within the complement(s), as in (20).

(18) President Bush would, **though**, be content to let regional powers contain and constrain the North Korean leadership if they were willing to do so (Dupont, 2015, p. 101).

(nearly-)fixed introductory expressions conveying the same meanings as comment adjuncts: in most cases, they can be replaced by equivalent comment adverbs (*it is clear that* ≈ *clearly; it is regrettable that* ≈ *regrettably*).

TABLE 6.1 *Summary of the classification of adverbial positions*

Positions	Examples
Thematic 1	Since the hearing is taking place during a presidential campaign, it's unlikely that a spirit of bipartisan decorum will prevail. **Nevertheless**, it's good to bring this debate out in the open.
Thematic 2	*Crucially*, **though**, the US was able to maintain the support of other countries.
Rhematic 1	→ **After an unmarked Theme** Past premiers would give just the occasional speech and the even more occasional one-to-one interview, and would otherwise make themselves accountable to MPs only at question time. *Mr Blair*, **on the other hand**, has rewritten the handbook on prime ministerial accessibility and accountability → **After a marked Theme** *When the surplus evaporated and turned into a huge deficit*, **however**, Bush did not reverse his arguments.
Rhematic 2	President Bush would, **though**, be content to let regional powers contain and constrain the North Korean leadership if they were willing to do so
Rhematic 3	Mr Straw played down the significance of the achievement. He should not be so modest. There are important caveats, **nevertheless**

(19) It is a matter of debate as to whether some of them would still be permissible under the Human Rights Act. They were, **nonetheless**, effective (ibid.).

(20) The Prime Minister cannot be completely confident, **however**, that this reasoned approach will pay dividends on his preferred timetable (ibid., p. 102).

Finally, **rhematic 3** connectors occur after all the verb complements. This position may (and frequently does) correspond to the final position, as in (21). However, some non-final connectors are also included in the rhematic 3 category, for example when the connector is followed by optional elements such as a sentential relative clause or a sentence adverbial, as in (22).

(21) Mr Straw played down the significance of the achievement. He should not be so modest. There are important caveats, **nevertheless** (Dupont, 2015, p. 102).

(22) The process of balancing continuity with change is a delicate one, **though**, especially so when it comes to the nature of the Royal Household.

Table 6.1 summarises the classification presented in this section, including one prototypical example for each of the five positions.

3 Data and Methodology

The study was carried out on the basis of a corpus of about 5.5 million words made up of texts from three language registers. The first subcorpus consists of c. 2 million words of quality newspaper editorials extracted from the *Multilingual Corpus of Editorials* (Mult-Ed).[8] The second subcorpus contains c. 2 million words of research articles in the humanities extracted from the *Louvain Corpus of Research Articles* (LOCRA).[9] The academic subcorpus includes data collected from top-rated, peer-reviewed journals from five disciplines, viz. anthropology, education, political science, psychology and sociology. The third subcorpus is made up of about 1.4 million words from *Europarl*, a multilingual corpus containing the minutes of debates from the European Parliament. I used the subpart of the Europarl corpus which distinguishes clearly between original and translated texts (see Cartoni & Meyer, 2012), so as to make sure to only include texts produced in original English. All the texts in the corpus are produced by native or expert users of the English language.[10] Table 6.2 provides the detailed breakdown of the corpus.

---

8 https://uclouvain.be/en/research-institutes/ilc/cecl/mult-ed.html. Last accessed 19 June 2017.

9 https://uclouvain.be/en/research-institutes/ilc/cecl/locra.html. Last accessed 19 June 2017.

10 This statement ought to be somewhat nuanced for the Europarl subcorpus. A study carried

TABLE 6.2 *Breakdown of the corpus*

Subcorpus	Text type	Number of words	Number of texts
Europarl	Parliamentary debates	1,381,368	245
LOCRA	Research articles in the Humanities (political science, anthropology, psychology, sociology, education)	2,006,998	262
Mult-Ed	Quality newspaper editorials (British papers, e.g. *The Guardian, The Telegraph* …)	2,010,799	4,185
TOTAL		5,399,165	4692

The three registers included in the corpus are all fairly formal registers sharing a combined argumentative and informative communicative purpose (although the balance between the two goals arguably varies between the three registers). As explained by Hyland (1998), writers of academic discourse aim at "both informing and persuading readers of the truth of their statements" (p. 440). The same goes for editorials, which are clearly considered to be an "opiniated genre intended to persuade the reader" (Biber, 1988, p. 148), but are also characterised by an informational component (Alonso Belmonte, 2007, p. 2). Parliamentary debates also display a mixed informational and argumentative communicative purpose (Granger, 2014, p. 62). The registers also display differences which make their comparison interesting. Firstly, while research articles and editorials fully resort to the written mode, parliamentary debates represent a more hybrid mode oscillating between writing and speech, some-

out by Nisioi, Rabinovich, Ordan and Wintner (2016) on a larger section of the Europarl corpus demonstrates that while a large majority (i.e. 80%) of the texts in their corpus are produced by native speakers of English, the corpus also contains some segments produced by non-native speakers of English. In line with what they explain, however, given that Members of the European Parliament can use any of the EU's 24 official languages when they speak in Parliament, the fact that these speakers choose to express themselves in English suggests that they are likely to be highly proficient users of the English language. In this respect, those texts are akin to those found in the LOCRA corpus: while all the researchers who publish in top-rated journals are not necessarily native speakers of English, the fact that they were able to publish in such high-quality journals suggests an excellent mastery of the English language.

times referred to as "written-to-be-spoken-as-if-not-written" (see Gregory & Carroll, 1978, p. 47). Finally, as Granger (2014) notes, the argumentative tone differs across the registers: in the debates, the tone is more directive, aiming "to influence the course of events" (p. 62). In the editorials, the tone is more reflective, as writers mainly interpret events that have already happened. Finally, in academic texts, the author seeks acceptance of his or her statements or findings within a given scientific community, to "negotiate academic knowledge in ways that are meaningful and appropriate to a particular disciplinary community" (Hyland, 1998, p. 440).

The corpus search relied on a previously-established list of 31 adverbial connectors of contrast (including both simple adverbs and adverbial phrases),[11] listed in Table 6.3. The occurrences of those connectors were extracted automatically from the corpus with WordSmith Tools 6 (Scott, 2012) and disambiguated manually in context,[12] so as to keep only the cases in which the items were used as adverbial connectors of contrast. Thus, for example, temporal uses of *still*, as in (23) were excluded from the data set. Similarly, examples such as (24), where *though* is used as a subordinator instead of an adverb, were discarded. Finally, items used below clause level, as in (25), were also weeded out.

(23) Skilled in war but also in the arts of peace, he was a seaman, naval officer, farmer and administrator whose vision of what Australia could become is **still** an inspiration (Mult-Ed).

(24) **Though** agencies like Oxfam are seeking to help 8,000 families per month, over 400,000 people have lost their belongings or their livelihoods (Europarl).

(25) The Government has a simple, but **nonetheless** excruciating, political difficulty (Mult-Ed).

The analysis of position was restricted to the most frequent connectors, i.e. markers that topped the natural cut-off point of 90 occurrences per million words after disambiguation in at least one of the three registers. This threshold

11 The list was obtained by pooling lists of connectors available in various reference books and studies, i.e. Biber et al. (1999); Castagnoli (2009); Chalker (1996); Halliday & Hasan (1976); Knott (1996); Quirk et al. (1985) and Rudolph (1996).

12 For *still*, random samples of 500 occurrences were used. This connector is particularly hard and time-consuming to disambiguate as it is usually very difficult to distinguish between its temporal and its contrastive uses.

TABLE 6.3 *List of adverbial connectors of contrast*[13]

– All the same	– Even so	– Nonetheless
– Anyhow	– For all that	– Notwithstanding
– Anyway(s)	– Having said that	– On the contrary
– At all events	– However	– On the other (hand)
– At any rate	– In any case	– Regardless
– At the same time	– In any event	– Still
– By comparison	– In comparison	– Still and all
– By contrast	– In contrast	– That (being) said
– Be that as it may	– Instead	– Though
– Contrariwise	– Meanwhile	
– Conversely	– Nevertheless	

was chosen because there was a striking gap in frequency between connectors with a frequency of 90 times per million words or more, and the other, less frequent connectors, which occurred 50 times or less per million words. This means that seven connector types were included in the study, viz. *however, instead, nevertheless, though, on the other (hand), still* and *in contrast*. The occurrences of these items were annotated for position according to the classification presented in Section 2.2.

4 Frequency of the Connectors across Registers

Table 6.4 provides the relative frequency per million words of each connector in each register.

In addition to their methodological interest—in determining which connectors are frequent enough to be included in the study—the figures in Table 6.4 are interesting in themselves. In line with Altenberg (1984, 1986), Greenbaum (1969) and Liu (2008), they show that both the total frequencies of connectors and the frequencies of each lexical item vary markedly across registers. Overall, adverbial connectors of contrast are markedly more frequent in the academic articles than in the editorials, which in turn display a much higher

13 Although *yet* is generally viewed as an adverbial connector, it is not included here because it not syntactically mobile, but instead restricted to sentence-initial position (see e.g. Quirk et al., 1985).

TABLE 6.4 *Frequency of the connectors per million words across registers*

Connector	Frequency in LOCRA (pmw)	Frequency in Mult-Ed (pmw)	Frequency in Europarl (pmw)
However	1144	601	737
Instead	178	183	39
Nevertheless	93	83	92
Though	26	163	19
On the other (hand)[14]	101	49	36
Still	67	157	40
In contrast	102	9	3
TOTAL	**1711**	**1245**	**966**

frequency of connectors than the debates.[15] The high frequency of connectors of contrast in academic texts is in line with Conrad (1999), as well as Hyland (1998), who uncovered a very high frequency of textual metadiscourse in a corpus of academic texts. It is also in accordance with the communicative purpose of the register, which seeks to "anticipate possible objections" and "negotiate knowledge" with respect to what has already been said in the relevant field (Hyland, 1998, p. 440). While doing this, authors integrate and position themselves in relation to a variety of different statements, which results in highly polyphonic texts (see Fløttum, Dahl & Kinn, 2006). Connectors of contrast, and more specifically, of concession (e.g. *nevertheless, still, though*), emerge as a valuable resource to do this, as they serve to accept another point of view as true whilst still establishing one's own as the most important one (Fløttum et al., 2006, p. 34), as in example (26) below, where the writer acknowledges and accepts another point of view, but sets up his/her own as the dominant one in this specific context.

14 Interestingly, the proportion of *on the other* vs. *on the other hand* varies across the corpora. The debates contain no occurrences of *on the other* (0/49). In the academic articles *on the other* accounts for no more than 2% of the occurrences of the sequence (4/203). In the editorials, however, 20% of the occurrences of *on the other (hand)* occur in the reduced form (20/98).

15 Admittedly, Table 6.4 does not include all the adverbial connectors in the corpus (since those that do not reach the frequency threshold of 90 pmw do not appear here). However, since all the frequent adverbial connectors are included, the total frequencies are never-

(26) Titmuss's foundational study of blood donation, The Gift Relationship (1997), compared the policy implications of the altruistic unpaid donation of blood under the British National Health Service with the payment of donors in the United States and elsewhere. His conclusion, that a system of unpaid donation was safer because it ruled out the intrusion of commercial interests into blood donation, has, in the light of infected blood scandals set in train by the HIV/AIDS pandemic in France, China, the United Kingdom, and elsewhere proven to be an oversimplification (Baud 2011, Chaveau 2011, Feldman & Bayer 1999, Laqueur 1999, Shao 2006, Shao & Scoggin 2009, Starr 1998). **Nevertheless**, Titmuss's insistence on the importance of attempting to ring-fence a purely altruistic system of blood donation to ensure the safety of transfused blood is worth considering more closely (LOCRA).

In sum, the large proportion of connectors of contrast in the academic subcorpus is in line with the features of the register. What is perhaps more surprising, by contrast, is the comparatively low frequency of those items in the Europarl subcorpus. As explained by Ilie (2003), parliamentary debates are governed by a dialectic process oscillating between cooperativeness and adversariality, between respect of power and struggle for power. Again, markers of concession seem to be an ideal tool in such a communicative situation, therefore we may have expected a greater frequency of connectors of contrast in the parliamentary debates. Finally, the lower frequency of connectors of contrast in the editorials as compared to the academic articles is partly in line with Biber et al. (1999), who find that the news register "uses far fewer linking adverbials than academic prose" (p. 882). For Biber et al. (1999), the explanation for this is that "reports of events are more common and arguments are rarer in news, and thus fewer linking signals are needed than in academic prose" (p. 882). That being said, editorials are only a subpart of the texts included in Biber et al.'s (1999) news register and, as explained in Section 3, are characterised by a strong argumentative component as compared to regular news reports. In fact, in Biber (1988), editorials are found to be one of the two most persuasive registers among a range of 22 genres, and appear to be markedly more persuasive than academic prose. As Biber explains, editorials display typical features of argumentation in that "[s]everal perspectives are considered, with arguments for and against them, but the overall discourse builds towards a final conclu-

theless revealing. It should also be noted that *however*, which is by far more frequent than all the other connectives, plays a large part in the differences observed.

sion and attempts to convince the reader that this conclusion is superior to any other" (p. 150). This description of the type of discourse strategy typically found in editorials is strikingly similar to the definition of concession. Therefore, we may have expected a higher frequency of connectors in the editorial corpus, especially as concessive discourse relations tend to be expressed explicitly: due to their high conceptual complexity, they are very difficult to infer in the absence of an explicit signal, and therefore unlikely to be left implicit (see e.g. Hoek & Zufferey, 2015). Note, however, the comparatively high frequency of the concessive connectors *still* and *though*, in line with the concessive tone of the register.

One possible explanation for the large gap in frequency between research articles and the other two registers might have to do with the use of the coordinator *but*. As the debates are associated with the spoken mode, this register may tend to resort to the coordinator *but* more frequently than adverbs to express a concessive relation. This seems to be the case, as a quick search for *but* returned 2368 occurrences per million words in the research articles, against 3762 in the parliamentary debates (i.e. 1.6 times more).[16] Similarly, the lower frequency of connectors of contrast in editorials as compared to academic prose seems to be compensated by a much more frequent use of *but*, which occurs with a frequency of 5908 per million words (i.e. 2.5 times more than in academic prose). By contrast, in academic writing inter-sentential *but* has long tended to be frowned upon (although this is gradually changing, see Bell, 2007), which might explain why adverbial connectors are preferred in this register.

Another observation emerging from Table 6.4 is that a given connector may be frequent in one register and infrequent in another. For example, *though* is very frequent in the editorials (163 pmw) compared to the research articles (26 pmw) and the debates (19 pmw); *in contrast* is quite frequent in the research articles (102 pmw) while it is infrequent in Mult-Ed (9 pmw) and Europarl (3 pmw). In fact, for most lexical items, two of the three registers pair up in terms of frequency while differing quite markedly from the third register and, strikingly, those pairings change according to the lexical item. *However, in contrast* and *on the other* (*hand*) are used with a similar frequency in the editorials and the debates, but are markedly more frequent in the research articles. For *though* and *still*, the research articles and the debates behave in a similar fashion, while the editorials stand out. Finally, for *instead* similarities are observed between the articles and the editorials, while the debates stand

16 Note that these figures are merely indicative, as the data has not been disambiguated.

out. Therefore, it seems misleading to claim that some registers attract more adverbial connectors of contrast than other registers overall. Although this statement is clearly true (as is clear from the comparison of the totals), it needs to be qualified, as it also appears that some lexical items, such as *though* and *in contrast*, are particularly attracted to specific registers as compared to others. In other words, as noted by Greenbaum (1969, p. 80), connectors seem to act as "style markers", with some individual items being typical of some communicative situations. Others, however, seem to be more stylistically neutral,[17] being (equally) frequent across the three registers investigated (e.g. *nevertheless, however*).

5 Connector Placement and Lexis: Individual Placement Patterns of Adverbial Connectors

Table 6.5 draws the positional profile of each adverbial connector investigated irrespective of register, i.e. for the corpus as a whole. The results are expressed in percent,[18] and the connectors are listed in increasing order of importance of the thematic 1 (i.e. initial) position, argued to be the unmarked position for connectors in the literature. The mean percentage of occurrences for each position was balanced so as not to give more importance to the very frequent connectors.[19]

The first observation emerging from Table 6.5 is that, in line with the statements found in the literature (see Section 1), the thematic 1 (or initial) position does seem to be the dominant position, with five connectors out of seven occurring in that position in more than 50% (and up to 90%) of the cases. Apart from *though* and *still*, at first sight the connectors investigated appear to display similar placement patterns, with a general preference for the thematic 1 position. However, a closer scrutiny of the frequencies of use of each position reveals some clear and statistically significant[20] differences between the seven

17 At least with respect to the registers investigated here; the picture would undoubtedly differ if conversations had been included in the data, for example.

18 See Appendix 1 for the raw frequencies.

19 This was done by adding up, for each position, the percentage of use of each connector in this specific position, and subsequently dividing the number obtained by the number of connectors investigated.

20 Chi-square tests of independence were used to assess the statistical significance of the differences observed. As the comparisons always involved tables of contingency with more than one degree of freedom (larger than 2-by-2 tables), whenever the chi-square

TABLE 6.5 *Placement patterns of connectors of contrast per lexical item (in percent)*

	Thematic 1	Thematic 2	Rhematic 1	Rhematic 2	Rhematic 3	Total
Though	4.7%[21]	7.4%	66.3%	10.6%	11.1%	100% (407 occ.)
Still	34.2%	2.6%	20.2%	43%	0%	100% (228 occ.)
However	56.8%	3%	26.3%	9.6%	4.4%	100% (4521 occ.)
Instead	68.7%	0%	4.6%	20.8%	5.9%	100% (779 occ.)
On the other (hand)	69.4%	0%	30%	0.3%	0.3%	100% (350 occ.)
Nevertheless	70.6%	1.3%	7.7%	17.9%	2.5%	100% (480 occ.)
In contrast	87.1%	0%	11.6%	0.9%	0.4%	100% (225 occ.)
Mean (balanced)	**56%**	**2%**	**23.8%**	**14.7%**	**3.5%**	**100% (6990 occ.)**

lexical items. Firstly, although the thematic 1 position is indeed dominant for most connectors, its importance varies very significantly between lexical items (χ^2=687.9, df = 6, p-value < 0.001): although *instead, on the other hand* and *nevertheless* behave in exactly the same way with respect to this position (post-hoc adjusted p-values = 1 for each pair), the thematic 1 position is used with significantly different frequencies for all the other connectors (post-hoc adjusted p-values = 0 for all the pairs of connectors).

A look at the other two frequent positions, i.e. rhematic 1 and rhematic 2, also reveals some degree of heterogeneity between the lexical items. The mean percentage of use of the rhematic 1 position is 23.8%. While some connectors, such as *however* (26.3%) and *still* (20.2%), behave in a way that is very consistent with this mean (see examples (27) and (28)), others diverge more or less markedly from it. *Instead* and *nevertheless*, for example, are used in rhematic 1 in only 4.6% and 7.7% of the cases respectively. *Though*, by contrast, is used in this position in as much as 66.3% of the cases, as in (29). A similar situation is observed with respect to the rhematic 2 position. While

test returned a significant result for the table as a whole, a post-hoc test was used in order to identify where exactly (i.e. for which pairs) the significant differences occurred in the frequency tables. The correction used was the Holm correction, and the significance threshold was set at 0.01.

21 Thematic 1 uses of *though* only correspond to cases in which the connector is used after another textual Theme, as in: *Still*, **though**, as Mr Chirac made clear, France and Britain also share a broad perspective on the challenges of what he likes to call a "multipolar" world (Mult-Ed).

nevertheless, with 17.6% of its occurrences used in rhematic 2 (see example (30)), is very close to the mean (i.e. 14.7%), we also find connectors which deviate considerably from it: *still* (43%) is used in rhematic 2 considerably more frequently than the mean (see examples (31) and (32)),[22] while *on the other hand* (0.3%) and *in contrast* (0.9%) are used markedly less frequently in this position. A chi-square test reveals significant differences in the use of the rhematic 2 position for most pairs of connectors (χ^2=384, df = 6, p-value < 0.001; post-hoc adjusted p-values < 0.001).[23]

(27) This newspaper has always argued that the cost, not only to the Exchequer but also to our liberties, far outweighs any possible benefits. Tony Blair, **however**, has been persuaded by the Home Secretary that identity cards might be the answer to the Government's own identity crisis (Mult-Ed).

(28) We will not use that word in these harsh economic times but it is not great amounts of money we are talking about. However, that cost **still** has to be borne by the taxpayers and by the Member States (Europarl).

(29) The SNP had a good 1990s, steadily increasing its share of the Scottish vote and boosting its toll of seats at Westminster and Strasbourg on a tide of rising national confidence as the Tory years came to an end. Devolution, **though**, has made the going tougher for the advocates of independence in both Scotland and Wales (Mult-Ed).

(30) The goal-setting theory states that goal specificity alone does not necessarily lead to high performance because specific goals vary in difficulty (Locke and Latham 2002). Specific goals are **nevertheless** important because they reduce the variance in performance by minimising

---

22 Interestingly, when *still* is used in rhematic 1 and rhematic 2 positions, it is very frequently accompanied by another marker of contrast (*but, however, even if*), as is the case in examples (28), (31) and (32). This type of co-occurrence is intriguing, and we may wonder whether the presence of another connective of contrast at the beginning of the clause may explain, at least partly, why *still* is placed sentence-medially. Also, when used sentence-medially, *still* was often fairly ambiguous, in the sense that it often expressed both contrast and temporality simultaneously; the meaning of *still* was much more clear-cut when the connector occurred in thematic 1 position (see Dupont, 2015 for a discussion).

23 Except for the following pairs (i.e. 4 out of 21 pairs): *instead* vs. *nevertheless* (post-hoc adjusted p = 0.72); *in contrast* vs. *on the other hand* (post-hoc adjusted p = 1), *however* vs. *though* (post-hoc adjusted p = 1) and *though* and *nevertheless* (post-hoc adjusted p =0.011).

role ambiguity and improving the clarity of the performance expected (Wright, Moynihan, and Pandey 2012) (LOCRA).

(31) It is not that long ago that a decision was reached on this but it was **still** seven or eight years ago (Europarl).

(32) His accusation was false, but it was **still** accompanied by a shocking internet smear campaign that caused considerable distress. (Mult-Ed)

So far, we have examined the adverbial positions separately, identifying the divergences between the connectors for a specific slot. However, the fact that two connectors display the same behaviour in one position in particular does not mean that they display the same patterns of placement overall. For example, although *instead* and *on the other hand* are strikingly similar in their use of the thematic 1 position (ca. 69% of the occurrences in both cases, see examples (33) and (34)), they differ significantly in their use of the rhematic positions, with *on the other hand* preferring the rhematic 1 position (30% vs. 4.6% for *instead*; post-hoc adjusted p=0; see example (35)) and *instead* preferring the rhematic 2 slot (20.8% vs. 0.3% for *on the other hand*; post-hoc adjusted p=0; see example (36)).

(33) We do not test the hypothesis that every parent or every teacher evaluates schools in a certain way. **Instead**, we are concerned with the question of whether aggregated parent and teacher evaluations can be useful indicators of school performance (LOCRA).

(34) Charles (fake name) was the person with the highest mean level of explanations (2.65) in this group, but his mean level of questions (2.29) ranked the second lowest. **On the other hand**, Vincent (fake name) had the highest mean level of questions (2.90), but his mean level of explanations (1.50) ranked the second lowest. (LOCRA).

(35) Morality expresses the most fundamental beliefs, but does not necessarily provide a means for resolving practical dilemmas. Ethics, **on the other hand**, does not only relate to beliefs but also to the way people determine how to act in practice (LOCRA).

(36) The truth is that there is no villain. There is **instead** a dilemma, admittedly a truly difficult one, which most destination countries have failed to fully address (Mult-Ed).

To conclude, the variation observed above demonstrates that connectors of contrast tend to display their own idiosyncratic placement patterns: in line with previous studies such as Altenberg (2006), each connector appears to have its own placement profile. Our corpus results thus clearly confirm the key role played by lexis in adverbial connector placement.

Finally, in light of the statements found in the reference literature, the positional patterns uncovered for *still* and *though* prove very surprising. While *still* is generally cited by descriptive grammars as one of the connectors that are restricted to initial position (see e.g. Quirk et al., 1972, 1985), the results show that it is actually used in this position in only about 35% of the cases (i.e. significantly less frequently than most other connectors), and tends to prefer the rhematic 2 position (43%; see examples (31) and (32) above). Similarly, while *though* is usually said to typically occur in final position, the results reveal that this is not the case, with only 11.1% of rhematic 3 uses, and an overwhelming majority of rhematic 1 uses (although *though* is the most frequent connector in rhematic 3), as in example (29) above.[24] In other words, the statements on the individual placement patterns of connectors found in the literature (and, more particularly, in descriptive grammars) are not confirmed by the corpus data analysed here.

6 Connector Placement across Registers

The second main objective of this study is to assess the impact of register on the placement patterns of adverbial connectors of contrast. Table 6.6 provides the frequency of use of each position per register in percent, independently of lexis (see Appendix 2 for the raw frequencies).

The most striking result emerging from Table 6.6 is that, while the thematic 1 position is clearly dominant in the debates (70.9%) and the research articles (65.5%), in the editorials it only accounts for about a third of the occurrences (i.e. 36.3%). In other words, thematic 1 connectors are nearly half as frequent in the editorials as in the other two registers. The differences in frequency of use of the thematic 1 position across registers are very significant (χ^2=591, df=2, p-value < 0.001; post-hoc adjusted p-values: LOCRA vs. Mult-Ed: p=0; Mult-Ed vs. Europarl: p=0; LOCRA vs. Europarl: $p < 0.001$). In fact, unlike the other two

24 Note that, when making claims about the position of *though*, the literature probably has speech in mind, in which situation the final slot may indeed be the dominant position (see Conrad, 1999, p. 13).

TABLE 6.6 *Adverbial connector placement across registers*

	Europarl	LOCRA	Mult-Ed
Thematic 1	70.9%	65.2%	36.3%
Thematic 2	2%	2.2%	3.5%
Rhematic 1	9.6%	21%	38.3%
Rhematic 2	15.8%	8.5%	14.5%
Rhematic 3	1.8%	3.2%	7.6%
Total	100% (1314 occ.)	100% (3414 occ.)	100% (2262 occ.)

registers, the editorials display not one but two important positions, with a roughly equal distribution of the connectors between the thematic 1 (36.3%) and rhematic 1 (38.3%) positions. The results reveal that the importance of the rhematic 1 position is highly variable across registers: it is quite infrequent in the debates (9.6%), fairly common in academic prose (21%), and even more frequent in the editorials. The quantitative differences in use of the rhematic 1 position are also statistically significant (χ^2=414, df=2, p-value < 0.001; post-hoc adjusted p-values: LOCRA vs. Mult-Ed: p=0; Mult-Ed vs. Europarl: p=0; LOCRA vs. Europarl: p=0). Significant differences in the use of the rhematic 2 and rhematic 3 positions are also uncovered, although they are less striking.

The results thus provide conclusive evidence of the impact of register on the placement patterns of adverbial connectors of contrast: depending on the communicative situation, writers tend to place connectors in different positions in the sentence. In addition, while the statements made in the reference grammars with respect to the initial position hold true in some communicative situations, they are not true across the board, as in the editorials the thematic 1 position is not strictly dominant. Rather, editorials have a marked tendency to use connectors rhematically. Note, however, that since *however* is by far the most frequent connector in all three corpora, the percentages presented in Table 6.6 are to some extent skewed due to the weight of *however* on these figures. In order to get a more accurate and nuanced picture of connector placement, in Section 7 the phenomenon is investigated from the angles of both lexis and register simultaneously.

7 The Combined Impact of Lexis and Register on Connector Placement

So far, lexis and register have been examined separately, and it was demonstrated that both factors have an impact on the placement patterns of adverbial connectors of contrast. In this section, we will consider the possible interaction between lexis and register in influencing connector placement, a factor which, to my knowledge, has not yet been considered in the literature. We will also try to discover whether one factor seems to be more influential than the other as regards connector placement. Tables 6.7 to 6.13 provide the placement patterns of each connector per register.

TABLE 6.7 *Placement patterns of* still *across registers*

	LOCRA	Mult-Ed	Europarl
Thematic 1	33%	41.6%	22.2%
Thematic 2	5.2%	0%	0%
Rhematic 1	23.5%	14.3%	22.2%
Rhematic 2	38.3%	44.2%	55.6%
Rhematic 3	0%	0%	0%
Total (raw)	115	77	36

TABLE 6.8 *Placement patterns of* instead *across registers*

	LOCRA	Mult-Ed	Europarl
Thematic 1	70.7%	67%	66.8%
Thematic 2	0%	0%	0%
Rhematic 1	8.1%	1.4%	3.7%
Rhematic 2	19.6%	21.8%	22.2%
Rhematic 3	1.7%	9.8%	7.4%
Total (raw)	358	367	54

TABLE 6.9 *Placement patterns of* nevertheless *across registers*

	LOCRA	Mult-Ed	Europarl
Thematic 1	70.4%	64.7%	78.7%
Thematic 2	0%	2.4%	1.6%
Rhematic 1	10.2%	6%	6.3%
Rhematic 2	17.2%	23.4%	11.8%
Rhematic 3	2.2%	3.6%	1.6%
Total (raw)	**186**	**167**	**127**

TABLE 6.10 *Placement patterns of* in contrast *across registers*

	LOCRA	Mult-Ed	Europarl
Thematic 1	88.4%	70.6%	75%
Thematic 2	0%	0%	0%
Rhematic 1	10.8%	17.6%	25%
Rhematic 2	0.5%	5.9%	0%
Rhematic 3	0%	5.9%	0%
Total (raw)	**204**	**17**	**4**

TABLE 6.11 *Placement patterns of* on the other (hand) *across registers*

	LOCRA	Mult-Ed	Europarl
Thematic 1	69%	59.2%	91.8%
Thematic 2	0%	0%	0%
Rhematic 1	30.5%	40.8%	6.1%
Rhematic 2	0%	0%	2%
Rhematic 3	0.5%	0%	0%
Total (raw)	**203**	**98**	**49**

TABLE 6.12 *Placement patterns of* however *across registers*

	LOCRA	Mult-Ed	Europarl
Thematic 1	64.6%	28.9%	72.5%
Thematic 2	2.6%	4.2%	2.3%
Rhematic 1	23%	46.9%	9.1%
Rhematic 2	6%	11.9%	14.8%
Rhematic 3	3.8%	8%	1.3%
Total (raw)	**2295**	**1208**	**1018**

TABLE 6.13 *Placement patterns of* though *across registers*

	LOCRA	Mult-Ed	Europarl
Thematic 1	1.9%	5.2%	3.8%
Thematic 2	15.1%	6.4%	3.8%
Rhematic 1	54.7%	70.1%	42.3%
Rhematic 2	9.4%	8.8%	34.6%
Rhematic 3	18.9%	9.5%	15.4%
Total (raw)	**53**	**328**	**26**

Two main types of placement profiles emerge from these tables. On the one hand, some connectors display fairly stable placement patterns across registers: no statistically significant differences are found between their positional patterns across registers. This is the case of *still*, *instead* and *nevertheless*.[25] In other words, those connectors appear to display strong lexical priming (see Hoey, 2005),[26] since lexis seems to be the most important factor determining their position. They have a fixed placement profile that seems to be independent of register. Other connectors, by contrast, exhibit variable positional patterns across registers: depending on the register in which they appear, they occupy

25 *In contrast* also seems to belong to that category, but due to its very low frequency in Europarl, no clear conclusions can be drawn about the cross-register patterning of this connector.

26 Hoey's theory of lexical priming postulates that each lexical item has a well-defined, idiosyncratic set of features in terms of collocation, colligation, semantic and pragmatic associations, stylistic features, position in the sentence, etc.

the various positions with significantly different frequencies across registers. This is the case of *however, on the other* (*hand*) and *though*.[27] Those connectors, in addition to some degree of lexical priming (e.g. *though* does seem to avoid the thematic 1 slot across the board), thus display what we might call strong stylistic priming,[28] as their placement patterns vary depending on the communicative situation in which they are used. Thus, for example, while (37) exemplifies a typical use of *however* in Europarl, in Mult-Ed the most typical use of *however* is illustrated by (38). LOCRA displays frequent instances of both, although with a marked preference for thematic 1 uses. Interestingly, *though* appears within the range of stylistically-primed connectors, which is surprising in view of the fact that it is generally presented by reference grammars as a typical example of a lexically-primed connector, distinctively prioritising final position.

(37) I note with satisfaction that Mr Medina Ortega's report largely supports the approach proposed by the Commission. **However**, he considers it regrettable that the measure proposed is reserved to a limited number of products and that it does not refer to the legal basis provided by Article 299(2) of the Treaty (Europarl).

(38) If the destabilisation of eastern Ukraine intensifies, tougher sanctions will be necessary. In present circumstances, **however**, the west ought to turn its attention to two other tasks (Mult-Ed).

Those results show that lexis and register do not seem to influence placement independently of each other, but instead appear to have a combined effect on connector placement. These two factors are therefore really worth investigating together: the difference between lexically- and stylistically-primed connectors

27 *Though* is a borderline case. The most striking differences between registers for this connector pertain to the rhematic 1 position. While, for this position, the *p*-value for the contingency table as a whole is statistically significant (χ^2=12, df=2, *p*-value=0.002), and therefore allows us to categorise this connector as a stylistically-primed one, the pairwise comparison by means of the post-hoc test does not make it possible to identify exactly where the significant differences occur (post-hoc adjusted *p*-values: LOCRA vs. Mult-Ed=0.08; LOCRA vs. Europarl=0.4; Mult-Ed vs. Europarl=0.02). This is probably due to the fact that the number of occurrences of *though* was fairly limited in LOCRA and Europarl. This is also due to the adoption of a 0.01 significance threshold, as a 0.05 threshold would have pointed to a significant difference between Mult-Ed and Europarl.

28 Special thanks to my supervisor Prof. Sylviane Granger for suggesting this term.

can only emerge by looking at both factors simultaneously. When lexis and register were considered separately in Sections 5 and 6, the interaction between the two factors went completely unnoticed. Finally, from these results, it does not seem to be the case that one of the two factors (i.e. lexis and register) is intrinsically more influential on placement than the other. The answer to this question seems to be dependent on the lexical item: while some items are lexically-primed, others are mostly stylistically-primed.

Against this backdrop, it is interesting to investigate the reasons why the placement patterns of some connectors vary across register, while those of others do not. One possible explanation has to do with the discourse effects achieved by connectors in particular positions (see Altenberg, 2006; Dupont, 2015; Lenker, 2010, 2011, 2014). In certain positions connectors perform discourse functions pertaining to information and thematic structure in addition to their regular linking function. Connectors used initially (thematic 1), as in (39), usually perform a strictly linking function. Rhematic 1 connectors, by contrast, in addition to signalling a link between two clauses, also have the effect of emphasising a fronted topical Theme, and of highlighting a topical shift in discourse. This is what happens in example (40), where the rhematic 1 connector clearly marks off the topical Theme (*After the demise of the revolution in 1990*), thus granting it more attention than if it had been fully integrated in the rest of the sentence. In addition, the rhematic 1 connector in (40) lays focus on a change in topical Theme happening between the first sentence, which is concerned with the 1970s, and the second one, which deals with the year 1990.

(39) The Commission agrees with the honourable Member that women are still under-represented at the higher levels of management in the Commission as well, indeed, as in other institutions. **However** I have to say with the very greatest respect to the honourable Lady that it is not accurate to say that women are excluded from those posts (Europarl).

(40) Starting in the 1970s, women enjoyed an unprecedented level of involvement in civil society, notably in community health committees (Garfield and Williams 1992). After the demise of the revolution in 1990, **however**, even militant Sandinista women began to feel drawn back into domesticity (LOCRA).

Rhematic 2 connectors also have the capacity to create discourse effects. As Lenker (2011) explains, they tend to emphasise not the Theme, but the Rheme of the sentence, by creating what Taglicht (1984, p. 20) refers to as a "marked Rheme" (see Section 2.1). A marked Rheme is a Rheme which, by being detached from the rest of the sentence, is granted more focus than it would have in the normal, uninterrupted sequence. An example of rhematic 2 connector creating a marked Rheme is provided in (41).

(41) We have received a number of important additions to the text. We have now given consumers seven working days in which to change their minds. They are going to be properly informed when they are going to be sent substitute goods. They are going to be reimbursed if they change their minds and they have the right to full reimbursement if the supplier goes bankrupt or fails to perform the service involved. Those are marvellous points and [...] they add up to a real degree of protection. There remains, **however**, the problem of financial services (Europarl).

A second effect of rhematic connectors is that they tend to act as partitions between given information and new information, i.e. to signal explicitly the boundary between what the reader already knows, and the genuinely new informational contribution of the sentence (see also Lenker, 2011). This is the case in example (41), in which what follows the connector adds a new point (i.e. *the problem of financial services*) to the components that were previously discussed. Another telling example is (42), in which we clearly see that what precedes the connector is taken to be known by the reader (with the determiner *this*), and what follows it provides the new information.

(42) This weaker support for the positive effect of issue linkage is, **however**, unsurprising (LOCRA)

Therefore, in examples (39) to (42), the same connector *however* achieves a different set of discourse functions depending on its position in the sentence. Interestingly, the two positions that are most apt to fulfil discourse effects (i.e. rhematic 1 and 2) are precisely those that have been overlooked in systemic functional research, which has mostly focused on the Theme and, on rare occasions, on the final part of the Rheme (see Section 2.1).

In view of this, we could postulate that the connectors displaying variable patterns of placement across registers might have a greater ability than the other connectors to create specific discourse effects in accordance with the communicative goals of a particular register. In other words, the greater mobility of stylistically-primed connectors across registers might be indicative of their capacity to better adapt to the communicative purposes of a given register than lexically-primed connectors. Stylistically-primed connectors may thus be said to be somewhat polyfunctional, while purely lexically-primed connectors would tend to be more monofunctional: due to a fixed positional profile, they are seemingly less apt to serve the rhetorical needs of the register in which they are used. Granted that this is the case, the editorial corpus seems to have a greater tendency to take advantage of the polyfunctionality of stylistically-primed connectors than the other two registers, since it often uses them in rhematic 1 positions (see e.g. Table 6.12 with *however*), and much less frequently in thematic 1—a discursively more neutral position—than the debates and the research articles. At this stage, however, this remains a hypothesis and needs to be further investigated.

8 Conclusion

This paper has emphasised the importance of taking both lexis and register into account when describing adverbial connector placement. The results have demonstrated an interaction between lexis and register, and have brought to light two major types of positional profiles for connectors: lexically-primed connectors, whose placement patterns are stable across registers; and stylistically-primed connectors, whose positional patterns vary depending on the register in which they are used. Lexically-primed connectors appeared to be rather monofunctional, while stylistically-primed connectors were associated with a greater ability to perform specific discourse effects in relation to the communicative goals of the register in which they were used, and thus with some degree of polyfunctionality. These findings add new perspectives to the previous statements about connector placement, and suggest that grammars of English should include more detailed descriptions, balanced with reflections about lexis and register. At the very least, it might be worth drawing attention to the ability of some connectors to fulfil various discourse effects according to their position, as such information could constitute a valuable resource for writers.

From a more theoretical perspective, the results demonstrate the usefulness of making distinctions within the Rheme. Failing to make distinctions within the rhematic part of the sentence would have left some interesting differences between lexical items and registers unnoticed. Subdividing the Rheme seems all the more relevant as the various rhematic positions were shown not to be equivalent in terms of the discourse effects that they produce. More generally, the findings illustrate the fruitful synergy between SFL and corpus linguistics. The corpus analysis made clear that, in its current state, the somewhat basic SFL system of thematic structure (with the Rheme viewed a one single unit) does not offer the necessary tools to provide a detailed account of the placement patterns of English connectors of contrast. Based on the corpus data, it was possible to adapt and refine the SFL system of thematic structure, so as to make it more apt to account for connector placement patterns in authentic language use. SFL in turn benefited corpus linguistics by providing the necessary theoretical tools to interpret (some of) the corpus results, as some of the placement patterns of adverbial connectors could be accounted for with reference to the SFL systems of thematic (Theme and Rheme) and information structure (given and new). This study therefore provides a good example of the ways in which "corpus data can inform and shape the [systemic functional] theory, and the theory can inform and give shape to the corpus data" (Halliday, 2006, p. 295).

Although this study provides some insights into the role played by lexis and register on connector placement, there is still much scope for follow-up research on this topic. Lexis and register are most probably not the only factors which influence placement. For instance, it would be interesting to see whether placement varies according to the subtype of contrast (i.e. opposition, correction or concession) expressed by a given connector. Another phenomenon that might be worth investigating is the patterns of co-occurrence of the connectors studied, in order to determine whether the tendency of some connectors to co-occur with other markers of contrast (e.g. *but ... still; but ... nevertheless*) has an impact on the position in which they are used.

References

Alonso Belmonte, M. (2007). Newspaper editorials and comment articles: A "Cinderella" genre? *Rivista Electrónica de Linguística Aplicada, 1*, 1–9.

Altenberg, B. (1984). Causal linking in spoken and written English. *Studia Linguistica, 38*(1), 20–69. DOI: 10.1111/j.1467-9582.1984.tb00734.x

Altenberg, B. (1986). Contrastive linking in spoken and written English. In G. Tottie & I. Bäckland (Eds.), *English in speech and writing. A symposium* (pp. 13–40). Uppsala: Acta Universitatis Upsaliensis.

Altenberg, B. (1998). Connectors and sentence openings in English and Swedish. In S. Johansson & S. Oksefjell (Eds.), *Corpora and cross-linguistic research: Theory, method, and case studies* (pp. 115–143). Amsterdam: Rodopi.

Altenberg, B. (2006). The function of adverbial connectors in second initial position in English and Swedish. In K. Aijmer & A.-M. Simon-Vandenbergen (Eds.), *Pragmatic markers in contrast* (pp. 11–37). Oxford: Elsevier.

Altenberg, B., & Tapper, M. (1998). The use of adverbial connectors in advanced Swedish learners' written English. In S. Granger (Ed.), *Learner English on computer* (pp. 80–93). London: Longman.

Bell, D. (2007). Sentence-initial *and* and *but* in academic writing. *Pragmatics, 17*(2), 183–201. DOI: 10.1075/prag.17.2.01bel

Biber, D. (1988). *Variation across speech and writing*. Cambridge University Press. DOI: http://dx.doi.org/10.1017/CBO9780511621024

Biber, D., Johansson, S., Leech, G., Conrad, S., & Finegan, E. (1999). *Longman grammar of spoken and written English*. London: Longman.

Bloor, T., & Bloor, M. (2004). *The functional analysis of English. A Hallidayan approach*. London: Arnold.

Cartoni, B., & Meyer, T. (2012). Extracting directional and comparable corpora from a multilingual corpus for translation studies. *Proceedings of the eighth Language Resources and Evaluation Conference* (LREC), Istanbul.

Castagnoli, S. (2009). *Regularities and variations in learner's translations. A corpus-based study of conjunctive explicitation*. (Unpublished doctoral dissertation). University of Pisa, Pisa.

Chalker, S. (1996). *Collins Cobuild English guides. 9: Linking words*. Glasgow: Harper Collins Publishers.

Conrad, S. (1999). The importance of corpus-based research for language teachers. *System, 27*, 1–18. DOI: 10.1016/S0346–251X(98)00046-3

Dupont, M. (2015). Word order in English and French. The position of English and French adverbial connectors of contrast. *English Text Construction, 8*(1), 88–124. DOI: 10.1075/etc.8.1.04dup

Field, Y., & Yip, L. (1992). A comparison of internal conjunctive cohesion in the English essay writing of Cantonese speakers and native speakers of English. *RELC Journal, 23*(1), 15–28. DOI: 10.1177/003368829202300102

Fløttum, K., Dahl, T., & Kinn, T. (2006). *Academic voices across languages and disciplines*. Amsterdam: John Benjamins. DOI: 10.1075/pbns.148

Foolen, A. (1991). Polyfunctionality and the semantics of adversative conjunctions. *Multilingua, 10*, 79–92.

Fries, P. (1994). On theme, rheme and discourse goals. In M. Coulthard (Ed.), *Advances in written text analysis* (pp. 229–249). London: Routledge.

Granger, S. (2014). A lexical bundle approach to comparing languages. Stems in English and French. *Languages in Contrast, 14*(1), 58–72. DOI: 10.1075/lic.14.1.04gra

Granger, S., & Tyson, S. (1996). Connector usage in the English essay writing of native and non-native EFL speakers of English. *World Englishes, 15*(1), 17–27. DOI: 10.1111/j.1467–971X.1996.tb00089.x

Greenbaum, S. (1969). *Studies in English adverbial usage*. London: Longman.

Gregory, M., & Carroll, S. (1978). *Language and situation: Language varieties and their social contexts*. London: Routledge.

Halliday, M.A.K. (1991). Corpus studies and probabilistic grammar. In K. Aijmer & B. Altenberg (Eds.), *English corpus linguistics: Studies in honour of Jan Svartvik* (pp. 30–43). London: Longman.

Halliday, M.A.K. (2006). Afterwords. In G. Thompson & S. Hunston (Eds.), *System and corpus: Exploring connections* (pp. 293–299). London: Equinox.

Halliday, M.A.K., & Hasan, R. (1976). *Cohesion in English*. London: Longman.

Halliday, M.A.K., & Matthiessen, C. (2004). *An introduction to functional grammar*. London: Hodder Arnold.

Hannay, M., & Gómez-González, M. (2013). Thematic parentheticals in Dutch and English. In M. Taboada, S. Doval Suárez & E. González Álvarez (Eds.), *Contrastive discourse analysis. Functional and corpus perspectives* (pp. 94–122). London: Equinox. DOI: 10.1558/lhs.v6i1–3.99

Hasselgård, H. (2004). The role of multiple themes in cohesion. In K. Aijmer & A.-B. Stenström (Eds.), *Discourse patterns in spoken and written corpora* (pp. 65–87). Amsterdam: John Benjamins. DOI: 10.1075/pbns.120.06has

Hasselgård, H. (2010). *Adjunct adverbials in English*. Cambridge: Cambridge University Press. DOI: 10.1017/cbo9780511676253

Hoek, J., & Zufferey, S. (2015). Factors influencing the implicitation of discourse relations across languages. In H. Bunt (Ed.), *Proceedings of the 11th Joint ACL—ISO Workshop on Interoperable Semantic Annotation* (pp. 39–45). Tilburg: Tilburg Center for Cognition and Communication.

Hoey, M. (2005). *Lexical priming. A new theory of words and language*. London & New York: Routledge. DOI: 10.4324/9780203327630

Hyland, K. (1998). Persuasion and context: The pragmatics of academic metadiscourse. *Journal of Pragmatics, 30*, 437–455. DOI: 10.1016/S0378–2166(98)00009-5

Ilie, C. (2003). Discourse and metadiscourse in parliamentary debates. *Journal of Language and Politics, 2*(1), 71–92. DOI: 10.1075/jlp.2.1.05ili

Izutsu, M. (2008). Contrast, concessive and corrective: Toward a comprehensive study of opposition relations. *Journal of Pragmatics*, 40, 646–675. DOI: 10.1016/j.pragma.2007.07.001

Jacobson, S. (1964). *Adverbial positions in English*. Stockholm: Studentbok.

Knott, A. (1996). *A data-driven methodology for motivating a set of coherence relations*. (Unpublished doctoral dissertation). University of Edinburgh, Edinburgh.

Kunz, K., & Lapshinova-Koltunski, E. (2014). Cohesive conjunctions in English and German: Systemic contrasts and textual differences. In L. Vandelanotte, K. Davidse, C. Gentens & D. Kimps (Eds.), *Recent advances in corpus linguistics: Developing and exploiting corpora* (pp. 229–262). Amsterdam: Rodopi.

Leech, G., & Svartvik, J. (1994). *A communicative grammar of English*. London: Longman.

Lenker, I. (2010). *Argument and rhetoric. Adverbial connectors in the history of English*. Berlin: Mouton de Gruyter.

Lenker, U. (2011). A focus on adverbial connectors: Connecting, partitioning and focusing attention in the history of English. In A. Meurmann-Solin & U. Lenker (Eds.),

Connectives in synchrony and diachrony in European languages. Helsinki: VARIENG. Retrieved from: http://www.helsinki.fi/varieng/series/volumes/08/lenker/. Last accessed 14 June 2016.

Lenker, U. (2014). Knitting and splitting information. Medial placement of linking adverbials in the history of English. In S. Pfenninger, O. Timofeeva, A.-C. Gardner, A. Honkapohja, M. Hundt & D. Schreier (Eds.), *Contact, variation and change in the history of English* (pp. 11–37). Amsterdam: John Benjamins.

Liu, D. (2008). Linking adverbials. An across-register corpus study and its implications. *International Journal of Corpus Linguistics, 13*(4), 491–518. DOI: 10.1075/ijcl.13.4.05liu

Morel, M.-A., & Danon-Boileau, L. (1998). *Grammaire de l'intonation. L'exemple du français oral*. Paris: Ophrys.

Nisioi, S., Rabinovich, E., Dinu, L., & Wintner, S. (2016). A corpus of native, non-native and translated texts. *Proceedings of the 10th Language and Resources Evaluation Conference (LREC)*, Porotrož.

Paquot, M. (2010). *Academic vocabulary in learner writing*. London: Continuum.

Prasad, R., Joshi, A., & Webber, B. (2010). Realization of discourse relations by other means: Alternative Lexicalizations. *Coling2010: Poster volume*. Beijing, August 2010, 1023–1031.

Quirk, R., Greenbaum, S., Leech, G., & Svartvik, J. (1972). *A grammar of contemporary English*. London: Longman.

Quirk, R., Greenbaum, S., Leech, G., & Svartvik, J. (1985). *A comprehensive grammar of the English language*. London: Longman.

Rudolph, E. (1996). *Contrast: Adversative and concessive expressions on sentence and text level*. Berlin: Mouton de Gruyter.

Scott, M. (2012). *WordSmith Tools 6* [computer software]. Liverpool: Lexical Analysis Software.

Taboada, M., & Gómez-González, M. (2012). Discourse markers and coherence relations: Comparison across markers, languages and modalities. *Language and the Human Sciences, 6*, 17–41. DOI: 10.1558/lhs.v6i1–3.17

Taglicht, J. (1984). *Message and emphasis. On focus and scope in English*. London: Longman.

Tankó, G. (2004). The use of adverbial connectors in Hungarian university students' argumentative essays. In J. Sinclair (Ed.), *How to use corpora in language teaching* (pp. 157–181). Amsterdam: John Benjamins. DOI: 10.1075/scl.12.13tan

Thompson, G. (2014). *Introducing functional grammar*. London & New York: Routledge.

Thompson, G., & Hunston, S. (Eds.) (2006). *System and corpus: Exploring connections*. London: Equinox.

Appendix 1. Placement Patterns of Connectors of Contrast per Lexical Item (Raw Frequencies)

	Thematic 1	Thematic 2	Rhematic 1	Rhematic 2	Rhematic 3	Total
Though	19	30	270	43	45	407
Still	78	6	46	98	0	228
However	2570	134	1188	432	197	4521
Instead	535	0	36	162	46	779
On the other hand	243	0	105	1	1	350
Nevertheless	339	6	37	86	12	480
In contrast	196	0	26	2	1	225
Total	3980	176	1708	824	302	6990

Appendix 2. Adverbial Connector Placement across Registers (Raw Frequencies)

	Europarl	LOCRA	Mult-Ed
Thematic 1	931	2227	822
Thematic 2	26	74	76
Rhematic 1	126	716	866
Rhematic 2	208	289	327
Rhematic 3	23	108	171
Total	1314	3414	2262

CHAPTER 7

Towards a Model of Co-collocation Analysis: Theory, Methodology, and Preliminary Results*

Moisés Almela and Pascual Cantos

1 Introduction

In corpus linguistics collocation is one of the primary sources of information for lexical semantic analysis. The search for distributional correlates of semantic properties is widely established as a fundamental methodological strategy in the discipline. At the same time, there is a general sense that the methods for filtering contextual information and selecting the relevant co-occurrence patterns need further improvement (Evert, 2009; Gries, 2013).

Although the extraction and analysis of collocations involves making decisions on several parameters (frequency threshold, collocation statistics, span, etc.), so far most of the efforts for developing a better methodology have been centred on the measure of lexical association. The result of these research efforts has been an extensive list of collocation statistics (t-score, z-score, MI, MI2, MI3, log-likelihood, logDice, *ΔP*, etc.) and the development of methods for their evaluation (Evert, 2005, 2009; Evert & Krenn, 2005). The question about the optimal collocational span has also been an object of inquiry and discussion (Mason, 2000), although to a lesser extent than the choice of collocation statistics. Other contributions have led to the addition of new dimensions of collocation analysis not taken into account in the received models, such as directionality and dispersion (Gries, 2013) or connectivity (Brezina et al., 2015).

An aspect of corpus collocational research that has remained virtually unrevised over the years—even over decades—is the node-collocate distinction. In the received models collocational relations are articulated in binary structures. This implies, among other things, that any member of a collocation must be either the node (i.e. the input term) or one of its collocates (statistically sig-

* The research we present here is framed in a project (Ref. FFI2012-38724) funded by the Spanish Ministry of Economy and Competitiveness. We are thankful for the support provided.

 | DOI: 10.1163/9789004361133_009

nificant co-occurrences of the node), and that any expansion of collocational relations into larger structures is derived from the concatenation of prior node-collocate pairs.

This paper takes issue with the node-collocate dualism and explores ways in which considering more complex forms of collocational association among words can help us arrive at more accurate descriptions of the semantic relations existing between a node and its lexical contexts. The goal of this paper is to explain the theoretical and methodological proposal that has resulted from this project and to illustrate its applicability with the analysis of some examples.

2 The Problem of Inter-collocational Dependency

Although the existence of correspondences between collocation and meaning is a well-established finding in corpus lexical studies, limitations and difficulties reported in previous research suggest that the mapping between collocates and semantic properties of the node cannot always be performed in a one-to-one fashion, and that it involves some complexities that cannot be adequately captured by the standard methods of collocation extraction and description.

One of the problems that complicate the mapping of collocates and meaning components is related to the attraction that the collocates of the node exert on other words occurring in the same textual window as the node. Stubbs (1995) pointed to this problem in a seminal article in which he examined the efficacy of three different association measures. In that article Stubbs concluded, among other things, that the lemma CAUSE is imbued with the negative semantic profile derived from an overwhelmingly large group of its collocates (e.g., *accident, poverty, death, illness*, etc.). However, he also observed that the collocational relations associated with the collocates themselves—and not directly with the node—pose a problem to the method of collocational description employed:

> The frequent collocation with *great* is partly due to phrases such as *cause for great concern*. Similarly, a frequent collocate of CAUSE is *driving*, not because the words directly collocate, but because of the phrase *reckless driving*, which in turn occurs in phrases such as *death caused by reckless driving*. Another collocate is *natural*: due to occurrences of *death from natural causes*. Another is *grievous*: due to *cause grievous bodily harm*. Another is *irreparable*: due to *cause irreparable damage*. Another is *untold*, due to phrases such as *cause untold damage / death and destruc-*

> *tion / heartache / misery / pain*. Such inter-collocations are beyond the scope of the method discussed here.
>
> STUBBS, 1995, pp. 44–45

Although the majority of collocates of CAUSE provides a reliable access to its meaning, some of its properties, particularly its negative semantic profile, can be obfuscated by the presence of collocates such as *driving, great*, or *natural*, which do not connote unpleasant things and are attracted to other collocates of CAUSE rather than being directly attracted to CAUSE itself. The existence of such inter-collocations[1] is an obstacle to the semantic description of CAUSE. Unless they are detected, they can distort our conclusions about the semantic properties of the node.

Almela (2011a) identified a similar problem in the collocational environment of the noun *incidence*. According to that study, the most statistically significant collocates of *incidence* can be classified into three broad conceptual groups: (1) magnitude (*high, increase, decrease, statistics, average*, etc.), (2) trouble/negativity (*sickness, disease, attack, stroke, problem, poverty, crime, violence*, etc.), and (3) anatomy (*heart, breast, skin, lung, dental*, etc.). Of the three groups, only (1) and (2) can be directly mapped onto specific components in the semantic structure of *incidence*, whose prototypical meaning can be paraphrased as 'the frequency with which something undesirable happens'. Collocates of group (3), referring to parts of the body (usually the human body), are attracted to the textual window of *incidence* not because of the influence directly exerted by *incidence*, but because of collocations with other collocates of *incidence*: (*incidence of*) *coronary heart disease/dental caries/skin cancer*, etc.

Thus, we know from previous research that some cases of *undesired* or potentially *misleading* collocation can be explained as by-products of INTER-COLLOCATIONAL DEPENDENCY, i.e. of situations in which the syntagmatic attraction between a node and a collocate is not self-contained, in the sense that it is a function not only of the relation between the node and the collocate but also of the influence exerted by other collocates of the same node—in

1 The term inter-collocation has also been used to refer to cases in which collocational attraction is observed in the two directions of a relationship between two given words—logically, this specification is necessary only in those cases in which the measure of association is sensitive to directionality. However, we think that the term RECIPROCAL COLLOCATION (or even BIDIRECTIONAL COLLOCATION) would provide a more accurate description of such cases of bidirectionality, while the term inter-collocation is best reserved for denoting relations of lexical association across different collocations, such as those described by Stubbs (1995) above.

other words, the strength of lexical association between the two members of the collocation is underdetermined by the internal structure of the collocation.

There are, in addition to undesired collocates, other effects of inter-collocational dependency. Some of them have been pointed out by Almela et al. (2013). Consider, for example, the following collocations with the noun *decision*: *face a decision, wise decision, tough decision*. The words *face, wise* and *tough* are relevant collocates of *decision*. The three of them are statistically significant co-occurrences of this noun and they are relevant for its semantic description (Almela et al., 2013). However, this does not mean that their respective potential for collocation with *decision* can be determined independently from one another. Interestingly, while the combination *face* (*a*) *tough decision*(*s*) is acceptable and relatively common, the combination *face* (*a*) *wise decision*(*s*) is odd—in fact, in a corpus as large as the enTenTen2012 (11,191,860,036 tokens)[2] there is no single instance of this combination, while in the same corpus the combination *face* (*a*) *tough decision* is registered 444 times. This suggests that the combinations of different collocations of *decision* are subject to restrictions. In the case mentioned above, we can observe that the selection of a collocate in the modifier slot is not independent of the selection of another collocate in the verbal slot. The probability of *tough* collocating with *face* is increased if *face* is selected as a verbal collocate (Almela et al., 2013; Almela, 2014), but the effect of this verb + noun collocation on the adjective *wise* is exactly the opposite. The choice of a collocate in a particular position is sensitive to the choice of another collocate in a different position with respect to the node.

The mainstream approaches to collocation are not equipped with the descriptive categories and the methodological tools necessary for identifying and analysing inter-collocational dependency relations. One of their limitations is that they fail to distinguish between strength of association and mode of association. The strength of association can be captured by the statistical scores available—as stated above, this is an aspect of collocational analysis on which the corpus linguistic tradition has been prolific, and we will not delve into it here. However, the different modes of lexical association represent a much less explored area of collocational research. By the notion of MODE OF ASSOCIATION we mean the configuration of relations between the internal

2 The TenTen family of corpora is a group of web corpora available at the Sketch Engine query system. English corpora from this family are called enTenTen. All of them are general corpora of English. At the time we conducted the research reported in Almela et al. (2013), enTenTen2012 was the largest version of this group of corpora.

structure of the collocation and the domains of lexical attraction that can be identified in a collocational window. A detailed explanation of this concept is provided in the next section.

3 Modes of Lexical Association: Unmediated and Mediated Collocation

The possibility to distinguish between different modes of lexical association is grounded in Cantos & Sánchez' (2001) proposal for a revision of Mason's (2000) notion of LEXICAL GRAVITY. In that article, Cantos and Sánchez argued that the influence exerted by a node on its environment is not unlimited, since some elements may be attracted to items other than the node. In a textual window there may be more than one domain of lexical attraction. This implies as a corollary that the items that determine—or contribute to determining—the strength of association between the node and other elements in a given collocational span or window may be both inside and outside the internal structure of the collocational pair under consideration. The different domains of lexical attraction into which the collocates in a textual window can be analysed were termed lexical constellations.

An important step in this line of argumentation is that, in the corpus linguistics literature, the distinction between node and collocate is purely methodological (not descriptive). Any word can be a node or a collocate, depending on the perspective adopted in each empirical investigation; or, to quote Sinclair, "[e]ach successive word in a text [...] is both node and collocate, though never at the same time" (1991, p. 115). Node and collocate are not different types of lexical items but simply different stages in the process of collocation extraction. The node is simply the search term, the item introduced as input, and the collocate is an item obtained as output. Given two words *a* and *b* that form a collocation, we could use both *a* and *b* as nodes, though in different processes of collocation extraction.

A logical consequence following from this is that the node is not necessarily the dominant source of syntagmatic lexical attraction in the text window in which it occurs. In the simplest possible case, the relationship between node and collocate is mostly determined by the internal structure of the collocation. If this is the case, we can speak of *unmediated* collocation (or, simply, collocation). In this mode of lexical association, the collocate features as a combinatorial quality of the node—or the node as a combinatorial quality of the collocate, depending on which direction of the relation is stronger. The implicit assumption behind the traditional methods of collocational analysis is that all

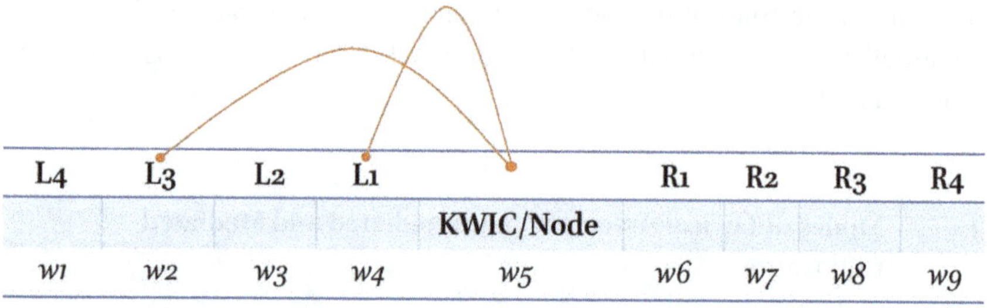

FIGURE 7.1 *Unmediated collocation*

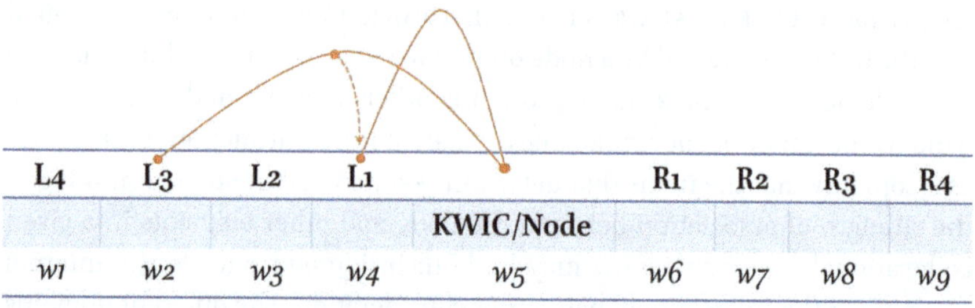

FIGURE 7.2 *Mediated collocation*

collocations are unmediated. However, as suggested in the previous section, several studies have reported situations in which the attraction between node and collocate is at least in part a function of items outside the collocational pair. The cases of inter-collocational dependency mentioned above qualify as examples of *mediated* collocation (or *co-collocation*, to use a shorter term).

The difference between these two modes of lexical association is graphically represented in Figures 7.1 and 7.2. Figure 7.1 represents unmediated collocation. There, the node relates individually with each of its co-occurrences in the textual window. Each line represents an unqualified relation of statistically significant co-occurrence. In contrast, Figure 7.2 represents a relationship of co-collocation. The dotted arrow indicates a reinforcement relation between a given collocation of the node and another collocation of the same node.

The fundamental difference between the structure represented in Figure 7.1 and the one in Figure 7.2 is that the latter is a multilateral relation. Strictly speaking, we cannot say that *w4* and *w5* form a collocation in Figure 7.2—even though they are statistically significant co-occurrences. The reason for this is that, since their mode of association is mediated by a third element (*w2*), the incorporation of both *w4* and *w5* within the same collocational structure cannot be made independently of the influence exerted by *w2*. It seems more accurate to suggest that the collocation is in this case formed by a relation involving more than two lexical domains, and not by a combination of two independently established collocational pairs. An important theoretical implication following from this is that co-collocations are not amenable to the traditional definition of collocation as a bipartite structure, because they are constituted by the interaction of more than two lexical domains. This issue is addressed in some more depth in the next section.

4 Collocation as a Multipartite Structure

The definition of collocation is a controversial issue. Nevertheless, the idea that it forms a bipartite structure is generally accepted by most scholars (Martin, 2008). In the Sinclairian corpus-linguistic tradition, the two parts are termed NODE and COLLOCATE; in other traditions, the two parts are called BASE and COLLOCATOR. There are some important theoretical differences underlying these two terminological pairs, which are by no means conceptually equivalent (see Hausmann, 1979; Hausmann & Blumenthal, 2006), but despite these differences, the idea that a collocation consists of two parts is shared as a common ground.

The traditional concept of collocation as a bipartite structure is suitable for describing cases of overlapping collocation, but not for describing cases of co-collocation. An overlap between collocations can be observed where two or more pairs of node and collocate (or of base and collocator) that are established independently of one another happen to share at least one member. In contrast, the concept of co-collocation implies that the node-collocate pair cannot be established independently of the influence exerted by an element outside the pair. Strictly speaking, a co-collocation consists of the relation between a node and two or more co-collocates, not of a combination of two collocations sharing the same node. In short: a co-collocation forms a multipartite structure, not a combination of bipartite structures.

Therefore, the notion of co-collocation should be distinguished from COLLOCATION CHAINS (Alonso Ramos & Wanner, 2007), which are combinations of two collocations with one member in common: *commit a violation of the law* (*commit a violation* + *violation of the law*), *take drastic measures* (*take measures* + *drastic measures*). The defining characteristic of a collocation chain is the existence of an overlap (a shared element) between the two adjoining collocations, without there being any specification concerning the dependency of one collocation on the other. As the authors explain, some collocation chains "can be treated as sequences of isolated collocations" (Alonso Ramos & Wanner, 2007, p. 11).

The criterion for distinguishing co-collocation and COLLOCATION NETWORKS is similar. Although the methods for building these networks have varied over time and across authors,[3] the strategy that generally characterises them is the successive connection of collocation pairs that have an element in common. For instance, if *time* is a collocate of *spend*, and *hours* is a collocate of *spend*, then the three items will be integrated in a collocation framework where *hours* features as a second-order collocate of *time* (Brezina et al., 2015, p. 152). Again, the fundamental difference with respect to the notion of co-collocation lies in the structural independence of the members of the network. Each new step *adds* connections to the network, but the new connections do not *feed back* on the previously established ones.

Co-collocations should also be distinguished from what García-Page (2005) and Koike (2005) have called COMPLEX COLLOCATIONS (Sp. *colocaciones complejas*), a special type of collocations that include a complex lexical item (more specifically an idiom) as one of their components. García-Page (2005) and Koike (2005) describe several examples in Spanish, e.g. *dar rienda suelta a + la imaginación* ('unleash one's imagination'). Complex collocations are bipartite structures—not multipartite structures—because the idiom (in the example above: *dar rienda suelta*) is considered as a single (multi-word) item.

The approach to SECOND-ORDER COLLOCATION devised by Mollet et al. (2011) differs from all the foregoing approaches. Mollet et al. (2011) use network modelling to describe the behaviour of a collocate towards other words within the node's co-occurrence patterns. The similarity with our approach is that both are interested in describing how the behaviour of a word towards a node can be influenced by the presence or absence of other items. For instance, Mollet et al. (2011) observe that the words that tend to co-occur with *order* when it is also accompanied by *social* are different from those that we find if *order* is accompanied by the expression of a mathematical formula. The essential difference, however, is that Mollet et al.'s (2011) approach does not examine the implications of second-order collocation for first-order collocation. They provide a separate model of analysis for each of the two. To this we must add the disadvantage that network modelling is a computationally heavy technique. The quantitative technique that we propose (see next section) is admittedly

3 The concept of collocation network is attributed to Phillips, and the idea has been later developed by Williams and his research team (Williams, 1998, 2012; Alonso et al., 2011) as well as by McEnery and, later, by Brezina et al. (2015). The latter author provides a useful overview of the evolution of the notion of collocation network as well as a useful comparison of different approaches.

less sophisticated than network modelling, but it offers the advantage of having an extremely low computational cost.

Finally, CO-VARYING COLLEXEME ANALYSIS (Stefanowitsch & Gries, 2005) investigates the statistical association of two different lexemes occurring in specific syntactic slots of a construction: for example, *fool* and *thinking* attract each other in the context of the *into*-causative construction (e.g., *fool sb. into thinking*), while *force* and *thinking* are repelled. In principle, the method employed in this approach could also be applied to the study of co-collocational relations, since it is possible to use the same technique in order to measure the statistical association of two different lexemes in the context of a given node. To the best of our knowledge, however, co-varying collexeme analysis has not been oriented to this goal yet; it has not been focused on the analysis of relations that restrict or modulate the influence of a node on its collocate inventory. At the initial stages of our project we considered utilising this technique but eventually we opted for a different type of statistics (see next section). The reason for this decision is that in the specialised literature there is a question as to whether statistical measures based on hypothesis testing are adequate for describing patterns of language use—see Kilgarriff (2005), counter-argued by Gries (2005). The objections are well-known: language is not random and statistically significant results grow with sample size.

5 Methodology

The existing collocation statistics are geared to measure the strength of binary relations—that is, of relations in which the strength of lexical syntagmatic association is a function of the relationship between two domains (one represented by the node and another represented by the collocate). Usually, the linguistic realisation of these two domains is either a pair of word forms or a pair of lemmas, but they might as well be more complex lexical items.

Crucially, the binary nature of the relation measured by standard collocation statistics is not altered by the internal complexity of each of the items associated. If we input a word pair as a node for collocate extraction and compute its frequency as a single element, we will obtain collocates of a collocation, but not co-collocations. Thus, in the enTenTen2013 corpus *enforce* is a statistically significant co-occurrence of *measure*, and it is also a statistically significant co-occurrence of *safety measure*. If we input *measure* as a search term (node), one of the statistically (logDice) significant co-occurrences we obtain is *enforce*; likewise, if we input *safety measure* as a search term (node) and compute its frequency as a single component, one of the statistically significant co-occurrences we obtain is, again, *enforce*. In both cases, the number of elements counted as single components in the relation is exactly the same, namely: two. Therefore, if we proceeded this way, it would be impossible to ascertain whether *enforce (a) safety measure(s)* is a multipartite collocational structure or merely a collocation consisting of two items of different internal complexity: a simple item and a multi-word item. Hence, if our goal is to describe co-collocational relations, the conventional collocation statistics alone will not do the work—they can be used as part of the methodology but will have to be complemented by some other type of measure.

As stated in Section 4, the step from collocation to co-collocation analysis does not consist in *adding* collocates or connections to an existing node-collocate pair but in *readjusting* the analysis of the initial node-collocate pair as it interacts with other elements in the environment. Therefore, we need a formula which allows us to reinterpret the output of a given lexical association measure after comparing their behaviour inside the collocation with some aspect of their behaviour towards elements outside the collocational pair.

The measure we adopted is based on comparisons of conditional probabilities (see the formula below in Step 4 of the methodology). This type of measure has been used earlier in approaches to collocation analysis, though with slight differences. Cantos & Sánchez (2001) used conditional probabilities to compare the attraction of a word towards different elements in a textual window. The difference between the formula applied in that study and the one used in the present one is twofold: first, the latter takes into account only frequency data in specific syntactic slots, and second, the comparison we make here is between intra- and inter-collocational levels of analysis. One of the terms of the comparison is the attraction between a collocate and a node (intra-collocational conditional probability) but the other term of the comparison is the attraction between that collocate and a given collocation (inter-collocational conditional probability), not the attraction between the collocate and another collocate. The reason for this modification lies in our attempt to describe modes of lexical association shaped by the interaction of more than two lexical domains (see Sections 3 and 4).

Comparisons of conditional probabilities have also been used as a measure of lexical association in collocate extraction. This is the case of ΔP (Gries, 2013). Again, the main difference between this use of conditional probabilities and ours is that in our study the lexical connections compared belong to different levels: intra-collocational and inter-collocational. Besides, in the methodology we propose conditional probabilities are not applied in the process of collocation extraction—we use logDice for that purpose—but in the process of distinguishing between mediated and unmediated collocational relations.

There are five different steps in the methodology we propose. These are arranged as follows:

Step 1. Obtain word sketch (using Sketch Engine) for a node word. Type of unit: lemma. Statistics: logDice. Frequency threshold: 3.

Step 2. Using multi-word sketches, obtain lemmatised co-occurrences in the context of the collocation (potential co-collocates) and in syntactically connected slots (e.g. Subject_of, Object_of, Modifier, etc.).

Step 3. Identify co-collocates based on comparisons of conditional probabilities at intra- and inter-collocational levels (see formula below).

Step 4. Apply the same formula to the measurement of relations between co-collocates obtained from Step 3 and other words standing in paradigmatic relation to the corresponding collocate.

Step 5. Apply the same formula to the measurement of relations between collocates analysed in Step 4 and other words standing in paradigmatic relation to the corresponding co-collocate.

Step 6. Classify collocates and co-collocates semantically and analyse their relation to the meaning of the node.

Steps 1–5 can be formalised in an algorithm. The motivation for the methodological decisions taken at each of these steps are briefly explained below. Only the last step requires subjective decisions on the part of the analyst—in the present state of the art this seems unavoidable if one of our aims is to arrive at semantic generalisations.

As stated above, the association measure used for the extraction of collocations in Step 1 is logDice:

$$14 + \log_2 \frac{2f_{xy}}{f_x + f_y}$$

One of the advantages of logDice is its stability across corpora of different size, and also across subcorpora (Rychlý, 2008). In the future, this can be useful for facilitating replications of the study using different types of corpora. Another advantage of logDice is its interpretability: the maximum value will always be 14, but usually less than 10, and negative values will mean no statistically significant co-occurrence (Rychlý, 2008). Admittedly, logDice has the disadvantage of not being a directional measure, while, as Gries (2013) rightly observes, directionality is one of the relevant parameters of collocation extraction and description. However, in the analysis of co-collocational relations this potential disadvantage of logDice is counteracted by the fact that the formula used for determining the mode of lexical association (mediated or unmediated) is sensitive to the directionality of the attraction (see description of Step 3 below).

The formula applied in Step 3 is sensitive to directionality, as stated above. We can distinguish between *node cued (n-cued)* and *collocate cued (c-cued)* conditional probabilities. The process for obtaining n-cued co-collocations is described in the following formulae:

(a) $P(c_1|n) = \frac{\textit{node word+collocate 1}}{\textit{node word+slot 1}} = P_1$

(b) $P(c_1|n, c_2) = \frac{\textit{node word+collocate 1+collocate 2}}{\textit{node word+slot 1+collocate 2}} = P_2$

(c) *If* $[P_2 > P_1]$ *then* c_2 *is a co-collocate of* c_1 *with respect to n; iff* $f(n, c_1, c_2) > 2$

First, we obtain the value of P_1: the probability that a given collocate occurs in a slot given the presence of the node. This value is calculated by dividing the joint frequency of node (n) and collocate 1 (c_1) in a specific syntactic relation by the overall frequency with which the node occurs in the same syntactic combination with any other word occupying the same slot as collocate 1. In the above formula this position is labelled *slot 1* (s_1). For example, we can divide the frequency of UNINTENDED + CONSEQUENCE (discontinuous sequences are also counted) by the frequency of 'Modifier' + CONSEQUENCE.

Then we calculate the value of P_2: this results from dividing the joint frequency of n, c_1 and c_2 (a second collocate of the node) by the overall frequency with which the collocation formed by n and c_2 occurs in a context defined by the co-presence of *slot 1*. For example, we can divide the frequency of MITIGATE + [UNINTENDED + CONSEQUENCE]$_{OBJ}$ (including the corresponding passive constructions) by the frequency of MITIGATE + ['Modifier' + CONSEQUENCE]$_{OBJ}$ (as before, the corresponding passive is also counted).

Finally, the values of P_1 and P_2 are compared. If P_2 is higher than P_1 and the joint frequency of n, c_1 and c_2 is higher than two, we can conclude that c_1 is not a direct collocate of n and that c_2 is a co-collocate of c_1 with respect to n.

The process for obtaining c-cued co-collocations is similar, with the only difference being the direction of the relation:

(a) $P(n|c_1) = \frac{\textit{node word+collocate 1}}{\textit{node slot+collocate 1}} = P_1$

(b) $P(c_1|n, c_2) = \frac{\textit{node word+collocate 1+collocate 2}}{\textit{node slot+collocate 1+collocate 2}} = P_2$

(c) *If* $[P_2 > P_1]$ *then* c_2 *is a co-collocate of n with respect to* c_1*; iff* $f(n, c_1, c_2) > 2$

In this case, the value of P_1 is calculated by dividing the joint frequency of n and c_1 by the overall frequency with which c_1 (not the node now) occurs in the same syntactic combination with any other word occupying the same slot as the node. In the above formula this position is labelled *node slot* (*ns*). For example, we can divide the frequency of UNINTENDED + CONSEQUENCE (again, discontinuous sequences are counted too) by the frequency of UNINTENDED + 'Noun'.

As for P_2, in the c-cued directionality this is calculated by dividing the joint frequency of n, c_1 and c_2 by the overall frequency with which the collocation formed by n and c_2 occurs in a context defined by the co-presence of *slot 1*. For example, we can divide the frequency of MITIGATE + [UNINTENDED + CONSEQUENCE]$_{OBJ}$ (including the corresponding passive constructions) by the frequency of MITIGATE + [UNINTENDED + 'Noun']$_{OBJ}$ (as before, the corresponding passive is also counted).

The formal conditions for the relation to qualify as a case of co-collocation are the same as those employed in the n-cued directionality. The value of P_2 must be higher than P_1 and the frequency of (n,c_1,c_2) must be above two. If the two conditions are met, we can say that c_2 is a co-collocate of the n with respect to c_1.

The formula for detecting co-collocations is applied again in Steps 5 and 6 to different sets of items. Suppose that in Step 4 we obtain a co-collocational pattern formed by (n,c_1,c_2), where c_2 is a verbal collocate that takes n as its direct object and c_1 is a modifier of n. In Step 5 we will apply the formula to other modifier collocates of n. This can be done using the *word sketch* tool in Sketch Engine, which groups collocates into categories according to their grammatical relation with the node. A hypothetical outcome of Step 5 is the following list of combinations: (n,c_1,c_2), (n,x_1,c_2), (n,y_1,c_2), (n,z_1,c_2), where c_2 is a co-collocate of x_1, y_1 and z_1, with the latter being modifier collocates of n. Then, in Step 6 we can apply the formula to combinations such as (n,c_1,x_2), (n,c_1,y_2), (n,c_1,z_2), (n,x_1,x_2), (n,x_1,y_2), (n,x_1,z_2), (n,y_1,x_2), etc., where x_2, y_2 and z_2 are different verbal collocates taking n as their direct object.

Steps 5 and 6 are similar in that they involve an extension of the application domain of the formula to include words standing in paradigmatic relation to the collocate and the co-collocate, respectively. This information can be useful for determining whether a given co-collocational pattern obtained from Step 4 reflects an idiosyncratic co-occurrence preference or forms part of a broader, more systematic semantic pattern. The justification of this search draws on findings from previous research. In the corpus linguistics literature on collocation there is a large amount of empirical evidence showing that collocational and colligational patterns tend to have both a syntagmatic and a paradigmatic dimension. Similarity of syntagmatic behaviour is a reliable predictor of paradigmatic relatedness. Several studies have shown that words which tend to occur in similar collocational and/or colligational contexts will also tend to be semantically related (Church et al., 1994; Renouf, 1996; Hunston & Francis, 2000; Jones, 2002; Stefanowitsch & Gries, 2003). Moreover, as the Behavioral Profile approach has shown, nuances of meaning distinguishing quasi-synonyms and opposites can be revealed or brought out by fine-grained examinations of distributional differences (Gries & Divjak, 2009; Gries & Otani, 2010; Liu, 2010). In principle, we can expect that similar correlations of contextual and semantic similarity—as well as of contextual and semantic differences—will emerge when the contextual features analysed are defined in terms of shared co-collocation. There is no reason to presume that co-collocational relations will represent an exception to the general principle of coordination between syntagmatic behaviour and semantic profile.

6 The Method at Work: The Case of *Unintended Consequence*

The corpus we have used in this study is *enTenTen2013*. With 19,717,205,676 tokens, this is at present the largest of the enTenTen family. Corpus size is a crucial factor in the methodology we propose. Many of the co-collocational patterns that can be obtained by means of this methodology do not emerge if we use smaller corpora. For instance, the combination *mitigate ... unintended consequence*(*s*) is not registered in the BNC, and consequently it does not reach the frequency threshold established in our methodology, but in the enTenTen2013 corpus this combination occurs 28 times.

The study has been focused on co-occurrences of lemmas (co-occurrences of word-forms were not computed) within one particular syntactic type of co-collocation: verb and modifier of an object noun. In an earlier paper, Almela (2011b) argued that transitive verbs can have collocational links with premodifiers of the object head noun. This suggests that the interaction of verbal and adjectival collocates of a noun can provide a fertile ground for applying the methodology proposed in the previous section and for comparing results obtained using conventional collocation analysis with those obtained from co-collocational analysis.

Observe the following concordances. The word we will take as node is in bold type and italics; the verbal and adjectival collocates we will focus on are in italics:

(1) It suggests that the political angle of AGW (that is, its close association with environmental statism) will *mitigate* the *long-term* **consequences** of its collapse.

(2) Members and witnesses discussed how to maintain the economic growth and success that this market sector currently enjoys while also *mitigating* the *unintended* **consequences** of regulation.

The conventional framework for analysing collocational relations allows us to state that *mitigate, long-term* and *unintended* are different collocates of *consequence*. The three of them attain a significant logDice score: *mitigate* (6.07), *long-term* (7.25), *unintended* (10.55) (the score is obtained automatically from the word sketch tool, so the context of co-occurrence of node and collocate is defined in terms of the specified syntactic relations: Modifier and Object_of).

However, since a node-collocate pair can be influenced by co-occurrence patterns outside the pair itself, the analysis of the three collocations above (*mitigate consequences, long-term consequences, unintended consequences*) is still incomplete. To determine the possible influence of one collocate on the other, we can compare the respective conditional probabilities at the intra- and inter-collocational level, as specified in Section 5. Since in this study we are interested in comparing the influence exerted by the node on its collocational environment with the influence exerted by other collocations of the node, we will adopt an n-cued directionality. Table 7.1 compares the capacity of the node for predicting the presence of a particular adjectival collocate (*long-term* or *unintended*) with the capacity of the verb-noun collocation (*mitigate consequences*) for predicting the presence of the same adjectival collocate. The inter-collocational probability (P_2) is higher than the intra-collocational probability (P_1) in the case of *unintended*, but not in the case of *long-term*. This means that *mitigate* strengthens the capacity of *consequence* for predicting *unintended* but not for predicting *long-term*. Only the former relation constitutes a co-collocational pattern.

The next step in our methodology involves making the same calculations with words that stand in paradigmatic relation to the collocate. This can help us determine whether the co-collocational relation we have identified forms part of a more general semantic pattern affecting other modifier collocates of *consequence*—notice that, in English, this grammatical category of collocates includes not only adjectives but also nouns, as in *tax consequences*. We have selected for this purpose a group of 25 collocates. The criterion has been purely statistical: the group includes the top 25 modifier collocates of *conse-*

TABLE 7.1 *Comparison of intra- and inter-collocational conditional probabilities*

c1	c2	f(n,c1)	f(n,s1)	f(n,c1,c2)	f(n,s1,c2)	P_1	P_2
long-term	*mitigate*	7381	481449	3	443	0.01533	0.00677
unintended	*mitigate*	25201	481449	28	443	0.05234	0.06321

TABLE 7.2 *Top modifier collocates of* consequence

1. *unintended* (10.55)	10. *inevitable* (7.37)	19. *unfortunate* (6.55)
2. *dire* (9.11)	11. *catastrophic* (7.36)	20. *direct* (6.48)
3. *negative* (8.59)	12. *long-term* (7.25)	21. *undesirable* (6.28)
4. *disastrous* (8.51)	13. *grave* (7.14)	22. *deadly* (6.23)
5. *devastating* (8.17)	14. *severe* (7.0)	23. *terrible* (6.22)
6. *adverse* (8.1)	15. *unforeseen* (6.76)	24. *harmful* (6.09)
7. *serious* (7.95)	16. *potential* (6.74)	25. *tax* (5.89)
8. *far-reaching* (7.5)	17. *logical* (6.72)	
9. *tragic* (7.39)	18. *fatal* (6.71)	

quence (again, the corpus is enTenTen2013, and the association measure used is logDice). In addition to *unintended* (10.55), which is the top collocate, the list includes the words in Table 7.2 (logDice scores in brackets).

The data used for calculating intra- and inter-collocational probabilities with *mitigate* as a potential co-collocate are available in the appendix. The results indicate that, in addition to *unintended,* there are five other modifier collocates of *consequence* that enter a co-collocational relation with *mitigate.* Those collocates are: *negative* (0.19838), *adverse* (0.11576), *potential* (0.03744), *disastrous* (0.00395) and *devastating* (0.00229) (the number in brackets is the difference between P_2 and P_1).

Finally, the methodology established in the previous section includes as a last step an extension of the analysis to include words standing in paradigmatic relation to the co-collocate. The goal of this step is to provide a more comprehensive view of the semantic patterns underlying the co-collocational relations detected. The verbs we have selected for this case study are *minimise/-ize* (with the two spelling variants computed as a single unit), *face* and *suffer*. The motivation for this choice has been to compare the effects of verbal co-collocates with different degrees of conceptual proximity and distributional similarity to *mitigate*. *Minimise* represents the closest proximity. In the context provided by *consequence*, *minimise* is a near-synonym of *mitigate*. Besides, with a score of 0.405, *minimise* ranks at the top of the distributional thesaurus obtained from enTenTen2013 for the verb *mitigate* (for an explanation of how distributional similarity is measured in Sketch Engine, see Rychlý & Kilgarriff, 2007). By contrast, *face* and *suffer* are much more distant both in terms of meaning and distribution. Their respective scores in the same thesaurus list are much lower than *minimise*: *suffer* (0.103), *face* (0.094). In turn, *face* and *suffer* are proximate to one another: their similarity score in the distributional thesaurus is 0.343, and in the context of *consequence* they have relatively similar meanings: both include the idea of 'being affected by a negative situation', although *face* further adds the meaning of 'accepting the situation / deciding to deal with it'. Our expectation is that, given their relative similarity, *face* and *suffer* will have a number of co-collocations in common which are not shared with *mitigate* and *minimise*—it should be noted that there is no circularity in making this prediction because the data used for calculating the similarity in the distributional thesaurus do not include contextual features defined in terms of co-collocation.

The data used for finding co-collocations of these verbs with the adjectives in Table 7.2 are shown in the appendix. Table 7.3 displays a summary of the results. Each cell shows the result of subtracting P_1 from P_2. Shaded cells stand for combinations which do not meet the frequency threshold requirement. Those cells whose value indicates the existence of a co-collocation have been highlighted in bold type.

TABLE 7.3 *Differences between* P_2 *and* P_1 *in the context of* consequence

	mitigate	*minimise/-ize*	*face*	*suffer*
adverse	**0.11576**	**0.08552**	−0.00115	**0.03469**
catastrophic	−0.00176	−0.00627	−0.00243	**0.00308**
deadly	−0.00383	−0.00383	−0.00021	−0.00144
devastating	**0.00229**	−0.01352	−0.00131	**0.00374**
dire	−0.01687	−0.01627	**0.06000**	**0.02823**
direct	−0.01398	−0.01398	−0.01150	−0.00823
disastrous	**0.00395**	−0.00558	−0.00439	**0.06379**
far-reaching	−0.00614	−0.00444	−0.00569	−0.00590
fatal	−0.00286	−0.00512	−0.00218	**0.00207**
grave	−0.00556	−0.00214	**0.00937**	**0.00739**
harmful	−0.00238	**0.01925**	−0.00305	−0.00008
inevitable	−0.00201	−0.00537	−0.00290	**0.00129**

TABLE 7.3 *Differences between* P_2 *and* P_1 *in the context of* consequence (cont.)

	mitigate	*minimise/-ize*	*face*	*suffer*
logical	−0.00613	−0.00613	−0.00545	−0.00493
long-term	−0.00856	−0.01533	−0.00990	−0.00071
negative	**0.19838**	**0.25839**	−0.02121	**0.00750**
potential	**0.03744**	**0.02879**	−0.00656	−0.01708
serious	−0.04210	−0.03748	**0.14398**	**0.03132**
severe	−0.00606	−0.01113	**0.05115**	**0.03774**
tax	−0.01680	−0.01680	−0.01680	−0.01680
terrible	−0.00330	−0.00385	**0.00462**	**0.01410**
tragic	−0.00531	−0.00416	−0.00169	**0.00298**
undesirable	0.00156	**0.01582**	−0.00160	−0.00224
unforeseen	0.00075	−0.00206	−0.00331	−0.00209
unfortunate	−0.00448	−0.00448	−0.00335	−0.00136
unintended	**0.01086**	**0.02445**	−0.04647	−0.04228

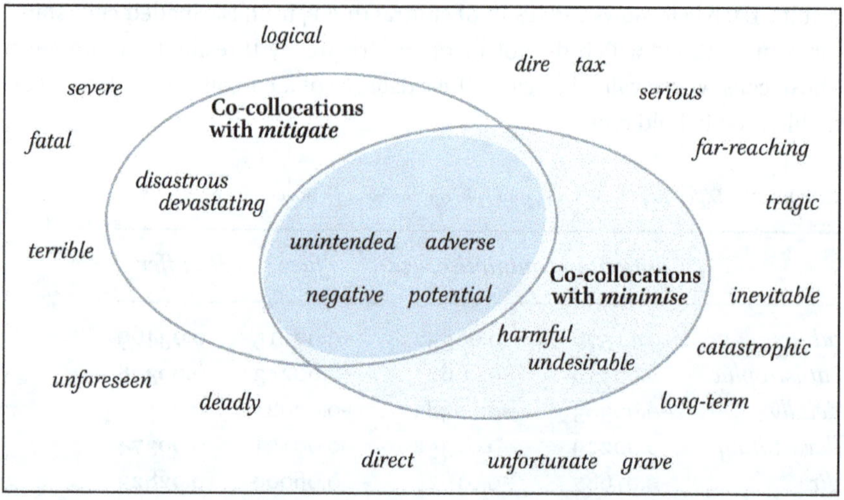

FIGURE 7.3 *Co-collocations in the framework* MITIGATE/MINIMISE + [*'Modifier'* + CONSEQUENCE]$_{OBJ}$

The results indicate that the collocates shared by *mitigate* and *minimise* are different from those shared by *suffer* and *face*. The adjectival co-collocates shared by *mitigate* and *minimise* are *adverse, negative, unintended* and *potential* (see Figure 7.3); those shared by *suffer* and *face* are *terrible, dire, grave, serious*

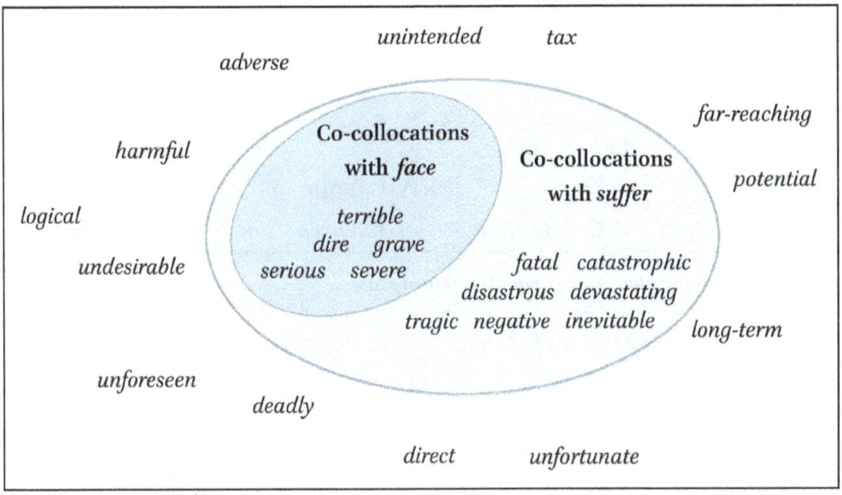

FIGURE 7.4 *Co-collocations in the framework* FACE/SUFFER + [*'Modifier'* + CONSEQUENCE]$_{OBJ}$

and *severe* (see Figure 7.4). The implications of these results for the analysis of the collocation *unintended consequence* are discussed in the next section.

7 Analysis and Discussion

The data obtained in Section 6 indicate that the distinction between mediated and unmediated collocation—and consequently between collocates and co-collocates—serves to capture some properties of word co-occurrences which a conventional approach to collocation cannot capture. First, we have observed that, when a node co-occurs simultaneously with two or more of its collocates, we should not assume that each of the collocations is established independently. While this seems to be the case in the combination *mitigate long-term consequences* in example (1) (see Figure 7.5), the combination *mitigate unintended consequences* in example (2) shows a kind of interaction between verb and modifier that escapes conventional collocation analysis. The data in Table 7.1 suggests that the overlap observed between the collocations *mitigate* + *consequences* and *unintended* + *consequences* is an instantiation of a multipartite structure (see Figure 7.6), rather than a mere overlap of two collocational pairs that happen to have one element in common but are independent from one another.

This does not mean that the co-occurrence with *unintended* is irrelevant for the semantic description of *consequence*, or that *unintended* is an undesired collocate. Mediated collocates are not necessarily equated with *false collocates*.

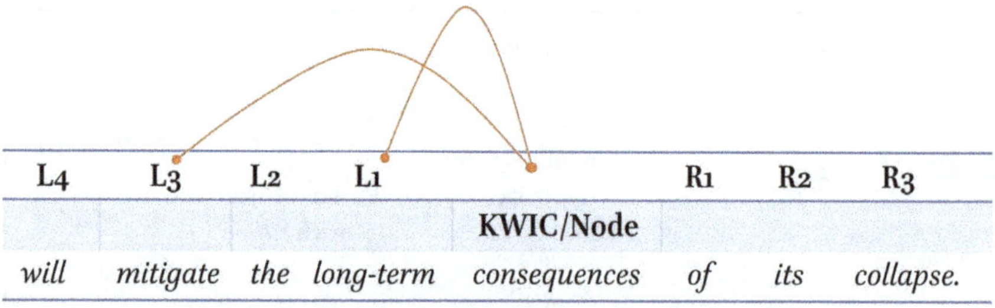

FIGURE 7.5 *Verb-modifier collocational overlap in example* (1)

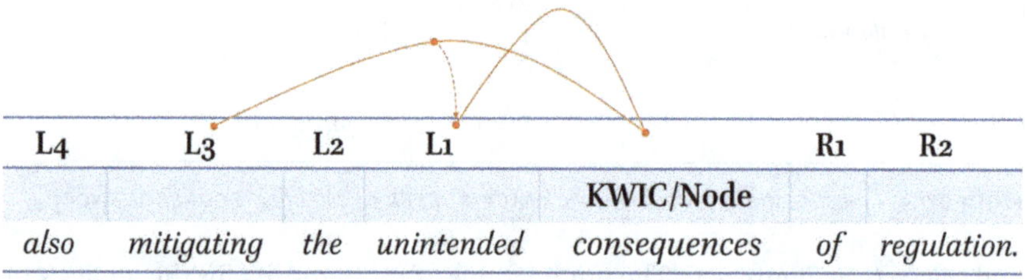

FIGURE 7.6 *Verb-modifier co-collocation in example* (2)

In fact, a close analysis of the syntagmatic behaviour of *consequence* and of its semantic relationship with *unintended* indicates that the collocation is indeed relevant. The meaning of *unintended* contains as one of its features an epistemic component of 'uncertainty'. Combined with the usually negative profile of *consequence*—see below—the resulting meaning for the collocation is roughly equivalent to 'risk'. Taken as a whole, the collocation refers to possible negative effects derived from an action meant to have positive effects. See, for instance, examples (3)–(7).

(3) Once again, this is an issue ACPET has advocated on extensively behind the scenes on behalf of its members and it is pleasing to see governments listening and keen to mitigate any *unintended consequences.*

(4) Third, transitional mechanisms need to be designed to minimise harmful *unintended consequences.*

(5) We worked very hard to educate our communities that battering affects children, and the community took leadership from our message. However we did not anticipate the consequences—that we would be losing our children to the system. Another *unintended consequence* that we are experiencing is with mandatory arrest policies, that we have embraced.

(6) Nzelibe argues that humanitarian interventions may have *unintended consequences* within the context of civil war. Because they tend to increase the chance that rebel leaders will achieve their political objectives, those leaders may feel incentivized to commit the kind of human atrocities that would lead to intervention in the first place.

(7) The result, if this degree of volatility persists, could be losses on a mammoth scale. This spike in interest rates is one of the many potential *unintended consequences* that could occur due to the huge amount of money that has been printed by the U.S. government along with the artificially low level of interest rates that has been engineered by the Federal Reserve's Ben Bernanke ...

Since the meaning of *unintended consequence* is nearly equivalent to the concept of 'risk', observing the collocational relationship between *mitigate* and *risk* can provide us with a clue to interpreting the role of *mitigate* as a co-collocate of *unintended*. With a logDice score of 6.6, *risk* is the top collocate of *mitigate* in the object slot; with the same score (remember that logDice is a non-directional association measure) *mitigate* is in turn the top verbal collocate of *risk* (again, in the syntactic framework of verb-object relations). This seems to indicate that there is an attraction between the argument type 'risk' and the predicative relation expressed by *mitigate*, which can be roughly paraphrased as 'reduce the effects of X'. This conclusion is further reinforced by the fact that *minimise/-ize*, a near-synonym of *mitigate*, also has *risk* as a highly significant collocate: the score is as high as 8.3 (for this calculation we have merged frequency data with the two spelling variants: *-ise* and *-ize*).

Based on these comparisons of collocational and co-collocational patterns, we can venture the explanation that the co-collocation of *mitigate* and *unintended* in the context of *consequence* reflects a more general semantic pattern of association between the concept of 'risk' and the predicative relation 'reduce the effects of X'. Expressions referring to the notion of 'risk'—including the collocation *unintended consequence*—are strongly attracted in the discourse to expressions denoting the predicative relation 'reduce the effects of X'. The association of these two concepts is manifested in several ways at the surface level of discourse. This implies that the semantic-associational pattern that motivates the attraction between *unintended* and *consequence* transcends the boundaries of this word pair. The expression *unintended consequence* is only a fragment of the structure from which the collocation itself is derived.

What we infer from this is not that *unintended* is an irrelevant collocate, but rather that its relevance is contingent on the influence from another collocate of *consequence*. When speakers use the noun *consequence* to refer to the risk associated with a well-meant and carefully planned action, they also tend to allude to other actions oriented to reducing the impact of such negative effects. Thus, the interaction between *unintended* and *mitigate* gives us more accurate information about the meaning of *consequence* than its collocation with *unintended* alone.

Concerning the relationship between semantic and behavioural profile, the data in Table 7.3 suggest that the co-collocation of *mitigate* and *unintended* is not an isolated lexical pattern. It forms part of a broader semantic framework. The co-collocations in the context of MITIGATE + ['Modifier' + CONSEQUENCE]$_{OBJ}$ can be classified into two semantic groups. The first one is formed by adjectives that activate a sense of 'risk' in the collocation when they function as modifiers of *consequence*. In addition to *unintended, potential* is also classified into this group. Observe how in examples (8)–(10) *potential* contributes an epistemic meaning of 'uncertainty' which in collocation with *consequence* contributes to activating the sense of 'risk'.

(8) But in the past few days, supporters of designating the group apparently eased most concerns or put forward contingencies to mitigate the risks and *potential consequences*.

(9) Those people that are caught up by drug addiction oftentimes do not realize the severity of their problem. They only care about their next usage, not *potential consequences*. Legal problems are not considered. Health problems are not considered.

(10) It's clear there are consequences to fighting back and taking action, ones which we can't necessarily predict or control. It's easy when thinking about the *potential consequences* of taking action to develop a sense of vertigo which might prevent us from standing up and walking forward, but the likely of effects [sic]of inaction will be more detrimental to us all.

The second group of adjectives in co-collocation with *mitigate* is more numerous. It is a group characterised by a negative semantic profile (*negative semantic prosody* is another term used in the corpus linguistics literature to describe this type of semantic patterning). The adjectives *negative, adverse, disastrous* and *devastating* convey a negative value judgment about the nature of the consequences referred to by the noun.

It should be noted that both groups are under-represented in the list of co-collocations: there are other collocates of *consequence* that belong to one of these semantic groups but fail to form co-collocations with *mitigate*. *Unfortunate, catastrophic, tragic* or *fatal*, among others, express a negative judgment but do not stand in co-collocational relation with *mitigate*, according to the data obtained and the calculations made. Likewise, *unforeseen* fails to share the co-collocate *mitigate* with the adjectives *unintended* and *potential*, even though it makes a similar semantic contribution, in the sense that it is associated with an epistemic meaning and with the sense of 'risk'—see examples (11)–(13):

(11) This is why it is customary after the wish is made for friends and family, magicians and fey folk in turn to make smaller wishes for the child in order to aid their wish along ... or to mitigate *unforeseen consequences*.

(12) In either case, this sort of "one-off" side-stepping of the proper solution, while seemingly innocent enough, can have additional, *unforeseen consequences*. Even if you catalogued this debt, can you really understand how it might compound in the future? Maybe the next developer comes along and builds off of your one-off, tacking on yet more debt.

(13) ... the application of antibiotics, it was thought, would lessen some of that risk. It also meant they could be raised in far less sterile conditions. But there was also an *unforeseen consequence*: the animals quickly grew fatter.

The problem observed here is the under-representation of semantic patterns at the surface lexical level. The number of word co-occurrence patterns that instantiate a semantic pattern is a subset of the total number of actual and possible word co-occurrences that instantiate the same semantic pattern. This problem is not specific of co-collocation analysis. Stubbs (1995) pointed out a similar problem in relation to collocation. He observed that some groups of collocates are semantically relevant even if the frequency data are too low to provide evidence of statistically significant association. Hoey (2005) makes a similar remark in his analysis of the relationship between collocation and semantic association as different layers of lexical priming.

The following example will serve to illustrate this problem. For instance, in enTenTen2013 the expressions *shoot a(n) animal(s)/elephant(s)/lion(s)/squirrel(s)/ buffalo(es)/coyote(s)*, etc., are statistically significant. These collocations are indicative of a semantic-associational pattern with the verb *shoot*: SHOOT + ['Noun: Animal']$_{OBJ}$. However, this semantic pattern is under-represented at the collocational level: the expression *shoot a beaver* is not statistically significant in the same corpus—hence, it does not qualify as a collocation—and yet, it is clearly another lexical realisation of the same semantic pattern. This does not imply that the association measure is ineffective; on the contrary, the association measure is a necessary tool for *indicating* or *pointing towards* the existence of the pattern, though admittedly not for *exhausting* its description. Locating the tip of the iceberg is a necessary step before we can dive and see what is below the surface; similarly, the most significant lexical manifestations of a semantic pattern often act as clues or signs telling us where we can look for more examples of the same pattern. The realisations of a semantic pattern found above the significance threshold are like signposts to those existing below that level.

We can follow the same line of reasoning in the analysis of semantic groups that are under-represented in co-collocational patterns: those groups of words that meet the quantitative criteria for being classified as co-collocates can be approached as lexical exponents of a semantic set that includes a much more extensive list of words which do not qualify as co-collocates. On this view, the most interesting aspect of the results from our study lies in the relationship between semantic groups of collocates and co-collocates, rather than in the distribution of individual items.

In the data obtained we can observe a certain alignment of semantic classes with distributional classes. First, we have observed semantic similarities related to distributional similarities at the co-collocational level: the two semantic groups of modifiers associated with *mitigate* (the epistemic group and the negative profile group) are also associated with *minimise*. Second, we have also observed that a difference in meaning can be related to a different co-collocational pattern: of the two semantic groups of co-collocates shared by *mitigate* and *minimise*, only one (adjectives that have a negative profile) is also shared with *face/suffer*. The epistemic group is not present among the co-collocations of *face/suffer*. These results suggest that the general principle of meaning-context correlation that previous research has documented for collocation might also be at work in the organisation of co-collocational relations.

8 Conclusions

In this study we have argued that the use of collocation in semantic description can be improved with the development of techniques for distinguishing between unmediated and mediated collocation. This also implies the need to reformulate the conventional definition of collocation to account for those cases in which the association between two or more different collocates of the node is integral to the structure of the collocation. While some collocations consist of a node and a collocate alone, other collocations include also a co-

collocate. Collocations of the latter type—consisting of node, collocate and co-collocate—have a multipartite structure which cannot be derived from the mere combination of collocational pairs that are established separately. This differentiates the structure of a co-collocational relation from that of a collocation network or a collocation chain.

We have also argued that the interaction of collocates and co-collocates has consequences for semantic description. When we use collocational data as a source of information for describing word meaning, considering the relation between collocates of different categories will help us provide a more comprehensive and precise picture than analysing the relation of the node with individual collocates alone or with specific sets of collocates. Although it is generally the case that distributional properties can be mapped onto semantic properties of words, the mapping between meaning and context often takes the form of multilateral relations which are not reducible to combinations of independent collocational pairs. As we have suggested, the attraction between *consequence* and its top modifier collocate *unintended* is derived from a semantic structure that includes elements—e.g. the verbal co-collocates *mitigate* and *minimise*—which lie outside the collocational pair.

Finally, it has also been observed that there is a certain relationship between semantic classes and distributional classes defined in terms of co-collocational relations. In the data analysed, near-synonymous verbal collocates of *consequence* were found to function as co-collocates of adjectives from well-defined semantic sets. Future research will determine the extent to which these findings can be generalised to co-collocational patterns obtained for nodes belonging to a variety of semantic fields.

References

Almela, M. (2011a). Improving corpus-driven methods of semantic analysis: A case study of the collocational profile of *incidence*. *English Studies, 92*(1), 84–99.

Almela, M. (2011b). The case for verb-adjective collocations. *Revista de Lingüística y Lenguas Aplicadas, 6*, 39–52.

Almela, M. (2014). *You shall know a collocation by the company it keeps*: Methodological advances in lexical constellation analysis. In J.R. Calvo Ferrer & M.Á. Campos Pardillos (Eds.), *Investigating Lexis: Vocabulary Teaching, ESP, Lexicography and Lexical Innovation* (pp. 3–25). Newcastle: Cambridge Scholars Publishing.

Almela, M., Cantos, P., & Sánchez, A. (2013). Collocation, co-collocation, constellation ... any advances in distributional semantics? *Procedia—Social and Behavioral Sciences, 95*, 231–240.

Alonso, A., Millon, C., & Williams, G. (2011). Collocational networks and their application to an E-Advanced Learner's Dictionary of Verbs in Science (DicSci). In I. Kosem & K. Kosem (Eds.), *Electronic Lexicography in the 21st Century: New Applications for New Users. Proceedings of eLex2011, Bled, 10–12 November 2011* (pp. 12–22). Ljubljana: Trojina.

Alonso Ramos, M., & Wanner, L. (2007). Collocation chains: How to deal with them? In K. Gerdes, T. Reuther & L. Wanner (Eds.), *Proceedings of the 3rd International Conference on Meaning-Text Theory. Klagenfurt, May 20–24, 2007. Wiener Slawistischer Almanach. Sonderband 69* (pp. 11–20). Wien. Retrieved from http://meaningtext.net/mtt2007/proceedings/. Last accessed 19 June 2017.

Brezina, V., McEnery, T., & Wattam, S. (2015). Collocations in context: A new perspective on collocation networks. *International Journal of Corpus Linguistics, 20*(2), 139–173.

Cantos, P., & Sánchez, A. (2001). Lexical constellations: What collocates fail to tell. *International Journal of Corpus Linguistics, 6*(2), 199–228.

Church, K.W., Gale, W., Hanks, P., Hindle, D., & Moon, R. (1994). Lexical substitutability. In B.T.S. Atkins & A. Zampolli (Eds.), *Computational approaches to the lexicon* (pp. 153–177). Oxford: Oxford University Press.

Evert, S. (2005). *The statistics of word cooccurrences. Word pairs and collocations.* PhD Thesis. http://dx.doi.org/10.18419/opus-2556

Evert, S. (2009). Corpora and collocations. In A. Lüdeling & M. Kytö (Eds.), *Corpus linguistics. An international handbook. Volume 2* (pp. 1212–1247). Berlin: Walter de Gruyter.

Evert, S., & Krenn B. (2005). Using small random samples for the manual evaluation of statistical association measures. *Computer Speech & Language, 19*(4), 450–466.

García-Page, M. (2005). Colocaciones simples y complejas: Diferencias estructurales. In R. Almela, E. Ramón Trives & G. Wotjak (Eds.) *Fraseología contrastiva: Con ejemplos tomados del alemán, español, francés e italiano* (pp. 145–168). Murcia: Servicio de Publicaciones de la Universidad de Murcia.

Gries, S.Th. (2005). Null-hypothesis significance testing of word-frequencies: A follow-up on Kilgarriff. *Corpus Linguistics and Linguistic Theory, 1*(2), 277–294.

Gries, S.Th. (2013). 50-something years of work on collocations. What is or should be next ... *International Journal of Corpus Linguistics, 18*(1), 137–165.

Gries, S.Th., & Divjak, D. (2009). Behavioral profiles: A corpus-based approach to cognitive-semantic analysis. In V. Evans & S. Pourcel (Eds.), *New directions in cognitive linguistics* (pp. 57–75). Amsterdam: John Benjamins.

Gries, S.Th., & Otani, N. (2010). Behavioral profiles: A corpus-based perspective on synonymy and antonymy. *ICAME Journal, 34*, 121–150.

Hausmann, F.J. (1979). Un dictionnaire des collocations est-il possible? *Travaux de Linguitique et de Litterature, 17*(1), 187–195.

Hausmann, F.J., & Blumenthal, P. (2006). Présentation: Collocations, corpus, dictionnaires. *Language Française, 150*, 3–13.

Hunston, S., & Francis, G. (2000). *Pattern grammar. A corpus-driven approach to the lexical grammar of English*. Amsterdam: John Benjamins.

Jones, S. (2002). *Antonymy. A corpus-based perspective*. London: Routledge.

Kilgarriff, A. (2005). Language is never, ever, ever, random. *Corpus Linguistics and Linguistic Theory, 1*(2), 263–276.

Koike, K. (2005). Colocaciones complejas en el español actual. In R. Almela, E. Ramón Trives & G. Wotjak (Eds.), *Fraseología contrastiva: Con ejemplos tomados del alemán, español, francés e italiano* (pp. 169–184). Murcia: Servicio de Publicaciones de la Universidad de Murcia.

Liu, D. (2010). Is it a chief, main, major, primary, or principal concern? A corpus-based behavioral profile study of the near-synonyms. *International Journal of Corpus Linguistics, 15*(1), 56–87.

Martin, W. (2008). A unified approach to semantic frames and collocational patterns. In S. Granger & F. Meunier (Eds.), *Phraseology. An interdisciplinary perspective* (pp. 51–65). Amsterdam: John Benjamins.

Mason, O. (2000). Parameters of collocation: The word in the centre of gravity. In J. Kirk (Ed.), *Corpora galore. Analyses and techniques in describing English* (pp. 267–280). Amsterdam/Atlanta, GA: Rodopi.

Mollet, E., Wray, A., & Fitzpatrick, T. (2011). Accessing second-order collocation through lexical co-occurrence networks. In T. Herbst, S. Faulhaber & P. Uhrig (Eds.), *The phraseological view of language: A tribute to John Sinclair* (pp. 87–121). Berlin: Walter de Gruyter.

Renouf, A. (1996). Les nyms: En quête du thésaurus des textes. *Lingvisticae Investigationes, 20*(1), 145–165.

Rychlý, P. (2008). A lexicographer-friendly association score. In P. Sojka & A. Horák (Eds.), *Proceedings of Recent Advances in Slavonic Natural Language Processing, RASLAN 2008* (pp. 6–9). Brno: Masaryk University. Retrieved from https://nlp.fi.muni.cz/raslan/2008/papers/13.pdf. Last accessed 19 June 2017.

Rychlý, P., & Kilgarriff, A. (2007). An efficient algorithm for building a distributional thesaurus (and other Sketch Engine developments). *Proceedings of the ACL 2007 demo and poster sessions* (pp. 41–44). *Prague, June 2007*. Retrieved from http://dl.acm.org/citation.cfm?id=1557783. Last accessed 19 June 2017.

Sinclair, J.M. (1991). *Corpus, concordance, collocation*. Oxford University Press.

Stefanowitsch, A., & Gries, S.Th. (2003). Collostructions: Investigating the interaction of words and constructions. *International Journal of Corpus Linguistics, 8*(2), 209–243.

Stefanowitsch, A., & Gries, S.Th. (2005). Covarying collexemes. *Corpus Linguistics and Linguistic Theory, 1*(1), 1–43.

Stubbs, M. (1995). Collocations and semantic profiles: On the cause of trouble with quantitative studies. *Functions of Language*, *2*(1), 23–55.

Williams, G. (1998). Collocational networks: Interlocking patterns of lexis in a corpus of plant biology research articles. *International Journal of Corpus Linguistics*, *3*(1), 151–171.

Williams, G. (2012). Bringing the data and dictionary together: Real science in real dictionaries. In A. Boulton, S. Carter-Thomas & E. Rowley-Jolivet (Eds.), *Corpus-informed research and learning in ESP. Issues and applications* (pp. 219–240). Amsterdam: John Benjamins.

Appendix: Data Used for Calculating Intra- and Inter-collocational Probabilities with *Mitigate* as a Potential Co-collocate

c1	c2	f(n,c1)	f(n,s1)	f(n,c1,c2)	f(n,s1,c2)	P_1	P_2
unintended	*suffer*	25201	481449	42	4172	0.05234	0.01007
unintended	*face*	25201	481449	26	4423	0.05234	0.00588
unintended	*mitigate*	25201	481449	28	443	0.05234	0.06321
unintended	*minimize/-ise*	25201	481449	45	586	0.05234	0.07679
dire	*suffer*	10298	481449	207	4172	0.02139	0.04962
dire	*face*	10298	481449	360	4423	0.02139	0.08139
dire	*mitigate*	10298	481449	2	443	0.02139	0.00451
dire	*minimize/-ise*	10298	481449	3	586	0.02139	0.00512
negative	*suffer*	25125	481449	249	4172	0.05219	0.05968
negative	*face*	25125	481449	137	4423	0.05219	0.03097
negative	*mitigate*	25125	481449	111	443	0.05219	0.25056
negative	*minimize/-ise*	25125	481449	182	586	0.05219	0.31058
disastrous	*suffer*	6793	481449	325	4172	0.01411	0.07790
disastrous	*face*	6793	481449	43	4423	0.01411	0.00972
disastrous	*mitigate*	6793	481449	8	443	0.01411	0.01806
disastrous	*minimize/-ise*	6793	481449	5	586	0.01411	0.00853
devastating	*suffer*	6507	481449	72	4172	0.01352	0.01726
devastating	*face*	6507	481449	54	4423	0.01352	0.01221
devastating	*mitigate*	6507	481449	7	443	0.01352	0.01580
devastating	*minimize/-ise*	6507	481449	0	586	0.01352	0.00000
adverse	*suffer*	7301	481449	208	4172	0.01516	0.04986
adverse	*face*	7301	481449	62	4423	0.01516	0.01402
adverse	*mitigate*	7301	481449	58	443	0.01516	0.13093
adverse	*minimize/-ise*	7301	481449	59	586	0.01516	0.10068
serious	*suffer*	24618	481449	344	4172	0.05113	0.08245
serious	*face*	24618	481449	863	4423	0.05113	0.19512
serious	*mitigate*	24618	481449	4	443	0.05113	0.00903
serious	*minimize/-ise*	24618	481449	8	586	0.05113	0.01365
far-reaching	*suffer*	2958	481449	1	4172	0.00614	0.00024
far-reaching	*face*	2958	481449	2	4423	0.00614	0.00045
far-reaching	*mitigate*	2958	481449	0	443	0.00614	0.00000
far-reaching	*minimize/-ise*	2958	481449	1	586	0.00614	0.00171
tragic	*suffer*	3645	481449	44	4172	0.00757	0.01055
tragic	*face*	3645	481449	26	4423	0.00757	0.00588

(cont.)

c1	c2	f(n,c1)	f(n,s1)	f(n,c1,c2)	f(n,s1,c2)	P_1	P_2
tragic	*mitigate*	3645	481449	1	443	0.00757	0.00226
tragic	*minimize/-ise*	3645	481449	2	586	0.00757	0.00341
inevitable	*suffer*	4228	481449	42	4172	0.00878	0.01007
inevitable	*face*	4228	481449	26	4423	0.00878	0.00588
inevitable	*mitigate*	4228	481449	3	443	0.00878	0.00677
inevitable	*minimize/-ise*	4228	481449	2	586	0.00878	0.00341
catastrophic	*suffer*	3019	481449	39	4172	0.00627	0.00935
catastrophic	*face*	3019	481449	17	4423	0.00627	0.00384
catastrophic	*mitigate*	3019	481449	2	443	0.00627	0.00451
catastrophic	*minimize/-ise*	3019	481449	0	586	0.00627	0.00000
long-term	*suffer*	7381	481449	61	4172	0.01533	0.01462
long-term	*face*	7381	481449	24	4423	0.01533	0.00543
long-term	*mitigate*	7381	481449	3	443	0.01533	0.00677
long-term	*minimize/-ise*	7381	481449	0	586	0.01533	0.00000
grave	*suffer*	2675	481449	54	4172	0.00556	0.01294
grave	*face*	2675	481449	66	4423	0.00556	0.01492
grave	*mitigate*	2675	481449	0	443	0.00556	0.00000
grave	*minimize/-ise*	2675	481449	2	586	0.00556	0.00341
severe	*suffer*	6178	481449	211	4172	0.01283	0.05058
severe	*face*	6178	481449	283	4423	0.01283	0.06398
severe	*mitigate*	6178	481449	3	443	0.01283	0.00677
severe	*minimize/-ise*	6178	481449	1	586	0.01283	0.00171
unforeseen	*suffer*	1813	481449	7	4172	0.00377	0.00168
unforeseen	*face*	1813	481449	2	4423	0.00377	0.00045
unforeseen	*mitigate*	1813	481449	2	443	0.00377	0.00451
unforeseen	*minimize/-ise*	1813	481449	1	586	0.00377	0.00171
potential	*suffer*	9145	481449	8	4172	0.01899	0.00192
potential	*face*	9145	481449	55	4423	0.01899	0.01243
potential	*mitigate*	9145	481449	25	443	0.01899	0.05643
potential	*minimize/-ise*	9145	481449	28	586	0.01899	0.04778
logical	*suffer*	2952	481449	5	4172	0.00613	0.00120
logical	*face*	2952	481449	3	4423	0.00613	0.00068
logical	*mitigate*	2952	481449	0	443	0.00613	0.00000
logical	*minimize/-ise*	2952	481449	0	586	0.00613	0.00000
fatal	*suffer*	2463	481449	30	4172	0.00512	0.00719
fatal	*face*	2463	481449	13	4423	0.00512	0.00294

c1	c2	f(n,c1)	f(n,s1)	f(n,c1,c2)	f(n,s1,c2)	P_1	P_2
fatal	*mitigate*	2463	481449	1	443	0.00512	0.00226
fatal	*minimize/-ise*	2463	481449	0	586	0.00512	0.00000
unfortunate	*suffer*	2156	481449	13	4172	0.00448	0.00312
unfortunate	*face*	2156	481449	5	4423	0.00448	0.00113
unfortunate	*mitigate*	2156	481449	0	443	0.00448	0.00000
unfortunate	*minimize/-ise*	2156	481449	0	586	0.00448	0.00000
direct	*suffer*	6733	481449	24	4172	0.01398	0.00575
direct	*face*	6733	481449	11	4423	0.01398	0.00249
direct	*mitigate*	6733	481449	0	443	0.01398	0.00000
direct	*minimize/-ise*	6733	481449	0	586	0.01398	0.00000
undesirable	*suffer*	1423	481449	3	4172	0.00296	0.00072
undesirable	*face*	1423	481449	6	4423	0.00296	0.00136
undesirable	*mitigate*	1423	481449	2	443	0.00296	0.00451
undesirable	*minimize/-ise*	1423	481449	11	586	0.00296	0.01877
deadly	*suffer*	1845	481449	10	4172	0.00383	0.00240
deadly	*face*	1845	481449	16	4423	0.00383	0.00362
deadly	*mitigate*	1845	481449	0	443	0.00383	0.00000
deadly	*minimize/-ise*	1845	481449	0	586	0.00383	0.00000
terrible	*suffer*	2675	481449	82	4172	0.00556	0.01965
terrible	*face*	2675	481449	45	4423	0.00556	0.01017
terrible	*mitigate*	2675	481449	1	443	0.00556	0.00226
terrible	*minimize/-ise*	2675	481449	1	586	0.00556	0.00171
harmful	*suffer*	2232	481449	19	4172	0.00464	0.00455
harmful	*face*	2232	481449	7	4423	0.00464	0.00158
harmful	*mitigate*	2232	481449	1	443	0.00464	0.00226
harmful	*minimize/-ise*	2232	481449	14	586	0.00464	0.02389
tax	*suffer*	8089	481449	0	4172	0.01680	0.00000
tax	*face*	8089	481449	0	4423	0.01680	0.00000
tax	*mitigate*	8089	481449	0	443	0.01680	0.00000
tax	*minimize/-ise*	8089	481449	0	586	0.01680	0.00000

CHAPTER 8

The Lexicogrammar of *Be Interested*: Description and Pedagogy*

Costas Gabrielatos

1 Introduction

This paper aims to contribute to the growing body of "pedagogy-driven corpus-based research" (Gabrielatos, 2006; see also Römer, 2004), with a focus on pedagogical lexicogrammar; that is, research which is situated at the intersection of language description, analysis of learner language, and evaluation of pedagogical materials, with the purpose of developing a body of corpus-based lexicogrammatical information for language learners.

The motivation for a study on *BE interested* is two-fold, stemming from both its nature and treatment in pedagogical materials (grammars and dictionaries for language learners). The adjective *interested* commonly features in pedagogical grammars, partly because of its contrast with the meaning of the adjective *interesting*, and the syntactic patterns each enters in, partly because of the variety of complementation patterns of *BE interested*. However, the information in pedagogical materials is not comprehensive (even at advanced levels), and no relevant frequency information is provided in corpus-based descriptive grammars (Biber, Johansson, Leech, Conrad & Finegan, 1999; Carter & McCarthy, 2006). The study can be seen as an example of the proposed approach to pedagogy-driven corpus-based lexicogrammatical research.

This paper examines lexicogrammatical patterns of *BE interested* in L1 and L2 (learner) corpora, representing both speech and writing. The analysis will compare learner and L1 use to establish similarities and differences. The above are then contrasted with the relevant information provided in pedagogical materials to establish the extent to which the latter provide an accurate and comprehensive account of the patterns, and the extent to which it can be hypothesised that learner use is influenced by the quality and quantity of the pedagogical information.

* The work on this paper was partly supported by the Edge Hill University Research Investment Fund.

 | DOI: 10.1163/9789004361133_010

2 Pedagogy-Driven Research

This study builds on the approach in Gabrielatos (2003, 2006, 2013), which combines corpus-based research on L1 and L2 use with the critical examination of the information provided in pedagogical materials. That is, in addition to comparing the information in pedagogical materials with L1 use (e.g. Biber, Conrad & Reppen, 1994), and comparing L1 and L2 use (e.g. Granger, Gilquin & Meunier, 2013, 2015), this approach attempts to triangulate the results of the above two comparisons by seeking explanations for differences between L1 and L2 use in the information provided in pedagogical materials.

Research in second language acquisition has indicated that explicit instruction, which includes providing learners with the type of metalinguistic information found in pedagogical materials, contributes to language learning (e.g. N. Ellis, 2015, pp. 13–14; R. Ellis, 2008, p. 863, 881, 883, 900–903; R. Ellis, 2015, pp. 264–265; Ortega, 2013, pp. 137–140). In this light, learner output can be expected to be influenced by the information in pedagogical materials, as their content greatly informs the input learners receive in class (Meunier, 2012, p. 113). This assumption also underlies the large body of studies critically examining the information in pedagogical materials in light of corpus evidence (e.g. Biber & Reppen, 2002; Gabrielatos, 2006; Harwood, 2005; Hunston & Francis, 1998; Kennedy, 1992; Meunier & Gouverneur, 2009; Owen, 1993; Römer, 2004). A shared finding in such studies is that pedagogical materials tend to provide partial, inaccurate, or misleading information. Another criticism of pedagogical materials concerns the mismatch between the frequency of a given structure in L1 use and its inclusion or prominence in pedagogical materials. Biber, Conrad and Reppen (1994, p. 171) observe that "some relatively common linguistic constructions are overlooked in pedagogic grammars, while some relatively rare constructions receive considerable attention." Although they acknowledge the importance of the difficulty and teachability of particular structures in the selection and prioritisation of content in pedagogical grammars, they also argue that the frequency of particular structures should be an equally important consideration (Biber, Conrad & Reppen, 1994, pp. 173–174; see also Biber & Reppen, 2002, pp. 206–207). Similarly, Leech (2011, pp. 12–15, 24) argues that frequent items must be prioritised in language teaching, as learners can be expected to encounter, and have a need to use, these items more often. An additional reason why the presence and prominence of particular items in pedagogical materials is worth investigating is related to Hasselgren's (1994) observation that the lexical repertoire of even advanced learners tends to be restricted to "lexical teddy bears" (ibid., p. 237): a relatively small group of words and expressions that learners feel comfortable

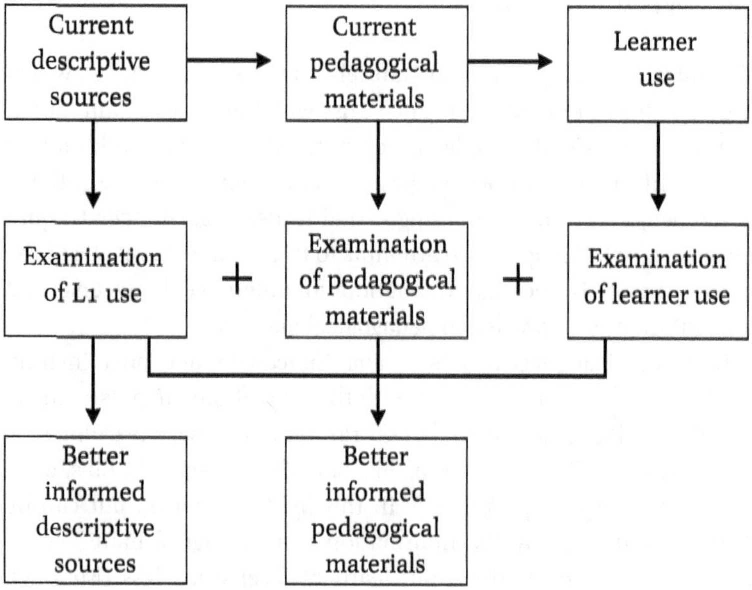

FIGURE 8.1 *Pedagogy-driven research: Components and interrelations*

to use because they have encountered and used them in the past. A similar effect can be achieved by the prominence of particular grammatical (and lexicogrammatical) items in pedagogical materials. For example, Gabrielatos (2013) found that, when compared to written L1 use, learners tended to overuse the types of conditionals specified in pedagogical materials and underuse those excluded. Overall, language items that are discussed explicitly and in some detail in pedagogical materials can be expected to be seen by learners as more salient than those only presented in examples or exercises, and, therefore, it is reasonable to expect them to be used more frequently by learners.

For the reasons outlined above, pedagogical materials are examined for the presence, comprehensiveness, and accuracy of the information they provide either directly (via explicit rules and guidelines) or indirectly (via examples and exercises). Of course, correlations between the frequency of particular patterns in L2 use and the presence/absence or prominence of relevant information in pedagogical materials should not be necessarily understood as indicating causation, as learner use is also influenced by non-pedagogical sources, such as films, TV, websites, social media, and computer games. Finally, in the approach taken here, the use of the language item in focus is examined in both native and learner corpora. Of course, pedagogy-driven research does not preclude, and frequently requires, primary descriptive research. That is, it does not simply contrast the information provided in pedagogical materials with that provided in descriptive grammars and dictionaries, as the latter may not be corpus-based, or may not cover the item comprehensively. Simply put, pedagogy-driven corpus research can also contribute to language description and theory. Figure 8.1 (adapted from Gabrielatos, 2005, p. 5; 2013, p. 160) summarises the elements of pedagogy-driven corpus-based research.

3 Conceptions of Lexicogrammar

Before moving to the focus and aims of this study, we must first discuss the notion of lexicogrammar, as views on its nature vary, and clarify the sense in which it is treated here. This section also provides a critical view of the primacy of lexis that is posited by most of the approaches to lexicogrammar (see Römer, 2009, pp. 141–147). What will be argued here, and what is emerging from the analysis, is that approaches treating lexis as primary and grammar as emerging from lexical patterning (as in Hoey, 2005, p. 1) are not grammar-free (as acknowledged in Hunston & Francis, 2000, pp. 1–2, 37; Stubbs, 1996, p. 40), nor can grammar be seen as secondary. The critical overview will start with approaches that posit the primacy of lexis, then look at Halliday's more balanced approach, and finally discuss the approach taken in this study.

Sinclair (1991, pp. 109–115) initially discussed the "idiom principle" (exemplified by collocation) as operating alongside the "open-choice principle", or "slot-and-filler model" (words chosen according to their semantic properties to fill in particular syntactic positions), and proposed the idiom principle as accounting for "the restraints that are not captured by the open-choice model" (ibid., p. 115). Sinclair (2004, p. 164) also distinguished between "lexicogrammar" and "lexical grammar", seeing the former as "fundamentally grammar with a certain amount of attention to lexical patterns within the grammatical frameworks; it is not in any sense an attempt to build together a grammar and lexis on an equal basis." However, his approach, later formalised as Lexical Grammar (Sinclair, 2004), does not treat lexis and grammar on an equal basis either, but clearly prioritises the idiom principle and a focus on lexis, with the "lexical item" (ibid., p. 141) as the unit of analysis. As Hunston and Francis (2000, p. 253) put it, lexical grammar "restored lexis in its rightful place at the centre of language description". The imbalance in favour of lexis becomes clear when we examine the components of the lexical item (Sinclair, 1996, p. 75; see also Stubbs, 2009, pp. 123–126): the core (i.e. a word or phrase), its collocates, its semantic preference, its semantic prosody, its colligations. The only component of a grammatical nature is colligation, defined as "the grammatical company a word keeps" (Hoey, 1997, p. 8), or "frequent co-selections of a content word and an associated grammatical frame" (Stubbs, 2002, p. 238). However, colligation is not an obligatory component, whereas collocation and semantic prosody are (Sinclair, 2004, p. 174; Stubbs, 2009, p. 124). Interestingly, despite the apparent prioritisation of lexis, Lexical Grammar does take account of grammar, albeit in an unacknowledged fashion. Collocation, a core component of the lexical item, is defined as relating to the co-occurrence of word-forms, as different forms of the same word can have different sets of collocates (e.g. Sinclair, 1991, pp. 53–56). However, this is tantamount to saying that morphological marking affects collocation patterns, and, therefore, implicitly accepting that collocation is not purely lexical, but is influenced by grammar. The primacy of lexis also underlies Hoey's work on lexical priming, which is very much in line with the tenets of Lexical Grammar. Hoey's (2005, p. 1) statement that "grammar is an outcome of lexical structure" clearly echoes Sinclair's (1991, p. 100) earlier view that "grammatical generalizations [...] are the accumulation of the patterns of hundreds of individual words and phrases". However, lexical priming analysis does make use of syntactic categories (e.g. Subject, Object, Complement) (ibid., p. 60).

An approach closely related to Lexical Grammar is Pattern Grammar; however, it differs from it in two important respects. First, its main focus is particular words or word classes and "the grammatical patterns they form part of" (Hunston & Francis, 2000, p. 1), while a pattern is seen as indicating "the behaviour of words that is typical of their word class" (Hunston & Francis, 2000, p. 202), and the description of particular patterns includes grammatical classes (e.g. *V of N*), and their discussion involves traditional syntactic categories (e.g. passive). In this light, its main focus can be described as colligation, which is only an optional component in Lexical Grammar. Second, in this approach, grammar can also be a starting point in the analysis: "a pattern can be seen to be associated with a variety of different words" (Hunston & Francis, 2000, p. 43). That is, Pattern Grammar reserves a larger role for grammar than Lexical Grammar. However, it retains lexis as its main focus: grammar patterns are seen as "belonging" to a particular word (Hunston & Francis, 2000, pp. 1–2).

Halliday proposed treating lexis and grammar as "complementary perspectives" (1991, p. 32), the combination of which comprises a single level of organisation in language, which he termed "lexicogrammar" (1992, p. 63). More precisely, Halliday conceived grammar and lexis as the notional ends of a lexicogrammatical continuum. He presented collocations and sense relations as examples of the lexis end, with polarity, mood and transitivity presented as examples of the grammar end, whereas prepositions and systems of modality were seen to occupy a middle ground (1992, pp. 63–64). Halliday argued that the reason lexis and grammar tend to be treated separately is because "they lend themselves to different techniques of analysis" (1992, p. 63), in that "if you interrogate the system grammatically you will get grammar-like answers and if you interrogate it lexically you get lexis-like answers" (1992, p. 64). Halliday described Sinclair's approach as "tunnelling through the system interrogating it lexically while moving further and further towards the grammatical end" (1992, p. 64) in order to identify aspects of language use that cannot be derived from a purely grammatical analysis (1966, p. 410). In contrast, Halliday's approach favours grammar-like answers (1992, p. 64), as he perceives lexis as "delicate grammar" (1961, p. 267), and his aim is "to build the dictionary out of the grammar" (1992, p. 63). A more recent approach that has grammar as its starting point is collostructional analysis (Gries & Stefanowitsch, 2004; Stefanowitsch & Gries, 2003), which examines the lexemes that are attracted or repelled by particular slots in a given construction.

Despite refuting the traditional distinction between lexis and grammar, all the above approaches isolate particular lexical or grammatical aspects in the analysis of research findings. That is, while discussing aspects of the lexis-grammar interaction they do focus on one or the other at different stages of the analysis. This practice is compatible with, and seems to support, Halliday's conception of the lexicogrammatical continuum described above. However, the relation between lexis and grammar is not only a matter of research angle (e.g. starting from the lexis or grammar end of the continuum), as lexis and grammar interact. Particular grammatical structures may tend to contain particular lexical items more frequently than others, or even be "lexically restricted" (Francis, 1993, p. 142; see also Stubbs, 1996, p. 40); in turn, particular lexis may be found more frequently within particular grammatical structures (e.g. Hunston & Francis, 2000, p. 1; Stefanowitsch & Gries, 2003). Combined, the two types of interaction can be seen as instances of "lexis-grammar co-selection" (Römer, 2009, p. 141).

The approach taken here is that grammar is always involved (Culicover, Jackendoff & Audring, 2017), and any apparent primacy of lexis is an effect of the research focus. For example, even the seemingly lexical starting point of the present study (i.e. the word *interested*) cannot be adequately defined without recourse to grammar. That is, a full description of the starting point needs to specify that the focus is *interested* when used as an adjective, rather than as the past tense of the verb INTEREST. Similarly, BE in *BE interested* needs to be specified as a copular verb in all its tense-aspect permutations. This study approaches *BE interested* lexicogrammatically to get lexicogrammatical answers—that is, the analysis will privilege neither lexis nor grammar—or, in Sinclair's terms, neither the idiom principle nor the open-choice principle. Wherever along the lexicogrammatical continuum the research starting point may be, the exploration can move towards either side. Support for this approach is provided in a study by Erman and Warren (2000), which examined the proportion of prefabs in texts from LOB and the London Lund corpus of Spoken English (using manual analysis). Prefabs are seen as manifestations of the idiom principle, and are defined as "a combination of at least two words favoured by native speakers in preference to an alternative combination which could have been equivalent had there been no conventionalisation" (ibid., p. 31). Erman and Warren (2000, pp. 50–53) report that choices consistent with the idiom or open-choice principle have fairly similar proportions in the texts they analysed, with choices consistent with the idiom principle being slightly more frequent on average (55%) and even more frequent in spoken texts, although the proportion in individual texts ranged from 40% to 60%. They concluded that their results support their hypotheses that "in producing utterances the language user alternates between the open choice principle and the idiom principle" (ibid., p. 30, 51). In this light, *BE interested* will be approached from both ends of the continuum, and the analysis will seek to derive not only grammar-like and lexis-like answers, but also answers reflecting instances of lexis-grammar co-selection. Similar examples of corpus-based lexicogrammatical research with a descriptive focus are McEnery and Xiao's (2005) examination of complementation patterns of the verb HELP, Hasselgard's (2016) examination of the patterns of '*the* N1 *of the* N2', and Rühlemann's (2007) study on the GET-passive, whereas examples of studies looking at both L1 and L2/learner use are Deshors' (2015) comparison of *to*-infinitival and gerundial complementation patterns, Gilquin's (2012) examination of the particular verbs and classes of verbs that occupy the non-finite verb slot in causative constructions, and Römer's (2009) study on the patterns of introductory *it*.

4 Focus and Aims

The main focus of this study is the complementation patterns of *BE interested*, and the extent to which relevant information about these patterns is provided in pedagogical materials. The study also examines the frequency of other copular verbs complemented by the adjective *interested*, in order to establish the extent to which the complementation pattern *BE interested* is frequent enough to merit examination. An initial analysis also suggested that the focus of the study could usefully be expanded to include the following: the presence or absence of modal marking of *BE* in *BE interested*, and the types of verbs found in two complementation patterns: '*BE interested* + *-ing* Clause' and '*BE interested*

+ *to*-inf Clause'. At this point, it must be clarified that the study does not aim to contribute to materials design, that is, the particular presentation of information in pedagogical materials (e.g. the wording of the information, and the selection of examples), or the design of exercises. However, it is hoped that the findings can inform this aspect of pedagogical materials.

As pedagogical grammars are expected to be informed by reference grammars, three major grammars were consulted for information pertaining to the focus and aims of this study: Carter and McCarthy (2006, pp. 21, 297, 300, 310, 439–445, 459, 462, 500, 508–509, 522, 546, 565–566), Huddleston and Pullum (2002, pp. 50, 83, 540–544, 658, 1230–1231), and Quirk et al. (1985, pp. 403, 413, 546, 576, 657–659, 740, 755, 774, 862, 979, 1061–1063, 1211, 1220–1292). All reference grammars mention *interested in* as a pattern—either by particular mention, or in lists of 'Adjective + Preposition' patterns, and they all discuss the following complementation patterns of *BE interested*:

1. *BE interested in* + NP
2. *BE interested in* + *-ing* participle Clause
3. *BE interested in* + Noun (*wh-*) Clause
4. *BE interested* + *to*-infinitive Clause
5. *BE interested* + ∅ (no complementation)

The study examines the presence, absence, and prominence of information regarding the above patterns in pedagogical materials. It also examines spoken and written L1 and L2 corpora for the frequency of a) different copular verbs complementing the adjective *interested*, b) different complementation patterns of *BE interested*, and c) modalised BE in *BE interested*. Comparison between L1 use and pedagogical materials is expected to establish the extent to which the latter represent L1 use and whether L1 use supports the inclusion or foregrounding of some patterns and the exclusion or backgrounding of others. Comparisons between L1 and L2 will establish the extent to which L2 use matches L1 use. Finally, comparisons between L2 and pedagogical materials will provide indications of the correlation between the information in pedagogical materials and learner use, which will be used as a proxy for determining the influence of pedagogical materials on learner use. In light of the above, the study addresses the following research questions:

In relation to pedagogical materials:

1. Do they treat *BE interested* explicitly as a pattern (i.e. do the materials reserve an entry for it)? If not, do they provide directly relevant lexi-

cogrammatical information, that is, information on the complementation patterns of 'Copula + Adjective'?

2. Do they provide information regarding other copular verbs complemented by the adjective *interested*?
3. Do they present all complementation patterns of BE *interested* (or just *interested*, irrespective of the copular verb)? If so, are these patterns treated explicitly (i.e. is information provided directly) or implicitly (i.e. do the patterns feature in examples or exercises)?
4. What other relevant information is provided (e.g. frequencies, collostructional choices)?

In relation to use, as evidenced in the corpora examined:

5. What is the frequency of different copular verbs of which *interested* is a complement?
6. What is the frequency of each complementation pattern of BE *interested*?
7. What is the extent of modal marking of BE in each complementation pattern?
8. Are particular types of verbs used more frequently in the non-finite slots in two of the complementation patterns ('BE *interested in* + *-ing* Clause' and 'BE *interested* + *to*-infinitive Clause').
9. Are there any differences between L1 and L2 use and between spoken and written production?

5 Data and Methodology

The study examines two types of data: pedagogical materials (grammars and dictionaries) and corpora (L1 and L2). The L2 corpora include learner writing and speaking at CEFR levels B2–C2 (see Section 5.2 for details).

5.1 *Pedagogical Materials*

The pedagogical materials examined are at the level that the learners whose use is represented in the corpora can be expected to have used (B1–C2). It must also be clarified that the grammars used in the study are not textbooks/coursebooks (i.e. they are not meant for use in class) but reference materials for learners (like dictionaries). Learners are not expected to plough through every page and learn everything contained in the book; rather, these types of pedagogical materials are to be used when a learner needs help in understand-

TABLE 8.1 *Pedagogical materials examined in this study*

Grammars	Dictionaries
– *English Grammar in Use* (B1–B2) – *Active Grammar Level 2* (B1–B2) – *Collins COBUILD English Grammar* (B1–C2) – *Grammar and Beyond 4* (B2–C2) – *Advanced Grammar in Use* (C1–C2) – *Active Grammar Level 3* (C1–C2)	– *Cambridge Dictionary Online*: dictionary.cambridge.org/dictionary/english/interested – *Collins Dictionary Online*: collinsdictionary.com/dictionary/english/interested – *Longman Dictionary of Contemporary English Online*: ldoceonline.com/dictionary/interested – *Macmillan Dictionary Online*: macmillandictionary.com/dictionary/british/interested – *Oxford Advanced Learner's Dictionary Online*: oxfordlearnersdictionaries.com/definition/english/interested

ing/using a particular language item (e.g. when writing an essay). For this reason, pedagogical materials can be comprehensive, without being intimidating for the learner. Although it is not assumed that learners will have necessarily consulted the specific pedagogical materials examined in the study, they can be expected to be largely representative of the kind of input L2 learners receive, as the content of pedagogical materials tends to be fairly uniform (e.g. Gabrielatos, 2003, 2006; Tomlinson, 2013, pp. 2–3, 17). Table 8.1 lists the pedagogical materials examined (for more details, see Appendix 1). Parentheses after the grammar titles indicate the range of CEFR levels each grammar is designed to address; links after dictionary titles lead to the entries examined.

In the case of pedagogical grammars, the information required to address questions 1–4 was sought using the tables of contents and indexes, and the examination of relevant entries ('rules'), examples and exercises. In the case of dictionaries, information was collected by looking up the entry for *interested*: definitions, examples, and other relevant information.

5.2 *Corpora and Methodology*

L1 use is examined via the BNC (written and spoken sub-corpora, henceforth BNCw and BNCs, respectively). Learner language is examined via two corpora: ICLE (Granger, Dagneaux, Meunier & Paquot, 2009), a corpus of essays written by upper intermediate to advanced learners of English (CEFR levels B2–C2)[1] and LINDSEI (Gilquin, De Cock & Granger, 2010), a corpus of elicited spoken English, produced by advanced learners (C1–C2).[2] It must be mentioned that the comparison between the learner corpora and the BNC is of course not ideal, as the BNC contains a variety of genres, whereas ICLE and LINDSEI are genre-specific. Therefore, comparisons between L2 and L1 use would in principle be more usefully carried out between corpora containing similar genres (Biber et al., 1994, p. 174, 183; Leech, 2011, p. 13); that is, between the above learner corpora, on the one hand, and LOCNESS and LOCNEC, on the other. In this light, the results of the comparisons between L1 and L2 use must be seen as tentative, as the study needs to be supplemented with comparisons between genre-compatible L1 and L2 corpora. However, LOCNESS and LOCNEC would not be useful in the evaluation of the pedagogical materials, which provide non-genre-specific information. In this light, the use of a general corpus (BNC) is essential.

The BNC was accessed via BNCweb (Hoffmann, Evert, Smith, Lee, & Berglund-Prytz, 2008), ICLE and LINDSEI via two versions of CQPweb (Hardie, 2012; Xu & Wu, 2014).[3] For aims 6–8, random concordance samples of 250 instances of the word-form *interested* were analysed. Samples were retrieved using this simple query, rather than using a complex query to return instances of *interested* used with the copular BE, for two reasons. First, it enabled the manual analysis to determine the proportion of BE in relation to other copular verbs complemented by the adjective *interested*. Second, it is expected to have resulted in very high recall (excluding instances of misspelling or mistranscription of *interested* in the corpora). This was particularly useful in the case of spoken corpora, in which features of spontaneous speech (e.g. fillers, repetitions, false starts) would make it likely that true positives would be missed and false positives would be included. For example, it would be difficult to formulate a complex query that could accommodate instances like (1) below, where a hesitation (*mm*) and a pause intervene between *interested in* and the *-ing* Clause complementing it. Samples were first examined in order to remove predicative uses of *interested* (2), learner mistakes (3), elliptical uses (4), and incomplete utterances (5).

1 https://uclouvain.be/en/research-institutes/ilc/cecl/icle.html. Last accessed 19 June 2017.

2 https://uclouvain.be/en/research-institutes/ilc/cecl/lindsei.html. Last accessed 19 June 2017.

3 I am grateful to Jajin Xu (Beijing Foreign Studies University) for cleaning and tagging LINDSEI (e.g. removing paralinguistic features from transcripts) and uploading it to BSFU CQPweb (http://111.200.194.212/cqp. Last accessed 19 June 2017).

(1) I I really I I don't know I don't have much preferences because (erm) *I'm very interested in* (mm). *talking* about this in (eh). (er) in literature written in English (LINDSEI IT:029)

(2) Is it not better off as a hidden surprise to be discovered by the *interested* tourist? (BNCw K5M:1867)

(3) I h= em I had in school and eh it eh is eh *interested* because. now I can do things that I want. and erm are eh eh of ver=. of *interested* to me. (LINDSEI GR:040)

(4) The people, who watch public television *are* in average more educated, often *interested in* politics and keenly following all daily events, they live with the rest of their society through television. (ICLE CZPU:1004)

(5) Margaret: Well, I mean we just said well that's, you know, an expensive place for a holiday by the sound of it, but erm we hadn't got into any details.
Raymond: Well this was erm Bulgaria
Margaret: Yes, yes
Raymond: Mm
Margaret: but er so I, I don't know if he'd *be interested in.* I certainly wouldn't coach it ⟨pause⟩ so ⟨pause⟩ I think you would be creased by the time you got there in two days. (BNCs KDM:6494–6499)

Frequency comparisons took into account both the size of frequency differences and their statistical significance (established using the log-likelihood test).[4] Sizeable differences were deemed those in which the frequency of a feature in one corpus was at least 25% higher than in the other; the threshold for statistical significance was set at $p \leq 0.05$ ($G^2 \geq 3.84$). It must be clarified that frequency differences will be presented in relation to the highest frequency, so that differences can be comparable. Although all sizeable differences will be discussed, only those that are also statistically significant will be deemed reliable. To facilitate reading the tables reporting on comparisons, in cases of

4 Calculations of frequency differences and statistical significance were carried out using Paul Rayson's spreadsheet (http://ucrel.lancs.ac.uk/people/paul/SigEff.xlsx. Last accessed 19 June 2017).

sizeable differences, the cell of the highest frequency will be shaded; if the sizeable difference is also statistically significant, the cell indicating the G^2 value will also be shaded.

In order to address question 8, an automated collocation analysis on the whole corpora was employed, so that the strength of collocation could be established (something that could not be achieved via the manual analysis). As the analysis of copular verbs complemented by the adjective *interested* (question 5) showed that BE is used in 92 %-99 % of instances, collocates were calculated on the queries "interested in" and "interested to". Right-hand collocates in position R1 for written corpora, and R1–R3 for spoken corpora (to allow for fillers and dysfluencies). Granted, the R1 position may exclude discontinuous constructions (e.g. As a result, economists are much more *interested than before in* correcting inefficiencies by reducing the costs of doing business [ABE:3219]; I *was interested last year to see* Tim Jonke's article and his method of spraying acrylic paint over oil paint [C89:1296]). However, such instances are extremely rare: in BNCw, queries with one and two intervening words between *interested* and *in* (followed by a verb) returned 34 and 3 instances, respectively, whereas there were 5016 instances of *interested in* followed by a verb. The corresponding results for *interested* and *to* were 7 and 9 instances, respectively, compared to 366 for *interested* followed by a *to*-infinitive. Therefore, the R1 span provides a dependable picture of collocates. The minimum frequency for both collocate and collocation was set at 1, so that even very infrequent collocates would be taken into account. For a word to be deemed a collocate, the MI score of the collocation had to be at least 3.

6 Results: Analysis and Discussion

6.1 *Pedagogical Materials*

Most of the pedagogical grammars examined present *interested* as an adjective, or make students aware that words ending in *-ed* can be adjectives (five out of six), and mention that *-ing* forms can function as nouns (four out of six). Dictionaries, due to their focus, do not provide any general grammatical information regarding *-ed* and *-ing* forms; however, they all contain an entry or subentry on *interested* as an adjective. When discussing complements of *interested in*, pedagogical materials (particularly dictionaries) rarely distinguish between *-ing* forms syntactically functioning as nouns and verbs, but tend to focus on reminding learners that a word with the suffix *-ing* must follow *interested in*. More to the point, they do not make it explicit that an *-ing* form may belong to a different part of speech according to the complementation pattern (and corresponding syntactic slot): a noun in '*BE interested in* + NP' or a verb in '*BE interested in* + *-ing* Clause'. Not all pedagogical grammars present *interested in* as a pattern, whereas most dictionaries (four out of five) explicitly include it in their entry for *interested*, and all provide examples with *interested in*. Only two grammars discuss both *interested in* and *BE interested in*, two provide partial treatment (i.e. *interested* is contained in lists of 'Adjective + Preposition' patterns), and two do not treat it at all. As a result, none of the grammars or dictionaries, individually, presents all complementation patterns, either regarding *interested* in particular, or adjectives in general.

The grammars and dictionaries examined overlap to some extent in the complementation patterns they prioritise, background, or omit. Two complementation patterns are mostly neglected in both pedagogical grammars and dictionaries: '*wh*-Clause' and zero complementation. No grammar or dictionary treats '*interested in* + *wh*-Clause' explicitly: only two grammars present information about the pattern in a section on adjective complementation, and one contains the pattern in an exercise. Three dictionaries do not treat the pattern at all (they contain no information or examples), and two only provide examples. Zero complementation is more neglected in grammars: none treats the pattern explicitly, one presents it in a list of adjectives complementing a copular verb, adding that the adjectives may not have complements themselves, and one elicits zero complementation in an exercise (one sentence). In dictionaries, zero complementation is neglected to a lesser degree: although dictionaries do not treat it explicitly, they all include the pattern in at least one example.

The pedagogical grammars examined, taken collectively, also underrepresent the other three complementation patterns. The NP complementation is completely absent from two grammars, the others providing relevant information when discussing 'Preposition + Noun' patterns. In dictionaries, although NP complementation is not completely neglected, it is only treated explicitly and fully in two dictionaries, the other three only providing examples. The '*-ing* Clause' complement is absent from one grammar, the others providing relevant information when discussing 'Preposition + V-*ing*' patterns. Only one dictionary neglects this pattern, with three treating it explicitly and fully, and one providing examples. The '*to*-inf' complement is absent from one grammar and four have sections on 'Adj + *to*-inf'. Only one grammar provides explicit treatment of the '*to*-inf' pattern, and contrasts it with the '*-ing* Clause' pattern. The '*to*-inf' pattern is the one receiving the most explicit attention in dictionaries, with four dictionaries explicitly mentioning the pattern (e.g. '*ADJ to*-inf'), and all five providing examples.

Finally, none of the pedagogical materials examined provides explicit information regarding alternative copular verbs, or makes distinctions between use in written and spoken language. They rarely provide frequency information regarding complementation patterns, or the likelihood of the copular verb being modalised in particular patterns—although some examples have modalised copulas. Also, no dictionary, and only one grammar, provide explicit information regarding the meaning of verbs that tend to be used in the '*to*-inf' complementation, and although all dictionaries but one provide relevant examples, only one grammar (the one offering the explicit treatment) does so. For an outline of the relevant content of each of the pedagogical materials examined here see Appendix 2.

From the perspective of the usual users of pedagogical materials, neither grammars nor dictionaries (individually) provide all the information that a learner may need when seeking to use *interested* as an adjective (whether they are aware that it is an adjective or not), but the two types of pedagogical materials seem to complement one another to some extent. Another interesting observation is that they do not provide information only on the grammar or lexis part of the lexicogrammatical continuum, respectively. Pedagogical grammars approach language from the grammar end of the lexicogrammatical continuum (morphology and syntax), but they also provide some information on the grammatical patterns of particular words (e.g. *interesting* vs. *interested*). However, if a student wants to know the grammatical patterns that a word can be used in, then pedagogical grammars are of limited help. Dictionaries, on the other hand, approach language from the lexical end (foregrounding senses and lexical relations), but they also provide related information regarding grammatical patterns—either directly (in a sub-entry) or indirectly (in examples).

6.2 *Corpus Analysis*

6.2.1 Copular Verbs Complemented by the Adjective *Interested*

The examination of the copular verbs complemented by the adjective *interested* revealed that BE is by far the most frequent copula complemented by *interested* in all four corpora, accounting for more than 92 % of the instances in all corpus samples (Table 8.2). The examination of the overall frequencies of the copulas shown in Table 8.2 in BNCw and BNCs showed that the proportion of BE in this group of copulas is 84.4 % and 79 %, respectively (compared to 92.6 % and 92.3 %, respectively, when complemented by *interested*). That is, the predominance of BE in the pattern in focus cannot be fully explained by its very high overall frequency in the BNC. This seems to support the examination of *BE interested* as a pattern which is not only by far the most frequent, but also somehow distinct. The frequency comparisons of the other copulas in the samples also show that there are clear differences between L1 and L2 use. Overall, L2 use

TABLE 8.2 *Copular verbs complemented by the adjective* interested

Copular verbs	BNCw (N=215)	*BNCw %*	BNCs (N=234)	*BNCs %*	ICLE (N=236)	*ICLE %*	LINDSEI (N=210)	*LINDSEI %*
BE	199	*92.6*	216	*92.3*	234	*99.2*	198	*94.3*
other	16	*7.4*	18	*7.7*	2	*0.8*	12	*5.7*
	BECOME (5)		BECOME (4)				BECOME (4)	
	FEEL (1)							
	GET (3)		GET (10)		GET (1)		GET (6)	
	KEEP (2)							
			LOOK (1)					
	MAKE (1)		MAKE (1)		MAKE (1)		MAKE (1)	
	REMAIN (2)							
	SEEM (2)		SEEM (2)					
							STAY (1)	

TABLE 8.3 *Proportion of copular verbs other than* BE*: Comparison of* ICLE *and BNCw*

	ICLE (N=236)	*ICLE %*	BNCw (N=215)	*BNCw %*	*%DIFF*	G^2
Other copular verbs	2	0.9	16	7.4	*722.2*	**13.74**

TABLE 8.4 *Proportion of copular verbs other than* BE*: Comparison of* LINDSEI *and BNCs*

	LINDSEI (N=210)	*LINDSEI %*	BNCs (N=234)	*BNCs %*	*%DIFF*	G^2
Other copular verbs	12	5.7	19	7.7	*35.1*	0.93

contains a smaller proportion of other copular verbs—particularly in writing. In learner writing, *interested* complements copulas other than BE in just above one-tenth of the corresponding frequency in the BNCw sample, and the difference has high statistical significance (Table 8.3). Learner speaking contains other copulas in about one-third of the frequency in the spoken BNC, but the difference is not statistically significant (Table 8.4). More importantly, learners seem to use a much smaller variety of other copular verbs compared to native speakers: 4 types as opposed to 8—with only BECOME, GET and MAKE being shared in the L1 and L2 corpus samples (Table 8.2).

6.2.2 Complementation Patterns of *BE Interested*

In all four corpora, the most frequent complementation pattern by far is '*BE interested in* + NP' (Table 8.5). However, this is where the similarities stop, as there are differences in the proportions of all complementation patterns (even in the case of NP complementation) between L1 and L2 corpora, as well as between speech and writing. For example, in writing (both L1 and L2), the second most frequent pattern is '*BE interested in* + *-ing* Clause' (23.62% in BNCw, 11.5% in ICLE), whereas in speech, the second most frequent pattern is 'BE interested ⌀' in BNCs (30.23%), but '*BE interested in* + *-ing* Clause' in LINDSEI. The remainder of this section will compare the frequencies of the patterns as follows:

a. speech and writing in L1
b. speech and writing in L2
c. writing in L1 and L2
d. speech in L1 and L2

TABLE 8.5 BE interested*: Proportion of complementation types in the four corpora*

Complementation pattern	BNCw (N=199)	*BNCw %*	BNCs (N=216)	*BNCs %*	ICLE (N=234)	*ICLE %*	LINDSEI (N=198)	*LINDSEI %*
BE interested in + NP	102	*51.3*	90	*41.9*	185	*79.1*	149	*75.3*
BE interested in + *-ing* Clause	47	*23.6*	27	*12.5*	27	*11.5*	24	*12.1*
BE interested in + *wh*-Clause	7	*3.5*	13	*6.1*	11	*4.7*	8	*4.0*
BE interested + *to*-inf	11	*5.5*	21	*9.8*	4	*1.7*	5	*2.5*
BE interested ⌀	32	*16.1*	65	*30.2*	7	*3.0*	12	*6.1*

Looking at L1 use (Table 8.6), the first observation is that the most frequent complementation pattern ('*BE interested in* + NP') is also the only one with similar frequencies in both speech and writing. The only pattern with higher frequency in writing is '*BE interested in* + *-ing* Clause', which shows almost double the frequency of the pattern in speech. The pattern that seems to characterise speech is zero complementation ('*BE interested* ⌀'), which has

TABLE 8.6 *Complementation patterns of* BE interested*: Comparison of* L1 *speech and writing*

Complementation pattern	BNCw (N=199)	*BNCw* %	BNCs (N=215)	*BNCs* %	*%DIFF*	G^2
BE *interested in* + NP	102	*51.3*	90	*41.9*	22.5	1.97
BE *interested in* + *-ing* Clause	47	23.6	27	*12.5*	*88.1*	7.13
BE *interested in* + *wh*-Clause	7	3.5	13	*6.1*	*74.3*	1.39
BE *interested* + *to*-inf	11	*5.5*	21	*9.8*	*78.2*	2.45
BE *interested* ∅	32	*16.1*	65	*30.2*	*87.6*	9.05

TABLE 8.7 *Complementation patterns of* BE interested*: Comparison of* L2 *speech and writing*

Complementation pattern	ICLE (N=234)	*ICLE* %	LINDSEI (N=198)	*LINDSEI* %	*%DIFF*	G^2
BE *interested in* + NP	185	*79.1*	149	*75.3*	*5.1*	0.20
BE *interested in* + *-ing* Clause	27	*11.5*	24	*12.1*	*5.2*	0.03
BE *interested in* + *wh*-Clause	11	*4.7*	8	4.0	*16.4*	0.11
BE *interested* + *to*-inf	4	*1.7*	5	2.5	*47.1*	0.34
BE *interested* ∅	7	*3.0*	12	*6.1*	*103.3*	2.30

almost double the frequency in speech compared to writing. The other two patterns ('BE *interested in* + *wh*-Clause' and 'BE *interested* + *to*-inf') also have higher frequency (about 75%) in speech, but due to their low raw frequency in the corpora, the differences are not statistically significant.

As in L1, 'BE *interested in* + NP' has very similar frequencies in L2 speech and writing (Table 8.7). However, the differences between speech and writing observed in the L1 corpora are not always mirrored in L2. The pattern 'BE *interested* ∅' is twice as frequent in speech, compared to writing, in both L1 and L2 corpora, but in the case of L2 use the difference is not statistically significant, as raw frequencies in both L2 speech and writing are very low (see below for a discussion).

Table 8.8 summarises the results so far: the symbol "=" indicates similar frequencies in writing (W) and speech (S) (i.e. any differences are non-sizeable); ">" indicates frequency differences that are both sizeable and statistically significant; parentheses indicate sizeable differences that are not statistically significant. Overall, L2 speech and writing show more similarities than differences,

TABLE 8.8 *Similarities and differences between L1 and L2 speech and writing*

Complementation pattern	L1 corpora	L2 corpora
BE *interested in* + NP	W=S	W=S
BE *interested in* + *-ing* Clause	W>S	W=S
BE *interested in* + *wh-* Clause	(S>W)	W=S
BE *interested* + *to*-inf	(S>W)	(S>W)
BE *interested* ∅	S>W	(S>W)

in contrast with the frequency differences in L1. In other words, L2 use seems more homogenised, in that it exhibits much less differentiation in the frequency of the five complementation patterns.

A more detailed picture of distributional differences emerges when we directly compare the frequencies of each complementation pattern in the written and spoken output of L1 and L2 users, respectively (Tables 8.9 and 8.10). In writing, four out of the five patterns show sizeable and statistically significant differences between L1 and L2. Learners tend to use three of the patterns less frequently than native speakers ('BE *interested in* + *-ing* Clause', 'BE *interested in* + *to*-inf', and 'BE *interested* ∅') and one pattern more frequently ('BE *interested in* + NP'). Focusing on differences that are both sizeable and statistically significant, the comparisons in this section indicate a correlation between L2 use and the presence/absence and detail of the information on (BE) *interested* and its complementation patterns in pedagogical materials (particularly grammars).

The most prominent difference is in NP complementation, which is the only pattern that learners overuse in both speech and writing. In fact, not only do learners use it much more frequently than L1 users, but they also use it so frequently that it dominates their relevant output, as learners opt for NP complementation in more than three-quarters of the instances in the corpus samples. At first glance, this does not seem to correlate with the treatment of NP complementation in the pedagogical materials examined: the pattern may be fairly prominent in the dictionaries, but it is less than prominent in the grammars. However, grammars for lower levels (A1–A2) tend to only treat NP complementation (e.g. Murphy, 2007, pp. 234–235). Therefore, it seems plausible to argue that NP complementation is rather neglected in grammars of higher levels (B1–C2), because the pattern is expected to be known. This is supported by the fact that two of the three B1–B2 grammars examined treat the

TABLE 8.9 *Complementation patterns of* BE interested *in L1 and L2 writing*

Complementation pattern	ICLE (N=234)	*ICLE* %	BNCw (N=199)	*BNCw* %	*%DIFF*	G^2
BE *interested in* + NP	185	*79.1*	102	*51.3*	*54.2*	12.78
BE *interested in* + *-ing* Clause	27	*11.5*	47	*23.6*	*105.2*	9.20
BE *interested in* + *wh*-Clause	11	*4.7*	7	*3.5*	*33.6*	0.37
BE *interested* + *to*-inf	4	*1.7*	11	*5.5*	*223.5*	4.63
BE *interested* ∅	7	*3.0*	32	*16.1*	*436.7*	21.66

TABLE 8.10 *Complementation patterns of* BE interested *in L1 and L2 speech*

Complementation pattern	LINDSEI (N=198)	*LINDSEI* %	BNCs (N=215)	*BNCs* %	*%DIFF*	G^2
BE *interested in* + NP	149	*75.3*	90	*41.9*	*79.8*	19.98
BE *interested in* + *-ing* Clause	24	*12.1*	27	*12.5*	*3.3*	0.02
BE *interested in* + *wh*-Clause	8	*4.0*	13	*6.1*	*52.5*	0.83
BE *interested* + *to*-inf	5	*2.5*	21	*9.8*	*292.0*	9.31
BE *interested* ∅	12	*6.1*	65	*30.2*	*395.1*	35.87

NP pattern in sections discussing 'Adjective + Preposition' patterns, whereas only one of the three B2–C2 grammars mentions the pattern (without listing *interested*, and with no related examples or exercises). Also, the two B1–B2 grammars include the NP complementation in order to contrast it with the '*-ing* Clause' pattern, which is introduced at B1–B2 level.

Learners underuse two patterns in both speech and writing: zero complementation and '*to*-inf'. Zero complementation shows by far the largest difference: learners use the pattern about five times less frequently in speech and six times less frequently in writing. This correlates with the pattern's virtual absence from grammars, and the lack of explicit treatment in dictionaries (which only include the pattern in examples). The '*to*-inf' pattern is also clearly underused by learners (about four times less in speech and three times less in writing). This correlates with its treatment in pedagogical grammars, in which it is only discussed indirectly (as part of the 'Adjective + *to*-inf' pattern), but not with its treatment in dictionaries, as four out of five present the pattern explicitly. Finally, one pattern ('*-ing* Clause') is underused in L2 writing only, with learners having less than half of the proportion in L1 writing. Again, this correlates with the treatment of the pattern in grammars rather than dictionaries. However, the underuse of '*to*-inf' and '*-ing* Clause' patterns, and the predominance of NP complementation in L2 speech and writing, may also be attributed to syntactic complexity. As NP complementation is syntactically much less complex than the other two, learners may have opted for the simpler complementation pattern to avoid errors (e.g. Davydova, 2011; Vyatkina, 2013).

6.2.3 Modalisation of BE in *BE Interested*

Looking at the complementation patterns of *BE interested* collectively in L1 use (Table 8.11), it becomes apparent that BE seems more likely to be modalised in speech than in writing, as modalised BE is about 70% more frequent in L1 speech, and the difference is statistically significant (G^2=4.87). In terms of individual complementation patterns, the '*to*-inf' pattern contains by far the higher proportion of modalised BE in both L1 speech (57.1%) and writing (36.4%). In L1 writing, all other complementation patterns have very similar proportions of modalised BE (between 12.5% and 14.9%). However, there are distinct differences in L1 speech, with proportions of modalised BE ranging from 15.4% ('*wh-* Clause') to 33.3% ('*-ing* Clause'). The above indicate that both the medium (speech or writing) and the particular complementation pattern have a bearing on the likelihood that BE (in *BE interested*) will be modally marked.

In this light, it is important to observe two differences between L1 and L2 use. First, BE is modalised less frequently in L2, particularly in speech, where the difference is statistically significant. It occurs about three times less frequently in L2 speech (G^2=15.69), and about a quarter less frequently in L2 writing (but G^2=1.01). This, of course, may be due to the general tendency of learners to use modal marking less frequently than L1 users (e.g. Flowerdew, 2000; Gabrielatos & McEnery, 2005); however, the lack of any explicit information in pedagogical materials regarding modalisation of BE in *BE interested* might also be a contributing factor. Second, L2 use does not mirror the differences observed between L1 speech and writing: on average, the five complementation patterns, collectively, show almost identical proportions of modalised *BE interested* (10.6 in speech and 10.7 in writing). As in the case of complementation types, L2 use regarding modalisation of *BE interested* seems fairly homogenised. The remainder of the section will discuss frequency comparisons of modalised *BE interested* between L1 and L2 speech and writing in relation to the five complementation patterns.

In L1, four out of the five complementation patterns have higher proportions of modalised BE in speech than in writing, although none of the differ-

TABLE 8.11 *Proportion of modalised* BE *in the complementation patterns of* BE interested

	BNCw	*BNCw %*	BNCs	*BNCs %*	ICLE	*ICLE %*	LINDSEI	*LINDSEI %*
in + NP	13/102	*12.8*	15/90	*16.7*	22/185	*11.9*	11/149	*7.4*
in + *ing* C	7/47	*14.9*	9/27	*33.3*	2/27	*7.4*	3/24	*12.5*
in + *wh* C	1/7	*14.29*	2/13	*15.4*	1/11	*9.1*	2/8	*25.0*
to-inf	4/11	*36.4*	12/21	*57.1*	1/4	*25.0*	0/5	*0*
∅	4/32	*12.5*	14/65	*21.5*	0/7	*0*	1/12	*8.3*
Total	29/199	*14.6*	52/216	*24.7*	26/234	*11.1*	17/198	*8.6*

ences is statistically significant (Table 8.12). L2 speech and writing also show differences, although not statistically significant (Table 8.13), but only in two instances do L1 and L2 show the same similarities/differences between speech and writing ('-*ing* Clause', zero). That is, L2 use shows few similarities with L1 use regarding the frequency of modalised BE in different complementation patterns of *BE interested* in speech and writing

L1 and L2 writing show large differences in the proportions of modalised BE (Table 8.14): in four out of the five complementation patterns, learners have clearly lower proportions of modalised BE, but due to the small number of modalised instances, the differences are not statistically significant. However, there is an important relevant similarity: in both L1 and L2 writing, '*to*-inf' has by far the highest modal marking compared to other complementation patterns. In other words, the learners' frequency of modalised BE in the '*to*-inf' pattern tends to conform to L1 use (albeit to a smaller extent), despite the lack of explicit information in pedagogical materials. What can be tentatively hypothesised is that learners pick up useful cues from the modal marking in examples and exercises, which they replicate in their writing.

The situation is similar, but not identical, in L1 and L2 speech (Table 8.15). As in writing, learners modalise BE much less frequently in four out of the five complementation patterns. The only case when spoken L2 has higher modal marking than spoken L1 is '*wh*-Clause' complementation, but the difference is not statistically significant. However, in two patterns, NP and '*to*-inf', the difference (lower proportions in L2) is so large that it is statistically significant despite the low frequencies involved. This may be explained by the almost identical proportions of modalisation in L2 speech and writing when complementation patterns are examined collectively (Table 8.11 above). As L1 shows much higher proportions in speech, the difference between L2 and L1 in speech

TABLE 8.12 *Proportion of modalised* BE *in the complementation patterns of* BE interested *in L1 speech and writing*

	BNCw	*BNCw %*	BNCs	*BNCs %*	*%DIFF*	G2
in + NP	13/102	*12.8*	15/90	*16.7*	*30.5*	0.50
in + *ing* C	7/47	*14.9*	9/27	*33.3*	*123.5*	2.57
in + *wh* C	1/7	*14.3*	2/13	*15.4*	*7.7*	0.00
to-inf	4/11	*36.4*	12/21	*57.1*	*56.7*	0.66
ø	4/32	*12.5*	14/65	*21.5*	*72.0*	1.01

TABLE 8.13 *Proportion of modalised* BE *in the complementation patterns of* BE interested *in L2 speech and writing*

	ICLE	*ICLE %*	LINDSEI	*LINDSEI %*	*%DIFF*	G2
in + NP	22/185	*11.9*	11/149	*7.4*	*61.1*	1.74
in + *ing* C	2/27	*7.4*	3/24	*12.5*	*68.8*	0.34
in + *wh* C	1/11	*9.1*	2/8	*25.0*	*175.0*	0.73
to-inf	1/4	*25.0*	0/5	*0*	*2.5E+19*	1.62
ø	0/7	*0*	1/12	*8.3*	*8.3E+18*	0.92

TABLE 8.14 *Proportion of modalised* BE *in the complementation patterns of* BE interested *in L1 and L2 writing*

	ICLE	*ICLE %*	BNCw	*BNCw %*	*%DIFF*	G2
in + NP	22/185	*11.9*	13/102	*12.8*	*7.6*	0.04
in + *ing* C	2/27	*7.4*	7/47	*14.9*	*101.4*	0.85
in + *wh* C	1/11	*9.1*	1/7	*14.3*	*57.1*	0.10
to-inf	1/4	*25.0*	4/11	*36.4*	*45.6*	0.12
ø	0/7	*0*	4/32	*12.5*	*1.25E+19*	1.58

TABLE 8.15 *Proportion of modalised* BE *in the complementation patterns of* BE interested *in L1 and L2 speech*

	LINDSEI	*LINDSEI %*	BNCs	*BNCs %*	*%DIFF*	G^2
in + NP	11/149	7.4	15/90	16.7	125.7	4.27
in + *ing* C	3/24	12.5	9/27	33.3	166.4	2.47
in + *wh* C	2/8	25.0	2/13	15.4	62.6	0.23
to-inf	0/5	0	12/21	57.1	5.71E+19	5.13
ø	1/12	8.3	14/65	21.5	159.0	1.11

is large enough to achieve statistical significance. Simply put, in the L2 corpora, speech tends to mirror writing.

6.2.4 Verb Types in Two Complementation Patterns of *Be Interested*: '*-ing* Clause' and '*to*-Inf'

The analysis of collocates in the two L1 corpora pinpointed a distinct difference between the meaning of verbs in the two complement types. In the case of '*BE interested in* + *-ing* Clause', there is no particular meaning group that is more frequent than others; the verbs in the complement seem to be topic-specific. On the contrary, more than half of the verbs in '*BE interested* + *to*-inf' have meanings that relate (directly or indirectly) to knowledge, or actions leading to knowledge (i.e. related to inquiry).

- Direct: *determine, discover, find out, know, learn, receive* (e.g. information), *share* (e.g. discovery), *study, understand.*
- Indirect: *analyse, assess, check, compare, contrast, discuss, examine, experience, explore, hear, identify, interview, listen, look, monitor, notice, observe, read, research, see, speak, study, talk, test, visit, watch, witness.*

Tables 8.16 and 8.17 show the proportions of knowledge-related verbs in the two complementation patterns (proportions are calculated on all collocates with MI≥3).

The proportion of knowledge-related verbs in '*BE interested* + *to*-inf', as compared to the proportion in '*BE interested in* + *-ing* Clause', is seven times higher in L1 writing and four times higher in L1 speech, and both differences are statistically significant despite the very low frequencies (G^2=36.85 and G^2=6.66 respectively). This suggests that the verbs in the '*to*-inf' complement

TABLE 8.16 *Proportion of knowledge-related verbs in the two complementation patterns: BNCw*

BNCw	Knowledge	All	%
BE *interested* + *to*-inf	22	41	*53.7*
BE *interested in* + *-ing* Clause	23	301	*7.6*

TABLE 8.17 *Proportion of knowledge-related verbs in the two complementation patterns: BNCs*

BNCs	Knowledge	All	%
BE *interested* + *to*-inf	8	14	*57.1*
BE *interested in* + *-ing* Clause	7	48	*14.6*

strongly tend to be pattern-specific. However, the preference for knowledge-related verbs is probabilistic rather than absolute. It is not that the '*-ing* Clause' complement does not contain knowledge-related verbs; rather, it seems much more likely for such verbs to be used in the '*to*-inf' complement. Before moving on to the comparisons with L2 speech and writing, we need to discuss the theoretical implications of these findings, particularly regarding the treatment of collocation in Lexical Grammar as "a purely lexical relation, non-directional and probabilistic, which ignores any syntactic relation between the words" (Stubbs, 2001, p. 64). The results contradict this treatment, as the adjective *interested* has distinctly different collocation patterns when the collocates are in different grammatical patterns (in our case, 'BE *interested in* + *-ing* Clause' and 'BE *interested* + *to*-inf'). The tendency to use knowledge-related verbs in '*to*-inf' complementation is also present in L2 use (Tables 8.18 and 8.19). However, differences are much less distinct (about 2.5 times more frequent in both writing and speech), and due to the extremely low frequencies they are not statistically significant (G^2=1.42 and G^2=0.58, respectively).

Looking at the results from a different angle, learners seem to use knowledge-related verbs in '*-ing* Clause' complements much more frequently than L1 users (about 3.5 times more in writing and about three times more in speech). In other words, when learners want to use a knowledge-related verb as a complement of the adjective *interested*, they tend to opt much less frequently for the complementation pattern preferred by L1 users.

TABLE 8.18 *Proportion of knowledge-related verbs in the two complementation patterns: ICLE*

ICLE	Knowledge	All	%
BE *interested* + *to*-inf	3	5	60.0
BE *interested in* + -*ing* Clause	10	39	25.6

TABLE 8.19 *Proportion of knowledge-related verbs in the two complementation patterns: LINDSEI*

LINDSEI	Knowledge	All	%
BE *interested* + *to*-inf	1	1	100
BE *interested in* + -*ing* Clause	6	15	40.0

7 Conclusions, Suggestions and Further Steps

The corpus analysis of L1 use revealed lexicogrammatical patterns that are not included in either reference or pedagogical materials, and showed that there are frequency differences not only between the complementation patterns of BE *interested*, but also that these patterns have different frequencies in speech and writing. Also, the analysis supports the conception of lexis and grammar as intertwined, without providing support for treating either as primary. Although the adjective *interested* can complement a number of copular verbs, the analysis revealed that BE is by far the most frequent copula. Also, some complementation patterns show a distinctly higher frequency of modalised BE, and others show a clear preference for verbs of a particular meaning in the complement. The latter indicates that a collocation analysis of the word form *interested* (particularly in the usual 5L-5R span) would mainly return collocates of *interested* in its most frequent word class, and in the most frequent syntactic patterns it is found. This type of analysis would be useful for the examination of the general semantic associations of a word-form (a common technique in corpus-based critical discourse studies—e.g. Partington, Duguid & Taylor, 2013), but it would not contribute to lexicogrammatical description or theory. That is, it would not reveal that '*BE interested* + *to*-inf' shows preference for a distinctive group of verb collocates in its complement, whereas '*BE interested in* + *-ing* Clause' does not. In fact, this grammar-specific collocation distinctiveness would not be observed even if the node was *interested* as an adjective, or if collocates were restricted to verbs, as it would fail to distinguish between co-occurrences within different syntactic structures. In light of the above, collocation can be more accurately described as a lexicogrammatical relation. Whatever the focus and starting point of the analysis, all patterns (and their components) can only be fully defined if both lexical and grammatical aspects are taken into account. We can, of course, focus on lexis to get lexis-like answers, but this should not mislead us to see grammar as secondary, or conclude that any patterns observed in such an approach can be explained in terms of lexis only, or that the lexis we choose to focus on (our starting point) is at the core of the patterns we observed. A related observation is that Halliday's (1992, p. 64) "tunnelling" metaphor may not be entirely useful, as it seems to imply both linearity and directionality in research: from the lexis end towards the grammar end of the continuum (or vice versa). Rather, the present analysis suggests that lexicogrammatical research cannot be mono-directional: at any given point of the analysis both grammar and lexis are involved. This observation is also related to the flexibility in the choice of the starting point of the analysis. For example, in Lexical Grammar the starting point is always a word/phrase, whereas in collostructional analysis the starting point is always a complex construction. In the same vein, whether the derived answer is perceived as lexis-like or grammar-like can be a matter of perspective or theoretical orientation. For example, a study may examine the frequency that a particular verb, or a semantically-defined group of verbs, is used in the progressive aspect, whereas another study may examine the frequency that the progressive aspect is used with particular verbs. Despite their different starting points, both studies would be essentially examining the same lexicogrammatical item.

Comparisons of L2 and L1 use revealed more differences than similarities. Overall, the results suggest a correlation between learner use and the treatment of *BE interested* in pedagogical materials, that is, the extent and detail of information they provide, and the relevant examples and exercises. Of course, it cannot be claimed that the correlations identified here necessarily point towards a direct influence of the content of pedagogical materials on learner use. However, these correlations are numerous and sizeable enough to merit consideration in decisions regarding the relevant content of pedagogical materials. More precisely, pedagogical materials at B1–C2 levels could usefully provide more comprehensive and nuanced information on the complementation and related lexicogrammatical patterns of *BE interested* (and, more generally, 'copula + *interested*'), and this information should be informed by the frequency of these patterns in speech and writing. In light of the differences in the focus and coverage of the two types of pedagogical materials examined here, L2 use seems to correlate with the information in grammars rather than dictionaries. This may be because lexicogrammatical patterns such as the ones examined in this study are presented to learners as grammatical points and/or that dictionaries are treated as sources for the meaning of words rather than their use (perhaps excepting collocation). Interestingly, the comparison between the grammars and dictionaries examined in this study (taken collectively) suggests that, in the case of lexicogrammatical patterns such as 'copula + *interested*', dictionaries would seem a more useful source for learners. Having said that, the overarching conclusion that can be drawn regarding pedagogical materials is that there is no single source which provides all the lexicogrammatical information that a learner may need in order to form a comprehensive picture of the use of 'copula + *interested*'. However, the analysis also indicated that some sources provide more information than others, which suggests that the selection of sources (by teachers or learners) is crucial. This also strongly indicates that consulting a single pedagogical source cannot be expected to be sufficient, and learners would be wise to combine sources, in particular grammars and dictionaries.

The analysis of pedagogical materials also showed that grammars and dictionaries overlap in their coverage: grammars also provide lexis-like information, and dictionaries also provide grammar-like information. However, the very existence of grammars and dictionaries for learners indicates that language teaching still treats grammar and lexis in a fairly compartmentalised fashion. When thinking of hard-copy publications, the distinction makes practical sense (as there are size and cost limitations); however, online publishing offers possibilities for more comprehensive learner resources that combine the features of pedagogical grammars and dictionaries: *pedagogical lexicogrammars*. Such resources would not only be easily updatable and expandable, but their content would also be interlinked. Using such a resource, learners would be able to access language information starting at any point of the lexicogrammar continuum, and then move back and forth along the continuum combining the information they access. For example, a learner looking up *interested* to find information on how to use it in a sentence (or wishing to check if their sentence contains a correct use of *interested*), that is, a learner starting at the lexis-end of the continuum, would not only encounter dictionary-like information, but also links to adjective complementation patterns, and complementation in general (the grammar end), as well as information on the types of verbs specific to particular patterns (more towards the lexis end), and issues of modal marking (around the middle). Finally, it would be feasible for entries to have links to corpora, so that learners could examine relevant concordance lines, a practice that, apart from providing a wealth of examples of actual use, would also allow for "serendipity" (Bernardini, 2000), that is opportunities for learners to discover language features other than the ones for which they accessed the pedagogical lexicogrammar.

Despite its multiple angles, the present study has not provided a full lexicogrammatical profile of the adjective *interested*. Further research needs to examine the complementation patterns of *interested* when it complements other copulas. The analysis of the modal marking needs to examine all copulas, and must be expanded to looking at the distribution of different modality types. In addition, an analysis of the type of subject of 'copula + *interested*' (e.g. noun, pronoun, impersonal *it*) can reveal correlations between type of subject and particular complementation patterns. Finally, it would be useful to examine whether these patterns are specific to *interested*, or whether the type of adjective (e.g. in terms of meaning) influences lexicogrammatical patterns. Of course, all the above lexicogrammatical patterns should also be examined in different varieties of English, and different genres within the same variety, as well as written and spoken L1 corpora comparable to ICLE and LINDSEI in terms of genre and user age (e.g. LOCNESS and LOCNEC).

References

Bernardini, S. (2000). Systematising serendipity: Proposals for concordancing large corpora with language learners. In L. Burnard & T. McEnery (Eds.), *Rethinking language pedagogy from a corpus perspective: Papers from the third international conference on teaching and language corpora. Lodz Studies in Language.* (pp. 183–190). Hamburg: Peter Lang.

Biber, D., & Reppen, R. (2002). What does frequency have to do with grammar teaching? *Studies in Second Language Acquisition, 24*(2), 199–208.

Biber, D., Conrad, S., & Reppen, R. (1994). Corpus-based approaches to issues in applied linguistics. *Applied Linguistics, 15*(2), 169–189.

Biber, D., Johansson, S., Leech, G., Conrad, S., & Finegan E. (1999). *Longman grammar of spoken and written English*. Harlow, Essex: Longman.

Carter, R., & McCarthy, M. (2006). *Cambridge grammar of English: A comprehensive guide*. Cambridge: Cambridge University Press.

Culicover, P.W., Jackendoff, R., & Audring, J. (2017). Multiword constructions in the grammar. *Topics in Cognitive Science*. Early view, 1–17. doi:10.1111/tops.12255.

Davydova, J. (2011). *The present perfect in non-native Englishes: A corpus-based study of variation*. Berlin: Walter de Gruyter.

Deshors, S.C. (2015). A multifactorial approach to gerundial and to-infinitival verb-complementation patterns in native and non-native English. *English Text Construction, 8*(2), 207–235.

Ellis, N.C. (2015). Implicit AND explicit learning: Their dynamic interface and complexity. In P. Rebuschat (Ed.), *Implicit and explicit learning of languages* (pp. 3–23). Amsterdam: John Benjamins.

Ellis, R. (2008). *The study of second language acquisition*. Oxford: Oxford University Press.

Ellis, R. (2015). *Understanding second language acquisition* (2nd ed.). Oxford: Oxford University Press.

Erman, B., & Warren, B. (2000). The idiom principle and the open choice principle. *Text*, *20*(1), 29–62.

Flowerdew, J. (2000). Investigating referential and pragmatic errors in a learner corpus. In L. Burnard & T. McEnery (Eds.), *Rethinking language pedagogy from a corpus perspective* (pp. 145–154). Frankfurt: Peter Lang.

Francis, G. (1993). A corpus-driven approach to grammar: Principles, methods and examples. In M. Baker, G. Francis & E. Tognini-Bonelli (Eds.), *Text and technology. In honour of John Sinclair* (pp. 137–156). Amsterdam: John Benjamins.

Gabrielatos, C. (2003). Conditional sentences: ELT typology and corpus evidence. *36th Annual BAAL Meeting*, University of Leeds, UK, 4–6 September 2003.

Gabrielatos, C. (2005). Corpora and language teaching: Just a fling, or wedding bells? *TESL-EJ*, *8*(4), 1–35. Retrieved from http://www.tesl-ej.org/wordpress/issues/volume8/ej32/ej32a1. Last accessed 19 June 2017.

Gabrielatos, C. (2006). Corpus-based evaluation of pedagogical materials: *If*-conditionals in ELT coursebooks and the BNC. *7th Teaching and Language Corpora Conference*, University Paris 7 Denis Diderot, Paris, France, 1–4 July 2006.

Gabrielatos, C. (2013). *If*-conditionals in ICLE and the BNC: A success story for teaching or learning? In S. Granger, G. Gilquin & F. Meunier (Eds.), *Twenty years of learner corpus research: Looking back, moving ahead* (pp. 155–166). Louvain-la-Neuve, Belgium: Presses Universitaires de Louvain.

Gabrielatos, C., & McEnery, T. (2005). Epistemic modality in MA dissertations. In P.A. Fuertes Olivera (Ed.), *Lengua y sociedad: Investigaciones recientes enlingüística aplicada. Lingüística y filología no.* 61 (pp. 311–331). Valladolid: Universidad de Valladolid.

Gilquin, G. (2012). The non-finite verb slot in English causative constructions: Comparing native and learner collostructions. In J. Leino & R. von Waldenfels (Eds.), *Analytical causatives: From "give" and "come" to "let" and "make"*. (pp. 41–63). München: Lincom Europa.

Gilquin, G., De Cock, S., & Granger, S. (Eds.) (2010). *LINDSEI: Louvain International Database of Spoken English Interlanguage*. Louvain, Belgium: UCL Presses.

Granger, S., Dagneaux, E., Meunier, F., & Paquot, M. (2009). *International Corpus of Learner English*. Presses universitaires de Louvain, Louvain-la-Neuve.

Granger, S., Gilquin, G., & Meunier, F. (Eds.) (2013). *Twenty years of learner corpus research: Looking back, moving ahead*. Louvain-la-Neuve, Belgium: Presses universitaires de Louvain.

Granger, S., Gilquin, G., & Meunier, F. (Eds.) (2015). *The Cambridge handbook of learner corpus research*. Cambridge: Cambridge University Press.

Gries, S.Th., & Stefanowitsch, A. (2004). Extending collostructional analysis: A corpus-based perspective on 'alternations'. *International Journal of Corpus Linguistics, 9*(1), 97–129.

Halliday, M.A.K. (1961). Categories of a theory of grammar. *Word, 17*(3), 241–292.

Halliday, M.A.K. (1966). Lexis as a linguistic level. In C.E. Bazell, J.C. Catford, M.A.K. Halliday & R.H. Robins (Eds.), *In memory of F.R. Firth* (pp. 148–162). London: Longman.

Halliday, M.A.K. (1991). Corpus studies and probabilistic grammar. In K. Aijmer & B. Altenberg (Eds.), *English corpus linguistics: Studies in honour of Jan Svartvik* (pp. 30–40). London: Longman.

Halliday, M.A.K. (1992). Language as system and language as instance: The corpus as a theoretical construct. In J. Svartvik (Ed.), *Directions in corpus linguistics: Proceedings of the Nobel Symposium 82, Stockholm, 4–8 August 1991* (pp. 61–77). Berlin: Mouton de Gruyter.

Hardie, A. (2012). CQPweb—combining power, flexibility and usability in a corpus analysis tool. *International Journal of Corpus Linguistics, 17*, 380–409.

Harwood, N. (2005). What do we want EAP teaching materials for? *Journal of English for Academic Purposes, 4*(2), 149–161.

Hasselgård, H. (2016). *The way of the world*: The colligational framework "the N1 of the N2" and its Norwegian correspondences. *Nordic Journal of English Studies, 15*(3), 55–79.

Hasselgren, A. (1994). Lexical teddy bears and advanced learners: A study into the ways Norwegian students cope with English vocabulary. *International Journal of Applied Linguistics, 4*, 237–258.

Hoffmann, S., Evert, S., Smith, N., Lee, D., & Berglund-Prytz, Y. (2008). *Corpus linguistics with BNCweb—a practical guide*. Frankfurt am Main: Peter Lang.

Hoey, M. (1997). From concordance to text structure: New uses for computer corpora. In J. Melia & B. Lewandoska (Eds.), *PALC '97: Practical applications in language corpora* (pp. 2–23). Łódź: Łódź University Press.

Hoey, M. (2005). *Lexical priming: A new theory of words and language*. London: Routledge.

Huddleston, R., & Pullum, G.K. (2002). *The Cambridge grammar of the English language*. Cambridge: Cambridge University Press.

Hunston, S., & Francis, G. (1998). Verbs observed: A corpus-driven pedagogic grammar. *Applied Linguistics, 19*(1), 45–72.

Hunston, S., & Francis, G. (2000). *Pattern grammar: A corpus-driven approach to the lexical grammar of English*. Amsterdam, Netherlands: John Benjamins.

Kennedy, G. (1992). Preferred ways of putting things with implications for language teaching. In J. Svartvik (Ed.), *Directions in corpus linguistics: Proceedings of the Nobel Symposium 82*, Stockholm, 4–8 August 1991 (pp. 335–378). Berlin: Mouton de Gruyter.

Leech, G. (2011). Frequency, corpora and language learning. In F. Meunier, S. De Cock, G. Gilquin & M. Paquot (Eds.), *A taste for corpora: In honour of Sylviane Granger* (pp. 7–31). Amsterdam: John Benjamins.

McEnery, A., & Xiao, Z. (2005). HELP or HELP to: What do corpora have to say? *English Studies, 86*(2), 161–187.

Meunier, F. (2012). Formulaic language and language teaching. *Annual Review of Applied Linguistics 32*(1), 111–129.

Meunier, F., & Gouverneur, C. (2009). New types of corpora for new educational challenges: Collecting, annotating and exploiting a corpus of textbook material. In K. Aijmer (Ed.), *Corpora and language teaching* (pp. 179–201). Amsterdam and Philadelphia: Benjamins.

Murphy, R. (2007) *Essential grammar in use* (3rd ed.). Cambridge: Cambridge University Press.

Ortega, L. (2013). *Understanding second language acquisition*. Oxford: Routledge.

Owen, C. (1993). Corpus-based grammar and the Heineken effect: Lexicogrammatical description for language learners. *Applied Linguistics, 14*(2), 167–187.

Partington, A., Duguid, A., & Taylor. C. (2013). *Patterns and meanings in discourse: Theory and practice in corpus-assisted discourse studies* (CADS). Amsterdam & Philadelphia: John Benjamins.

Quirk, R., Greenbaum, S., Leech, G., & Svartvik, J. (1985). *A comprehensive grammar of the English language*. London: Longman.

Römer, U. (2004). Textbooks: A corpus-driven approach to modal auxiliaries and their didactics. In J. McH Sinclair (Ed.), *How to use corpora in language teaching* (pp. 185–199). Amsterdam: John Benjamins.

Römer, U. (2009). The inseparability of lexis and grammar. *Annual Review of Cognitive Linguistics, 7*, 140–162.

Rühlemann, C. (2007). Lexical grammar: The GET-passive as a case in point. *ICAME Journal, 31*, 111–128.

Sinclair, J. (1991). *Corpus concordance collocation*. Oxford: Oxford University Press.

Sinclair J. (1996). The search for units of meaning. *Textus*, 9(1), 75–106.

Sinclair, J. (2004). *Trust the text: Language, corpus and discourse*. London: Routledge.

Stefanowitsch, A., & Gries, S.Th. (2003). Collostructions: Investigating the interaction of words and constructions. *International Journal of Corpus Linguistics, 8*(2), 209–243.

Stubbs, M. (1996). *Text and corpus analysis: Computer-assisted studies of language and culture*. Oxford: Blackwell.

Stubbs, M. (2001). *Words and Phrases: Corpus studies of lexical semantics*. Oxford: Blackwell.

Stubbs, M. (2002). Two quantitative methods of studying phraseology in English. *International Journal of Corpus Linguistics, 7*(2), 215–244.

Stubbs, M. (2009). The search for units of meaning: Sinclair on empirical semantics. *Applied Linguistics, 30*(1), 115–137.

Tomlinson, B. (2013). Introduction: Applied linguistics and materials development. In B. Tomlinson (Ed.), *Applied linguistics and materials development* (pp. 1–7). London: Bloomsbury.

Vyatkina, N. (2013). Specific syntactic complexity: Developmental profiling of individuals based on an annotated learner corpus. *Modern Language Journal* 97, 11–30.

Xu, J., & Wu, L. (2014). Web-based fourth generation corpus analysis tools and the BFSU CQPweb case. *Waiyu dianhua jiaoxue* [Computer-assisted Foreign Language Education]. Retrieved from http://en.cnki.com.cn/Article_en/CJFDTotal-WYDH201405002.htm. Last accessed 19 June 2017.

Appendix 1: Pedagogical Materials Examined in This Study

Bunting, J.D., Diniz, L., & Reppen, R. (2012). *Grammar and beyond, level 4. Student's book.* Cambridge: Cambridge University Press.

Davis, F., & Rimmer, W. (2011). *Active grammar, level 2*. Cambridge: Cambridge University Press.

Hewing, M. (2013) *Advanced grammar in use* (3rd ed.). Cambridge: Cambridge University Press.

Lloyd, M., & Day, J. (2011). *Active grammar, level 3*. Cambridge: Cambridge University Press.

Murphy, R. (2012). *English grammar in use* (4th ed.). Cambridge: Cambridge University Press.

Cambridge Dictionary Online. Retrieved from http://dictionary.cambridge.org. Last accessed 19 June 2017.

Collins COBUILD English grammar (3rd ed.) (2011). Glasgow: Harper Collins.

Collins Dictionary Online. Retrieved from https://www.collinsdictionary.com/. Last accessed 19 June 2017.

Longman Dictionary of Contemporary English Online. Retrieved from http://ldoceonline.com. Last accessed 19 June 2017.

Macmillan Dictionary Online. Retrieved from http://macmillandictionary.com. Last accessed 19 June 2017.

Oxford Advanced Learner's Dictionary Online. Retrieved from http://oxfordlearnersdictionaries.com. Last accessed 19 June 2017.

Appendix 2: Critical Review of Pedagogical Materials: Summary of Findings

Key to notation

Y	The information specified in the row heading is provided directly, or the pattern specified in the row heading is treated explicitly (an entry in dictionaries; a chapter/section in pedagogical grammars).
(Y)	The information is not provided directly, or the pattern does not have an entry/section, but a) (*BE*) *interested* is listed among the items conforming to a particular pattern, or b) the pattern is used in an example, or c) the pattern is used in an exercise.
((Y))	The information is not provided directly, or the pattern does not have an entry/section, but the dictionary/grammar provides information (e.g. a 'rule') that is relevant to (*BE*) *interested* (e.g. 'we can use a noun or a word ending in *-ing* after an adjective').
+	It indicates additional information provided.
=	It is used after (Y) or ((Y)) to indicate the particular way that the indirect information is provided (e.g. an example or 'rule').
No	Not mentioned/treated at all.
NA	Not applicable (i.e. not expected to be provided in the particular type of pedagogical materials).

Dictionaries

	Cambridge	Collins	Longman	Macmillan	Oxford
-ed forms can be adjectives	NA	NA	NA	NA	NA
interested can be an adjective	Y	Y	Y	Y	Y
-ing forms can be nouns	NA	NA	NA	NA	NA
Mention of *BE interested* (*in*)	(Y) = example	Y	Y	Y	Y
Mention of '*BE interested in* + NP (*-ing* form)'	(Y) = example	(Y) = example	No	No	No
Mention of '*BE interested in* + NP (noun)'	No	(Y) = example	Y + example	(Y) = example	Y + example
Mention of '*BE interested in* + *-ing* Clause'	(Y) = example	No	Y + example	Y + example	Y + example
Mention of '*BE interested in* + *wh-* Clause'	(Y) = example	No	No	No	(Y) = example
Mention of '*BE interested* + *to*-inf'	(Y) = example	Y + frequent	Y + example	Y + example	Y + example
Mention of '*BE interested* ø'	(Y) = example	(Y) = example	(Y) = example	(Y) = example	(Y) = example
Information regarding knowledge verb collocations	(Y) = example	No	(Y) = example	(Y) = example	(Y) = example
Information regarding modalisation patterns	(Y) = example	(Y) = example	(Y) = example	(Y) = example	(Y) = example

Pedagogical grammars	**English Grammar in Use (B1–B2)**	**Active Grammar 2 (B1–B2)**	**Collins COBUILD (B1–C2)**	**Grammar and Beyond (B2–C2)**	**Advanced Grammar in use (C1–C2)**	**Active Grammar 3 (C1–C2)**
***-ed* forms can be adjectives**	Y	Y	Y	No	Y	Y
***interested* can be an adjective**	Y	Y	Y	No	(Y) = included in list of adjectives	Y
***-ing* forms can be nouns**	(Y) = included in list of 'noun + noun' compounds	No	Y	Y (gerund) But mostly treated as verb	(Y) = included in list of (un)count nouns	Y
Mention of *BE interested* (*in*)	(Y) = included in examples and exercises + contrast with '*to*-inf'	(Y) = included in 'adjective + preposition' list	Y But not (*BE*) ***interested in***	No	No	(Y) = included in 'adjective + preposition' list
Mention of '*BE interested in* + NP (*-ing* form)'	(Y) = included in exercises	((Y)) = information on 'preposition + noun / V-*ing*'	No	No	((Y)) = information on 'preposition + noun / V-*ing*'	No
Mention of '*BE interested in* + NP (noun)'	(Y) = included in 'adjective + preposition' examples	((Y)) = information on 'preposition + noun / V-*ing*'	No	No	((Y)) = information on 'preposition + noun / V-*ing*'	No

	English Grammar in Use (B1–B2)	Active Grammar 2 (B1–B2)	Collins COBUILD (B1–C2)	Grammar and Beyond (B2–C2)	Advanced Grammar in use (C1–C2)	Active Grammar 3 (C1–C2)
Mention of 'BE *interested in* + *-ing* clause'	(Y) = 'preposition + V-*ing*' example + Contrast with '*to*-inf'	((Y)) = information on 'preposition + noun / V-*ing*'	No	((Y)) = information on '*by/in* + "participle phrases"'	((Y)) = information on 'preposition + V-*ing*'	((Y)) = information on 'preposition + V-*ing*'
Mention of 'BE *interested in* + *wh*- clause'	(Y) = included in an exercise	No	((Y)) = information on *wh*-clauses (*interested* not listed)	No	((Y)) = information on complementation patterns of adjectives (*interested* not listed)	No
Mention of 'BE *interested* + *to*-inf'	Y + contrast of '*in* + N-*ing*' vs. '*to*-inf'	((Y)) = information on 'adjective + *to*-inf'	(Y) = included in list of adjective complements	No	((Y)) = information on complementation patterns of adjectives (*interested* not listed)	((Y)) = information on 'adjective + *to*-inf'
Mention of 'BE *interested ø*'	No	No	(Y) = included in list of adjectives taking zero complementation	No	((Y)) = included in an exercise (one sentence)	No

Pedagogical grammars (cont.)

	English Grammar in Use (B1–B2)	Active Grammar 2 (B1–B2)	Collins COBUILD (B1–C2)	Grammar and Beyond (B2–C2)	Advanced Grammar in use (C1–C2)	Active Grammar 3 (C1–C2)
Information regarding knowledge verb collocations	Y = information (knowledge verbs included in list of examples of verbs used in '*interested to*-inf' pattern)	No	No	No	No	No
Information regarding modalisation patterns	(Y) = included in examples	No	No	No	No	No

CHAPTER 9

Tracking L2 Writers' Phraseological Development Using Collgrams: Evidence from a Longitudinal EFL Corpus

Yves Bestgen and Sylviane Granger

1 Introduction

One of the major contributions of learner corpus research is the light it sheds on phraseological aspects of learner language. For too long, studies of L2 lexis have been dominated by single words. For example, multiword units have been absent from measures of lexical richness which rely exclusively on single word forms or lemmas (Wolfe-Quintero, Inagaki, & Kim, 1998; van Hout & Vermeer, 2007; Milton, 2009). Admittedly, a few lists of multiword units have been developed of late (Simpson-Vlach & Ellis, 2010; Martinez & Schmitt, 2012; Ackermann & Chen, 2013) and Cobb (2013) has recently made the case for including multiword units alongside single words in lexical profiling software. However, as pointed out by Treffers-Daller et al. (2016) in relation to measures of lexical diversity, studies are still "based on analyses of single words and do not take into account formulaic language". This is hardly justifiable today, as a range of increasingly sophisticated tools and methods can be used to extract word combinations of all types automatically or semi-automatically from corpora. When applied to learner corpora, these techniques help identify the phrases that are typically used by foreign or second language (L2) learners. Comparisons with native corpora make it possible to tease out the word combinations that are used correctly and idiomatically by learners from those that are incorrect or less appropriate and/or occur with unusual (i.e. too high or low) frequency in learner productions.

Learner corpus research to date has focused on two main types of phraseologisms, i.e. collocations and lexical bundles. Collocations can be defined as pairs of significantly associated words which may—but need not—be contiguous. Among the most studied collocation types are verb + noun collocations, especially those containing delexical verbs (*make a comment, give a talk, take a walk*) which have been shown to be particularly error-prone (Nesselhauf, 2005). Collocations can be extracted manually on the basis of linguistic criteria, in particular restricted lexical range, syntactic fixedness and seman-

 | DOI: 10.1163/9789004361133_011

tic non-compositionality, or automatically, using word co-occurrence metrics, such as mutual information (MI), t-score and z-score (Evert, 2009). The other type of phraseologism that has attracted a great deal of interest is the category of lexical bundles (Biber, Johansson, Leech, Conrad, & Finegan, 1999). These are n-grams, i.e. sequences of n words, which tend to recur in a particular register. Unlike collocations, they are contiguous word sequences of (usually) more than two words which frequently co-occur but whose strength of association is usually unspecified. Lexical bundles have been particularly investigated in academic writing because of the routine characteristics of the genre (Chen & Baker, 2010; Hyland, 2012; Durrant, 2015).

Corpus-based studies of the L2 phrasicon have generated a wealth of results. Unfortunately, these are not easy to synthesise, partly because of the different qualitative and quantitative criteria used to identify the sequences that count as phraseological (for surveys, see Paquot & Granger, 2012, and Ebeling & Hasselgård, 2015). A few general trends can, however, be observed. For collocations, one of the most noticeable results is the high rate of errors, even at fairly advanced proficiency levels. For example, Nesselhauf (2005) reported a 25% error rate for verb + noun combinations produced by advanced German learners of English. A large proportion of collocation errors are due to the influence of the mother tongue: about 50% for Nesselhauf (2005) and up to 67% for Wanner et al. (2013), who investigate miscollocations of all types produced by Spanish learners. Learners also tend to underuse the most collocationally restricted combinations. This is shown, for example, by Granger's (1998) study of adjective intensifiers, which highlights a clear tendency to underuse stereotypical combinations involving *-ly* adverbs (*acutely aware, vitally important*) and overuse combinations with the all-round amplifier *very*. For lexical bundles, learner data gives evidence of unidiomatic use rather than errors. One commonly observed result is learners' tendency to repeat the same multiword units, which suggests that their repertoire is more limited than that of native speakers. For example, Ädel and Erman's (2012) analysis of four-word lexical bundles in native and learner academic texts highlights a considerably wider range of these sequences in native texts, with a total of 130, as compared to 60 in learner texts. Another prevalent result is the high degree of variability in the frequency of individual phraseological units: while some are overused, others are significantly underused. In academic writing, for example, Chen and Baker (2010) note an overuse of some—usually informal—lexical bundles (e.g. *all over the world, in the long run*) in L2 compared to L1 academic writing, and an underuse of many formulaic sequences typical of academic texts (e.g. *can be seen in, to a certain extent*). Likewise, for speech, De Cock (2000) notes an overuse of some sequences, notably vagueness tags (*or something, and things,* *sort of*) coupled with atypically high frequency of use of others (*yes of course, for example, and so on*) As is the case for collocations, L1 transfer also proves to play a major role (Paquot, 2013; Parkinson, 2015).

Though highly informative, studies to date have suffered from one major limitation: the vast majority are cross-sectional, i.e. they explore learner populations at a particular point in time and therefore cannot be used as a basis to track the development of learners' phraseological proficiency over time. The issue of gradual progression towards mastery of phraseological skills has not been altogether absent from the learner corpus scene, however. A few recent studies (Chen & Baker, 2016; Granger & Bestgen, 2014) have compared groups of learners at different proficiency levels, adopting an approach that is referred to as "pseudolongitudinal" by Gass (2013, p. 36): "[O]ne can use a cross-sectional design to create a pseudolongitudinal study. In such a study, the emphasis, like that of a longitudinal study, is on language change (i.e., acquisition), with data being collected at a single point in time, but with different proficiency levels represented". By using this method, "a longitudinal picture can be then constructed by comparing the devices used by the different groups ranked according to their proficiency" (Ellis & Barkhuizen 2005, p. 97). These studies reveal that both the type and the number of multiword units vary with language proficiency. For example, Chen and Baker (2016), relying on data from learners at levels B1, B2 and C1 of the Common European Framework of Reference for Languages (CEFR) (Council of Europe, 2001), found that lower-level learners tended to use lexical bundles typical of conversation, while the bundles used by higher-level learners were closer to those found in academic prose. A study of oral L2 French by Forsberg and Bartning (2010) showed significant differences in the number of lexical formulaic sequences between low and high levels of the CEFR scale, but no significant differences between neighbouring levels, a result which suggests that the acquisition of these sequences is relatively slow.

While these studies have brought to light some interesting proficiency-related trends, they should ideally be complemented by truly longitudinal studies that track the phraseological development of the *same* learners over an extended period of time. This has been near-impossible until now because of the lack of longitudinal learner corpora. Fortunately, the situation is beginning to change thanks to recent corpus collection initiatives launched with a view to filling that gap.

In the current study, we investigate aspects of the learner phrasicon based on a section of the *Longitudinal Database of Learner English* (LONGDALE), made up of written data produced by learners of English as a Foreign Language (EFL) followed over a period of three years. Section 2 describes the phraseological measure used in the study, which we refer to as collgram. After providing information on the data and methodology used (Section 3), we present the main developmental trends displayed by the data (Section 4). In Section 5, two caveats are highlighted—one related to the density of the data collection, the other to the variability of learners' trajectories. Section 6 presents our conclusions and outlines some potential applications of collgram-based research.

2 Collgrams

Our study relies on collgrams, a category of phraseological unit that combines the strengths of both collocations and lexical bundles. The main advantage of collocations is that they involve an association score, which makes it possible to tease out collocational combinations of various strengths from non-collocational ones. On the downside, however, collocation-based studies tend to have limited scope, as they are often restricted to some predefined words (e.g. the verb *make* in Altenberg & Granger (2001) or the verbs *cause* and *lead to* in Pan (2010)) or parts of speech (e.g. high-frequency prepositions in Groom (2009)). In comparison, lexical bundles have a wider coverage: they involve sequences of words of all types, the only limitations being the size of the bundles and their frequency. The disadvantage, however, is that the extracted sequences are very numerous and not necessarily strongly associated. As pointed out by Ellis, Simpson-Vlach, Römer, O'Donnell and Wulff (2015, p. 361), "[d]efinitions in terms of frequency alone result in long lists of recurrent word sequences that collapse distinctions that intuition would deem relevant". Collgrams combine the best of both phraseological units: they are essentially n-grams to which an association score has been assigned. Although there are already plenty of terms to refer to phraseological units, we are introducing this new term to avoid any confusion with collocations, which may not be contiguous, and lexical bundles, which are contiguous but whose strength of association is usually not measured.

The identification of collgrams proceeds in two steps: (1) extraction of n-grams of a given length and frequency threshold from a learner corpus; and (2) computation of the degree of association of the words that compose them on the basis of a large reference corpus, such as the *British National Corpus* (BNC) for English. Collgrams are particularly well suited for the analysis of L2 productions, as the different association scores enable a representation of phraseological proficiency as a continuum, from the best, most closely associated units to the downright incorrect ones, through a range of intermediary stages—good, weak and dubious.

A small number of learner-corpus-based studies have made use of methods that bear similarities with the collgram method, albeit with a range of different terms (collocations, lexical bundles, formulas, formulaic sequences, etc.). For example, Serrano, Stengers and Housen (2015) used MI scores extracted from the *Corpus of Contemporary American English* as an additional criterion to identify formulaic verb sequences (e.g. phrasal and prepositional verbs) produced by L1 Spanish/Catalan learners of English in an intensive language programme compared with learners who followed a regular programme as well as native speakers. The study shows that intermediate learners benefited most from intensive instruction in terms of production of formulaic sequences and that advanced learners' use of these sequences was still quite far from native speakers' use. It is important to note that MI scores were not used to analyse the degree of formulaicity of learners' verb sequences. Siyanova and Schmitt (2008) used both frequency and MI association scores in the BNC to assess the appropriateness of adjective-noun combinations (e.g. *social services*) produced by Russian learners of English. They found that around 45% of the combinations were both frequent and strongly associated. A comparison with native speaker data revealed very little difference in the use of appropriate collocations. One limitation of the study is that less appropriate or inappropriate collocations were not investigated. Parkinson (2015) compared MI-scored noun-noun combinations produced by Chinese, Tswana and Spanish learners of English and demonstrated that both transfer from the L1 and the context in which English was learned had an influence on the quantity and quality of the combinations.

The most direct inspiration for the collgram-based approach is a study by Durrant and Schmitt (2009), which investigated modifier + noun combinations in a corpus of texts written by learners of English from several L1s and used the BNC to assign two association scores to each combination: MI, which highlights bigrams composed of relatively rare words, and the t-score, which brings out those made up of relatively frequent words (Clear, 1993). They found that, compared with native writers, learners tend to overuse high-frequency collocations such as *long way* (identified on the basis of t-score) and underuse lower-frequency, but strongly associated, collocations, such as *tectonic plates* (identified by their MI score). Adopting this type of approach, Granger and Bestgen (2014) showed that intermediate learners of English tend to overuse collocations made up of frequent words and underuse those containing rare words, while advanced learners display the opposite tendency. A second study demonstrated that the collgram scores are good predictors of text quality as determined by human raters (Bestgen & Granger, 2014).

3 Data and Methodology

3.1 *Data*

For our study, we made use of a subcorpus of the *Longitudinal Database of Learner English*[1] consisting of 178 argumentative essays written by 89 French-speaking English language and literature undergraduates at the University of Louvain (72 female and 17 male). The subcorpus contains approximately 100,000 words in total (see Table 9.1). Each learner contributed an essay in their first year at university (T1) and another in their third year (T3). The length requirements ranged between 500 and 700 words. For the first essay, they had a choice between four topics; for the second, they were required to use the same topic as in Year 1 to ensure maximum comparability. The breakdown is given in Table 9.2.

TABLE 9.1 *Subcorpus of* LONGDALE

	T1	T3	Total
Number of texts	89	89	178
Total number of words	52635	51490	104125
Mean number of words per text	591.4	578.5	
Standard deviation	101.8	88.23	
Minimum	183[2]	417	
Maximum	884	897	

The students wrote their essays in a computer lab using Notepad, with no access to reference tools (grammar, dictionary, spellchecker). The allotted time (90 minutes) also included the time needed to fill in the learner profile questionnaire and a short vocabulary placement test. All the students proved to have enough time to write their essay. Although the exercise was compulsory,

1 https://uclouvain.be/en/research-institutes/ilc/cecl/longdale.html. Last accessed 19 June 2017.

2 This is an outlier. The next shortest text totals 393 words. It is worth noting that the analyses reported in this chapter were conducted both with and without this text, without producing any noticeable difference. We therefore decided to keep it so as to preserve the integrity of the data.

TABLE 9.2 *Essay titles*

Title	No. of essays
Lying is immoral and should always be condemned	13
In our modern world, dominated by science, technology and industrialisation, there is no longer a place for learning and imagination	33
Money is the root of all evil	18
Violent films are harmful and should be banned	25
Total	89

it was not part of a formal exam. However, the students did take it seriously, as they were promised individual feedback on the quality of their text.

3.2 *Methodology*

As statistical inferential tests based on corpus data considered as a whole have been questioned because they do not take into account the real sampling unit, which is the text and not the word, the bigram or the syntactic construction (Kilgarriff, 1996, 2005; Bestgen, 2014), all the analyses were conducted on the individual texts. The procedure used to gather the necessary data is described in detail in this section.

Before collgrams can be extracted, each learner text must be subjected to a pretreatment process involving orthographic correction, tokenisation and part-of-speech tagging with CLAWS7 (for more details, see Granger & Bestgen (2014)). The first step of the collgram method proper consists in extracting the bigrams from each text. For this study, we extracted all the bigrams whatever their part of speech (POS), a category referred to as ALL,[3] and three POS bigram categories: noun-noun (NN), adjective-noun (JN) and adverb-adjective (AJ). The breakdown of the extracted bigrams is shown in Table 9.3.

The next step was to search for each bigram in the BNC, a 100 million word collection of samples of written and spoken language.[4] The sequences that had fewer than five occurrences in the BNC were categorised as below threshold

3 The bigrams made up of two proper nouns were excluded. Thus, *John Huston* was excluded but *European country* was kept.

4 http://www.natcorp.ox.ac.uk/corpus/. Last accessed 19 June 2017.

TABLE 9.3 *Number of bigrams in T1 and T3 corpora: breakdown per bigram category*

	T1			T3		
	Total number of extracted bigrams	Average number of bigrams per text	Average number of bigrams per 1000 words	Total number of extracted bigrams	Average number of bigrams per text	Average number of bigrams per 1000 words
NN	336	3.78	6.42	355	3.99	6.80
JN	2002	22.49	38.48	2271	25.52	44.18
AJ	595	6.69	11.32	496	5.57	9.59
ALL	46247	519.63	878.50	45849	515.16	889.89

(BT). Their association strength was not computed, as association measures computed for bigrams below this threshold are thought to be unreliable (Durrant & Schmitt, 2009, p. 168). The word sequences that reached the frequency threshold of five were assigned two association scores, MI score and t-score, computed by means of the formulas reported in Evert (2009, p. 1225). As a measure of strength of association, MI tends to highlight collgrams made up of words that are rarely found independently of each other. Even a rare bigram can have a very high MI score if it comprises very infrequent words. Compared to MI, the t-score, which measures the degree of confidence we can have about the existence of an association, gives much more weight to the number of times a collgram has been observed. It therefore prioritises frequently occurring collgrams that are very often made up of frequent words.

A graphic representation of the method is shown in Figure 9.1. Four bigrams extracted from the LONGDALE subcorpus—*vicious circle, an opposite, accept to* and *moving society*—are assigned their corresponding MI score in the BNC. *Vicious circle*, with a highly significant MI score, can be considered a highly idiomatic combination, while the non-significant MI score of *an opposite* points to a less typical combination. Serious doubts can be raised about the appropriateness of the other two bigrams: *accept to* has a negative MI score, which means that the bigram is less often used in the BNC than chance would predict, while *moving society* does not reach the frequency threshold in the BNC.

Each bigram that has been assigned an association score is then classified as displaying one of four degrees of collocational strength: non-collocational (NC), collocational: low (L), collocational: medium (M) and collocational: high

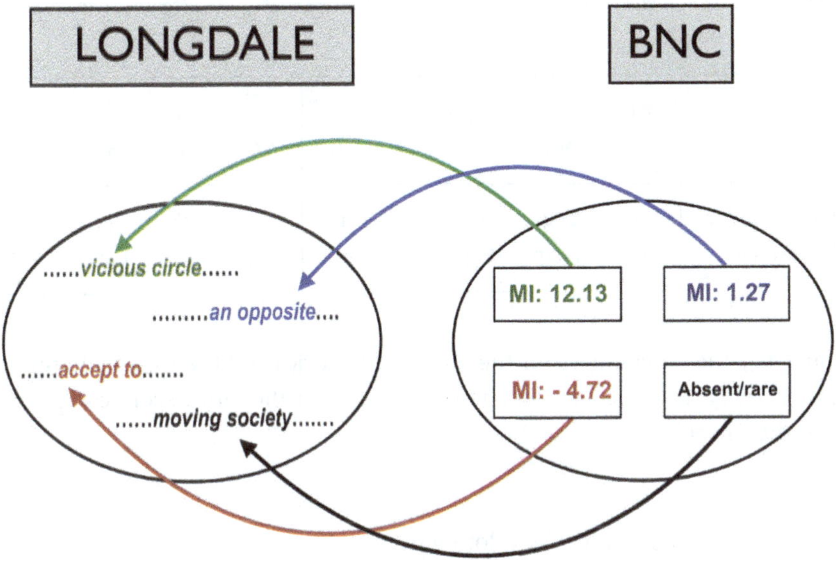

FIGURE 9.1 *Assignment of* BNC *scores to* LONGDALE *data*

TABLE 9.4 *Thresholds used for the association measures*

Bigram category	MI	t-score
Non-collocational	< 3	< 2
Collocational: Low	≥ 3 and < 5	≥ 2 and < 6
Collocational: Medium	≥ 5 and < 7	≥ 6 and < 10
Collocational: High	≥ 7	≥ 10

(H). The thresholds used for the MI and t-scores are given in Table 9.4 (see Durrant & Schmitt (2009) and Granger & Bestgen (2014) for justification).

Finally, the percentage of bigrams in each of the five collgram categories (BT, NC, L, M and H) was computed for both association measures (MI and t-score). This was done independently for each learner text and each of the four bigram categories (NN, JN, AJ and ALL). The values were computed on the basis of all the bigrams present in the learner texts (tokens) as well as all the *different* bigrams present in each text (types).

By way of illustration, the results for one bigram category (ALL) in one learner text are presented in Table 9.5. The 527 bigrams contained in the text are broken down into the different degrees of collocational strength in terms of raw frequencies (first line) and percentages (second line). As can clearly be seen in

TABLE 9.5 *Raw frequencies and percentages for the bigrams in the ALL category in one learner text*

	BT	MI				t-score			
	BT	NC	L	M	H	NC	L	M	H
Raw frequency	107	284	97	27	12	65	58	32	265
Percentage	20.30	53.89	18.41	5.12	2.28	12.33	11.01	6.07	50.29

Table 9.5, the percentages for the four MI categories and the BT set add up to 100%; this is also the case for the percentages for the four t-score categories and the BT set.

4 L2 Phraseological Development

4.1 *Longitudinal Trends*

To determine whether there was a statistically significant impact of the time of collection (T1 and T3) on the average percentages of each collocational type (BT, NC, L, etc.) in each bigram category (NN, JN, AJ and ALL), we used randomisation tests for matched samples, which are equivalent to Student's t-tests for comparing means, but do not require any assumption of normality (Howell, 2013). For each test which was based on one million random permutations, we report whether the effect of the time factor was statistically significant for three conventional thresholds ($p \leq .05$, $p \leq .01$ and $p \leq .001$). To gauge the importance of the impact of the time factor, we provide a measure of effect size, Cohen's d (Cohen, 1988). This measure expresses the difference between the means of the two collection times in standard deviation units. We used the standard deviation of the T1 scores to avoid overestimating the actual effect size (Dunlop, Cortina, Vaslow, & Burke, 1996). Following Cohen (1988), we consider that a d of about 0.20 indicates a small effect, one of about 0.50 a medium effect, and one of about 0.80 a large effect. As can be seen in Table 9.6, we found a large number of significant differences between T1 and T3 essays.

The bigram category that has the largest number of significant results turns out to be the category that offers the broadest picture of learner performance, i.e. the ALL category. The most outstanding result is that non-collocational bigrams (*past people, relevant in, more little*) are particularly good discriminators: there are consistently fewer of these in Year 3 than in Year 1, for both MI

TABLE 9.6 *Association scores (MI and t-score) for the four bigram categories (types and tokens) at T1 and T3*

			MI				t-score				BT
			NC	L	M	H	NC	L	M	H	BT
NN	Tokens	T1	5.2	4.1	7.8	21.0	4.8	11.5	13.3	8.6	61.9
		T3	3.4	4.8	11.3	22.3	1.6	14.7	14.2	11.3	58.2
		p									
		d									
	Types	T1	5.3	4.1	7.7	20.2	4.8	11.3	12.7	8.6	62.7
		T3	3.5	4.6	12.0	20.1	1.8	15.1	12.6	10.7	59.8
		p									
		d									
JN	Tokens	T1	12.2	18.4	25.7	9.9	3.6	24.7	10.9	27.0	33.9
		T3	10.0	16.0	27.4	13.4	2.3	27.5	12.2	24.8	33.3
		p	*			**	**				
		d	0.30			0.48	0.29				
	Types	T1	13.4	18.7	21.7	10.2	4.0	22.0	11.3	26.7	36.1
		T3	10.3	17.0	24.2	13.2	2.5	25.3	12.6	24.3	35.3
		p	**			**	*	*			
		d	0.40			0.42	0.29	0.30			
AJ	Tokens	T1	19.0	26.4	25.8	8.2	8.2	17.6	14.0	39.5	20.7
		T3	14.8	28.1	25.3	4.1	3.7	24.6	12.7	31.4	27.7
		p				*	**	*		*	*
		d				0.29	0.43	0.39		0.37	0.40
	Types	T1	19.6	25.5	25.6	8.3	8.5	17.8	13.7	39.0	21.1
		T3	14.9	27.6	25.6	3.9	3.8	24.8	12.4	31.1	28.0
		p				*	**	*		*	*
		d				0.31	0.43	0.39		0.37	0.39
ALL	Tokens	T1	56.6	25.6	6.7	1.2	14.6	10.1	7.0	58.5	9.9
		T3	55.5	25.0	6.8	1.7	13.7	10.8	7.4	57.2	11.0
		p	**			***	***	**	*	**	**
		d	0.42			0.78	0.48	0.36	0.29	0.28	0.42
	Types	T1	58.0	23.6	6.0	1.3	16.0	10.7	7.5	54.7	11.1
		T3	56.1	23.8	6.3	1.7	14.8	11.4	7.7	53.9	12.2
		p	***			***	***	**			**
		d	0.68			0.68	0.60	0.38			0.41

Significance level (* = $p \leq .05$, ** = $p \leq .01$, *** $p \leq .001$); size of the effect (*d*, Howell, 2013, pp. 203–204) and t-score.[5] This is an important result, as the non-collocational category contains sequences that are atypical in the target language (represented here by the reference corpus). The strongest effect, as measured by Cohen's *d*, is the higher percentage of High-MI scores for tokens at T3, an effect that is also quite high for types. This is also a telling result, as these scores signal sequences such as *paramount importance, funnily enough, life expectancy* that indicate advanced lexico-grammatical proficiency (Granger & Bestgen, 2014).

The fact that high-scoring collgrams are the most significant and that medium strength does not appear to be a useful category could act as a prompt to revise the cut-off points used to identify significant collocations. Our results are consonant with those of Durrant and Doherty (2010, p. 145). Based on the fact that collocational priming was only demonstrated "between pairs with MI scores of at least 6 and t-scores of at least 7.5", these two authors suggest that the lower scores that are commonly used in the applied linguistics literature "need to be revised upwards".

For t-scores, the analysis based on tokens reveals significant differences for the three collocational types (L, M and H) but the effect sizes are rather weak. The results for the High category (*in particular, close to, there is, of course, a few, I mean, the same, such as*) are consistent with Durrant and Schmitt's (2009) observation that non-native writers use more high t-scores than native writers. This more frequent use of high-t collgrams at T1 is counterbalanced by a weaker use of less strongly associated t-score collgrams (L and M) (*make profits, personal opinion, proper use, make films, almost everybody*).

Finally, Table 9.6 also reveals a higher percentage of BT bigrams at T3 than at T1, a finding which again concurs with Durrant and Schmitt (2009), who found more of these bigrams in native-speaker texts than those by non-native writers. Interpreting this result is not straightforward, however, as some bigrams are inappropriate (e.g. *responsible of, adults life, controversed question, importantly responsible, scientifics researches*), while others are perfectly acceptable combinations which simply fail to appear or are rare in the BNC (e.g. *ban violence, a smartphone, emotional intelligence*). There are also some creative combinations (e.g. *anatomically precise, candle-lit nights, emotionless violence*) which point to learners leaving their comfort zone and experimenting with more sophisticated combinations. Space limitations do not allow for further analysis of this heterogeneous category, which clearly deserves careful investigation.

5 It is important to note that this category partly contains the same bigrams for MI and t-score. The reason is that bigrams which are found in the reference corpus with a frequency lower than chance would necessarily have a negative score for the two association indices and are therefore found in the same collgram category (NC).

One particularly striking finding for the remaining three POS-bigram types (NN, JN and AJ) is that the results show marked differences. No significant results are found for the NN category. This may be due to the sparseness of the data for this category. As shown in Table 9.3, NN is the least populated category in the corpus with fewer than four occurrences per text.[6] It is also the category that contains the highest number of BT bigrams (approximately 60 %) whose association scores have not been computed. A frequency of fewer than two MI-scored NN bigrams per text (40 % of four) is not sufficient to assess the learner's phraseological use of this category. The results for the other two POS-bigram types (JN and AJ) are very similar to those observed for ALL: when an effect is significant for one of these two categories, it is also significant for ALL. The only exception is the percentage of the High-MI collgrams in the AJ category, which is lower at T3 than at T1, while in all the other categories it is higher. A look at the lists of collgrams helps clarify this apparent contradiction. Most of the sequences at T1 contain high-frequency intensifying adverbs (*most, completely, totally, much, too, that*), bigrams with *most* (*most important, most enjoyable*) accounting for 50 % of the sequences. According to Lorenz (1998, p. 55), this frequent use of adjective intensification is a sign of novice writing, while "low adjective intensifier counts correlate with linguistic maturity and native-like argumentative writing". Our results confirm this observation: at T3 the number of such sequences decreases and students start using less frequent adverbs ending in *-ly* (*perfectly happy, easily accessible, widely available*).

4.2 *Longitudinal vs. Pseudolongitudinal Design*

As longitudinal data are difficult to collect, it seems reasonable to examine whether the results obtained with this approach are similar to those that can be obtained on the basis of a pseudolongitudinal approach, i.e. an approach which relies on cross-sectional corpora that include proficiency information for each learner. As pointed out by Forsberg (2010, p. 32), the advantage of this type of corpus is that it enables us "to get an idea of how the second language develops, from beginner levels to very advanced levels, even though we only can study selected 'stations' on the L1 learners' journey towards ultimate attainment".

6 Interestingly, Parkinson (2015) also establishes a very low rate of NN collocations in Spanish learners of English, a finding which she attributes to the absence of this type of structure in Spanish. Transfer may also be at play here, as this structure is not available in French either.

TABLE 9.7 *The* ALL *category in* L *and* ψ*L studies*

			MI				t-score				BT
			NC	L	M	H	NC	L	M	H	BT
L	Tokens	T1	56.6	25.6	6.7	1.2	14.6	10.1	7.0	58.5	9.9
		T3	55.5	25.0	6.8	1.7	13.7	10.8	7.4	57.2	11.0
		p	**			***	***	**	*	**	**
		d	0.42			0.78	0.48	0.36	0.29	0.28	0.42
	Types	T1	58.0	23.6	6.0	1.3	16.0	10.7	7.5	54.7	11.1
		T3	56.1	23.8	6.3	1.7	14.8	11.4	7.7	53.9	12.2
		p	***			***	***	**			**
		d	0.68			0.68	0.60	0.38			0.41
ΨL	Tokens	B	57.9	22.8	6.7	1.7	14.2	10.4	6.9	57.6	10.9
		C	55.1	23.2	6.7	2.5	12.9	11.3	7.8	55.6	12.5
		p	***			***	***	***	***	**	**
		d	0.88			0.84	0.71	0.56	0.67	0.43	0.45
	Types	B	57.9	21.9	6.2	1.7	15.5	11.2	7.4	53.5	12.3
		C	54.7	22.6	6.5	2.4	13.8	12.2	8.2	52.0	13.8
		p	***			***	***	***	***	*	**
		d	1.01			0.89	0.88	0.58	0.64	0.33	0.39

In this section, we compare the results of the current longitudinal study with those of a previous pseudolongitudinal study (Granger & Bestgen, 2014) in which the same method was applied but with learner groups at different proficiency levels. The learner corpus consisted of 223 essays from the *International Corpus of Learner English* (ICLE; Granger et al., 2009) which had been graded according to the Common European Framework of Reference for Languages (CEFR) by two professional raters. The collgram method was used to compare the intermediate (level B) with the advanced texts (level C).

Apart from some minor differences, the pseudolongitudinal (ΨL) study displays very similar trends to those obtained with a longitudinal (L) design. In other words, the differences in collgram use between intermediate and advanced learners are completely in line with those obtained when the start and end stages of development are compared over a three-year span. The results for the ALL category presented in Table 9.7 show this very clearly. As was the case in the longitudinal study, the strongest effect is the higher percentage of High-MI scores in the more advanced learner texts. It is sequences of this type that mark learners' development in both longitudinal and pseudo-longitudinal data. A look at the top 100 collgrams at T3 for LONGDALE and the advanced (C) level for ICLE (see Appendix for the full list) highlights the diversity of these sequences. Besides NN (*drug addiction, refugee camps*) and JN collgrams (*vast majority, conscientious objector*), which together account for 70–80% of the top 100 units, and AJ collgrams (*easily accessible, mentally ill*), the lists also feature a range of other types of closely associated bigrams (verb + object: *commit suicide*; subject + verb: *doorbell rang*; verb + adverbial particle: *torn apart*; numeral + noun: *twentieth century*; noun + preposition: *grudge against*; verb + reflexive pronoun: *manifests itself*).

In this study, the results of the longitudinal and pseudolongitudinal studies are very close. It would be wrong, however, to assume that the two approaches will always generate the same results. One factor which may account for the closeness of the results in this case is the fact that the time period covered by the longitudinal study is very long. If the period covered had been much shorter, the longitudinal study might well have yielded very few significant changes.

5 Two Caveats

Although the results of our study look promising, it is important to mention two caveats: the first concerns the density of the data collection, the second the variability of learners' development.

In longitudinal studies, the denser the data collection, the better. Lowie and Vespoor (2015, p. 84), for example, advocate "frequent measurements over a long period of time". In second language acquisition (SLA) terms, "frequent measurements" means weekly, biweekly or monthly collections; the notion of "long period of time" is more fluid: "as short as three or four months and as long as six years, in very few cases" (Ortega & Byrnes, 2008, p. 6). While our study meets the requirement in terms of time span, it clearly falls short on the number of measurements, as we only compared two data points. The data collection is therefore particularly sparse. For the type of study we had in mind, however, dense collection would have been very problematic. While for morphology and (albeit to a lesser extent) grammar, it is acceptable to have learners write on different topics for each collection, for lexical studies it is essential to control for topic and it would clearly not be an option to ask learners to write on the same topic repeatedly. The fact that the texts written at T1 and T3 were comparable in terms of topic is clearly a strong point of our study. The downside, however, is that we only have a start point and an end

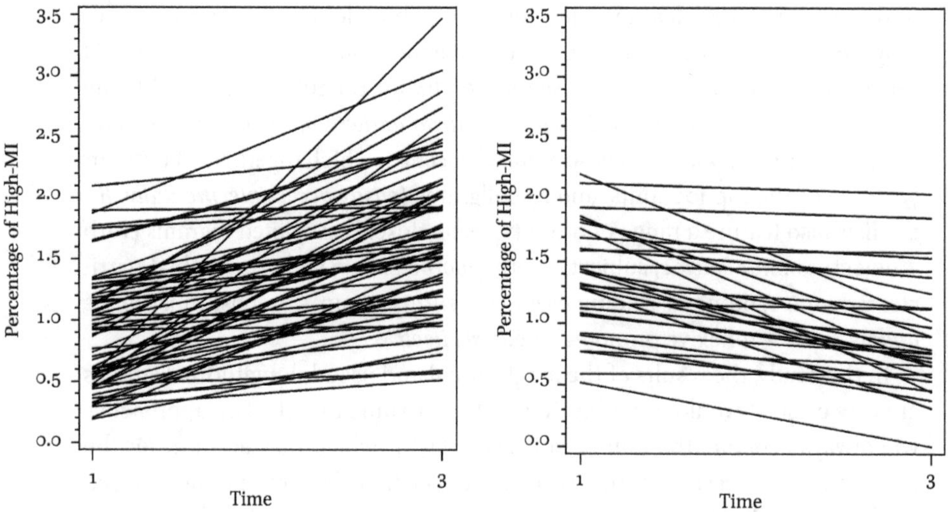

FIGURE 9.2 *Individual trajectories of the percentage of the High-MI category (in tokens)*

point and no intermediary stages. It is important to bear in mind that, as shown by Dynamic Systems Theory (De Bot et al., 2007), a lot can happen between these two stages and our data are not capable of capturing this information.

The second caveat pertains to the group perspective adopted in the study. Longitudinal studies "are generally case studies [...], with data being collected from a single subject (or at least a small number of subjects)" (Gass, 2013, p. 34). Our study is not a case study: it focuses on group rather than individual trajectories. This group perspective is criticised by many SLA researchers, who argue that second language acquisition is characterised by a high degree of variability and "there can be no logical expectation that the pattern found in generalisations at the group level is the same as the actual development of the individual learner" (Lowie & Verspoor, 2015, p. 84). While our study is clearly and indeed purposely not focused on individuals, it departs from most learner corpus studies in factoring in individual variation: in all the quantitative analyses, the learner corpus is considered as a series of individual texts rather than one long text.

It remains true, however, that the comparison involves groups of learners. The differences are general trends, which may hide marked differences between individuals. This can be seen very clearly in Figure 9.2, which shows the development of High-MI collgrams for each of the 89 learners. The left-hand diagram represents the learners who have a higher score at T3 than at T1, and the diagram to the right those who have a lower score at T3. As the percentage of High-MI is significantly higher at T3 than at T1 and the effect size is large, more learners can be expected to have a higher score at T3. The left-hand diagram shows that this is indeed the case for two-thirds of the learners (60 out of 89). However, the right-hand diagram indicates that one-third of the learners have a lower score at T3. While the statistical analyses in Table 9.6 highlight general tendencies, Figure 9.2 makes it clear that the general trend only applies to part of the data. Determining why the scores of some learners increase, while in others the opposite trend is observed would require access to the numerous variables that can affect learners' performance, such as their level of motivation, their initial proficiency level in English, their familiarity with the essay topic, etc. This type of information needs to be gathered at the time of data collection, which unfortunately was not the case for the LONGDALE data used for this study.

The fine-grained view provided by the individual results compared with the group ones should not be seen as a reason for rejecting the use of mean scores for groups of learners. In this study, the general trend observed in the group results is found in two-thirds of the learners, which is far from negligible. Focusing exclusively on the existence of individual differences would amount to throwing out the baby with the bathwater. Lowie and Verspoor (2015, p. 79) themselves recognise the value of the stages identified by developmental studies of groups of learners "especially if the groups consist of similar learners that acquire the language in a similar context". The fact that the learners in the LONGDALE are particularly homogeneous (same mother tongue background, same learning setting, similar age) strengthens the validity of our findings. We fully subscribe to Lowie and Verspoor's (2015, p. 79) view that "the two perspectives, the dynamic development of the individual and the grand sweep development of groups, can exist side by side. The perspective taken depends on the preferred methodology and the preferred theoretical framework."

6 Conclusion

This study shows that the collgram method is capable of tracking learners' development over the course of the learning process. One of the main advantages of the method is that it presents a fine-grained picture of the L2 phrasicon: rather than labelling sequences into discrete categories of right and wrong, it highlights degrees of appropriateness, which makes it particularly well-suited to trace L2 development.

The results identify clear development in the three-year span covered by the study, both for the total set of bigrams (ALL category) and for the three POS-bigram categories (NN, JN and AJ). Over time the use of collgrams becomes increasingly more sophisticated, as evidenced by a lower frequency of non-collocational bigrams and a concomitant increase in lower-frequency, but strongly associated, collgrams. The results also confirm the very infrequent use of NN bigrams by L2 learners recently reported by Parkinson (2015). The highly significant results obtained for the ALL category are particularly encouraging for future applications, as this category does not require any morpho-syntactic processing. However, as proved by the analysis of intensifying adverbs, it remains very fruitful to carry out detailed analyses of particular categories of collgrams.

These developmental trends are valid for the group as a whole but do not necessarily reflect the development of each individual learner in the group. In view of the applied objective of our research, we have opted for a group perspective, but the learner corpus data, which we have taken care to analyse as a series of individual texts rather than an aggregate set, also allow for investigations of individual development.

Since a longitudinal design is very difficult to implement on a large scale, it makes sense to compare the results with those obtained from pseudolongitudinal data, which are much easier to collect. Gass (2013, p. 37) warns us, however, that we should not necessarily assume that the two approaches will yield the same results: "[t]he extent to which the assumption is warranted is controversial". Our study shows that the two approaches may well yield very similar results in *some* circumstances, which as such is already a very interesting finding. However, it can be expected that differences in proficiency level (beginners instead of intermediate/advanced) or the time span of the data collection (a few months rather than three years) will lead to radically different results. There is clearly scope for further research to circumscribe the specificities of each approach.

The results of studies such as the one conducted here could inform a wide range of applications. The least appropriate collgrams could be used for remedial exercises. Overused collgrams could serve as a basis for rewriting exercises prompting learners to use more advanced combinations. Insights from collgram-based studies could also help prioritise phraseological expressions in the new pedagogically oriented phrasal lists such as those compiled by Simpson-Vlach and Ellis (2010) and Martinez and Schmitt (2012). They could also contribute to fleshing out the CEFR descriptors (Chen & Baker, 2016) and be integrated into automated scoring algorithms alongside traditional measures such as orthographic or grammatical errors (Futagi, Deane, Chodorow & Tetreault, 2008).

Admittedly, there is more to phraseology than collgrams; other types of multiword units—larger n-grams, non-contiguous combinations such as collocations or phrase-frames—are also worth investigating. Each of these types of phraseologisms could form the basis of a new multiword-based measure of lexical richness, which would complement the traditional single word-based measures. It is not only the field of foreign language learning, teaching and testing that could benefit from these developments, however. A recent application of the collgram method to translations (Bestgen & Granger, in press) has shown that it can be used to compare phraseological units in original and translated texts and serve as an objective method to test predictions based on translation universals (Baker, 2007). These applications highlight the potential of the collgram method, but further research is necessary to fine-tune its implementation.

References

Ackermann, K., & Chen, Y.-H. (2013). Developing the Academic Collocation List (ACL)—A corpus-driven and expert-judged approach. *Journal of English for Academic Purposes*, *12*(4), 235–247.

Ädel, A., & Erman, B. (2012). Recurrent word combinations in academic writing by native and non-native speakers of English: A lexical bundles approach. *English for Specific Purposes*, *31*(2), 81–92.

Altenberg, B., & Granger, S. (2001). The grammatical and lexical patterning of *make* in native and non-native student writing. *Applied Linguistics*, *22*(2), 173–194.

Baker, M. (2007). Patterns of idiomaticity in translated vs. non-translated text. *Belgian Journal of Linguistics*, *21*, 11–21.

Bestgen, Y. (2014). Inadequacy of the chi-squared test to examine vocabulary differences between corpora. *Literary and Linguistic Computing*, *29*, 164–170.

Bestgen, Y., & Granger, S. (2014). The use of collocations by intermediate vs. advanced non-native writers: A bigram-based study. *International Review of Applied Linguistics in Language Teaching* (*IRAL*), *52*(3), 229–252.

Bestgen, Y., & Granger, S. (in press). Collocation et traduction. Analyse automatique au moyen d'indices d'association. In M. Kauffer & Y. Keromnes (Eds.), *Theorie und Empirie in der Phraseologie / Approches théoriques et empiriques en phraséologie*. Tübingen: Stauffenburg Verlag.

Biber, D., Johansson, S., Leech, G., Conrad, S., & Finegan, E. (1999). *Longman grammar of spoken and written English*. London: Longman.

Chen, Y.-H., & Baker, P. (2010). Lexical bundles in L1 and L2 academic writing. *Language Learning & Technology*, *14*(2), 30–49.

Chen, Y.-H., & Baker, P. (2016). Investigating criterial discourse features across second language development: Lexical bundles in rated learner essays, CEFR B1, B2 and C1. *Applied Linguistics*, *37*(6), 849–880.

Clear, J. (1993). From Firth principles: Computational tools for the study of collocation. In M. Baker, G. Francis, & E. Tognini-Bonelli (Eds.), *Text and technology: In honour of John Sinclair* (pp. 271–292). Amsterdam: John Benjamins.

Cobb, T. (2013). Frequency 2.0: Incorporating homoforms and multiword units in pedagogical frequency lists. In C. Bardel, C. Lindqvist, & B. Laufer (Eds.), *L2 vocabulary acquisition, knowledge and use* (pp. 79–108). Eurosla Monographs Series 2.

Cohen, J. (1988). *Statistical power analysis for the behavioral sciences* (2nd ed.). New Jersey: Lawrence Erlbaum.

Council of Europe (2001). *Common European Framework of Reference for languages: Learning, teaching, assessment*. Cambridge: Cambridge University Press.

De Bot, K., Lowie, W., & Verspoor, M. (2007). A dynamic systems theory approach to second language acquisition. *Bilingualism: Language and Cognition*, *10*(1), 7–21.

De Cock, S. (2000). Repetitive phrasal chunkiness and advanced EFL speech and writing. In C. Mair & M. Hundt (Eds.), *Corpus linguistics and linguistic theory* (pp. 51–68). Amsterdam: Rodopi.

Dunlop, W.P., Cortina, J.M., Vaslow, J.B., & Burke, M.J. (1996). Meta-analysis of experiments with matched groups or repeated measures designs. *Psychological Methods, 1*, 170–177.

Durrant, P. (2015). Lexical bundles and disciplinary variation in university students' writing: Mapping the territories. *Applied Linguistics*. First published online April 19, 2015, doi:10.1093/applin/amv011.

Durrant, P., & Doherty, A. (2010). Are high-frequency collocations psychologically real? Investigating the thesis of collocational priming. *Corpus Linguistics and Linguistic Theory*, *6*(2), 125–155.

Durrant, P., & Schmitt, N. (2009). To what extent do native and non-native writers make use of collocations? *International Review of Applied Linguistics in Language Teaching* (*IRAL*), *47*, 157–177.

Ebeling, S.O., & Hasselgård, H. (2015). Learner corpora and phraseology. In S. Granger, G. Gilquin, & F. Meunier (Eds.), *The Cambridge handbook of learner corpus research* (pp. 207–229). Cambridge: Cambridge University Press.

Ellis, R., & Barkhuizen, G. (2005). *Analysing learner language*. Oxford: Oxford University Press.

Ellis, N., Simpson-Vlach, R., Römer, U., O'Donnell, M.B., & Wulff, S. (2015). Learner corpora and formulaic language in second language acquisition research. In S. Granger, G. Gilquin, & F. Meunier (Eds.), *The Cambridge handbook of learner corpus research* (pp. 357–378). Cambridge: Cambridge University Press.

Evert, S. (2009). Corpora and collocations. In A. Lüdeling & M. Kytö (Eds.), *Corpus linguistics. An international handbook* (pp. 1211–1248). Berlin: Mouton de Gruyter.

Forsberg, F. (2010). Using conventional sequences in L2 French. *International Review of Applied Linguistics in Language Teaching* (*IRAL*), *48*, 25–51.

Forsberg, F., & Bartning, I. (2010). Can linguistic features discriminate between the communicative CEFR-levels? A pilot study of written L2 French. In Bartning, I., Martin, M. & Vedder, I. (Eds.), *Communicative proficiency and linguistic development. Intersections between SLA and language testing research* (pp. 133–158). EUROSLA monographs series 1.

Futagi, Y., Deane, P., Chodorow, M., & Tetreault, J. (2008). A computational approach to detecting collocation errors in the writing of non-native speakers of English. *Computer Assisted Language Learning, 21*(4), 353–367.

Gass, S. (2013) (with J. Behney, & L. Plonsky). *Second language acquisition: An introductory course.* (4th ed.). New York: Routledge.

Granger, S. (1998). Prefabricated patterns in advanced EFL writing: collocations and formulae. In Cowie A. (Ed.), *Phraseology: Theory, analysis and applications* (pp. 145–160). Oxford: Oxford University Press.

Granger, S., & Bestgen, Y. (2014). The use of collocations by intermediate vs. advanced non-native writers: A bigram-based study. *International Review of Applied Linguistics in Language Teaching (IRAL), 52*(3), 229–252.

Granger, S., Dagneaux, E., Meunier, F., & Paquot, M. (2009). *International Corpus of Learner English v2* (Handbook + CD-Rom). Louvain-la-Neuve: Presses universitaires de Louvain.

Groom, N. (2009). Effects of second language immersion on second language collocational development. In A. Barfield & H. Gyllstad (Eds.), *Researching collocations in another language* (pp. 21–33). London: Palgrave Macmillan.

Howell, D. (2013). *Statistical methods for psychology* (8th ed.). Wadsworth, Cengage Learning.

Hyland, K. (2012). Bundles in academic discourse. *Annual Review of Applied Linguistics, 32*, 150–169.

Kilgarriff, A. (1996). Comparing word frequencies across corpora: Why chi-square doesn't work, and an improved LOB-Brown comparison, *Proceedings of ALLC-ACH Conference* (pp. 169–172).

Kilgarriff, A. (2005). Language is never, ever, ever random. *Corpus Linguistics and Linguistic Theory, 1*, 263–275.

Lorenz, G. (1998). Overstatement in advanced learners' writing: stylistic aspects of adjective intensification. In S. Granger (Ed.), *Learner English on computer* (pp. 53–66). London & New York: Addison Wesley Longman.

Lowie, W., & Verspoor, M. (2015). Variability and variation in second language acquisition orders: A dynamic reevaluation. *Language Learning, 65*(1), 63–88.

Martinez, R., & Schmitt, N. (2012). A phrasal expressions list. *Applied Linguistics, 33*(3), 299–320.

Milton, J. (2009). *Measuring second language vocabulary acquisition.* Bristol: Multilingual Matters.

Nesselhauf, N. (2005). *Collocations in a learner corpus*. Amsterdam & Philadelphia: John Benjamins.

Ortega, L., & Byrnes, H. (2008). The longitudinal study of advanced L2 capacities: An introduction. In L. Ortega & H. Byrnes (Eds.), *The longitudinal study of advanced L2 capacities* (pp. 1–20). New York & London: Routledge.

Pan, F. (2010). Lexical acquisition viewed from a contrastive analysis of collocational behaviour of near synonyms. *Chinese Journal of Applied Linguistics, 33*(5), 52–64.

Paquot, M. (2013). Lexical bundles and L1 transfer effects. *International Journal of Corpus Linguistics, 18*(3), 391–417.

Paquot, M., & Granger, S. (2012). Formulaic language in learner corpora. *Annual Review of Applied Linguistics, 32*, 130–149.

Parkinson, J. (2015). Noun-noun collocations in learner writing. *Journal of English for Academic Purposes, 20*, 103–113.

Serrano, R., Stengers, H., & Housen, A. (2015). Acquisition of formulaic sequences in intensive and regular EFL programmes. *Language Teaching Research, 19*, 89–106.

Simpson-Vlach, R., & Ellis, N.C. (2010). An academic formulas list: New methods in phraseology research. *Applied Linguistics, 31*(4), 487–512.

Siyanova, A., & Schmitt, N. (2008). L2 learner production and processing of collocation: A multi-study perspective. *Canadian Modern Language Review, 64*(3), 429–458.

Treffers-Daller, J., Parslow, P., & Williams, S. (2016). Back to basics: How measures of lexical diversity can help discriminate between CEFR levels. *Applied Linguistics*. First published online: April 7, 2016. DOI: 10.1093/applin/amw009

van Hout, R., & Vermeer, A. (2007). Comparing measures of lexical richness. In H. Daller, J. Milton, & J. Treffers-Daller (Eds.), *Modelling and assessing vocabulary knowledge* (pp. 93–115). Cambridge: Cambridge University Press.

Wanner, L., Alonso Ramos, M., Vincze, O., Nazar, R., Ferraro, G., Mosqueira, E., & Prieto, G. (2013). Annotation of collocations in a learner corpus for building a learning environment. In S. Granger, G. Gilquin, & F. Meunier (Eds.), *Twenty years of learner corpus research. Looking back, moving ahead* (pp. 493–503). Louvain-la-Neuve: Presses universitaires de Louvain.

Wolfe-Quintero, K., Inagaki, S., & Kim, H.-Y. (1998). *Second language development in writing: Measures of fluency, accuracy and complexity*. Honolulu: Second Language Teaching and Curriculum Center, University of Hawaii.

Appendix: List of the Top 100 Collgrams in LONGDALE (T3) and ICLE (Advanced), Classified in Decreasing Order of MI Score

ALL bigrams in LONGDALE T3	MI	ALL bigrams in ICLE advanced	MI
modus_operandi	19.7	woe_betide	19.4
mentally_disordered	14.2	homo_sapiens	18.9
global_warming	13.9	spaghetti_bolognaise	18.3
downward_spiral	13.7	alma_mater	17.7
curriculum_vitae	13.5	self-raising_flour	16.3
mobile_phones	13.1	cayenne_pepper	16.2
swimming_pool	12.8	conscientious_objectors	15.9
stumbling_block	12.6	chewing_gum	15.8
heinous_crimes	12.6	conscientious_objector	15.4
commit_suicide	12.4	tabasco_sauce	15.1
law-abiding_citizens	12.4	barbed_wire	14.9
tuition_fees	12.1	juvenile_delinquents	14.8
committing_suicide	12.0	conveyor_belt	14.8
austerity_measures	12.0	baked_beans	14.6
nineteenth_century	11.9	soap_operas	14.2
twentieth_century	11.8	mentally_handicapped	14.2
human_beings	11.8	lunatic_asylum	14.1
sleeping_soundly	11.8	dear_sirs	14.0
eighteenth_century	11.7	doorbell_rang	14.0
mentally_ill	11.7	old-age_pensioners	14.0
artificial_intelligence	11.6	arabian_peninsula	13.9
technological_advances	11.6	global_warming	13.9
nuclear_weapons	11.5	lemon_juice	13.9
innermost_thoughts	11.5	ozone_layer	13.8
drug_addiction	11.5	high-heeled_shoes	13.7
deeply_rooted	11.5	pink_floyd	13.5
funnily_enough	11.4	corporal_punishment	13.4
industrialised_countries	11.4	universal_suffrage	13.3
alarm_clocks	11.4	zebra_crossing	13.3
twenty-first_century	11.4	transformational_grammar	13.3
paramount_importance	11.4	refugee_camps	13.3
broadly_speaking	11.3	chilli_sauce	13.1
concluding_remarks	11.3	baltic_republics	13.1
twenty-four_hours	11.2	fairy_tales	13.0

(cont.)

ALL bigrams in LONGDALE T3	MI	ALL bigrams in ICLE advanced	MI
concentration_camps	11.1	swimming_pool	12.8
life_expectancy	11.0	khaki_shorts	12.8
carefully_crafted	11.0	second-class_citizens	12.8
easily_accessible	10.9	comfortably_furnished	12.7
native_speakers	10.9	steering_wheel	12.7
vast_majority	10.8	tropical_forests	12.6
marble_statues	10.7	sesame_seed	12.6
washing_machine	10.6	armani_suits	12.6
colourless_liquid	10.6	chocolate_mousse	12.5
mental_disorder	10.6	racial_hatred	12.5
severely_punished	10.6	drug_addict	12.4
torn_apart	10.5	second-class_citizen	12.3
horror_movies	10.3	star_trek	12.3
capitalist_societies	10.3	sore_throat	12.2
wide_range	10.2	tiny_tots	12.2
deep_breath	10.2	channel_tunnel	12.2
closely_related	10.1	ice_cream	12.2
clear-cut_distinction	10.1	martial_arts	12.1
unskilled_workers	10.1	vicious_circle	12.1
strongly_influenced	10.1	silk_stockings	12.0
commit_crimes	10.0	rice_pudding	12.0
mobile_phone	9.9	poached_eggs	12.0
visual_arts	9.9	raw_materials	11.9
interest_rates	9.9	mountain_bikes	11.9
unbearable_suffering	9.9	silk_scarf	11.9
structuralist_theories	9.9	nineteenth_century	11.9
bad_tempered	9.8	civil_servants	11.9
secondary_schools	9.8	ice-cream_parlour	11.8
developing_countries	9.7	leather_jackets	11.8
younger_brother	9.7	tsarist_regime	11.8
amazonian_forest	9.7	import_tariffs	11.8
every-day_life	9.7	roam_freely	11.8
hollywood_movies	9.7	twentieth_century	11.8
grudge_against	9.7	human_beings	11.8
multinational_companies	9.6	apple_pie	11.8
supernatural_powers	9.6	silk_blouse	11.7

ALL bigrams in LONGDALE T3	MI	ALL bigrams in ICLE advanced	MI
worldly_goods	9.6	god_bless	11.7
newly_acquired	9.6	mentally_ill	11.7
oddly_enough	9.6	taxi_driver	11.7
horror_movie	9.6	tomato_soup	11.7
years_ago	9.6	straw_hat	11.7
million_dollars	9.5	artificial_intelligence	11.6
utter_chaos	9.5	armed_forces	11.6
bus_stops	9.5	sandy_beach	11.6
thorny_issue	9.5	junk_mail	11.6
tentative_steps	9.5	favourite_pastime	11.6
catastrophic_consequences	9.5	prime_minister	11.5
attitude_toward	9.5	sun_shines	11.5
nowhere_near	9.4	industrialized_countries	11.4
tv_screens	9.4	alarm_clocks	11.4
mental_illnesses	9.4	video_recorder	11.4
religious_traditions	9.4	19th_century	11.4
well-paid_job	9.3	curly_hair	11.4
detrimental_effects	9.3	mitigating_circumstances	11.4
heavily_criticised	9.3	manifests_itself	11.3
mental_health	9.3	alarm_clock	11.3
corruption_allegations	9.3	taken_aback	11.3
darkest_hour	9.3	fifteenth_century	11.2
generally_speaking	9.3	plastic_beaker	11.2
somebody_else	9.3	20th_century	11.2
video_clips	9.3	poole_harbour	11.2
politically_correct	9.2	elder_brother	11.2
higher_education	9.2	male_chauvinists	11.2
hollywood_movie	9.2	neatly_stacked	11.1
industrial_revolution	9.2	shaven_heads	11.1
mass_murderer	9.2	minced_meat	11.1

Index of Concepts

Index of Corpora and Databases

www.ingramcontent.com/pod-product-compliance
Lightning Source LLC
LaVergne TN
LVHW020633300926
849161LV00004B/689